Country Climbs

Mark Glaister

A rock climbing guidebook to the best climbs
in the West Country of England

Text, computer artwork, layout, topos and editing by Mark Glaister,
Stephen Horne and Alan James
All uncredited photos by Mark Glaister
Original ROCKFAX design Mick Ryan and Alan James
Printed by John Browns Printers, Nottingham
Distributed by Cordee (www.cordee.co.uk)

All maps by ROCKFAX

Published by ROCKFAX Ltd. July 2010
© ROCKFAX Ltd. 2010
www.rockfax.com

ISBN 978 1 873341 37 7

Cover photo: Rich and Sam Mayfield on *Solid Air* (VS 4b) - *page 126* - at Gull Rock,
one of the Culm Coast's many isolated sea-cliffs.
This page: The steep and exposed *Incubus* (E1 5b) - *page 367* - on the grossly
overhanging Sanctuary Wall, Torquay, Devon. Climbers: Marti Hallett and Helen Dudley.

Avon Somerset

North Devon

Culm Coast

Inland Cornwall

Atlantic Coast

West Penwith

The Lizard

Inland Devon

Torbay

Dorset

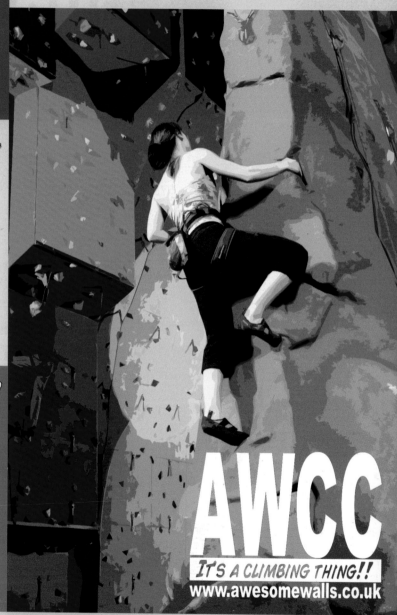

Contents

Photo: Steve Crowe nearing the finish of *Break on Through* (E4 5c) - *page 142* - Lower Sharpnose, Cornwall. Photo: Dave Pickford

Avon Somerset

North Devon

Culm Coast

Inland Cornwall

Atlantic Coast

West Penwith

The Lizard

Inland Devon

Torbay

Dorset

Avon Somerset | North Devon | Culm Coast | Inland Cornwall | Atlantic Coast | West Penwith | The Lizard | Inland Devon | Torbay | Dorset

West Country Climbs is a selective guide to the finest rock climbing in Cornwall, Devon, Dorset, Somerset and Avon in western England. The area has hundreds of fantastic routes of all grades and styles, on a variety of rock types, and these are presented here in one concise guidebook.

For many climbers, the golden granite sea cliffs of Cornwall will be considered the jewel in the West Country's crown, however there are many more outstanding climbing destinations on offer. The broad choice ranges from the dark lava and culm of the north coast of Devon and Cornwall, to the granite of Bodmin and Dartmoor and to the lighter limestone of Torbay, the Avon Gorge, Somerset and Dorset. Whatever grade of climb, and whatever preferred style of climbing is sought, the West Country caters for all options - long, adventurous climbs on remote sea cliffs, modern sport climbs above the beach, short bouldery routes on granite tors, and everything in between.

Mid-grade traditional classics on perfect granite? - West Penwith.
Huge, committing sea cliff adventures? - The Atlantic and Culm coast.
Sunny, limestone sport routes? - Portland, Brean Down and Torquay.
Exhilarating sea-cliff trad climbs with a holiday ambience? - Berry Head and Swanage.
Technical sport and trad routes on moorland granite? - Dartmoor and Inland Cornwall.
Rural, or ultra-urban climbing? - The Dewerstone and Chudleigh or the Avon Gorge.

West Country Climbs brings all of these cliffs and their
climbs alive with clear approach information, huge
photo-topos, detailed route descriptions and inspiring
action photography.

But it's not all about the climbing. The West
Country is one of Europe's most enchanting
corners. Its rugged coastline, wind-swept
moors, traditional rural pubs, gorgeous
beaches and picturesque villages make any
visit an unforgettable experience, but when
combined with the excellence of the climbs
on offer and a bit of decent weather it is
without a doubt one of the finest places
to climb anywhere.

Alex Mason on the Great Zawn gem *Green Cormorant Face* (E2 5c) - *page 216* - at Bosigran, West Penwith. Photo: Duncan Skelton/Offwidth Images

Avon Somerset

North Devon

Culm Coast

Inland Cornwall

Atlantic Coast

West Penwith

The Lizard

Inland Devon

Torbay

Dorset

This Guidebook

This 2010 first edition of West Country Climbs is a selective guidebook that details the prime rock climbs of the major cliffs in the West Country. In general, only the best routes on the best cliffs are described, although on some buttresses (mainly the sport crags) all the lines are described to avoid confusion where many lines exist on uniform looking faces. In total there are 884 routes described in detail which will be more than enough to keep the majority of climbers happy for a lifetime's worth of visits.

Route Lines - The photo-topos in this book are large and detailed. These qualities enable the route lines to be seen very clearly, showing intricate detail of where the routes go. Great care has been taken when adding the route lines but it is inevitable that some may not be exactly right, especially on the more obscure routes and on routes where there is no precise line. If unsure then use personal judgement to pick out a line, and let us know of any discrepancies by commenting on the Rockfax Route Database (**www.rockfax.com**).

Other Guidebooks

There are thousands of routes in the West Country which are not covered in this book. The Rockfax guidebook to Dorset covers all the routes in the last section of this book. For bouldering information have a look at Dave Henderson's excellent website - **www.javu.co.uk**. For other areas consult the books from the following:

The Climbers' Club - www.climbers-club.co.uk
Cordee - www.cordee.co.uk
Cheddar Gorge and Caves - www.thegorgeoutdoors.co.uk

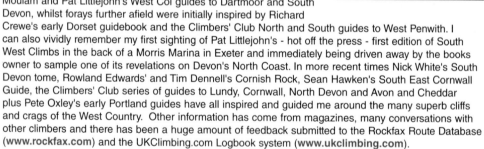

The information that is included in this guidebook has been gathered together over my climbing life, distilled and built upon to produce the guidebook that you now have in your hands. My guidebook shelf charts my association with climbing in the West Country - having been born in Devon my first steps were guided by the contents of Tony Moulam and Pat Littlejohn's West Col guides to Dartmoor and South Devon, whilst forays further afield were initially inspired by Richard Crewe's early Dorset guidebook and the Climbers' Club North and South guides to West Penwith. I can also vividly remember my first sighting of Pat Littlejohn's - hot off the press - first edition of South West Climbs in the back of a Morris Marina in Exeter and immediately being driven away by the books owner to sample one of its revelations on Devon's North Coast. In more recent times Nick White's South Devon tome, Rowland Edwards' and Tim Dennell's Cornish Rock, Sean Hawken's South East Cornwall Guide, the Climbers' Club series of guides to Lundy, Cornwall, North Devon and Avon and Cheddar plus Pete Oxley's early Portland guides have all inspired and guided me around the many superb cliffs and crags of the West Country. Other information has come from magazines, many conversations with other climbers and there has been a huge amount of feedback submitted to the Rockfax Route Database (**www.rockfax.com**) and the UKClimbing.com Logbook system (**www.ukclimbing.com**).

I would like to acknowledge the effort put in by all those who have worked on documenting the climbing in the West Country over the years. The West Country is a huge area with complex access where quick and easy research is hampered by the difficulties of viewing many of the routes properly, except from the sea. It is an impossible task to document everything with 100% accuracy, but hopefully this guidebook can at least record routes in a way that inspires those who want to explore some of the lesser known parts of the West Country, and provide good information for those who want to climb the classics.

Mark Glaister, June 2010

Avon Somerset
North Devon
Culm Coast
Inland Cornwall
Atlantic Coast
West Penwith
The Lizard
Inland Devon
Torbay
Dorset

Max Bonniot on *Pyjamarama* (E4 6b) - *page 236* - at
Longships Wall, Land's End. Photo: Rob Gibson

Having climbed in the West Country since I was a young teenager it is impossible to thank all those who I have climbed with on the routes included in this guidebook - so it will have to suffice to say that without your company the experiences would have been far less memorable and fun.

Many people have helped me compile this book, their help ranging from posing for pictures and checking lines, to proof reading and providing route descriptions – Gordon Jenkin, Ray Mardon, John Warner, Carrie Hill, Marti Hallett, Anna Rayner, Paul Cox, Bev Connor, Rob Knight, Lee Proctor, Jonny Aylwin, Tom Skelhon, Dave Henderson, Brian Wilkinson, Bruce Woodley, Rich White, Rob Kennard, Mark Tomlinson, Rich Mayfield, Sam Mayfield, Ken Palmer, Pete Saunders, Barney Carver, Dave Pickford, Chris Savage, Dave Turnbull, Emma Medara, Stu Bradbury, Dave Johnson, Rob Byrom, Caz Neely. Iain Peters, Pat Littlejohn, Frank Cannings, Nick Hancock, Darren Russell, Toby Keep, Neil Foster, Duncan Critchley, Alison Martindale, Bridget Collier, Phil Black, Paul Carling, Wilf and Jane Williamson, Bill Birkett, Mikey Robertson, Steve Thorpe, Trev Ford, James Forbes, Martin Cathrow, Shane Ohly, Chad Harrison, Dave Hope, Rob Greenwood, Adrian Berry, Ben Hall, Chris Sims, Gavin Symonds, Danie Rushmer, Rich Kirby, Sue Hazel, Helen Dudley, Jack Geldard, Guy Blackwood, Martin Perry, Andy Long, Al Ashmore, Neal and Helen Heanes, Mick Ward, Steve Watt, Steve Taylor - without all of your help the book would never have seen the light of day.

A special thanks to the fishermen, and women, especially Richard Cook and David Bliss, who I managed to cajole in to taking me around some of the wilder sections of the West Country's coastline.

A huge amount of appreciation to those who supplied the stunning action photographs - Bev Connor, Dave Pickford, Carrie Hill, Grant Farquhar, Dave Johnson, Pete Saunders, Nick Hancock, Adrian Berry, Ian Parnell, Tobi Carver, Chris Sims, Virgil Scott, Sam Mayfield, Bridget Collier, Ian Wilson, Alex Ekins, Sean Kelly, Martin Perry, Nick Arding, Mike Robertson, Sue Hazel, Mark Davies, Rob Gibson, Duncan Skelton.

Much of my climbing life, especially in the early days, has been inspired and influenced to a large degree by the various rock climbing guidebooks to the West Country and to all those authors I owe a huge amount of gratitude.

It's been a long haul this one, and I owe a massive thanks to the team at UKC/Rockfax - Alan, Stephen, Chris, Sherri, Mick and Jack for all their hard work and encouragement along the way.

Mark Glaister, June 2010

Photo: Bridget Collier

Barry Durston nearing the end of the crux-pitch of the super steep *Guernica* (E6 6a) - *page 178* - at Carn Gowla. Photo: Ian Parnell

Avon Somerset

North Devon

Culm Coast

Inland Cornwall

Atlantic Coast

West Penwith

The Lizard

Inland Devon

Torbay

Dorset

Equipment Manufacturers

Black Diamond - *Outside back cover*
Tel: 01629 580484
www.blackdiamondequipment.com

Entre Prises - *Page 27*
Kelbrook, Lancashire. Tel: 01282 444800
www.ep-uk.com

Climbing Walls

Awesome Walls - *Page 2*
St. Alban's Church, Liverpool.
Tel: 01512 982422
The Engine House, Stockport.
Tel: 0161 494 9949
Sefton Road, Stoke-on-Trent.
Tel: 01782 341919
www.awesomewalls.co.uk

Barn Climbing Centre - *Inside back cover*
Milton Abbot, Tavistock. Tel: 01822 870521
www.barnclimbingwall.co.uk

Boulders - *Page 33*
Pengam Road, Cardiff. Tel: 0845 52 118 50
www.bouldersclimbingcentre.co.uk

Dartrock - *Page 19*
Old Totnes Road, Buckfastleigh.
Tel: 01364 644 499
www.dartrock.co.uk

The Climbing Academy - *Page 25*
Charlton Street, Bristol. Tel: 0117 907 2956
www.theclimbingacademy.com

Undercover Rock - *Page 17*
Mina Road, Bristol. Tel: 01179 413489
www.undercover-rock.com

Shops

Taunton Leisure - *Front cover*
East Reach, Taunton. Tel: 01823 275121
www.tauntonleisure.com

Rock On - *Page 15*
Mile End, London. Tel: 0208 981 5066
Craggy Island, Guildford. Tel: 01483 565635
Redpoint, Birmingham. Tel: 01213 598709
www.rockonclimbing.co.uk

Holidays / Guidance / Accommodation

Rock and Sun - *Back cover flap*
Mina Road, Bristol. Tel: 08456 864586
www.rockandsun.com

Dartmoor Adventures - *Page 31*
Dartmoor, Devon. Tel: 01752 690292
www.dartmooradventures.co.uk

Southwest Adventures - *Page 21*
Bampton, Devon. Tel: 07870 451827
www.southwestadventures.co.uk

3 Great Parks - *Page 29*
Sea Barn Campsite. Tel: 01305 782218
www.seabarnfarm.co.uk
West Fleet Holiday Farm. Tel: 01305 782218
www.westfleetholidays.co.uk
Bagwell Farm Touring Park.
Tel: 01305 782575
www.bagwellfarm.co.uk

Wall-Crawler - *Page 21*
Welcombe, near Bude. Tel: 01288 331145
www.wall-crawler.co.uk

The Orange House - *Page 31*
Finestrat, Alicante, Spain. Tel: 01752 690292
www.theorangehouse.co.uk

Avon Somerset | North Devon | Culm Coast | Inland Cornwall | Atlantic Coast | West Penwith | The Lizard | Inland Devon | Torbay | Dorset

Avon Somerset
North Devon
Culm Coast
Inland Cornwall
Atlantic Coast
West Penwith
The Lizard
Inland Devon
Torbay
Dorset

Midnight Express (E1 5b) - *page 271* - at St. Levan's Wall, West Penwith. Photo: Paul Cox

West Country Logistics

Avon Somerset | North Devon | Culm Coast | Inland Cornwall | Atlantic Coast | West Penwith | The Lizard | Inland Devon | Torbay | Dorset

Avon Somerset

North Devon

Culm Coast

Inland Cornwall

Atlantic Coast

West Penwith

The Lizard

Inland Devon

Torbay

Dorset

An incoming tide hastens the retreat from the top of the Middle Fin at Lower Sharpnose on the Atlantic Coast in the late afternoon. Time to retreat to the pub.

Avon Somerset
North Devon
Culm Coast
Inland Cornwall
Atlantic Coast
West Penwith
The Lizard
Inland Devon
Torbay
Dorset

In Emergency
Dial 999 and ask for 'COASTGUARD'
They have knowledge of the climbing areas and routes and can co-ordinate any rescue efforts.

Mobile Phones
Mobile phone coverage at many of the sea-cliffs in this guidebook is not good. There is often no signal at all at the base of many of the sea-cliffs and even at the top of the cliffs a strong signal can not be relied upon. This is especially the case on Lundy and the north coasts of Devon and Cornwall. Be prepared to seek out higher ground in an emergency. For those climbing on Portland it is worth checking where the signal is being picked up from as it is not uncommon that a French operators signal will be picked up if the phone is set to roaming mode. Mobile coverage is reasonable for all of the inland cliffs.

Tourist Information
For help and information on all aspects of a visit to the West Country the tourist information centres and websites listed below are a good starting point. The major TICs, closest to the climbing, are listed.

Bristol - Anchor Road, Harbourside, Bristol, BS1 5DB   Tel: 0906 711 2191
Bideford - The Quay, Bideford, Devon, EX39   Tel: 01237 477676
Bude - The Crescent, Bude, Cornwall, EX23 8LE   Tel: 01288 354240
Camelford - The Clease, Camelford, Cornwall, PL32 9PL   Tel: 01840 212954
St. Ives - Street-an-Pol, St Ives, Cornwall, TR26   Tel: 01736 796297
Penzance - Station Road, Penzance, Cornwall, TR18 2NF   Tel: 01736 362207
Bodmin - Mount Folly Square, Bodmin, Cornwall, PL31 2DQ   Tel: 01208 76616
Torquay - Vaughan Parade, Torquay Devon, TQ2 5JG   Tel: 01803 211211
Swanage - Shore Road, Swanage, Dorset, BH19 1LB   Tel: 01929 422885

www.visitbristol.co.uk
www.visitsomerset.co.uk
www.visitdevon.co.uk
www.visitcornwall.com
www.visit-dorset.com

Port Issac near Doyden Point and Pentire Head

Bulging with Climbing Gear!

Many shops claim to be climbing specialists.

At Rock On we sell climbing/ mountaineering equipment

and books, and absolutely NOTHING ELSE.

Now thats specialist.

Mile End Climbing Wall
Haverfield Road,
Bow, London,
E3 5BE.
Tel: 0208 981 5066

Craggy Island
9 Cobbett Park,
Slyfield Estate,
Guildford, GU1 1RU.
Tel: 01483 565635

Redpoint Climbing Centre
77 Cecil Street,
Birmingham,
B19 3ST.
Tel: 0121 359 8709

www.rockonclimbing.co.uk

Dominic Sutcliffe on Outward Bound, HVS.

Avon Somerset | North Devon | Culm Coast | Inland Cornwall | Atlantic Coast | West Penwith | The Lizard | Inland Devon | Torbay | Dorset

Camping

Camping in pleasant surroundings near to many of the cliffs is one of the West Country's great appeals. There are many camping options and the limited number of sites listed below is only a pointer to what is available. The West Country being the UK's premier summer holiday destination is extremely busy at peak times and the larger campsites are expensive and also get fully booked well in advance. However, a drive out into the sticks, up onto the moors or along the remoter sections of coastal roads usually turns up a basic farm camping field or less well known site that are often cheaper and less busy. It is also worth remembering that many family campsites do not allow large and/or single sex groups.

Somerset and Avon
Cheddar Camp - *Shipham, Nr. Cheddar. Tel: 01934 743 166* www.cheddarcamp.com

North Devon and Lundy
Lundy Shore Office - *Bideford, Devon. Tel: 01237 477779* www.lundyisland.co.uk
Stoke Barton Farm - *Stoke, Hartland, Devon. Tel: 01237 441238* www.westcountry-camping.co.uk

North Cornwall and Bodmin Moor
South Penquite Farm - *Blisland, Bodmin, Cornwall. Tel: 01208 850491* www.southpenquite.co.uk

West and South Cornwall
Treen Campsite - *Treen, Penzance, Cornwall. Tel: 01736 810273* www.treenfarmcampsite.co.uk
Henry's Campsite - *The Lizard, Helston, Cornwall. Tel: 01326 290596* www.henryscampsite.co.uk

Torbay and Dartmoor
Runnage Campsite - *Postbridge, Dartmoor. Tel: 01822 880222* www.runnagecampingbarns.co.uk

Portland
Sea Barn Farm - *Fleet, Weymouth, Dorset. Tel: 01305 782218* www.seabarnfarm.co.uk

Swanage
Acton Field - *Langton Matravers, Swanage, Dorset. Tel: 01929 439424* www.actonfieldcampsite.co.uk
Tom's Field - *Langton Matravers, Swanage, Dorset. Tel: 01929 427110* www.tomsfieldcamping.co.uk

Not Camping

Many other options for self-catered accommodation near to the climbing are available. Two increasingly popular options are Camping Barns/Bunkhouses and Backpacker Hostels. The YHA also has flexible and very competitively priced accommodation www.yha.org.uk. B&B's and holiday cottages are ubiquitous.

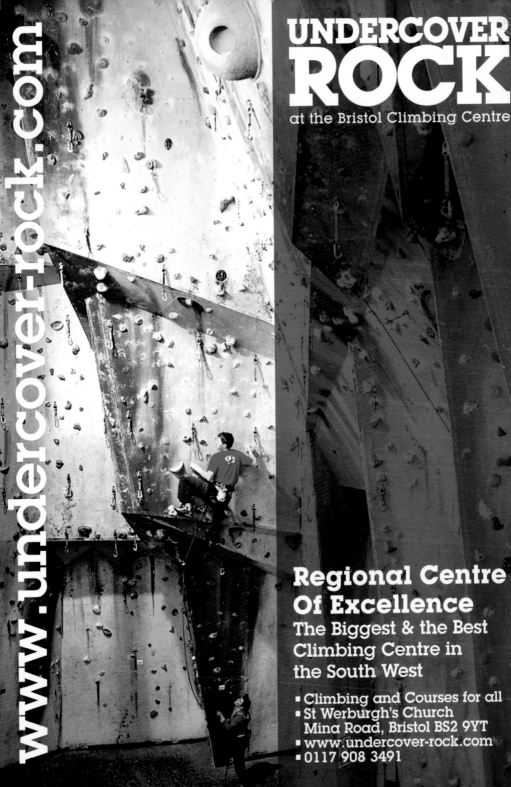

Avon Somerset | North Devon | Culm Coast | Inland Cornwall | Atlantic Coast | West Penwith | The Lizard | Inland Devon | Torbay | Dorset

Climbing Walls (and Gear Shops)

There are a number of climbing walls scattered sporadically around the West Country. Most of these walls have a reasonable stock of climbing gear as well.

Undercover Rock www.undercover-rock.com
St.Werburghs's Church, Mina Road
Bristol. S2 9YT Tel: 0117 941 3489
See advert on page 17

The Climbing Academy
www.theclimbingacademy.com
Charlton Street, Bristol. BS5 0FD Tel: 0117 907 2956
See advert on page 25

Dart Rock Climbing Centre www.dartrock.co.uk
Dart Mills, Old Totnes Road
Buckfastleigh. TQ11 ONF Tel: 01364 644499
See advert opposite

The Barn Climbing Centre
www.barnclimbingwall.co.uk
Eastacott Barton, Milton Abbot. PL19 0QP Tel: 01822 870521
See advert inside back cover

Rock and Rapid Adventure Centre
www.rockandrapidadventures.co.uk
Hacche Mill, South Moulton, Devon. Tel: 01984 623989

Climbing Gear Shops

There are a number of specialist outdoor shops in the West Country but many of the cliffs, especially in Cornwall and North Devon, are not close to the shops so a bit of a drive will be required if the need for a visit arises.

Somerset and Avon

Taunton Leisure www.tauntonleisure.com
38-42 Bedminster Parade, Bristol. BS3 4HS. Tel: 0117 9637640

Taunton Leisure www.tauntonleisure.com
40 East Reach, Taunton. TA1 3ES. Tel: 01823 332987
See advert inside front cover

CaveClimb www.caveclimb.com
Cheddar Business Park, Cheddar. Tel: 01934 741623

Dick's Climbing www.dicksclimbing.co.uk
26 West Street, Bristol. Tel: 0117 9555 243

The Gorge Outdoors www.thegorgeoutdoors.co.uk
Cheddar Gorge, Somerset. Tel: 01934 742 688

North Devon

Rock and Rapid www.rockandrapid.co.uk
Hacche Mill, South Moulton. Tel: 01984 623 989

South Devon

Taunton Leisure www.tauntonleisure.com
110 Fore Street, Exeter. EX4 3JF. Tel: 01392 410534
See advert inside front cover

Cotswold Outdoors www.cotswoldoutdoor.com
Darts Farm, Topsham. Tel: 01392 878313

Cotswold Outdoors www.cotswoldoutdoor.com
Drakes Circus, Plymouth. Tel: 01752 672024

Moorland Rambler www.moorland-rambler.co.uk
148-149 Fore Street, Exeter. Tel: 01392 321065

Trail Venture www.trailventure.co.uk
North Street, Ashburton. Tel: 01364 652522

Dorset

Great Western Camping www.greatwesterncamping.co.uk
High East Street, Dorchester. Tel: 01305 266800

Kayaking off Portland.

Pubs

Below is a list of some of the West Country's best pubs that are within a quick stroll or drive of the cliffs. Some have good beer and cider, some have great food, most have both.

Photo: Dave Pickford

The Coronation Tap - Handy for the Avon Gorge, just above the suspension bridge.
Coxes Mill - Big bar at the entrance to Cheddar Gorge.
The Thatch Inn - Lively pub in Croyde close to Baggy Point.
The Old Smithy - Nice old pub at Welcombe village, handy for the Culm Coast.
The Bush Inn - Good spot at Morwenstow, close to Sharpnose Point.
The Port Garvene Inn - A pub in a quiet fishing cove. Good for Doyden Point and Pentire.
The Tinner's Arms - An atmospheric pub in Zennor close to Bosigran and Gurnard's Head.
The Logan Rock Inn - Good for south coast granite in the village of Treen.
The Cadgwith Cove Inn - Lovely pub close to The Lizard and its beaches.
The Meavy Inn - On Meavy village green close to the Dewerstone and Sheeps Tor.
The Rugglestone - Great Dartmoor pub with a fine beer garden.
The Berry Head Hotel - Great views across Torbay, close to The Old Redoubt.
The Carey Arms - Close to Anstey's Cove at Babbacombe Beach.
The Cove House - Good spot to watch the sun go down after climbing on Portland.
The Square and Compass - Popular haunt and convenient for the Swanage cliffs.

Cafes

It is impossible to provide a guide for all the cafes and tearooms in the West Country since that would be a guidebook as thick as this one in itself. Suffice to say that a decent cafe or tearoom selling diet-busting cream teas or pasties is never more than a brief drive from most of the cliffs.

Sundown over Lyme Bay from Chesil Beach, Dorset

Side tabs: Avon Somerset | North Devon | Culm Coast | Inland Cornwall | Atlantic Coast | West Penwith | The Lizard | Inland Devon | Torbay | Dorset

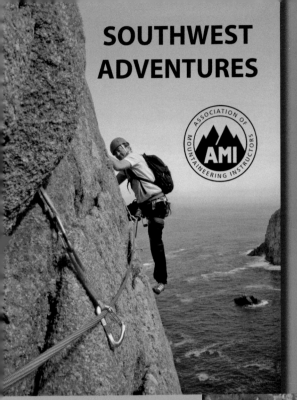

Avon Somerset | North Devon | Culm Coast | Inland Cornwall | Atlantic Coast | West Penwith | The Lizard | Inland Devon | Torbay | Dorset

West Country Climbing

Avon Somerset

North Devon

Culm Coast

Inland Cornwall

Atlantic Coast

West Penwith

The Lizard

Inland Devon

Torbay

Dorset

Steve Monks midway up the leaning corner of the classic Bosigran extreme *Raven Wall* (E3 5c) - *page 203* . Photo: Dave Pickford

Access to the sea-cliffs and the inland crags, quarries and gorges covered in this guidebook is on the whole uncomplicated. There are few problems at most crags and this has been the case for many years.

The greatest restrictions on access to the cliffs are for the protection of bird nesting sites, these restrictions are seasonal and predominately on the sea-cliffs but also on some inland cliffs. All the relevant restrictions and their current durations are covered under the introductions to the venues affected. These restrictions may vary from year to year and new ones may be imposed, so it is important that a check on the BMCs Regional Access Database (RAD) site is made to get the latest up-to-date

information available - **www.thebmc.co.uk/bmcCrag**. It is also good practice to keep an eye out for any signs and notices at the cliffs that may give new or updated information on the extent or duration of restrictions.

Access restrictions for environmental concerns are only in effect on a small number of cliffs, however many of the cliffs are in protected areas such as SSSIs and great care to minimise the impact of climbing must be made. Again reference to the BMCs RAD can be made to gain information on any current access restrictions.

A number of the cliffs are privately owned and great care must be taken not to damage relationships with landowners - one major climbing site which needs considerable care when planning a climbing visit is Cheddar Gorge (see page 84).

In the majority of cases all that is required to ensure continued freedom of access to the cliffs, and to maintain good relations with landowners and stewards is a responsible approach and level of behaviour. This includes sticking to footpaths, not climbing over walls and fences, not lighting fires or leaving litter, parking considerately, keeping noise down, closing gates and not gardening routes excessively.

Freedom of access to climb is easily lost but far harder, if not impossible, to regain.

Should any access problems arise at the climbing sites covered in this guidebook please refer details to the BMC Access Officer, 177-179 Burton Road, West Didsbury, Manchester, M20 2BB **www.thebmc.co.uk**

THE CLIMBING ACADEMY

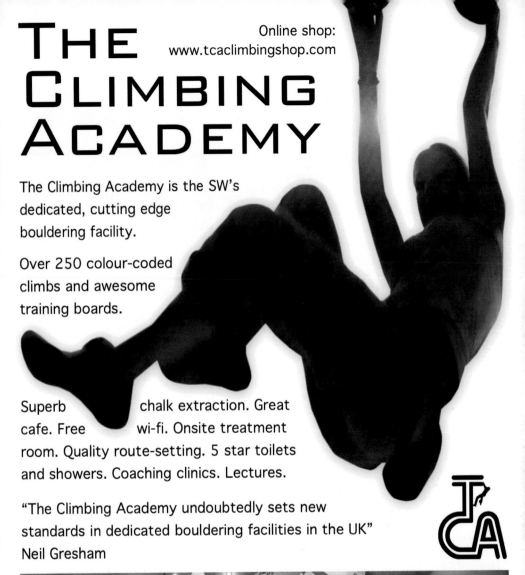

Rack

The basic UK traditional rack of wires, large nuts, cams, quickdraws, slings and double ropes is the very minimum requirement of equipment needed to climb the traditional routes in the West Country. It is difficult to generalise about how much to carry but on the limestone and culm routes wires will normally be required in larger numbers (maybe 3 sets or more) whilst on the granite lines cams and large nuts will be used more often, however there are exceptions so use your own judgement. On the sport routes 14 quickdraws is sufficient for virtually all the routes included in this book.

Climbing Ropes

The normal practice for leading routes is to use double 50m x 9mm ropes. This allows the routes to be climbed with greatly reduced rope-drag than would be possible on a single rope as many climbs do not follow direct lines. For the sport climbs in this guidebook a single 60m rope will suffice, although one route - *Infinite Gravity* at Swanage - requires a longer one.

Rope Buckets - One of the problems when at the sea-cliff bases can be keeping the rope dry and away from rock pools or the sea. A useful tool for routes with a hanging stance at the end of an abseil is a rope bucket. You can feed your twinned 9mm ropes into the bucket before you abseil down and clip the bucket onto the belay. If you have done it correctly then the ropes will feed easily out of the bucket as the leader climbs.

Abseiling in to Compass Point on the Culm Coast.

Abseil Ropes

An abseil rope is essential to reach the base of many of the sea-cliffs and it is hardly ever possible to abseil on your climbing ropes due to the belays being set well back from the edge. A single rope of 50m is the minimum requirement but preferably 60m if you have one. Often when you arrive at the crag you may well find an ab rope in place. In such circumstances it is accepted practice to use ropes that are in place rather than clutter up belays with an extra rope.

Helmets and Loose Rock

Many routes have loose rock on them, especially on their final sections. Always wear a helmet since rock can be dislodged at any time, and always put an extra runner in before the last moves, no matter how easy it looks. Test every hold and be especially careful early in the season, or on days after heavy rain. When belaying keep out of the fall zone especially when the leader is finishing a pitch.

Other Gear

Prusik Loops - A prusik loop is useful for protecting you when you abseil and having 2 is invaluable if you fall off when seconding or leading a steep route, although make sure you know how to use them if you suspect you might struggle - learning 'on the job' is not much fun! Prusik loops (or rope ascenders) should always be carried or left on the base of the abseil rope in case of emergency or failure on a route and an escape up the rope needs to be undertaken.

Abseil Rope Protectors - These are useful for the cliff-top edges particularly if the rope runs over an abrasive edge or will be used for a lot of abseil traffic.

Avon Somerset | North Devon | Culm Coast | Inland Cornwall | Atlantic Coast | West Penwith | The Lizard | Inland Devon | Torbay | Dorset

Fixed Gear

Pegs - Over the years many of the routes throughout the West Country have been climbed using pegs for protection. On the sea-cliffs, due to accelerated corrosion in the salty environment, most of these pegs should now be regarded as untrustworthy, this includes stainless steel pegs. Current thinking is for the use and replacement of pegs on the sea-cliffs in the West Country to be phased out. The highest profile route to see the effect of this thinking in this guidebook is the famous route *Eroica* at the incomparable Pentire Head. For many years *Eroica* was graded E2 with a point of aid from a blade peg. The peg corroded quickly (it was replaced at least once) and, although various solutions as to its possible long-term replacement were aired, its latest demise bought about a consensus that it should not be replaced. The route has now been climbed on a number of occasions without the peg and re-graded at E4. Therefore, even though many sea-cliff

A rotting old abseil station on the Culm Coast.

routes in this guidebook have pegs mentioned in their descriptions, a good deal of caution should be exercised when climbing these routes as some of the pegs mentioned in descriptions may have corroded away altogether or be in a very poor state - they will probably not be replaced.

On the inland crags, pegs have also been used in abundance for protection, however they are less prone to corrosion and are often replaced. Nevertheless the same level of caution should be applied to the reliability of the pegs as even away from the sea-cliff environment corrosion is still fairly rapid. At Chudleigh great care should be taken to back-up the 'ring' style pegs.

Threads - Fixed threads in the West Country are not common. Threads tend to be more accepted than pegs since they make use of natural features without damaging the rock, and they are more easily replaced. Care must still be taken to assess the state of the thread - pull it around so that you can examine all of it and leave a different section in the rock. If you decide to replace a thread, remove all the old ones since one brand new thread is a lot better than a few dodgy old ones.

Bolts and Staple Bolts - Bolts are used extensively for protection on both sport and traditional climbs in the West Country. On the sea-cliff sport climbs (covered in this guide) of Swanage, Portland, Anstey's Cove and Brean Down, marine-grade staples and bolts are used almost exclusively. On the inland crags and quarries, stainless steel bolts and staples are also widely used, however non-stainless steel bolts will also be encountered. As with pegs and threads always check the placement and state of the bolt before trusting your life to it.

Abseil points - On a number of cliffs it is necessary to descend by abseil after completing a climb. If there is an abseil point in place - ALWAYS CHECK ITS RELIABILITY! Some abseil points were originally set up using pegs and many of these are now in a dangerous state. If in any doubt always back-up the abseil point.

Chesil Beach looking towards Portland. Photo: Chris Craggs

The traditional routes in this book are graded using the British Traditional Grading system. The sport routes are graded using the French Sport Grading system.

British Trad Grade

1) Adjectival grade (Diff, VDiff, Severe, Hard Severe (HS), Very Severe (VS), Hard Very Severe (HVS), E1 and upwards)
How well-protected a route is, how sustained and a general indication of the level of difficulty of the whole route.

2) Technical grade (4a, 4b, 4c,..... to 7b)
The difficulty of the hardest single move.

Sport Grade

The sport routes in this book are graded using the familiar 'sport grade', or 'French grade' as it is often know. The overall difficulty of a route is rated on a scale in this guidebook from **4** to **8c+**.

More information on grades:
www.rockfax.com/publications/grades.html

Deep Water Solo Grades

Four routes in this book are described as deep water solos. They have been given a British technical grade and an S grade within their descriptions. The simple S Grade consists of a 0, 1, 2 or 3. S0 gives relative safety, with S3 offering considerable possibility of injury in the event of a fall.
The routes in this book that are described as deep water solos are all hard and a degree of experience is essential (and the ability to swim!) if you intend to climb them un-roped.

ROUTE GRADES

BRITISH TRAD GRADE	Sport Grade	UIAA	USA
Mod *Moderate*	1	I	5.1
Diff *Difficult*	2	II	5.2
VDiff *Very Difficult*	2+	III	5.3
HVD *Hard Very Difficult*	3-	III+	5.4
Sev *Severe*	3	IV	5.5
HS *Hard Severe* 4a BOLD SAFE	3+	IV+	5.6
VS *Very Severe* 4a 5a BOLD SAFE	4	V-	5.7
HVS *Hard Very Severe* 4b 5b BOLD SAFE	4+	V	5.8
E1 5c BOLD SAFE	5	V+	5.9
E2 5a 6a BOLD SAFE	5+	VI-	5.10a
E3 6a BOLD SAFE	6a	VI	5.10b
E4 5c 6b BOLD SAFE	6a+	VI+	5.10c
E5 6a 6c BOLD SAFE	6b	VII-	5.10d
E6 6b 6c BOLD SAFE	6b+	VII	5.11a
E7 6c 7a BOLD SAFE	6c	VII+	5.11b
E8 7a 7a BOLD SAFE	6c+	VIII-	5.11c
E9 7a 7b BOLD SAFE	7a	VIII	5.11d
E10 7b SAFE	7a+	VIII+	5.12a
	7b	IX-	5.12b
	7b+		5.12c
	7c	IX	5.12d
	7c+	IX+	5.13a
	8a	X-	5.13b
	8a+	X	5.13c
	8b	X+	5.13d
	8b+		5.14a
	8c	XI-	5.14b
	8c+	XI	5.14c
	9a	XI+	5.14d
	9a+		5.15a

Colour Coding

The trad routes and sport routes are all given a colour-coded dot corresponding to a grade band.

● **Green Routes** - Everything at grade **Severe** and under, and **4a+** and under for sport routes. Good routes to start out your climbing career on.

● **Orange Routes** - **HS** to **HVS** inclusive, and **5** to **6a+** for sport routes. General ticking routes for those with more experience, a large range of excellent routes is available across this band.

● **Red Routes** - **E1** to **E3** inclusive, and **6b** to **7a** for sport routes. For the experienced and keen climber. Anyone operating at this level can expect to enjoy some of the best climbing in the book.

● **Black Routes** - **E4** and above, and **7a+** and above for sport routes. The hard stuff! Have a go at some major national testpieces, plus you can do all the red, orange and green routes as well. Can't be better than that!

Avon Somerset | North Devon | Culm Coast | Inland Cornwall | Atlantic Coast | West Penwith | The Lizard | Inland Devon | Torbay | Dorset

Avon Somerset

North Devon

Culm Coast

Inland Cornwall

Atlantic Coast

West Penwith

The Lizard

Inland Devon

Torbay

Dorset

Tides are a crucial consideration when climbing on the sea-cliffs of the West Country since the access to, or escape from, many of the cliffs, is affected by the state of the tide. The West Country has huge differences in tidal range that varies from one of the largest in the World on the North Devon and Culm Coast - with tides swings as big as 8 metres - to some very small swings at Swanage. Understanding more about tides can be a great help in making the most out of your visit.

About Tides

Throughout one lunar month there are two *spring* or high-range tides, and two *neap* or low-range tides. *Spring* tides occur during the full and new moons, when the sun and moon are in line and the combined gravitational pull causes the highest tides, which then ebb to the lowest level. During *spring* tides the low tides will always fall towards the middle of the day.

During the first and third quarters of the moon, when the sun's and moon's attractional forces are at right angles, we experience less extreme high and low tides. *Neap* tides will always be low at either end of the day with the high tide occurring in the middle.

By knowing the current phase of the moon you can roughly work out what kinds of tide you are going to get. Local tide tables (displayed in local newspapers, and available from the Climbers' Club web site - www.climbers-club.co.uk) will give you precise times and levels of high and low tide.

From high tide to low tide takes approximately 6 hours, which means that there are two high tides and two low tides in every 24 hour period. The average time for the tide to turn around is actually slightly longer than 6 hours. This means that each day the high and low tide times are between 30 and 80 minutes later than the previous day.

The most dramatic *spring* tide swings range from a massive 8m (spring and autumn) to usually at least 6.5m (summer and winter), and *neap* tide swings range from around 2.5m (spring and autumn) to 4.5m (summer and winter). Along the south coast towards Swanage and Portland the tides have a significantly reduced range.

Important Considerations

1) During the middle hours between low and high tide, the sea comes in MUCH faster and areas of flat rock and boulder beach can disappear rapidly so escape routes can be cut off. This means that you may have spent a few hours at the crag and not noticed much tide movement when suddenly there is water lapping around your ankles. This is significantly more pronounced during *spring* tides.

2) The smaller fall to low *neap* tides may give much less access than low spring tides to certain cliffs. For example, The Blisterin' Barnacle Slab, the routes at Gurnard's Head, and the ledges at the base of The Amnesty Wall on The Lizard are either inaccessible or only barely uncovered during low *neap* tides.

3) The lower level of high *neap* tides may allow access to certain routes which are cut off in high *spring* tides.

4) Persistent and strong onshore winds can prolong or even slightly raise high tide levels as can a high swell from some distant ocean storm.

Low tide at Bude's surf beach on the Culm Coast, Cornwall.

Crag Table 1

Region	Crag	Routes	up to Sev	HS to HVS	E1 to E3	E4 and up
Avon and Somerset	Avon Gorge	68	9 ✓✓	23 ✓✓✓	25 ✓✓✓	11 ✓✓✓
Avon and Somerset	Portishead Quarry	5	- ✗	4 ✓✓	- ✗	1 ✓✓
Avon and Somerset	Split Rock Quarry	8	- ✗	- ✗	3 ✓✓	5 ✓✓
Avon and Somerset	Brean Down and Uphill	22	- ✗	1 ✓	5 ✓✓	16 ✓✓✓
ND	Baggy Point	25	5 ✓✓✓	12 ✓✓✓	6 ✓✓✓	2 ✓
ND	Blackchurch	8	- ✗	2 ✓	5 ✓✓	1 ✓
Culm Coast	Smoothlands to Dyer's	8	- ✗	1 ✓	3 ✓✓	4 ✓✓✓
Culm Coast	Screda Point	11	- ✗	4 ✓	6 ✓✓	1 ✓
Culm Coast	Gull Rock and Cornakey	13	- ✗	7 ✓✓	5 ✓✓	1 ✓✓
Culm Coast	Vicarage and Oldwalls'	11	2 ✓✓	6 ✓✓	3 ✓✓	- ✗
Culm Coast	Lower Sharpnose	21	- ✗	3 ✓	8 ✓✓✓	10 ✓✓✓
Culm Coast	Compass Point	6	2 ✓	3 ✓✓	1 ✓✓	- ✗
Inland Cornwall	Cheesewring Quarry	18	1 ✗	7 ✓	6 ✓✓	4 ✓✓
Inland Cornwall	Roche Rock and Devil's Jump	10	4 ✓✓	4 ✓✓	1 ✗	1 ✓
Atlantic Coast	Tintagel	3	- ✗	- ✗	- ✗	3 ✓✓✓
Atlantic Coast	Doyden Point	4	- ✗	1 ✓	2 ✓✓	1 ✓
Atlantic Coast	Pentire Head	6	- ✗	- ✗	- ✗	6 ✓✓✓
Atlantic Coast	Carn Gowla	14	1 ✗	2 ✓	7 ✓✓✓	4 ✓✓✓

Quality and range of routes in different grade bands: ✓✓✓ - Excellent ✓✓ - Good ✓ - Okay ✗ - Not worth a visit

Side tabs: Avon Somerset | North Devon | Culm Coast | Inland Cornwall | Atlantic Coast | West Penwith | The Lizard | Inland Devon | Torbay | Dorset

Approach	Sun	Tides	Abseil	Restrictions	Summary	Page
0 to 15 min	Lots of sun			1 wall only	A spectacular gorge in a noisy urban setting. Numerous limestone walls of up to 70m in height, some natural and others quarried. Lots of great climbs both single and multi-pitch.	44
5 min	To mid afternoon				A good quarried face that gets plenty of morning sun with a small line-up of mid-grade trad lines.	70
5 min	To mid afternoon				The best of the Somerset quarries, and a good venue for teams operating in the mid to high-grades. The rock is superb and the climbing hard, but fairly well protected.	72
2 to 5 min	Afternoon	Tidal			A popular beachside sport crag with some mid-grade and hard lines that get a lot of sun. Uphill Quarry has a trio of good fingery face-climbs.	76
25 min	From mid morning	Tidal	Abseil in	1 wall only	A long-established slab climbing venue, close to a great surf-beach. Plenty of good single and multi-pitch climbs, with the bulk of the climbing in the mid grades.	92
25 min	Not much sun	Tidal			Blackchurch draws few climbers to it loose, shady and vegetated face, although for those in search of an adventure, the place might meet the brief.	110
15 to 25 min	Evening	Tidal			The two most impressive sweeps of steep culm on the coast. The big lines are amongst the hardest in the West Country.	114
5 min	Afternoon	Tidal			Easy access ensures that the routes at Screda Point get plenty of attention. The lines are predominantly in the mid-grades, and are tidal, although nearby Speke's Mill is not.	120
25 min	Lots of sun	Tidal			A great venue, although some of the routes are now more serious than they once were. Cornakey is home to a famous multi-pitch culm classic.	124
30 to 40 min	Lots of sun	Tidal			Vicarage Cliff is an excellent fin of culm with easy access and a number of good lower-grade lines. Oldwalls' Point is a large face of culm with a couple of intimidating cracklines on it.	130
35 min	Sun and shade	Tidal	Abseil in		The Culm's finest cliff. A unique set of three gravity-defying fins of rock with a host of mid and hard-grade classics on the faces of the fins. Sun and shade available.	136
10 min	Lots of sun	Tidal			A popular cliff, close to the busy beach at Bude. The rock needs careful handling, especially near the finishes of the climbs.	144
13 min	Lots of sun				Cornwall's premier inland crag. Best visited in dry and warm weather, as it is high on Bodmin Moor. Both trad and sport routes on solid quarried granite.	152
1 min	Lots of sun				Good crags for some lower-grade climbing. Both cliffs have good rock and are situated in interesting landscapes.	158
20 min	Afternoon			Restrictions	A big, well hidden cliff on the Island of Tintagel. The multi-pitch climbs here are amongst the most serious of their grades in the West Country. Permission required to climb.	166
10 min	Afternoon		Abseil in		Close to the quaint fishing hamlet of Port Quin and has couple of popular climbs that pack a punch.	170
15 min	Evening				Pentire's Great Wall is the West Country's finest face. All the routes are hard and brilliant.	172
5 min	Sun and shade	Tidal	Abseil in		One of the most remote and wild sections of coast in England. Big routes with committing approaches and serious climbing.	176

Shaded means that only some of the routes are tidal / require an abseil / are restricted

	Routes	up to Sev	HS to HVS	E1 to E3	E4 and up
Gurnard's Head Area Zennor, Gurnards, Carn Gloose, Robin's Rocks	10	- ✗	4 ✓✓	5 ✓✓✓	1 ✓
Bosigran	42	12 ✓✓✓	13 ✓✓✓	14 ✓✓✓	3 ✓✓✓
Kenidjack	6	- ✗	3 ✓✓	3 ✓✓	- ✗
Sennen	34	10 ✓✓✓	17 ✓✓✓	5 ✓✓	2 ✓✓
Lands End and Pordenack	10	2 ✓✓	4 ✓✓	2 ✓✓	2 ✓✓
Carn Les Boel to Fox Carn les Boel, Zawn Kellys, Carn Barra, Fox Promontory	36	3 ✓	17 ✓✓	10 ✓✓	6 ✓✓
Chair Ladder	17	4 ✓✓✓	8 ✓✓✓	5 ✓✓✓	- ✗
Porthgwarra to St. Levans Porthgwarra, Hella Point, Vessacks West, St. Levan's	12	4 ✓✓	4 ✓✓	4 ✓✓	- ✗
Cribba Head to Tater Du Cribba Head, St. Loy, Tater Du	14	- ✗	4 ✓✓	3 ✓✓	7 ✓✓
Trewavas Head	7	2 ✓	4 ✓✓	1 ✓	- ✗
Lizard Point	26	9 ✓✓	9 ✓✓	5 ✓✓	3 ✓✓
Chudleigh	36	6 ✓✓	13 ✓✓✓	12 ✓✓✓	5 ✓✓
Torbryan Quarry	23	- ✗	- ✗	13 ✓✓	10 ✓✓
Haytor and Hound Tor	36	13 ✓✓	10 ✓✓	9 ✓✓	4 ✓✓
Bench Tor and Sheeps Tor	16	10 ✓✓	5 ✓✓	1 ✓	- ✗
The Dewerstone	19	7 ✓✓	9 ✓✓✓	3 ✓✓	- ✗
Berry Head	13	- ✗	5 ✓✓	5 ✓✓✓	3 ✓✓✓
Daddyhole	21	3 ✓	8 ✓✓	6 ✓✓	4 ✓✓
Anstey's and Long Quarry	32	1 ✗	2 ✗	8 ✓✓	21 ✓✓✓
Portland	81	- ✗	11 ✓✓✓	41 ✓✓✓	29 ✓✓✓
Swanage	62	6 ✓✓	19 ✓✓✓	20 ✓✓✓	17 ✓✓✓

Side tabs (left margin): Avon Somerset | North Devon | Culm Coast | Inland Cornwall | Atlantic Coast | West Penwith | The Lizard | Inland Devon | Torbay | Dorset

Region groupings (left of crag names): West Penwith | Lizard | Inland Devon | Torbay | Dorset

Quality and range of routes in different grade bands: ✓✓✓ - Excellent   ✓✓ - Good   ✓ - Okay   ✗ - Not worth a visit

Approach	Sun	Tides	Abseil	Birds	Summary	Page
15 to 25 min	From mid morning	Tidal	Abseil in		Three atmospheric tidal cliffs that can be combined in a single visit plus the nearby Zennor cliff if conditions are poor. The main three cliffs can retain dampness.	188
10 min	Afternoon		Abseil in		Cornwall's best known cliff set high above the sea with no tidal problems. Something for all - long, short, easy or hard. Also includes The Great Zawn and Bosigran Ridge areas.	198
20 min	Lots of sun		Abseil in		Kenidjack's shear looking killas slate face is a popular place that is sheltered, non-tidal and home to one of the finest HVSs on the coast.	220
12 min	Afternoon	Tidal			An array of superb pitches on super-solid granite. The grade span is wide and the plentiful easier and mid-grade lines are some of the best on the coast.	224
5 to 15 min	Afternoon	Tidal	Abseil in		A complex area with some mixed quality granite but a number of good pitches and a great ridge route. Pordenack Point has better rock, is barely tidal and has some classic routes.	232
10 to 25 min	Afternoon	Tidal	Abseil in		Carn Les Boel and Zawn Kellys are two remote and quiet cliffs with great atmosphere. Carn Barra is great for harder single pitch climbs. Fox Promontory is a quiet location.	242
12 min	From mid morning	Tidal	Abseil in		A fantastic sea-cliff with superb low and mid-grade multi-pitch routes Can be frustrating to get perfect conditions, as the cliff is tidal and nesting birds are a big problem at times.	256
5 to 20 min	Lots of sun	Tidal	Abseil in		An often-overlooked section of the coast, with a number of worthwhile routes on a diverse set of crags.	266
25 to 40 min	Lots of sun	Tidal	Abseil in		A long strip of coastline that presents some diverse climbing styles and aesthetically interesting cliffs.	272
20 min	Sun and shade				An increasingly popular crag, set high above the sea. Sheltered with some good pitches on granite. Can be combined with other crags at Lizard Point.	282
10 to 15 min	Lots of sun	Tidal	Abseil in		A collection of dark sea-cliffs dotted around the UK mainland's most southerly point. The climbs are excellent and in a superb location.	286
5 min	Lots of sun				A very popular limestone cliff, set in the depths of rural Devon, but not too far from Dartmoor and Torbay. The climbs are all trad and up to four pitches long.	300
4 min	Afternoon				A small but excellent limestone sport crag. Takes a bit of finding, but the fine climbs are well worth the battle with the Devon rural roads.	310
5 min	Sun and shade				Dartmoor's largest tor that is rarely quiet. Brilliant rock and routes. Hound Tor is a friendly venue with plenty of short, fun pitches.	314
5 to 15 min	Lots of sun				Sheeps Tor is a very popular place, with a lot of short, easier lines, whereas Bench Tor has a limited number of lines, and one athletic classic. Sheeps Tor is often used by groups.	324
10 to 15 min	Lots of sun				One of the West Country's finest cliffs for the lower and mid-grade trad climber. The climbs are up to 3 pitches long, on excellent granite and in a magical setting.	330
3 to 10 min	Morning	Tidal		Most areas	Classic multi-pitch lines that soar up and out of the Great Cave, and two sea level traverses that radiate from the Great Cave. Some nesting restrictions.	344
5 to 12 min	Morning	Tidal			Sunny, adventurous and spectacular climbing on the Main Cliff contrasts with more technical climbing in the quarries. Sheltered and non-tidal.	354
9 to 10 min	Lots of sun	Tidal			A picturesque setting above a gorgeous cove, with hard sport routes and serious trad climbs. Can be very warm in the summer.	360
10 to 20 min	Afternoon	Tidal			The UK's most popular sport climbing destination with hundreds of routes across a broad spread of grades. Good weather and quick-to-dry but can get busy.	374
10 to 45 min	Lots of sun	Tidal	Abseil in	2 areas	A massive cliff with a mix of sport and trad climbs in an adventurous setting. Most climbs require committing abseil approaches. Fewer tide problems but some bird restrictions.	390

Avon Somerset | North Devon | Culm Coast | Inland Cornwall | Atlantic Coast | West Penwith | The Lizard | Inland Devon | Torbay | Dorset

Shaded means that only some of the routes are tidal / require an abseil / are restricted

Avon Somerset

North Devon

Culm Coast

Inland Cornwall

Atlantic Coast

West Penwith

The Lizard

Inland Devon

Torbay

Dorset

This is a very rough graded list of the best routes. As ever, it will not be found accurate by eveyone. If you disagree strongly with it, then please let us know via the voting on the Route Database on the web site - **www.rockfax.com**

Top 50 - The 'Top 50' are not necessarily the best 50 routes in the book, just 50 great challenges through the grade range.

Sport Routes

8c+
		Page
***	Brian	363

8b
***	A Fisherman's Tale	363
***	Tuppence	363
***	Brean Topping	80

8a+
| *** | Palace of the Brine | 402 |
| Top 50 | Infinite Gravity | 401 |

8a
| *** | The Cider Soak | 363 |

7c+
***	Shadow Beast	368
***	La Créme	363
***	Monoculture	380
***	Smashing of Amps	75
***	Psychokiller	156
***	Temple Redneck	402
***	Avenged	362
***	Storm Warning	80
***	Total Seizure	403

7c
***	Return of the Gunfighter	86
***	Hall of Mirrors	389
***	El Chocco	80

7b+
***	The Lynch	363
***	Bird of Paradise	86
Top 50	Empire of the Sun	362
***	Waves Become Wings	403
***	Chulilla	80
***	Starscrape	86
***	Zinc Oxide Mountain	383

7b
***	Want Out	389
***	Rampage	155
***	More Steam, Bigger Women!!!	365
***	Living Dead	77
***	Halfway to Heaven	385
***	Tessellations	403
***	Thread Flintstone	313
***	Paradise Lost	86

7a+
		Page
***	Chiming for You	77
***	Pump Hitler	382
Top 50	England's Dreaming	376
***	Victims of Fashion	380
***	Barney Rubble	313
***	Reverence	385

7a
***	Portland Heights	378
***	Superfly Guy	386
***	Get that Man!	86
***	Shakin' Like a Leaf	86
**	Chepito	79
***	Pearl Harbour	79

6c+
| *** | Best Fingers Forward | 384 |
| *** | Nothing but the Groove | 386 |

6c
***	Mayday	313
***	Burning Skies	378
**	Coral Sea	79

6b+
***	Buoys Will Be Buoys	382
***	Lord Stublock Deepvoid	379
***	The Jewel of the Isle	384

6b
| *** | The Watchman | 384 |

6a+
***	Reptile Smile	376
***	Stalker's Zone	385
***	Trad Free World	385

5
| *** | Slings Shot | 376 |

Trad Routes

E9
| Top 50 | The Walk of Life | 118 |
| ** | Question Mark | 274 |

E8
***	Pre-Marital Tension	274
***	Wall of Spirits	175
Top 50	The Monk's Satanic Verses	143

E6
***	Hellbound	116
***	Savage Earthsea	348
***	Watching the Ocean	105
***	The Jimi Hendrix Experience	77
***	Free the Spirit	367
***	Booby Prize	127
***	Coronary Country	143
***	Pink Ginsane	59
***	The Mind Cathedral	402
***	Caribbean Blue	367
**	The Earthsea Trilogy Part 1	118
Top 50	Caveman	348
***	Edgemaster	54
***	Demolition	227

E5

E4

E3

E2

E1

Avon Somerset · North Devon · Culm Coast · Inland Cornwall · Atlantic Coast · West Penwith · The Lizard · Inland Devon · Torbay · Dorset

E1 continued ...   Page

HVS

VS

HS

S   Page

HVD

VDiff

Diff

Pippa Froggatt finishing the exposed final pitch of the Top 50 route *Right Angle* (HS 4b) - *page 192* - at Gurnard's Head, West Penwith. Photo: Chris Sims

Avon Somerset

North Devon

Culm Coast

Inland Cornwall

Atlantic Coast

West Penwith

The Lizard

Inland Devon

Torbay

Dorset

Avon and Somerset

Avon Somerset

North Devon

Culm Coast

Inland Cornwall

Atlantic Coast

West Penwith

The Lizard

Inland Devon

Torbay

Dorset

The exposed single-pitch climbs above the ramp at the Avon Gorge's Unknown Buttress are some of the Gorge's best Extremes. Dan Donovan on *Arms Race* (E4 5c) - *page 50*

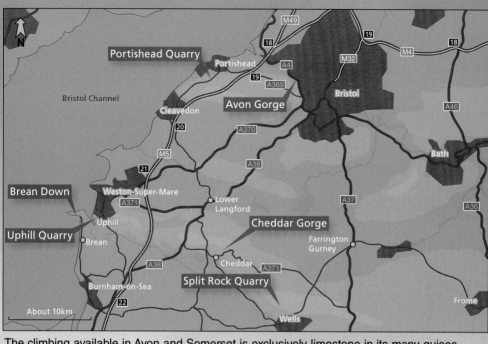

The climbing available in Avon and Somerset is exclusively limestone in its many guises. Routes here range from well-equipped beach-side sport climbs to intense multi-pitch traditional climbs on the walls of the impressive Cheddar Gorge and the Avon Gorge. A good deal of the rock in the area is quarried giving climbs that often rely upon a fair amount of fixed protection. At the Avon Gorge, the style of the climbing can be a little unsettling on first acquaintance, however a number of its climbs are superb challenges. The fine faces of Split Rock, Portishead and Uphill quarries have a mix of the traditional and sport ethic whilst the short and intense seaside sport climbs of Brean Down contrast with the awesome walls of the south side of Cheddar Gorge. The ambience of the climbing is not as enticing as that found on many of the cliffs deeper into the region and, although the intrusion of road noise and the nature of the quarried environment will erode some of the enjoyment for many, the quality of the climbing still shines through.

Getting Around

Travel to the cliffs in Avon and Somerset is relatively simple - all being quickly reached from the M5 motorway - making a flying visit on the way out west an attractive option.

Brean Down

Avon Somerset

North Devon

Culm Coast

Inland Cornwall

Atlantic Coast

West Penwith

The Lizard

Inland Devon

Torbay

Dorset

The deceptively steep sport routes at Brean Down are just one facet of the limestone climbing experience on offer in Avon and Somerset. *Pearl Harbour* (7a) - *page 79* - Photo: Bev Connor (Glaister collection)

	No star	☆	☆☆	☆☆☆
Mod to S	1	3	5	-
HS to HVS	-	7	11	5
E1 to E3	-	2	12	11
E4 and up	-	-	3	8

The huge winding gash of the Avon Gorge holds the UK's biggest and best urban crag. Brunel's famous suspension bridge spans the gorge, providing a magnificent backdrop to the climbing and, even though the cliffs are blighted by traffic noise, the climbing experience is memorable. The crags rise to around 70 metres and for the most part are composed of high quality quarried limestone, the one exception being the grand natural buttress beneath the suspension bridge itself.

The Gorge is basically a traditional venue and caters for most tastes and abilities, offering single and multi-pitch climbs throughout the grade range. Each of the cliffs has a distinct style. The compact and quarried nature of the Sea Walls and Main Wall take a bit of getting used to, their profusion of flat or sloping holds and often-spaced protection exercising the mind as much as the body. In contrast the Suspension Bridge Buttress and Unknown Area offer a more conventional limestone experience with better protection possibilities and generally steeper faces.

Access to the Gorge and its climbing is simple and for the travelling visitor makes a convenient stop-off on the way to, or return from, locations deeper into the West Country.

Approach   See main area map on page 44

From junction 18 on the M5, follow the A4 Portway into Bristol and after 4 miles the road passes directly underneath the crags. The first crag encountered is the towering Unknown Area whilst 200m further on and set back from the road are the Sea Walls. The parking for both of these crags is on the ground directly beneath the right-hand side of the Sea Walls. The turning into this parking area is sharp and great care is needed. The Main Wall is another 500m further on and has a parking layby directly below. The Suspension Bridge Buttress and neighbouring Giant's Cave Buttress are directly under, and adjacent to, the bridge a further 800m beyond the Main Wall and the parking and approach are more complicated here - see individual approaches for detail.

A fine evening on *The Arete* (VDiff 4a) - *page 63* - on the Morning Slab at the Avon Gorge.

Access

The only restriction, due to nesting birds, is on the Pink Wall section of the Main Wall, which is in force from March 1st to June 30th - the exact extent of this restriction is posted at the approach to the bottom of the crag. Climbing from the top of Suspension Bridge Buttress onto the suspension bridge itself is not allowed and descent must be made by abseil.

Conditions

Some of the more popular routes on the quarried walls are polished and in warm or humid weather they can be unpleasant and much harder. The rock dries quickly and there is little seepage, however there is little opportunity for climbing in the rain. Climbing during cold but clear spells in the winter is a possibility. A good deal of the protection, especially on Main Wall, is from fixed gear in the form of pegs and bolts. Many of the pegs are old and should be backed-up, whereas many of the bolts do get replaced from time to time.

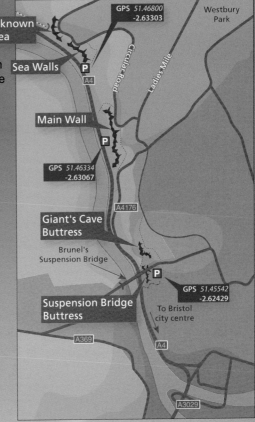

GPS 51.46800 -2.63303

Westbury Park

Unknown Area

Sea Walls

Circular Road

Ladies Mile

P

A4

Main Wall

P

GPS 51.46334 -2.63067

A4176

Giant's Cave Buttress

Brunel's Suspension Bridge

P

GPS 51.45542 -2.62429

To Bristol city centre

Suspension Bridge Buttress

A369

A4

A3029

Avon Somerset

North Devon

Culm Coast

Inland Cornwall

Atlantic Coast

West Penwith

The Lizard

Inland Devon

Torbay

Dorset

Avon Somerset

North Devon

Culm Coast

Inland Cornwall

Atlantic Coast

West Penwith

The Lizard

Inland Devon

Torbay

Dorset

Descent

Them - page 50

New Horizons - page 50

Lots of sun | 3 min | Multi-pitch

Unknown Wall

The left side of the area is a huge mass of variable-quality rock (the Unknown Wall) up which some big multi-pitch classics wend their way. In contrast, the right-hand side of the area (the Unknown Buttress) is divided into two walls by a huge ramp, and has consistently excellent rock and some superb single-pitch wall and crack-climbs.

Approach - Park in the Sea Walls car park and walk 100m towards the huge ramp. For the upper wall scramble up the ramp. For the remainder of the routes walk along the road and hop over the wall to gain the base of the crag.

Descent - For the climbs that top-out, walk left (facing out) along the pavement to the end of the cliff edge wall and then head down a good climbers' path through woods that ends back at the road. For climbs on the upper wall it is easiest to abseil down to the huge ramp. For those routes that end on the huge ramp either abseil down or scramble back down the ramp.

Conditions - Once the sun hits the face it can be either heaven, in cool conditions, or exactly the opposite in hot weather. The face does get a breeze and dries very quickly, although it does not stay dry in the rain.

❶ Desecrator . . . . 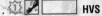 **HVS 5a**

Tucked away high above the traffic on the extreme left of the Unknown Wall is this exciting and very exposed pitch. Approach via a path that rises up leftwards under the wall from the base of the face. Follow the path for 100m to a final steep step which ends at a good ledge and small tree-belay on the right, with a cave 5m above and right.

28m. Move up a small rib to a spike at its top and step right to a ledge beneath the left side of the overhung cave. Climb very steeply through the overhang on loose looking, but good solid holds to a small tree. Move up to a peg and then follow thin cracks to the top.
FA. Mick Putman, Peter Hicks, Paul Todd 16.10.1972

❷ The Blik **E3 5b**

A stern test of both mind and strength on one of Avon's most impressive walls. Start about 45m up the path from the base of the crag at a well-worn gearing-up spot below a tree on a ledge at 3m.

1) 5b, 25m. Climb up vegetated ground above the tree and work easily rightwards to a peg under an overhang. Move down left, then make committing moves up the wall to better holds which lead leftwards again to a small overhang. Move over the overhang rightwards to a small ledge and climb the groove above to a small stance.

2) 5b, 25m. Continue up the groove to an overhang and pull out right and then up into the crack that splits the spectacular final wall. Follow the crack to the left end of the capping overhangs and finish leftwards.
FA. Ed Ward Drummond, Pete Morgan, Cathy Woodhead 5.67 (1pt)

❸ Unknown Wall . . . . **VS 4c**

A shy gem of a climb that builds to a dramatic climax in its upper reaches. The first pitch is vegetated but the holds are clean. Start at the well-worn gearing-up spot as for *The Blik*.

1) 10m. Climb up rightwards on easy but vegetated ground to a good belay ledge right of a projecting block.

2) 4c, 27m. Continue above the belay and take the line left of the overhang (double pegs) that ends at a bulge. Move right and up past a peg with difficulty to an open corner and belay ledge.

3) 4c, 18m. Climb up to the overhang, pegs, and traverse left beneath them for 6m to where they fade. Move up past double pegs to easier ground and the top.
FA. Mike Thompson, R.Harris 1961

❹ Amanita Muscarina . . **E4 6a**

Remarkably varied, exposed and sustained climbing from start to finish sets this route firmly in the mold of "modern classic". Start 20m up from the base of the wall on a ledge next to a short slab and below a precarious-looking flake.

1) 5c, 22m. Gain and layback the flake to a ledge. Move up rightwards to a borehole and peg. Climb the borehole via some difficult moves and traverse right to a good ledge and various belays, including an old spike.

2) 6a, 25m. Flip the rope over a spike high on the right for a runner and then make fingery moves direct to a pocket and crack. Climb the crack above the pocket and gain a small ledge, peg. Stand on the ledge and move up the wall to easier ground. Traverse left to a good calcite thread, at the base of an impending corner above. Climb the corner to an awkward stance on a block with various belays.

3) 5c, 23m. Move up right and climb past old bolts to some steep moves on good holds that lead to a prominent peg and small pancake of rock (good thin sling runner). Move up to and over the bulge above and finish leftwards past a short crack and a final steep move to ledges.
FAA. Tony Willmott, Dave Hermalin 2.5.1971 (A5).
FFA. Steve Monks 1979

❺ Yellow Edge **E3 5c**

A steep and exciting journey up the very centre of the wall - a Gorge classic. Start 20m left of the huge corner at a well-trodden patch of ground clear of brambles, beneath a bolt at 9m.

1) 5c, 26m. Move up shale covered ledges to the bolt. Make an awkward short traverse left and up to better holds and another bolt above. Trend right and move up into a vertical borehole and good small wires. Move up to the top of the borehole, peg, and traverse steeply left to a grassy ledge and pull onto it. Move up right to another good ledge with a double staple bolt belay.

2) 5b, 22m. Clip a ring peg above the ledge on the right and make surprisingly difficult moves up the wall and onto a hollow flake/ledge. Move up leftwards and clip a peg before traversing left on good pockets to a peg and deep pocket (just above a prominent metal spike). Climb a crack above the pocket and gain a small ledge, peg. Stand on the ledge and move up the wall to easier ground. Traverse left past a good calcite thread, and the base of the impending corner above, and make steep moves up past a couple of pegs to a hanging belay on a spike and good nuts.

3) 5b, 22m. Climb rightwards on great holds with feet above the overhang past a thread to a harder section where the wall turns smoother. Gain a small pancake of rock (good thin-sling runner) and prominent peg. Now gain the right-to-left sloping ramp and follow this on rounded but plentiful holds to a steep exit near its end. A wildly exposed pitch.
FA. Terry Gloag, P.Johnston 5.1972 (1pt)

Top
50

Avon Somerset

North Devon

Culm Coast

Inland Cornwall

Atlantic Coast

West Penwith

The Lizard

Inland Devon

Torbay

Dorset

❶ **New Horizons** E3 5c

The huge arete on the right-hand side of the lower wall is a good but slightly bold route. Start 3m to the left of the arete.

1) 5c, 23m. Move up to the base of a small corner and traverse right across the bottom of a grey slab to the arete. Ascend the arete to an overhang, peg. Make a perplexing move through the overhang via a short hanging corner and climb a little way above to a ledge and a belay on the arete.

2) 5c, 22m. Move right and climb a short crack and wall above the stance to a thread (thin sling needed). Move left to the arete and make delicate moves to a peg from where easier climbing up the arete finishes at the apex of the lower wall.
FA. Richard Harrison, Andy Hall 7.8.1977

❷ **Hocus Pocus** E4 6a

The towering face right of the arete is taken centrally by this superb and sustained route. Start just to the left of the large corner at the base of the face.

1) 6a, 18m. Move up to and climb a thin crack and wall to a bolt. Pass the bolt leftwards via some fingery moves to a thin horizontal break. Traverse left with difficulty and move up a tiny corner to a good crack, then climb up it to the next set of ledges. Move left to a belay on the arete as for *New Horizons*.

2) 5c, 20m. Move back right and climb a short crack and wall above the stance to a thread (thin sling needed). Continue in the same line up a little corner, peg, to a prominent peg on the right. Climb past the peg to a lighter band of rock and a peg on the left below a small white corner. Climb the wall right of the white corner, past a peg, to the top.
FA. Martin Corbett, Steve Bell 29.4.1981

❸ **M1** E1 5b

A fabulous single-pitch, fully loaded with a great deal of excellent and varied climbing. Start beneath the large corner/groove at the base of the face.

35m. Follow the blank corner/groove to ledges before heading right along a break to the base of a scoop. A few difficult moves up the right-hand side of the scoop, peg, gain the base of a right-leaning groove which leads to a ledge and easier ground.
FA. Tony Willmott, Mike Spring 1971 (1pt)

❹ **Ladder of Desire** E3 5c

An enthralling wall-pitch composed of numerous testing parts and culminating in an exciting finish. Start at a blank section of wall 7m right of the long corner groove of *M1*.

35m. Make some bouldery moves up the initial wall before moving left and climbing a corner/groove to a break and two pegs. Make bold moves rightwards up the wall to a ledge. From a short crack on the left, move up left to pockets that lead to a concrete block. Move right to a narrow groove and climb this and the wall above with difficulty past a pocket and bolt on the left to better finishing holds that lead to the ramp.
FA. Richard Harrison, Andy Hall 7.2.1978

The rest of the routes start from the ramp.

❺ **Them** E3 6a

A thrilling pitch combining a head-spinning position with faultless wall-climbing. Start at the top of the ramp.

26m. Traverse out left for 3m along the break, level with the ramp, to a tiny ledge. Climb slightly rightwards up the wall, past 2 pegs, to good nuts in the cracks above. Move up leftwards with difficulty to the base of an open groove and a peg on the right and proceed up the groove to where it fades. Finish up the fingery final wall passing a peg.
FA. Pat Littlejohn, Chris King 17.11.1977

❻ **New Horizons II** E2 5c

A good pitch that takes on a fine corner-crack close to the top of the ramp. Start at a right-facing flake-crack 10m down from the top of the ramp.

20m. Climb the corner past some difficult moves midway, to where it ends at a short steep headwall. Traverse right to better holds and easier ground leading back left to belays. The short headwall can be climbed directly via a long move at 6a.
FA. Richard Harrison, Steve Findlay 18.7.1977

❼ **Mirage** E3 6a

An upper wall testpiece that features a hard but well-protected crux. Start at a right-leaning crack, the base of which disappears into a hole in the ramp.

18m. Follow the crack pleasantly to a hand-ledge. Continue more steeply to where it thins, and make a couple of urgent pulls up the wall just left of the crack to an easy finish up a tiny corner.
FA. Richard Harrison, Andy Hall 11.2.1978

❽ **Arms Race** E4 5c

A popular pumper that folows a fine, well-protected finger-crack. The rock anchor bolts are out-of-bounds for holds! Start at the bottom of a thin right-trending crack below an overhang at 7m with a couple of massive rock anchors just above it.
Photo on page 43.

18m. Climb the strenuous crack past the overhang and up the grey wall until it fades below a massive ring bolt. Move up to just below the ring bolt (runner only!) traverse the thin break left and move up to a short crack and easier climbing to the top.
FA. Steve Monks, Paul Newman 18.10.1979

❾ **Low Profile** E5 6b

Superb and very sustained wall-climbing. Start at pockets in the wall just left of a small overhang, 4m right of the start of *Arms Race*.

20m. Climb up the pockets to meet the base of a short right-trending crack. Climb the crack to a peg and step right to a thinner crack. Climb this past another peg to a move right and a shakeout on the blunt arete. Move up to a peg and then climb the steepening wall past a peg on the left to the top.
FA. Andy Hall, Pete Long 10.5.1980

❿ **Rancho Cucamonga** . . . E3 5c

Smart climbing that is low in the grade. Start at a pocketed yellow streak just left of *Banshee's* thin crack.

16m. Reach up to the pockets and take these to a peg. Move up to another peg on the right (on *Banshee*) and make a long move to a flat hold at the base of a slim groove, peg. Climb the left wall of the groove to meet a horizontal crack and finish on good holds to the right. Cable abseil station above and left.
FA. Gordon Jenkin, Matt Ward, Martin Crocker, Tony Penning 3.6.1989

⓫ **Banshee** E2 5c

A neat little pitch. Start 50m up the ramp at the first section of pocketed wall below a thin crack in the grey wall 2m left of two rock anchor bolts.

16m. Climb the crack until level with two pegs on the left. Step left to the pegs and then climb the left-hand side of the shallow arete above to a final mantel onto a sloping ledge. A cable abseil station is a few metres up to the left.
FA. Gordon Jenkin, Dave Viggers 16.6.1984

Avon Somerset
North Devon
Culm Coast
Inland Cornwall
Atlantic Coast
West Penwith
The Lizard
Inland Devon
Torbay
Dorset

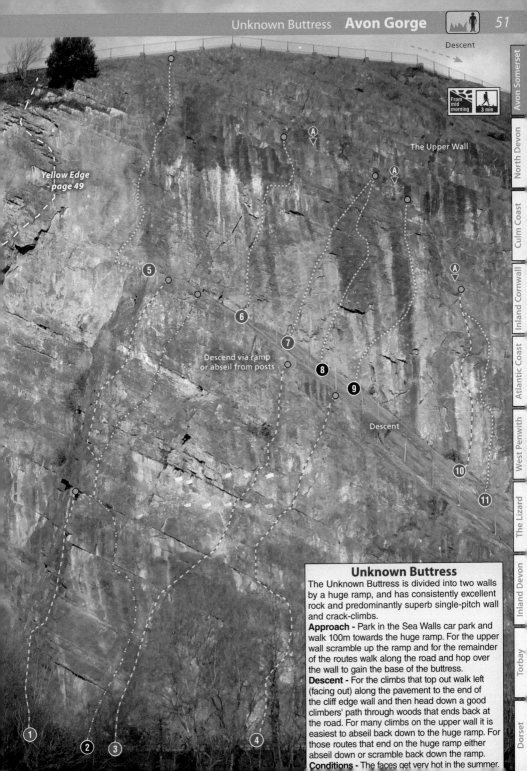

Descent

The Upper Wall

*Yellow Edge
page 49*

Descend via ramp
or abseil from posts

Descent

Unknown Buttress

The Unknown Buttress is divided into two walls
by a huge ramp, and has consistently excellent
rock and predominantly superb single-pitch wall
and crack-climbs.

Approach - Park in the Sea Walls car park and
walk 100m towards the huge ramp. For the upper
wall scramble up the ramp and for the remainder
of the routes walk along the road and hop over
the wall to gain the base of the buttress.

Descent - For the climbs that top out walk left
(facing out) along the pavement to the end of
the cliff edge wall and then head down a good
climbers' path through woods that ends back at
the road. For many climbs on the upper wall it is
easiest to abseil back down to the huge ramp. For
those routes that end on the huge ramp either
abseil down or scramble back down the ramp.

Conditions - The faces get very hot in the summer.

Avon Somerset
North Devon
Culm Coast
Inland Cornwall
Atlantic Coast
West Penwith
The Lizard
Inland Devon
Torbay
Dorset

Avon Somerset

North Devon

Culm Coast

Inland Cornwall

Atlantic Coast

West Penwith

The Lizard

Inland Devon

Torbay

Dorset

Sea Walls

The Sea Walls are the most popular section of The Avon Gorge and have a line-up of easily-accessed routes to please most tastes, these range from the super serious to the amenable ramble. The most popular climbs are polished, although in cool conditions it isn't a problem.

Approach - The car park is directly below the cliff and care should be taken when pulling in from the main road.

Descent - Walk off to the left (looking out) down through woods on a good climbers' path.

Conditions - The crag becomes an oven in hot weather and there is no shade. Many of the climbs dry quickly after rainfall.

Descent

❶ Gronk . . . . 🗒️🏃📦 VS 4c

A fascinating outing that takes in plenty of exciting situations and has some surprisingly difficult moves. The first pitch is at the top of the grade and care is needed to protect the second on the traverses on pitches 3 and 4. Start at a short, well-scratched thin crack.

1) 4c, 26m. Climb up past the crack and continue in the same line to a peg and a couple of good nuts just above. Gain the ledge above via a perplexing move before heading left to a short corner that ends at vegetated ledges. Various belays.

2) 4b, 10m. Above are two corners right of a big blank wall with bolts in it. Climb up the right-hand corner a metre or so and move right out to the arete and flake-crack just beyond. Climb the flake-crack to a good ledge in a corner up and left. Poor belays.

3) 4b, 15m. Climb out right and make some awkward moves diagonally rightwards to a perch on a small ledge. Step down and right and move into the wide corner-crack which is climbed to a ledge belay. It is probably wise to place a runner in the diagonal break above the belay in order to protect the second on the traverse.

4) 4b, 20m. Follow the exposed left-trending diagonal breaks with good gear and holds to a tree belay.

5) 4a, 10m. Climb the corner above the tree to the first overhang, pull left to an easy gully and finish up this,

FA. Barry Annette, Mike Thompson 2.1961

❷ Morpheus . . . . 🗒️✒️🏃📦 HVD

A long and popular trip that has masses of interesting climbing punctuated with good belay ledges. The climbing is fairly tough in places but these sections are well-protected. Begin at a short wall just right of the thin crack at the start of *Gronk*.

1) 4a, 28m. Boulder up the short steep wall to a big ledge and a good nut runner. Wander right to an easy-angled blocky corner. Follow the corner for a couple of moves until easy-angled slabs and short walls lead back leftwards to a belay in a little bay at a tall white-stained flake.

2) 16m. Layback up to the top of the flake and move right and up. Continue up short walls slightly right until a move left gains easy ground and a block covered belay ledge which is below a corner with an intermittent wide crack in it.

3) 10m. Climb the corner to an old peg and overcome the next section of the corner by moving right and up. Continue to a good stance on the right. Climbing the corner and wide crack direct is much harder.

4) 12m. Move up to below a small bush and then climb diagonally right to a ledge and the top.

FA. Mike Rhodes, P.Ford 1956

❸ Sleepwalk . . . . 🗒️✒️📦 S 4a

A Sea Walls classic that sees plenty of action. The climbing is bold on the third pitch but is fairly straightforward and not polished. Start at a short wall just right of a thin crack, as for *Morpheus*.

1) 4a, 18m. Boulder up the short steep wall to a big ledge and a good nut-runner. Wander right to an easy-angled blocky corner and follow this for 5m to a belay ledge and rock spike.

2) 16m. Move leftwards up a smooth slab to a broken corner-line, follow this to a good ledge and belay on its right side. The lower belay nuts are poor but the best placement is just above and not easily seen when standing on the belay ledge.

3) 17m. Climb the right-trending slabs above in a fine position, but with no protection, to a good crack where the wall steepens. A quick pull gains a belay ledge.

4) 4a, 10m. Climb the steep, well-protected corner-crack behind the belay to finish.

FA. Mike Thompson, W.Nissin 2,1960

The next set of routes is centred around a large, smooth walled open corner at the base of the crag, that is covered in graffiti.

❹ Ffoeg's Folly . . . . 🗒️🏃📦 E2 5c

A great combination of pitches taking the left-hand of two parallel grooves in the centre of the walls - the visually striking first pitch being a good HVS in its own right. Start at the shallow open corner with a large 'starfish' shaped piece of graffiti on its right wall.

1) 5a, 16m. Forcefully climb the steep corner-crack to a ledge. Bolt belay.

2) 5c, 23m. Take the groove above the stance, which can sprout various plants in the summer, to where it steepens. Move up past a peg and then pull right to the arete. Step back left to the short blank corner, small wire, and climb this to a huge jug at its top, and a hard-to-spot ring peg on the right. Climb the short slab above to a terrace and belay. Move down and right to the large fir tree and abseil off.

FA. Ed Ward Drummond, Pete Morgan 3.1967

❺ Last Slip . . . . 🗒️📷📦 E3 5c

A superb bold and memorable climb taking the blank wall and soaring groove right of *Ffoeg's Folly*. Start right of the 'starfish' graffiti at the base of the open corner of *Ffoeg's Folly*.

1) 5b, 16m. Move right up an easy sloping ramp to its highest point and then make some fingery wall moves to easier ground and the first belay of *Ffoeg's Folly*. This is a very bold pitch that is unprotected and is often swapped for the first pitch of *Ffoeg's Folly*.

2) 5c, 24m. Traverse right and climb up to reach a bolt on the left rib of the lower groove, move right and up to a small overhang. Enter the groove above with difficulty and climb boldly to a peg. Continue up the narrowing groove that curves right, before heading up a short corner on the left with a hard-to-spot ring peg at its top, then take the short slab above to a terrace and belay. Move down and right to the large fir tree and abseil off.

FA. Ed Ward Drummond, Cathy Woodhead 1966 (1pt)
FFA. Chris Perry 1969

❻ Nightmare . . . . 🗒️✒️📷📦 S 4a

An Avon trade route that, although polished, is still a very classy piece of climbing. It is worth noting that the long runout on the second pitch is not polished. Start at a corner, right of some vegetation. High in the grade.

1) 4a, 12m. Bridge up the corner to below a small overhang and cracked block. Traverse left awkwardly and move up to a small tree and belay ledge just above.

2) 4a, 22m. Pull out right to a ledge beneath a corner. Move up and right around the arete and follow the magnificent line of good holds and ledges boldly rightwards and up to a grassy ledge. Continue to the fir tree belay above with a difficult move to access the ledge.

3) 4a, 20m. Above the fir tree is a right-slanting corner, move up to its start and then traverse right for around 4m to a line of well-used holds on the wall. Climb the wall to an easing and then head left on easy ground to finish.

FA. Mike Thompson, W.Nissin 2,1960

Avon Somerset | North Devon | Culm Coast | Inland Cornwall | Atlantic Coast | West Penwith | The Lizard | Inland Devon | Torbay | Dorset

Avon Somerset | North Devon | Culm Coast | Inland Cornwall | Atlantic Coast | West Penwith | The Lizard | Inland Devon | Torbay | Dorset

❼ Edgemaster E6 6b

A stunning line and very hard climbing combine to yield a memorable testpiece. Start below a steep wall with a narrow, white stained, rightward-trending ramp-line at mid-height.
28m. Move up to, and past a peg with difficulty to the base of the ramp-line, bolt. Ascend the ramp-line to a big flake and then head for the large fir tree on easier ground. Abseil off.
FA. Martin Crocker, Gordon Jenkin, Dave Viggars 1.1.1985

❽ Padansac. E2 5c

A popular little climb that follows the tapering open groove right of the steep white-stained wall. Start below the open groove.
27m. Climb the technical groove, past 2 pegs, to a ledge and big flake. Finish up easier ground to a belay at the large fir tree. Abseil off.
FA. M.Jeffs, Dave Mortimer 1968

❾ Simian . . . . HVS 5a

A butch exercise. Start below a recess 3m above the ground with a borehole strike at its back.
30m. Move up to the borehole, and then climb the right-hand wall to an easing below a steep crack and undercut wall, some good gear here. Make big moves to jugs over the lip and haul up to a resting place. Climb more easily to a bolt and then head right to finish up the cleanest line.
FA. Fred Bennett 8.5.1966

❿ Daydream . . . . VS 5a

One of the best single-pitch climbs on this section of the cliff, high in the grade. Start below a thin crack-line just right of the low recess at the base of *Simian*.
28m. Make some hard, technical starting moves up the thin crack and continue to an overhang. Move left to below a steep corner and climb this to an interesting exit rightwards on some amazingly high friction rock. Take the long narrow corner more easily to the top.
FA. Geoff Mason, Robert Walker 1966

⓫ Idleburger Buttress . . . . VDiff

A popular line that, although well-travelled, is still worthwhile. It is endowed with good gear on its hardest moves at mid-height. Start at a low ledge on the nose of the buttress.
26m. Move onto the ledge and work left on ledges for a few metres until it is possible to pick the easiest line up, then move rightwards to below a big overhang. Move right and then step up left to clear the overhang. Continue more easily past a cluster of bolts and finish leftwards.
FA. Fred Bennett, John Nixon, E.M.Baldwin 1956

⓬ Floating Voter . . . . VS 4c

A snaking line that possesses a couple of testing moves. Start at a rightward-leading narrow ramp, left of a brown-stained wall.
26m. Move up the ramp and make a puzzling move up the narrow corner above. Continue more easily, passing an overhang on its right, then climb a crack through the next overhang and move right to finish up the grey wall, above some bolts.
FA. M.Taylor, Robert Walker 30.3.1966

⓭ Jasper. . . . . HVS 5b

A very polished local classic that is high in the grade, but does involve some fine climbing. Start at the corner right of the brown-stained wall.
24m. Climb the right wall of the corner, with little gear at hand, to easier ground and good gear in the wider flakes midway up the corner. Steeper moves lead to the overhang where hard moves over it gain the tree. Move up leftwards and then finish direct past bolts.
FA. M.Taylor, Robert Walker 4.1966

From mid morning | Roadside

Abseil from tree

Descent

Avon Somerset

North Devon

Culm Coast

Inland Cornwall

Atlantic Coast

West Penwith

The Lizard

Inland Devon

Torbay

Dorset

Embarking on the steep ground of the sustained *Central Wall* (E4 6a) - *page 59* - on the Main Wall at Avon Gorge.

The Main Wall Overview

The Main Wall is an impressive curve of quarried lime-stone with a vast amount of great climbing on its various sectors, which rise to a height of 70m. The climbing is all traditional with most of the routes being multi-pitch. This is a good venue for all teams with fine climbs throughout the grades.

Approach - All the climbs are very easily viewed from the parking area. Many of the climbs require a scramble up ledges to reach the first belays.

Descent - To regain the base of the cliff is very straightforward. A descent can be made at either end of the crag. The left side of the crag has a number of steep and muddy paths that are easily located, which drop down to meet the base of the crag, close to the road. The right-hand side of the crag has a much cleaner descent. Follow a surfaced path along the cliff edge. When it turns inland, take the right-hand branch and after a short distance cut down a climbers' path, through trees, to pick up another surfaced path that meets the main road. Walk along the bus lane to the base of the crag.

Conditions - Fast drying and sunny, this wall is a fine winter venue, though it can be very unpleasant in hot weather.

❶ Choker . . . . 🔲🔲🔲 **E1 5a**
Stylish and exposed climbing up the left side of the buttress. Start on a belay ledge beneath a black-streaked groove.
1) 5a, 20m. From the left side of the ledge take a narrow, diagonal ramp out leftwards to two good hidden pegs at the base of a white wall. Climb the wall to another peg and then move up and left to a big quarry-spike just left of the arete. Move around to the left side of the arete and climb up over an overhang and belay below a rickety tree.
2) 4c, 16m. Move rightwards onto the face and make intricate moves right to the base of a shallow groove in the centre of the face. Climb the groove past a peg, all the way to a large tree at the top of the crag. Walk off or abseil from the tree.
FA. Greg Lyne, Terry Taylor 1963

❷ The Corpse . . . . 🔲🔲🔲 **HVS 5a**
A strong line, good gear, and plenty of variety make this a worthwhile and popular route. Start on a belay ledge beneath a groove.
30m. Move easily up the wall right of the streaked groove and then step left to a small corner at 5m. Take the corner past a peg, and the relatively bold wall above on good holds to a ledge at the base of a right-leaning corner, where there are some more pegs. Climb the corner to a difficult and polished exit onto a ledge. Finish up easier rock to a large tree at the top of the crag. Walk off or abseil from the tree.
FA. Chris Jones, John Wooton 1964 (1pt)

❸ Zombogies Direct . . . . . 🔲🔲🔲 **E1 5b**
An excellent pitch on superb rock. The start is a touch bold. Start on a belay ledge up and right from the larger belay ledge at the base of *The Corpse*.
26m. Step up to a smaller ledge on the right and from its left side boldly climb leftwards from a vertical borehole with a low peg at its base, to good holds. A stretch gains a jug and further good, but concealed holds that lead up and then leftwards to a junction with the ledge at the base of the upper corner of *The Corpse*. Now head off rightwards following the pleasant right-trending narrow groove to easier ground and a big tree belay. Walk off or abseil from the tree.
FA. Oliver Hill, D.Bradley 4.1967

❹ The Lich . . . . 🔲🔲🔲 **HVS 5a**
An Avon favourite, featuring fine climbing, protection and posi-tions. Start on a belay ledge up and right from the larger belay ledge at the base of *The Corpse*.
30m. Step up to a smaller ledge on the right. Follow the line of weakness left of the blunt right-hand arete to a peg underneath a shattered overhang, and pull over the overhang with care. Move up to another small overhang and move left past a peg, and then up and back right towards the arete. Take the thin crack to a final overlap and move left and up the final slab. Various tree belays. Walk off or abseil from the trees.
FA. Barry Annette, Mike Thompson 1961 (1pt)

❺ Bonbogies . . . . 🔲🔲🔲 **HVS 5a**
A well-travelled and testing pitch that wanders up to, and past the left side of the prominent triple pointed overhang midway up the crag. Start at a narrow ledge and stunted tree directly below the triple pointed overhang.
30m. Move leftwards for 4m and then climb up to the left end of an 'eyebrow' overhang, large cams. Pull up its left side to a small ledge and then stride right above the overhang into a corner that is bridged to the left side of the triple pointed overhang, peg. Pull over the overhang and follow the slab to the base of a stepped white rib on the left. Follow the rib to a tree belay. Scramble to the top and walk off or abseil.
FA. Mike Rhodes, P.Ford 1957

Lich Area

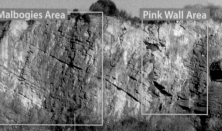
Malbogies Area

Pink Wall Area

Morning Slab and Evening Wall

Central Buttress

The Lich Area

The left side of the Main Wall has a number of good and popular routes that are a nice introduction to the climbing style on these walls.

Approach - Scramble up ledges to various belays.
Descent - Either by abseil or walk off. Abseil is preferable if more that one route is to be attempted.

Lots of sun | Roadside | Multi-pitch

Avon Somerset

North Devon

Culm Coast

Inland Cornwall

Atlantic Coast

West Penwith

The Lizard

Inland Devon

Torbay

Dorset

Descent

2

7

6

3 4

This belay ledge is reached via the start of route 1

Very loose

Original start

5

1

7

Approach scramble

❶ Pink Ginsane . . 🔲🔲🔲🔲 ⬜ **E6 6b**

A very exposed and runout pitch that takes on the blank central section of the pink wall, high on the left side of the face. Start via a scramble to a good ledge directly below the wall.

1) 5a, 30m. Move up a rib and wall on the left to ledges (belay of *Krapp's Last Tape* and *Main Wall Eliminate* on the right). Move up and traverse left until a rib can be climbed past a spike to a bulge and peg. Pull up into the groove above the bulge, peg, and climb it until a belay can be taken at some horizontal breaks.

2) 6b, 25m. Move up to the pink wall and clip two bolts above (on *Think Pink*). Move left and then up a line of holds into the middle of the wall. Climb rightwards, bolt, and then up, bolt, before traversing right into a groove (on *Think Pink*), bolt. Hard moves out left into a shallow niche are followed by a big runout above it which ends at a peg and better holds. A short bulging section gains a belay ledge and tree on the right.

3) 6b, 13m. Climb a slim groove past a peg and make a long move up the wall above to another peg. Finish leftwards.

FFA. Richard Harrison, Derek Carter 20.3.1981

❷ Think Pink . . . . 🔲🔲🔲 ⬜ **E3 6a**

The central line of weakness in the suspended white and pink wall is brilliant. Start via a scramble to a good ledge directly below the wall, as for *Pink Ginsane*.

1) 5a, 30m. As for *Pink Ginsane*, then traverse right to a stance at a quarry spike and bolt at the top off *Krapp's Last Tape*.

2) 6a, 25m. Move left from the spike belay to a steep wall below a small overhang with two bolts in it. Climb with difficulty past the bolts and over the left end of the overhang to an easing and a peg at the base of a long groove. Climb the groove to a bolt and stretch past it to a better series of cracks that are climbed to a belay ledge and tree.

3) 5c, 14m. Move left along the break to below a right-slanting thin crack with a peg near its base. Climb past the peg and continue a short distance before better holds lead leftwards up the wall away from the crack to the top and a tree belay.

FFA. Richard Harrison 4.12.1977

❸ Krapp's Last Tape . . 🔲🔲🔲 ⬜ **E3 5b**

An Avon rite of passage. Good climbing with a bold feel, although the gear improves as height is gained. Start at a peg and nut belay on a high ledge reached via the initial 9m of *Pink Ginsane's* first pitch.

30m. Take the easy-angled groove above the belay to a peg. Step up above the peg and pull out left on to the wall, good small nut. Move up and bridge right to a point below an overhang with pegs below it. Pull over the overhang, good nut in borehole, to a peg before moving down right and then up to an overhang, peg and another good nut. Traverse left below the overhang past a peg to a stance at a quarry spike and bolt. Finish up *Think Pink* or abseil off.

FA. Ed Ward Drummond, Cathy Woodhead 5.1967

❹ Main Wall Eliminate 🔲🔲🔲 **E4 6a**

An intimidating pitch featuring both delicate and strenuous climbing. Start at the peg and nut belay of *Krapp's Last Tape*.

28m. Climb up rightwards past a peg and up a shallow corner to an overhang, pegs. Pull over the overhang at a tiny corner, 2 pegs, and continue to a bolt. Steep climbing through the overhangs above on reasonable holds gains a break and bolt above. Head upwards to a shallow depression with two bolts in its left wall and climb it to its end, from where moves left reach an abseil station.

FFA. Chris King 6.1978

Malbogies Area

The right-hand side of the Main Wall has a number of long, hard routes that typify the best of what the Avon Gorge has to offer on its quarried walls.

Approach - Scramble up ledges to various belays.
Descent - Either by abseil or walk off.
Conditions - The wall is very exposed to wind and sun and dries quickly. There is little seepage.

❺ Malbogies . . . . 🔲🔲🔲🔲 ⬜ **HVS 5a**

Main Wall's most famous line is a fine climb that follows a subtle left-to-right line of weakness through an intimidating rockscape. A classic. Start on a grassy ledge at the base of the line.

1) 5a, 25m. From the left-hand side of the ledge move boldly up a small corner in the blunt arete to double pegs (as for *Central Wall*). Traverse right, beneath a line of overhangs past a number of pegs to a ledge under a shattered looking wall. Climb up rightwards across the wall to a corner and take this to a peg and nut belay on a slab, 5m below the main line of overhangs.

2) 4b, 32m. Climb up past a peg to the overhang and move over it on good holds. Move rightwards and up a broken rib before heading back leftwards under a line of overhangs until is possible to gain the base of a wide depression. Climb up the middle of the depression, passing a peg, to an exit left at the very top.

FA. Chris Bonington, G.Francis, H.Rogers 23.10.1957

❻ Central Wall . . . . . . 🔲🔲🔲 ⬜ **E4 6a**

A high-quality climb on very good rock, with a lot of fixed protection. Start on a grassy ledge at the base of the line. *Photo on page 55*.

28m. From the left-hand side of the ledge, climb boldly up a small corner in the blunt arete to double pegs. Move up to a peg in the wall above and traverse left to a small corner which leads to a hole, thread, peg and good nut. Move up to the overhang above, peg, and make a difficult move to get established above it, peg. Climb the weakness above to the shallow depression with two bolts in its left wall and climb it to its end, from where moves left reach an abseil station.

FFA. Richard Harrison 7.1.1978

❼ The Preter . . . . 🔲🔲🔲🔲 ⬜ **E2 5b**

An airy voyage taking in some of the Main Wall's best positions. The climbing is very sustained and some of it serious. Nevertheless, the gear - when present - is good. The first pitch is dangerously loose, however the original start to *Malbogies* provides a worthy alternative. Start at a small tree on a ledge down and right of *Malbogies*.

1) 5a, 23m. Move up the blunt rib on the left to a gap between two overhangs and pull up right into a corner. Climb the corner (very loose) to an overhang and bush (thread above). Pull over the overhang and move left to the shattered wall of *Malbogies*. Follow the wall and corner to the first stance of *Malbogies*.

1a) 5b, 23m. *The Original Malbogies Start.* From the *Malbogies* stance, move up a right-trending groove to a slim overhang and a peg. Pull over and climb the wall above with difficulty to a ledge. Continue as for *Malbogies* to its first stance.

2) 5b, 28m. Downclimb from the stance for 5m and traverse left on good holds before moving up to good small wires. Move left again and then down to a small overhung niche. Reach left to good holds and move up to a peg. Climb the excellent groove past a peg to the overhang and traverse left for 6m to a peg and large cam belay.

3) 5b, 26m. Traverse back right for 3m to a gap in the overhangs and make a puzzling move up to get established above them. Climb the groove and wall on its left past various pegs to an overhang and move out left around the blunt arete. Finish up the easier wall.

FA. Ed Ward Drummond, W.Hill 1.5.1966

Avon Somerset
North Devon
Culm Coast
Inland Cornwall
Atlantic Coast
West Penwith
The Lizard
Inland Devon
Torbay
Dorset

Avon Somerset

North Devon

Culm Coast

Inland Cornwall

Atlantic Coast

West Penwith

The Lizard

Inland Devon

Torbay

Dorset

❶ Dawn Walk .... S 4a

A long, diagonal expedition crossing the Morning Slab (page 62) that is serious for both leader and second. Start by scrambling to a tree next to a yellow crumbling wall. The final pitch is shown on page 62.

1) 4a, 20m. Climb easily to a cave and move right up a slab then pull into a groove on the right. Move up this and its right wall to an iron spike. Pull up the short steep wall to Breakfast Ledge and a withering tree belay plus low back-up nuts.

2) 4a, 27m. Move right to a vegetated corner and head out along a grass ledge before moving rightwards up the slab to a good, long foot ledge and peg. Shuffle along the ledge till it fades and then climb up the slab to bolt and tree belays.

3) 18m. Climb rightwards to a crack and climb this to the Lunchtime Ledge.

❷ Lich Gates E2 5c

Marvellous climbing and wildly exposed positions combine to make this route one of Avon's greatest excursions. The first pitch is serious for the second whilst the hard moves on pitch two are perfectly protected. Start on Breakfast Ledge.

1) 5a, 30m. From the left end of the higher ledge climb a groove to a good peg and wires. Traverse left to a poor peg and then downclimb left past a distinct finger edge to small ledges. Traverse left again until beneath a corner with a high prominent peg in its left wall. Move left again past a well fingered crack and a hidden peg via steep moves that allow a big quarry spike to be reached a little higher. Move left on easier rock to a stance in a yellow niche and good quarry spike belay 3m above.

2) 5c, 24m. Move up to the right-hand side of the big overhang, peg, and step right and up to a good ledge. Move up the left wall above the overhang with difficulty, 2 pegs, to easier ground. Move up to the leaning headwall and 2 pegs before traversing delicately right into a superbly-positioned groove, peg. Finish up the groove.

FA. Barry Annette, G.Clarke 1961 (5pts)

❸ Peryl........... E4 6a

Quarried perfection. Sustained and intricate climbing with good protection and rock. Start on Breakfast Ledge.

1) 6a, 30m. Follow *Lich Gates* to its second (poor) peg and step up left to below a small overhang. Good nuts in a short crack down to its left. Move up over the overhang, 2 pegs, and then climb a flared groove below a pink wall, peg on left, rightwards to a difficult exit, 2 pegs, and a rest on the right. Traverse the fingery break left, 2 pegs, to a bolted stance.

2) 6a, 25m. Climb up the wall on the right, peg out left and a bolt on the right, to a groove and 2 pegs. Follow the groove to a left-trending break and move left, peg, and up into a small overhang capped corner/groove, peg. At the overhang go left, peg, and pull over the overhang to finish.

FA. Chris Perry, Dave Pearce 28.6.1968 (4pts)
FFA. Richard Harrison, Gordon Jenkin 18.12.1977

❹ Changeling E5 6b

An excellent route incorporating a lot of difficult and tenuous climbing as well as some serious situations on the first pitch. Start on Breakfast Ledge.

1) 6b, 42m. Follow *Lich Gates* up its initial groove to a peg and then move carefully up and slightly right to another peg and wires. Make bold moves diagonally left past a poor peg to join *Peryl* at a peg. Follow *Peryl* up right to a rest and then back left past pegs and move into a shallow groove with difficulty. From two bolts move up slightly right to 2 pegs and make some final pressing moves to a belay.

2) 6b, 12m. Climb up rightwards to a peg and wires, or, up left to a break and a thread and move right and down to the peg. From the peg move up and right to another peg and wires and so on to the top. A committing and exciting pitch.

FA. Richard Harrison, Gordon Jenkin 2.11.1985 (as described)

❺ Pink Wall Direct E2 5c

An engrossing and adventurous tour of the wall. The second pitch is no place for a timid second. Start on Breakfast Ledge. *Photo on page 67.*

1) 5b, 20m. From the right side of the ledge above the tree pull over an overhang and head up and slightly right to a slim corner. Follow this to an overhang and move over it rightwards to a hanging stance on pegs and an old bolt plus nuts.

2) 5c, 26m. Traverse left beneath the overhang to pegs and gear where it fades. Move up and left to a pocket, peg, and then left again to the base of corner groove, peg. Climb the groove and then romp up the three iron spikes on the left wall to a fine stance - the Aerodrome stance.

3) 5a, 14m. Hand traverse left along the exposed rising break, pegs, and finish up the short easy corner.

FA. Barry Annette, C.Jones 2.1964 (4pts)

❻ Pink Wall Traverse .... HVS 5a

Exposed and quirky traversing taking in some of Avon's most impressive locations. Start from The Gallery to the left of Lunchtime Ledge (see page 62 for access to this ledge). Combined with *Mike's Mistake* (page 62) it forms a classically varied way up the cliff. The last pitch and a half is shared with *Pink Wall Direct.*

1) 16m. Traverse easily left beneath an overhang to a tree. Continue in the same line to pegs and a stance under the leaning headwall.

2) 4c, 22m. Downclimb the groove on the left to point level with the lowest of the three huge iron spikes in the sheer left wall. Make a tricky move to grab the first spike and then romp up the spikes to a fine and very exposed stance - the Aerodrome stance.

3) 5a, 14m. Hand traverse left along the exposed rising break, pegs, and finish up the short easy corner.

FA. Barrie Page, H.Morgan (aid) 1955
FFA. Mike Harvey 1956

Lich Area
Malbogies Area
The Pink Wall
Morning Slab and Evening Wall

Central Buttress

Avon Somerset

North Devon

Culm Coast

Inland Cornwall

Atlantic Coast

West Penwith

The Lizard

Inland Devon

Torbay

Dorset

Lots of sun | Roadside | Multi-pitch

Access - A bird ban is in effect on this face between April 1st and June 30th.

Descent

The Gallery

Breakfast Ledge

Approach scramble

The Pink Wall

The steep, white and pale-pink wall that leans out over the left-hand side of Morning Slab is the canvas for a number of brilliant multi-pitch routes. The climbs have bags of atmosphere and although runout in places the rock and protection are generally good.
Approach - All of the climbs except for *Pink Wall Traverse* start from the Breakfast Ledge which is normally gained via the first pitch of *Dawn Walk*. The start of *Dawn Walk* is accessed by walking up the slope from the base of Morning Slab.
Descent - Walk off either left or right.
Conditions - The face dries very quickly following rain and does not seep badly. The face is also a suntrap in the afternoon which is perfect in winter but can become too hot in the warmer months.

Avon Somerset

North Devon

Culm Coast

Inland Cornwall

Atlantic Coast

West Penwith

The Lizard

Inland Devon

Torbay

Dorset

Descent

Pink Wall Traverse - page 60

The Gallery

6 7 8 9

A

Lunchtime Ledge

Dawn Walk - page 60

Breakfast Ledge

1 2 3 4 5

1 Mike's Mistake . 〈✂🖊✍🐦 [ ] E1 5b

Spicy climbing up the centre of Morning Slab. High in the grade. Start at an old, small tree-stump just before the ground rises up to the left.

1) 5b, 35m. Climb to the first overhang and pull over it into a right-leaning groove. Move up to a bolt and then step right and upwards with difficulty to easier ground and a peg. Climb up to the second band of overhangs past another peg, and pull through to the slab above. Pad up this to a tree and bolted belay.

2) 18m. Finish up the third pitch of *Dawn Walk*.

FA. Mike Harvey, E.Baldwin 1956

2 Clarion . . . . 〈✂🖊🖊 [ ] VS 4c

Lovely climbing on an enticing line, and with much better gear than first appearances would suggest. Start below a slim snaking groove-system where the upper overhangs fade.

1) 4c, 28m. Climb to the first band of overhangs and step up into an open groove. Follow the open groove to its end at the next horizontal break before stepping left and up into the final rounded groove. Intricate climbing up the groove gains a small tree and nut belay.

2) 4a, 20m. Climb above the stance, moving rightwards to the base of a wide rounded crack. Move insecurely up the crack to a small tree and finish on easy ground to Lunchtime Ledge.

FA. M.Ward 6.1956

3 Sinister . . . . 〈✂🖊🖊 [ ] HS 4b

Pleasant, popular and polished climbing with three good pitches. Start below a small broken rib at 4m, just right of *Clarion*.

1) 4b, 22m. Climb the broken pillar to good gear in the break at the first set of overhangs. Step over the overhang onto a large, slick foothold and move up the short slab to the base of a narrow corner. Follow the corner to a bulging wall above and devise an exit right to a tree belay.

2) 4b, 10m. Move left and up to a football sized hold. Step left and pull on to a slab. Traverse left to a small tree and nut belays.

3) 4a, 20m. Finish up the wide rounded crack of *Clarion's* second pitch.

FA. Geoff Sutton, B.Dowman, Pat Browne 1950

4 Dexter . . . . 〈✂🖊🐦 [ ] HS 4b

A worthwhile and pulse enhancing route making the most of the slabby wall left of *The Arete*. Start 2m left of *The Arete*.

1) 25m. Climb up and diagonally left without much gear to a gap in the bushes. Move left across and up a slab to a tree belay below a wide rounded runnel.

2) 4b, 26m. Take the smooth wide runnel onto the open smooth slab. Move up a thin, fading crack to its end and then up the bold slab to an easing. Continue up the steadier slab above to Lunchtime Ledge.

FA. Geoff Sutton, B.Dowman, Pat Browne 1950

5 The Arete. . . . . 〈✂🖊 [ ] VDiff 4a

Enjoyable, clean climbing on a strong line make this the area's best route at the grade and an Avon favourite, though now well-glossed. Start at the base of the arete. *Photo on page 46*.

1) 13m. Take the arete to a tree belay.

2) 13m. Continue up the groove and arete to a ledge.

3) 4a, 14m. The ledge above is very awkward and slippery to stand on! Thankfully the rest of the pitch to gain Lunchtime Ledge is far easier.

FA. Geoff Sutton (solo) 1940's

Morning Slab and Evening Wall

Morning Slab is a massive hulk of compact rock, split in its lower half by bands of narrow overhangs. The upper Evening Wall is steeper and has much stronger lines. A good deal of the routes on the Morning Slab are runout, although the rock is generally excellent. The large tree-covered ledge that splits Morning Wall from Evening Wall is known as Lunchtime Ledge and is a pleasant place to relax between routes.

Approach - Walk through gaps in the iron fence to the base of the climbs.

Descent - Walk off to the left (facing out) along paths that descend well to the side of the cliff and end at the road from where a quick walk along the bus lane regains the parking layby below the Main Wall. Alternatively, from Lunchtime Ledge, make a 50m abseil to the ground from the tree at the left end (facing in) of the ledge.

Conditions - On hot days the polish shines through and can make the climbs unpleasant and more difficult.

The next four climbs all start from the Lunchtime Ledge.

6 Bob's Climb . . . . 〈✂🖊 [ ] VDiff

A fantastic climb covering some impressive ground for the grade. Start at a large tree belay on the left of Lunchtime Ledge.

1) 24m. Traverse left across the smooth slab and then move left around the base of a big block overhang. Follow the corner above past a small tree to another tree and belay ledge.

2) 18m. Behind the tree is a blank looking wall. Climb this rightwards on good hidden holds to reach a big rock anchor bolt. Continue up a corner to a big overhang and pass it steeply using huge holds to easier ground and an abrupt finish.

FA. R.Smith, J.Clark 1956

7 Petros . . . . 〈✂🖊 [ ] VS 4c

A fun pitch that requires a number of interesting manoeuvres not found in the average rock climbing manual. Start at a large tree close to the back of the ledge, next to two acute overhangs.

25m. Climb up the tree and fix a runner in the branches before stepping onto the slab above the overhangs. Without the aid of a large rock anchor bolt climb the slab to a peg at the base of a right-leaning flake. Climb the flake, peg, to its end and a useful iron spike runner. Pull up the steep wall above the flake and finish steeply leftwards on good holds, passing another iron spike runner midway.

8 Direct Route. . . . . . 〈✂🖊🐦 [ ] S 4a

A well-travelled line up the slab and corner in the centre of Evening Wall. Start at the left side of the slab where it abuts a steep wall.

23m. Make a bouldery move over the low overhang to get established on the slab. Climb the polished slab, with a move right to runners in a thin horizontal crack halfway. Gain a ledge at the base of the steeper upper corner. Follow the corner to an exit on the left. A variation finish up the wall and overhang right of the final corner is also worthwhile.

FA. Geoff Sutton (solo) 1940s

9 Original Route . . . . [ ] Diff

The easiest way off of Lunchtime Ledge. Start on the far right-hand side of Lunchtime Ledge.

23m. Follow a rightward trending line of grooves, ledges and trees to the top.

FA. Geoff Sutton (solo) 1940s

Avon Somerset

North Devon

Culm Coast

Inland Cornwall

Atlantic Coast

West Penwith

The Lizard

Inland Devon

Torbay

Dorset

Avon Somerset
North Devon
Culm Coast
Inland Cornwall
Atlantic Coast
West Penwith
The Lizard
Inland Devon
Torbay
Dorset

① Central Rib . . . . VS 4b

A shy line that winds its way up some intimidating ground. The climbing is a touch runout and the finish exposed. Start by scrambling to a stance beneath a shallow groove, topped by an overhang.
1) 4b, 20m. Climb the groove to a peg under a small overhang on the left, then move up to the larger overhang and pull over. Move right to a stance in a sloping niche, peg and nut belays.
2) 4a, 15m. Step left and move up a shallow corner to an overhang and peg. Traverse leftwards below small overhangs to a sapling and then climb direct, passing a small tree on the right, to a short steep crack that is climbed to a larger tree and belay.
3) 4b, 26m. Traverse right to a grey-stained niche, pegs. Move right again to the end of the overhang and pull up and then back left above the overhangs. Climb flakes and then short walls to an easy slab which is followed to the top.
FA. Barrie Page, A.Clarke 1954

② Great Central Route . . . HVS 5a

An all-time winner finding its way through steep territory on the first pitch and in airy locations on the second. Start by scrambling to a belay at the lowest of three small trees.
1) 5a, 23m. Climb small corners to the highest tree and then climb the wall on the right to the overhangs and a peg. Pull over the overhang past another peg, and traverse right between the overhangs until good holds allow a stiff pull to be made through the second overhang, peg. Climb the rib and step left to a short corner and an awkward stance just above, at the base of a corner below a steep wall.
2) 4c, 45m. Move left around the edge of the steep wall and into a corner, peg. Climb up right to the arete and then with hands on the lip of an overhang traverse back left and pull over the overhang on good holds. Move right once again to the arete and gain the long, easy-angled finishing slab.
FA. Hugh Banner, L.J.Griffin 1953

③ Piton Route . . . . . . VS 4c

A 'Classic Rock' tick taking on the well defined right-to-left diagonal line that slants up the left side of the crest of the buttress. Start at a peg and nut belay at the top of Exhibition Slab.
1) 4c, 20m. Move left 6m to a wide corner. Climb the corner to a peg and the make a precarious sequence of moves left across the wall to an easing. Continue traversing left beneath the overhangs and then step down to a sloping niche and peg and nut belays.
2) 4a, 14m. Step back right and move up and then left to pass the overhang. Climb a slab on the left to a small tree and then continue up a short steep crack to a larger tree and belay.
3) 4b, 24m. Behind and left of the tree is a wall with a borehole. Take the wall via diagonal cracks, steep at first, to an easing up and left. Continue up ledges past a vertical iron spike and then via easier ground to the top and a substantial twin tree belay.
FA. Graham Balcombe 1936 (1pt)

④ Central Buttress . . . E1 5a

A classic and very bold line that gives a memorable climb. Start at a peg and nut belay at the top of the Exhibition Slab, as for *Piton Route*.
1) 5a, 23m. Climb straight up the blunt rib to a horizontal break, peg. Climb past the break on the right with difficulty and continue straight up to a second break and overlap, pegs. Pull over and climb boldly up and left, to gain a left-facing flake. Once again climb boldly up and left to a belay on a small sloping ledge below the midpoint of a red leaning wall. Poor 8mm bolt, good medium cam, peg and nuts up to the left.
2) 5a, 27m. Move right under the steep wall, pegs, until a dramatic step around the overhangs can be made to gain a good horizontal slot. Step right and up past a hidden pocket in the steep wall to a final pull over the lip that gains an easy slab above. Continue to the top past several small trees (possible belays).
FA. L.J.Griffin, Hugh Banner, 1952

Central Buttress

The long narrow rib at the far right-hand end of the cliff holds some high quality climbs, though they are limited in number. Some of the climbing is polished and protection is at times poor.

Approach - At the base of the buttress is a low-angled slab, the Exhibition Slab. To its left is a broken area of rock. Both of these features are easily ascended to the various first stances and belays.

Descent - Walk off to the left (facing out) along paths that descend well to the side of the cliff and end at the road from where a quick walk along the bus lane regains the parking layby below the Main Wall.

Conditions - The climbs get some useful shade in the mornings. The rock dries very quickly but offers no shelter from rain.

Avon Somerset

North Devon

Culm Coast

Inland Cornwall

Atlantic Coast

West Penwith

The Lizard

Inland Devon

Torbay

Dorset

Descent

The Arete - page 63

② ①

③④ Peg-belay

Exhibition Slab

Approach scramble

Approach scramble

Avon Somerset

North Devon

Culm Coast

Inland Cornwall

Atlantic Coast

West Penwith

The Lizard

Inland Devon

Torbay

Dorset

Giant's Cave Buttress

Approach-scramble

Suspension Bridge Buttress

Giant's Cave Buttress

A long undulating series of steep buttresses dropping the full-height of the Gorge define the line of this entertaining multi-pitch urban classic.

Approach - From the parking adjacent to the suspension bridge walk down to the left of the bridge and take the zig zag public footpath down to the road. Walk through the rockfall tunnel below the bridge, and hop over the fence. Scramble up 30m to the base of the climb.

Descent - Follow the cliff-top path back to the parking.

Conditions - The ridge is very exposed but dries quickly after rainfall.

① Giant's Cave Buttress . . . . 🔆 🧗 ✏️ ☐ **VS 4c**

A long and very popular route most suited to those who appreciate an audience. The climbing is fairly tricky in places but the belays are comfortable and the views of the suspension bridge spectacular. Start on a sloping ledge at the toe of the buttress with good nut belays in a small corner.

1) 4c, 25m. Move up and step right to a small corner just right of the arete. Make some technical moves on sloping holds up the small corner, before it becomes possible to move back left onto the front face of the buttress and climb a narrow corner to a bulging arete above, peg. Pull awkwardly left around the arete and climb to easier ground that leads to a large belay beneath an overhang.

2) 4a, 23m. Skirt the overhang on the left before heading back right and following short walls and ledges up to another large belay ledge below an overhanging wall.

3) 4c, 25m. Pull left around the arete to a hand-ledge and make a difficult move up to attain a standing position on it. Move left a little way to a corner and climb up to a ledge. Continue up the wall above to a corner and climb this before trending slightly right to the top.

FA. Alan Hicklin, Fred Bennett 1958

| ☀️ Lots of sun | 🧗 15 min | 🧗 Multi-pitch |

Suspension bridge and parking

Approach scramble

Avon Somerset

North Devon

Culm Coast

Inland Cornwall

Atlantic Coast

West Penwith

The Lizard

Inland Devon

Torbay

Dorset

Tackling the slim corner on the first pitch of the sustained
Pink Wall Direct (E2 5c) - *page 60* - at the Avon Gorge.

Avon Somerset
North Devon
Culm Coast
Inland Cornwall
Atlantic Coast
West Penwith
The Lizard
Inland Devon
Torbay
Dorset

Suspension Bridge Buttress

Located under the Suspension Bridge, this fine crag is home to some Avon Gorge classics. The rock is un-quarried, solid and the lines are peppered with a multitude of pockets and threads. Protection is generally good. Due to the tunnel that extends over the road below the crag it is not as noisy as might be anticipated.

Access - Topping out onto the bridge or its retaining walls is not permitted. Always descend by abseil.

Approach - From the parking in the streets adjacent to the Suspension Bridge walk down to the left of the bridge and take the zig zag public footpath path down to the road. Walk right (best on the opposite side of the road) to the start of the tunnel and scramble up the landward side of the rock-catch fence to a gap that allows access to the grassy platform below the buttress.

Descent - All climbs require an abseil from fixed points.

Conditions - The buttress gets lots of sun but is exposed and can be windy. The climbs dry quickly after rain.

① **Suspension Bridge Arete** 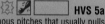 **HVS 5a**
One of the Avon Gorge's most famous pitches that usually pulls in a crowd of viewers on the suspension bridge. Start on a good ledge 5m right of the arete below a pocketed crystal crack and just right of a vegetated groove.
30m. Move up the crack and then head left to a small groove that leads to a ledge system at 10m. Head left to the arete and make some tricky moves to a wide, pocketed runnel. Take the runnel to a horizontal break and move right into an easier finishing corner. Belay and abseil post on the left.
FA. Mike Harvey 1956

② **Suspense** . . . . **HVS 5a**
Brilliant climbing on the wall just right of the arete. Start as for *Suspension Bridge Arete* at a pocketed crystal crack.
30m. Move up the crack and then head left to a small groove that leads to a ledge system at 10m. Climb up the wall rightwards on good pockets to a large hole. Follow the crack-system leftwards to the finishing corner of *Suspension Bridge Arete*. Abseil off the post.

③ **Baby Duck** **E1 5b**
Fine wall-climbing that requires some care with route finding. Start just right of the crystal crack of *Suspension Bridge Arete*.
30m. Follow the crack-system just right of the starting crack of *Suspension Bridge Arete* to the horizontal break at 10m. Climb up right to a steep pocket line and follow this with difficulty, to a point level with a small overhang just down and right of the hole on *Suspense*. Move up right to stand on a good hold and climb thin cracks up the wall to a break. Climb the pocketed crack above to a traverse line that leads up leftwards to the abseil post.
FA. Richard Nicholas, J.Moss 8,1971

④ **Limbo** **E1 5b**
Immaculate and intricate face climbing up the pockets and grey wall left of the steep black bulges in the middle of the wall. Start on a ledge at the base of the wall beneath the black bulges.
1) 5b, 33m. Climb the left-hand-crack-system to ledges below the black bulges. Move left to the pocket line and climb up past a thread to a peg on the left wall. Make technical moves left, up and back right to the pocket line and continue to a horizontal break. Climb up right to a stance below a corner.
2) 4b, 12m. Climb the corner to a belay and abseil point at a large rock anchor.
FA. Ed Ward Drummond, Oliver Hill 1966

⑤ **GT Special** **E4 6a**
A challenging pitch that makes a direct assault on the black bulges. Start as for *Limbo* beneath the black bulges.
41m. Climb to the ledges beneath the black bulges and locate a series of pockets that breach them on their left side. Difficult climbing and fiddly gear accesses the easier wall above and a horizontal break. Continue direct up a thin crack in a smooth, white wall and then via a small groove that leads to a belay and abseil point at a large rock anchor.
FFA. Andy Sharp, Steve Lewis 26.10.1976

⑥ **The Earl of Perth** . . . **E1 5b**
A great route giving steep climbing on an uncompromising line. Start on the ledge at the base of the wall just right of *Limbo*.
1) 5b, 23m. Take the right-hand line of thin cracks to ledges beneath the right side of the black bulges, thread. Steep climbing through the bulges on good pockets gains a strenuous perch at a large pocket. Pull steeply out right and up to better holds and a little further a hanging stance at a horizontal break.
2) 5a, 23m. Enter the long groove above the stance and follow it all the way to ledges that allow a short traverse left to a belay and abseil point at a large rock anchor.
FA. Ed Ward Drummond, Hugh Drummond 27.10.1965

⑦ **Hell Gates** . . . . **HVS 5a**
Fun and intriguing climbing that gives a memorable outing. Start at a ledge just to the left of a slim curving crack on the right side of the face.
1) 5a, 20m. Climb the wall just left of the crack, joining it at 4m. Follow the crack to ledges and a massive thread just above. Pull steeply through the bulge, thread, and continue past another thread to a body-size circular cave. Belay in the cave, and be sure to search out and sign the visitors' log book. Alternatively; from just below the massive thread, traverse up and rightwards to the base of a small corner and follow this to the lower of two horizontal breaks. Traverse the break left, past a peg, to the body-size circular cave.
2) 5a, 12m. Climb steeply out of the cave on the right, peg, and follow a short groove to easier ground and belay on a ledge.
3) 4b, 14m. Traverse left around the exposed arete into a corner (junction with *Earl of Perth*). Continue traversing left for 5m to a peg and climb up 5m to an abseil point at a large metal rock anchor.
FA. Ed Ward Drummond, Hugh Drummond 15.5.1965

Do not exit onto the bridge

Belay and abseil slings around large rock bolt with a square metal plate

Abseil from metal post Ⓐ

Approach

Just to the west of the M5 south of Bristol is a limestone quarry that offers a number of high quality traditional pitches covering a reasonable grade span. The quarry is an extensive working that has two walls of interest to climbers. The rock and protection are good and, although the quarry is not exactly a beauty spot, it is quiet and clean.

Access
Please keep noise to a minimum when passing the houses on the way to the quarry and do not park in the residential layby closer to the start of the footpath than the one described.

Approach
From junction 19 on the M5, follow the A369 in the direction of Portishead and then take the B3124 to Weston in Gordano. 400m before Weston in Gordano is a small layby on the left opposite a field gate - park here. Walk back along the road to some houses (do not park here - residents' parking only) and pick up a footpath on the left that leads to a track which quickly gains the entrance to the quarry.

Conditions
Portishead is sheltered from westerly winds. The walls get the sun from first thing in the morning and dry quickly after rain.

Brian Mullan climbing *Highway One* (E4 6a) - *opposite* - at Portishead. Photo: Mark Davies

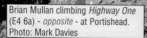

Bristol Channel · Portishead Quarry · Portishead · Bristol · Weston in Gordano · B3124 · Clevedon · M49 · 18 · M5 · A4 · 19 · A369 · GPS 51.466387 -2.787834 · About 5km · 20 · A370 · A38 · N

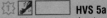

❶ Highway One . . . . . 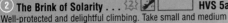 **E4 6a**
Take a few small wires, although the bulk of the hard climbing is
bolt protected. Start on blocks below a thin left-slanting seam.
40m. Follow the thin, left-slanting seam (wires) until just before a
big flake-crack that comes in from the left. Now follow the line of
bolts rightwards up a shallow depression to a steep finish.
Photo opposite.
FA. Richard Harrison, J.Edwards 24.8.1983

❷ The Brink of Solarity . . . **HVS 5a**
Well-protected and delightful climbing. Take small and medium
size wires. Start 2m right of the large vegetated corner that
defines the left side of the slab.
36m. Move up the slab to a narrow right-facing corner/groove
and climb this to a small ledge. Continue up a thin crack and at
its end move up right slightly on pockets at the change in angle
to below another thin crack. Take the thin crack and easier ground
above to the top.
FA. Martin Crocker, Keith Williams 7.8.1975

❸ Pickpocket . . . . **HVS 5a**
Another enticing climb in a similar mold to *The Brink of Solarity*
but slightly tougher, and with a bold start. Start at the base of a
long thin crack 5m right of the vegetated corner.
23m. Climb carefully to good wires at 7m and then take the
well-protected remainder of the crack to a double bolt lower-off
just beyond where the crack curves left and fades.
FA. Robert Walker, Keith Williams 8.1971

❹ The Baldest . . . . **HVS 5a**
The parallel thin cracks just left of the slab's most prominent
crack, climbed by *Pharos*, is yet another enjoyable pitch. Start at a
smooth slab below the cracks.
22m. Climb up the smooth lower slab to the cracks and follow
these all of the way to a double bolt lower-off.
FA. Frank Thompson, Andy March 18.5.1983

❺ Pharos . . . . **HS 4b**
A very popular, well-travelled crack-line that has good protection.
Start at the base of the widest crack in the slab.
22m. Climb the crack in its entirety and then move left to a
double bolt lower-off.
FA. J.Hanz, K.Burton 12.1962

To mid afternoon | 5 min | Sheltered

Descent

Avon Somerset · North Devon · Culm Coast · Inland Cornwall · Atlantic Coast · West Penwith · The Lizard · Inland Devon · Torbay · Dorset

Avon Somerset

North Devon

Culm Coast

Inland Cornwall

Atlantic Coast

West Penwith

The Lizard

Inland Devon

Torbay

Dorset

	No star	⚝	⚝⚝	⚝⚝⚝
Mod to S	-	-	-	-
HS to HVS	-	-	-	-
E1 to E3	-	-	1	2
E4 and up	-	1	2	2

Well concealed on the lower slopes of the rolling tree-covered Mendip Hills is this gem of a quarry. There are only a few routes here but the quality of the rock and climbing is fantastic and, for any team up to the task, a visit will be well rewarded.

The routes are predominantly traditional, albeit with a smattering of fixed kit in the form of threads, pegs and bolts. The well-featured rock face gives the climbs a great deal of diversity, often linking pockets, cracks and breaks via thin face holds. Protection is normally good and the climbing is sustained and technical plus, on the harder lines, it is extremely fingery. The quarry is also popular with cavers, rescue teams and management training groups who use the cliff for practice and instruction from time to time.

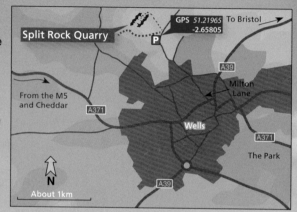

Access
Climbing is not permitted on the more broken crags on the east side of the cutting.

Approach
Split Rock Quarry lies close to the cathedral town of Wells which is best reached from the M5 by exiting at junction 22 and following the A38 and A371, first to Cheddar and then on to Wells. On entering Wells, pick up signs for the A39 to Bristol and follow the road out of the town and turn left onto Milton Lane - a minor road. Follow Milton Lane and cross Ash Lane. A little further up the road, pass Reservoir Lane on the right, continue past some blocks on the left and park on the verges next to a locked, gated track and path on the left. Take care not to block the road. Walk along the path to the edge of the woods and, either follow a path just inside the woods along its edge to the cliff, or a path through the field next to the woods to the same point (5 minutes).

Conditions
The climbs get plenty of morning and early afternoon sun and are a suntrap in good weather. In warm weather the climbs are best attempted in the cool of the evening when they are in the shade. The wind can funnel down the cutting but the crag is actually very well sheltered from strong westerly winds. The crag dries quickly but is not quite steep enough to allow climbing in the rain.

Glastonbury Tor.

Avon Somerset

North Devon

Culm Coast

Inland Cornwall

Atlantic Coast

West Penwith

The Lizard

Inland Devon

Torbay

Dorset

Moving up the pumpy lower wall of *Certain Surprise* (E3 5c) - *page 75* - on the trademark red-rock of Split Rock Quarry.

Avon Somerset

North Devon

Culm Coast

Inland Cornwall

Atlantic Coast

West Penwith

The Lizard

Inland Devon

Torbay

Dorset

Certain Surprise Wall

A fabulous wall of red-stained limestone peppered with a multitude of pockets, thin cracks and deep horizontal breaks. The climbing is excellent.

Approach - The wall is at the left-hand end of the steepest section of the crag's east facing wall.

Descent - Walk off down to the left (facing out).

Conditions - The crag forms one side of a cutting through the hillside and can funnel wind. However the crag is very sheltered from westerly gales. Some of the pockets and breaks can become slightly muddy.

❶ Sahara . . . . . . ☆ 🖐️🕳️🐾 ⬜ E5 6b

A pokey route with good, but hard and bold climbing in its lower reaches. Start at a tree below a prominent hold at 5m.

27m. Boulder up to the prominent hold and some good small wires. Stand on the hold and stretch right around a slight rib to a tiny corner and use this to start a reachy sequence that leads to an easing, bold. Continue to a peg at the midway break and move right for 5m to a thin crack. Climb the thin crack to a vegetated niche and finish up the rightward-trending thin crack.

FA. Richard Broomhead, Andy Hall 17.9.1982

❷ Crimson Dynamo ☆ 🖐️🕳️🔩 ⬜ E6 6b

Fine, intense and highly technical climbing on excellent rock. Start 5m right of *Sahara* below some pockets and an eco bolt at 7m.

26m. Stretch up the pockets to the bolt and use a thin sidepull on the left to start a difficult, crimpy sequence up the wall above before trending right to the midway break and a thread. Climb up the wall above the thread past a hidden finger-jug to a good horizontal break and then make some long moves up the wall above slightly leftwards to join and finish as for *Sahara*. Lower-off.

FA. Martin Crocker, Richard Harrison 9.9.1984

❸ Rustic Wall Direct. . . . . ⬜3⬜ 🔩📷 ⬜ E3 5c

Immaculate wall-climbing described here with the now popular direct and logical upper variation. Start 6m left of a small shallow cave at ground level below a thin right-leaning crack.

26m. Pull up to a small hand-ledge just left of the crack and move left and stretch for a positive pocket, bolt above. Climb directly to a good break and continue in the same line to an incut horizontal break and large cam placement. Pull straight up the wall above and finish steeply on good holds.

FA. Richard Harrison, Richard Broomhead 9.5.1980

FA Martin Crocker 27.6.1990 (Direct finish - The Video Kills)

❹ Red Rag to a Bull . . ☆ 🔩📷 ⬜ E5 6b

A quality excursion packed with hard climbing and topped off with a well-positioned steep slab. Start at the thin right-leaning crack as for *Rustic Wall*.

27m. Move up the thin crack-line to a peg and make a couple of hard moves up left to a good pocket. Climb up right past a bolt to gain and follow a rightward trending, strenuous thin diagonal crack to a good hidden hold. Make a powerful pull up to a short crack in the wall above to good holds. Gain the recess above and from its right side move up onto the slabby wall and traverse left above two bolts to a small niche. Climb the slabby wall boldly, first up and then right to the top.

FA. Martin Crocker, Matt Ward 31.5.1986

To mid afternoon | 5 min | Sheltered

Descent

5 Certain Surprise **E3 5c**
The trade route at Split Rock Quarry is a brilliant classic. Start at a small, shallow cave at ground level. *Photo on page 73.*
26m. Hard moves up the crack sprouting from the cave lead to an easing at 6m. Follow the steepening crack past two threads and climb the wall above to a large niche, bolt. Move up and left out of the niche on big holds to a small corner and follow this on more good holds to a move right at its end to finish.
FA. Richard Harrison, Richard Broomhead 9.5.1980

6 Corsican Days **E3 5c**
Sustained and surprisingly pumpy climbing on generally good holds with good gear. The upper wall requires a degree of lateral thinking. Start as for *Certain Surprise.*
27m. Climb the steep cracks of *Certain Surprise* and, at its second thread, move right to a slight groove. Climb the hold-infested wall above past double bolts where more good holds allow a peg on the blank wall out right to be clipped. Step down and execute a precarious sequence right to another duo of bolts. Another stiff pull gains positive holds and a final peg. The top is just above.
FA. Gordon Jenkin, J.Allum 17.5.1999

Just over to the right is the Tricky Dicky Wall.

7 Smashing of Amps . **7c+**
The stunning thin right-leaning crack is the line of the crag and a must for anybody up to the mission. Start at the base of the crack.
26m. Intense and precarious progress up the crack gains a good jug. Now devise a method of reaching a good hold and ramp on the wall above and left of the crack and finish up the still difficult wall above.
FA. Martin Crocker 19.4.1986

Tricky Dicky Wall
A sheer wall of compact limestone scored by a thin crack and split by a couple of narrow ledges.
Approach - The wall is the first encountered at the right-hand end of the steepest section of the crag.
Descent - Walk off down to the left (facing out).
Conditions - The crag forms one side of a cutting through the hillside and can funnel wind. This being said, the crag is very sheltered from westerly gales. The pockets at the start of *Tricky Dicky* can be slightly muddy after rainfall.

8 Tricky Dicky **E5 6a**
A classic mixture of the bold and technical gives a memorable pitch. Start below a narrow ledge at 8m with an eco bolt just under its lip.
26m. Climb the smooth, pocketed initial wall to gain the bolt and narrow ledge at 8m - bold. Make an awkward mantleshelf on to the ledge, and from its left-hand side, make some fingery moves up and left to join the thin crack of *Smashing of Amps* and stick in some good nuts. Follow the crack to a resting ledge before tackling the thin continuation seam and crack via some technical and fingery moves to a lower-off just below the top.
FA. Paul Smith, Richard Cary 5.1983

Descent

Other bolts on this wall

The Lizard | Inland Devon | Torbay | Dorset | Avon Somerset | North Devon | Culm Coast | Inland Cornwall | Atlantic Coast | West Penwith

7

8

Uphill Quarry is a towering sheet of blank limestone that faces out across a boat park and marshland to the sea beyond. The climbs on the main face are extremely sustained and technical and provide some of the area's best wall-climbing. The rock is generally very good.

Approach   See main area map on page 44

From exit 21 on the M5, follow the A370 until road signs to Uphill (a village) can be picked up on the outskirts of Weston-Super-Mare. Once at Uphill, drive through it and, at a bend with a large wall next to it, park on the left. Walk through an entrance to a boat yard and the crag is easily viewed directly ahead. Note that Uphill can also be reached by exiting the M5 at junction 22 and following the A38 and A370 to the outskirts of Weston-Super-Mare from where Uphill is signposted - this is the best approach from the south. From the parking, walk through the sea-defence gates, and the quarry is just along the track on the left.

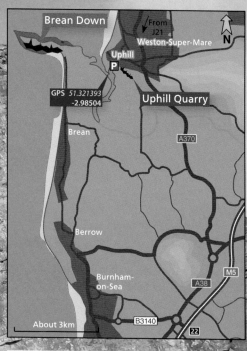

Conditions

The cliff is exposed to the elements. It can be an oven here but can also be freezing if there is a cold westerly wind. Often though, it is a perfect spot. There is no seepage.

Dave Henderson on the fingery and technical wall climb of *Living Dead* (7b) - *opposite* - at Uphill Quarry, a good winter venue in an unusual setting.

❶ The Jimi Hendrix Experience

E6 6b

A high-quality pitch which relies mostly on well-spaced fixed protection. The route follows the tall white wall left of the central broken corner. Start below a prominent peg at 10m, left of the broken corner.

30m. Climb easily to below the peg, pull up to it then step right and move up to a bolt. Make hard fingery moves to the next bolt and then, with little respite, make some insecure reaches to a positive diagonal break and good wires. Move right and up to a small ledge and a rest. Climb the wild upper wall on much better holds past a good thread and a bolt.
FA. Martin Crocker, Gordon Jenkin 17.9.1987

❷ Living Dead . . . 7b

Precise, fingertip wall-climbing on superb crystalline edges builds to a final testing climax at the top of the pitch. Start just right of a left-trending broken ramp-line at the base of the face. *Opposite.*

25m. Move up easy rock to a sloping ledge at 9m. Pull through the slim overlap above to a sidepull and continue up the wall to a resting ledge. Move slightly right and follow the steepening wall up a slight depression until a final hard sequence gains a ledge and lower-off 5m below the top of the crag. The top of the cliff can be gained via a short HVS 5a pitch.
FA. Martin Crocker, Damien Carroll 16.6.1984

❸ Chiming for You . . . 7a+

A beautiful wall pitch that gradually picks its way up the central face and culminates in a technical finish. Start at a right to left sloping ramp, 5m right of the start of *Living Dead.*

25m. Take the straightforward gangway to a sloping ledge at 9m. Climb the steep wall above and slightly right on small positive holds past a slim overlap to a good ledge (small cam optional). Move up the steepening wall on diminishing holds to the final bolt, from where a very thin move gains a good hold and ledge just above, lower-off on the left. The top of the cliff can be gained via a short HVS 5a pitch.
FA. Martin Crocker, Damien Carroll 29.6.1984

Descent

Belay on large bolts

Short 5a pitch to top

Avon Somerset · North Devon · Culm Coast · Inland Cornwall · Atlantic Coast · West Penwith · The Lizard · Inland Devon · Torbay · Dorset

	No star	⚝	⚝⚝	⚝⚝⚝
Mod to S	-	-	-	-
HS to HVS	-	2	-	-
E1 to E3	1	2	2	1
E4 and up	3	4	6	4

The south-facing line of low limestone crags that stretch out into the Bristol Channel offer up some intriguing and esoteric climbs. Brean Down started its climbing life as an out-of-the-way trad venue but it has now become popular as a fine sport climbing location, tucked away on its own above a busy beach that looks out over extensive tidal flats. It is a suntrap that suffers from little seepage, and offers the chance of warm conditions even in the middle of winter.

The sport climbs at Boulder Cove are very popular and are always chalked-up, whilst the trad climbs are far more serious undertakings and see little traffic and, as a result, have become slightly vegetated. The traditional lines require the use of stake-belays in the steep sandy slope above the crag.

The limestone is not as reliable as that found elsewhere locally, and great care is needed with the placing of gear, and use of the sometimes-fragile holds. Having said this, the routes in this book are on the best rock at Brean Down.

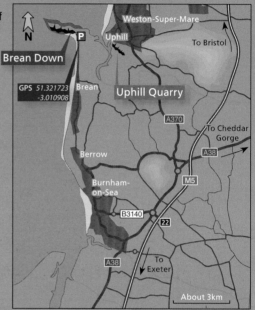

Approach   See main area map on page 44

From Junction 22 on the M5, take the road westwards to a small roundabout and follow signs for Berrow and Brean. Continue for approximately 15 minutes, through various small towns, and passing many holiday parks, to the end of the road and a car park (fee). The crag and approach across the beach are obvious from here.

Conditions and Tides

The tide is not much of a problem. Boulder Cove is not accessible for around 1 to 2 hours either side of high water but access to the Great Corner and Ocean Wall is less restricted. There is little shelter from westerly winds but, if the sun is out, the crag gets hot very quickly, and in summer it is an oven. In cold, settled weather with a northerly breeze the conditions are normally ideal. There is little seepage and some possible dry spots in the rain.

Avon Somerset | North Devon | Culm Coast | Inland Cornwall | Atlantic Coast | West Penwith | The Lizard | Inland Devon | Torbay | Dorset

Boulder Cove

An excellent, beautifully located wall of compact limestone with a number of worthwhile sport routes.
Descent - All routes have lower-offs in place.

① Brean Dream . . . . . 6a+

The first and easiest line on the wall, but no pushover. Start just right of some very poor rock at the far left end of the crag.
15m. Move up the initially technical wall to an easing. Continue slightly leftwards to a lower-off well below the top of the crag.
FA. Francis Haden, Gordon Jenkin, Ed Heslam, S.Cook 23.4.1995

② Kraken . . . . 6b+

A pleasing pitch as long as the correct line is taken. Start at a steep 3m flake-crack.
18m. Take the stiff layback crack to a rest. Move left and pick a way up the wall which reveals some surprising holds.
FA. Francis Haden, Ian Parnell, J.Hunt 7.11.1993

③ Bikini Atoll . . . . 6c+

This good line up the centre of the wall is spoilt by some sharp rock and lichen. Start at the 3m flake-crack as for *Kraken*.
18m. Start up the stiff layback and climb direct on increasingly sharp edges to a step left at the fifth bolt.
FA. Francis Haden, Ian Parnell, J.Hunt 7.11. 1993

④ Coral Sea 6c

Intricate and surprisingly steep wall-climbing. Start just left of a wide diagonal crack that sprouts from the beach.
Photo on page 83.
20m. Move easily up the wall just left of the diagonal crack until the wall steepens. Fingery moves up the steeper wall and then rightwards lead to less pressing ground.
FA. Matt Ward, Martin Crocker 10.12.1988

⑤ Chepito 7a

The first of the steeper sports routes has some excellent moves but ageing bolts. Start at the diagonal crack.
20m. Nip up the easy crack and then tackle the sustained leaning wall on good but at times hard-to-spot holds passing a good pocket on the steep bit.
FA. Martin Crocker, Jim Robertson 19.12.1992

⑥ Pearl Harbour 7a

Fine and pumpy. Start at the diagonal crack as for *Chepito*.
Photo on page 45.
18m. Move up easily, step right and then attack the spaced horizontal breaks on good holds to less steep but more technical ground up the groove and wall above.
FA. Martin Crocker, Matt Ward 10.12.1998

❼ Tide Rising . . . . . . 7b+

Hard and fingery wall-climbing that is at the top of the grade. Start just right of the diagonal crack of *Chepito*.
20m. Take the wall to the break and the high first bolt. Make some fingery moves to larger holds and then climb with increasing difficulty to a final easing on the top wall.
FA. Francis Haden, Gordon Jenkin, Ed Heslam 23.4.1995

❽ Clashing Socks 7b

One of the longer lines on the wall that features a tough section on the final headwall. Start below an ivy patch.
24m. Climb to a rope thread. Ascend the wall on the left of the ivy patch and continue past the right side of an overhang at two-thirds height. Climb the steep headwall with difficulty to finish.
FA. Martin Crocker 25.11.1990

Lots of sun | 5 min | Tidal

High-tide exit or approach on unstable ground 10m

Brean Topping - page 80

Scramble up boulders to access right-hand section of cliff

Avon Somerset | North Devon | Culm Coast | Inland Cornwall | Atlantic Coast | West Penwith | The Lizard | Inland Devon | Torbay | Dorset

Avon Somerset

North Devon

Culm Coast

Inland Cornwall

Atlantic Coast

West Penwith

The Lizard

Inland Devon

Torbay

Dorset

⑨ Black Snake Moan . . . . 🔲📷⬜ **8a**
A smart line. Start on the ledges just left of the gearing-up block.
20m. Climb the fingery brown wall to the break and finish up the black streak above.
FA. Dave Pickford 2010

⑩ Brean Topping . . . . 🔲📷🔲 **8b**
The testpiece of the sport routes at Brean Down and one of Somerset's most difficult undertakings. Start on the raised ledges just left of the gearing-up block.
20m. Climb the fingery brown wall to the mid-height break, step right and climb the fierce upper wall.
FA. Steve McClure 1.1.2002

⑪ Storm Warning . . . . . . 🔲📷⬜ **7c+**
An excellent and much-attempted link-up. Start on the raised ledges just left of the gearing-up block. *Photo this page.*
20m. Start up the fingery initial brown wall of *Black Snake Moan* and move right to finish up the pumpy top wall of *Chulilla*.
FA. Francis Haden 22.3.1995

⑫ Chulilla . . . . 🔲📷⬜ **7b+**
Brean Down's best sport route is well worth tracking down. Start on the large block as the ledge levels out.
17m. Step off the block into a steep corner and follow it strenuously to a semi-rest at the mid-height break. Step left and crank up the fingery wall before moving left to join *Brean Topping* at its last bolt.
FA. Martin Crocker 10.2.1990

⑬ Prisoner of Conscience . 🔲🔲⬜ **7b+**
A short bouldery start gets you going on this one. Start just right of the large block.
20m. The bouldery lower wall gains a good break. Finish up the easier corner above.
FA. Martin Crocker 4.2.1990

Lee Proctor sneaking in some New Year exercise on the classic sport climb at Boulder Cove, *Chulilla* (7b+) - *this page* - at Brean Down, Somerset.

⑭ Milky Bar Kid . . . . 🏁 📏 ⬜ 8a
A link-up that takes in the crux moves of three lines. Start just right of the large block as for *Prisoner of Conscience*.
24m. Climb the lower wall moving right to the crux of *Bullworker* and finally move right to finish as for *El Chocco*.
FA. Chris Savage 2009

⑮ The Guilt Edge . . . . 🏁 ✊ 📏 ⬜ 7c
The arete above the initial wall of *Prisoner of Conscience* extends the quality climbing. Start just right of the large block.
20m. Follow *Prisoner of Conscience* to the good break. The hanging arete above has some perplexing moves that gain easier but bold climbing rightwards to a lower-off.
FA. Martin Crocker, Francis Haden 13.8.1994

⑯ Bullworker . . . . 🏁 ✊ ▮ ⬜ 7c
Butch stuff, and a touch reachy with it. Start at a small corner 3m right of the large block.
17m. The overhanging, narrow corner is followed to a good break and a move left, from where a long, powerful move accesses still steep ground, though with more positive holds.
FA. Martin Crocker, Matt Ward 1.1.1989

⑰ El Chocco . . . . 🏁 🧗 ⬜ 7c
Quality climbing with a sting in the tail. Start 6m right of the large block.
17m. Leave the ground with some difficulty and continue past the break and up the small steep corner to the crux rock-over that provides access to the final short slab.
FA. Martin Crocker, Matt Woodford 3.3.1990

⑱ Global Solutions . . . . . . 🏁 ✊ ⬜ 7c
A worthwhile link-up. Start 6m right of the large block. as for *El Chocco*.
24m. Climb *El Chocco* until it is possible to make hard moves to the final moves of *Bullworker* and finish up this.
FA. Ally Smith 2008

⑲ The Roof of Inequity . . . 🏁 ✊ ⬜ 7a+
An entertaining and spectacular pitch. Start 6m right of the large block, as for *El Chocco*.
17m. The right-hand line of bolts above the difficult start of *El Chocco* points the way up steep ground on good holds to a powerful finish rightwards, through the capping roof.
FA. Martin Crocker, Matt Ward 3.1.1987

Lots of sun | 5 min | Tidal

From left-hand section of cliff

Avon Somerset | North Devon | Culm Coast | Inland Cornwall | Atlantic Coast | West Penwith | The Lizard | Inland Devon | Torbay | Dorset

Avon Somerset | North Devon | Culm Coast | Inland Cornwall | Atlantic Coast | West Penwith | The Lizard | Inland Devon | Torbay | Dorset

Boulder Cove

① Great Corner E2 5a

Brean Down's classic trad line is a serious undertaking. The climbing is both sustained and on variable quality rock. The pitch can be split at the big ledge at 9m. Start below the corner.
23m. Gain the large horizontal break and ledge at 8m via the narrow corner and wall. Ascend the sustained continuation corner to an exit up the final vegetated crack. Stake belays and additional belays in the rock outcrops further up the slope.
FA. Pat Littlejohn, Richard Broomhead 31.8.1975

② The Brean Machine. E5 6b

The thin crack-line in the bulging central area of the wall is an extremely impressive and tough trad pitch. Start at a crack in the lower half of the wall right of an old concrete structure at the base of the wall.
22m. Move up the lower wall via a crack to the halfway break. Pull through the overhang and take the thin crack passing a peg close to the top. Stake belays and additional belays in the rock outcrops further up the slope.
FA. Martin Crocker, Matt Ward 3.8.1985

③ Pandora's Box .... VS 4c

A well-defined corner on the right-hand side of the wall provides the best of the sub-extreme routes at Brean Down. Start at a left-slanting flake-crack that leads up to the corner.
22m. Approach the mid-height break via the right-to-left-slanting flake-line. The steep corner above is sustained but has plenty of gear and a few plants. Stake belays and additional belays in the rock outcrops further up the slope.
FA. Geoff Mason, I.Adams 1963

Great Corner and Ocean Wall

Midway along the crag is the striking line of *Great Corner* whilst the Ocean Wall is directly above the beach nearest to the sea wall. These steep and sunny walls have a lot of climbs on them, however the rock is not uniformly solid and the fixed gear is old. The slopes above the wall are steep and are composed of grass and sand. The stakes on the grass slope maybe missing or old in which case an extra rope will be needed to reach the rock walls above to secure a belay.

Approach - Walk along the beach from the sea wall.

Conditions and Tides - The Ocean Wall is barely tidal whilst the Great Corner Area is cut off at high tide. Seepage is not really a problem but in warm sunny weather the cliff becomes unbearably hot.

Lots of sun | 4 min | Tidal

Stake belays in the unstable slope

Great Corner and Boulder Cove - 100m

Avon Somerset

North Devon

Culm Coast

Inland Cornwall

Atlantic Coast

West Penwith

The Lizard

Inland Devon

Torbay

Dorset

The sport routes at the suntrap of Brean Down come into their own during the cooler months from October to May. Here, Paul Cox makes the most of some November sunshine to bag *Coral Sea* (6c) - *page 79* - at Boulder Cove.

Cheddar Gorge is a major West Country landmark that attracts thousands of visitors a year to view its stalactite caverns and towering limestone crags. It is also a tremendous climbing venue that has a total of over 1,000 climbs on its north and south sides. The climbing available offers a good spread of style from single to multi-pitch sport and traditional lines whilst the grade spectrum accommodates all from beginner to expert. Nearly all of the climbing is easily viewed from the bottom of the Gorge with many of the most popular climbs being merely a few steps from the car. However many of Cheddar Gorge's most impressive and highest quality lines are perched way up on the bulging walls and buttresses that appear to lean out over the road.

At the request of *Cheddar Caves and Gorge* only a selected list of the best climbs have been included in this book.

Access and climbing information

The climbing situation at Cheddar Gorge is unique. The current arrangements arose as a result of a local initiative driven by Martin Crocker in collaboration with *Cheddar Caves and Gorge* and with the support of the BMC, the Climbers' Club and The National Trust. A detailed and progressive climbing access agreement between the BMC and *Cheddar Caves and Gorge* is now in place. As a result, access to some of the best of the 1,000 climbs in the Gorge is permitted most of the year round. On public safety and conservation grounds, climbing on the south (*Cheddar Caves and Gorge*) side is not permitted at all during peak holiday periods, and many other routes are necessarily limited to the winter months. *Cheddar Caves and Gorge* has published a guidebook to the climbs. It can be purchased from shops in the Gorge, from the Cargo Cult shop at Gough's Cave (Tel: 01934 742343) and from The Gorge Outdoors (www.thegorgeoutdoors.co.uk).

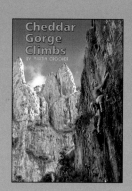

Important Information on Access for Climbing

It is imperative that reference to the detailed access information in the Cheddar Gorge Climbs guidebook, and on the BMC Regional Access Database (RAD) www.thebmc.co.uk, site must be read before attempting to climb or view the cliffs in the gorge. Below is the basic information and requirements that are needed for a trip to climb at Cheddar Gorge.

- ALL climbers must abide by the Cheddar Gorge Climbers Code of Conduct (see BMC RAD) and have third party insurance. The Gorge is policed regularly and climbers will be asked to leave if proof of insurance cannot be demonstrated.
- Access to climbing on the cliffs varies according to the time of year, and reference to the guidebook and the BMC RAD website must be made prior to a visit in order to identify which cliffs are open and which are closed.
- The designated access routes to individual cliffs must be utilised.

Approach   See main area map on page 44

Cheddar Gorge is quickly accessed from Junction 22 of the M5 and is well sign-posted via the A38, A371 and finally the B3135.

Avon Somerset | North Devon | Culm Coast | Inland Cornwall | Atlantic Coast | West Penwith | The Lizard | Inland Devon | Torbay | Dorset

Avon Somerset

North Devon

Culm Coast

Inland Cornwall

Atlantic Coast

West Penwith

The Lizard

Inland Devon

Torbay

Dorset

Heading for the majestically-positioned upper corner of the multi-pitch sport route *Paradise Lost* (7b) - *page 86* - on Sunset Buttress at Cheddar Gorge.

Avon Somerset

North Devon

Culm Coast

Inland Cornwall

Atlantic Coast

West Penwith

The Lizard

Inland Devon

Torbay

Dorset

Cheddar's most gorgeous climbs

Below is a listing and brief summary of Cheddar Gorge's most revered and popular climbs. With around 1000 climbs - both sport and trad - on its north and south sides, and a wide spectrum of grades, the list below is only a pointer to the potential climbing available.

1 Smooth Operator **6a**
Many choose this and its neighbouring sport climbs as a first taste of Cheddar climbing. Fun climbing.

2 Dinner Date **E1 5b**
A well-protected corner climb that gets the morning sunshine.

3 British Summertime **6b+**
Sustained and varied climbing from start to finish.

4 The Numb Ones . . . . . . **6b+**
Top five in the list of Cheddar's best grades 6s.

5 Space Tourist . . . . **6b+**
A fine, multi-pitch journey with magnificent exposure.

6 Coronation Street **E1 5b**
THE route of the gorge. 120m of climbing from the road.

7 Castles Made of Sand **6c**
A full-height sport climb that is endowed with varied climbing and a stunning finish.

8 Brainbiter **E3 5c**
Tough climbing in a high-rise situation that most still need a few aid points as a helper to start the second pitch.

9 Crow **E3 5c**
A long, exposed and very sustained classic that now sees regular ascents and stays clean.

10 Shakin' Like a Leaf . **7a**
Immaculate wall-climbing. One of the best single-pitches at Cheddar.

11 Ahimsa **E3 5c**
The soaring second pitch of this Cheddar classic is a stunner.

12 Speedfreak **7a**
A steep corner that provides a pumpy and enjoyable pitch.

13 Get that Man! **7a**
Mighty fine roadside climbing that links a corner, wall and impressive bulge.

14 Warlord **E4 6b**
An eye-catching two pitch climb high above the road.

15 Paradise Lost **7b**
A phenomenal line way up in the sky. *Photo on page 85*.

16 The Empire **E5 6a**
Hidden from view but worth the hunt is this fine thin crack.

17 Starscrape . . . . **7b+**
A superlative sport pitch way up above the road.

18 Shock of the New . . **7b+**
A fine and much-attempted pitch with a fingery start.

19 Bird of Paradise . . . . **7b+**
Varied climbing and an outrageously exposed last pitch.

20 Return of the Gunfighter . . . **7c**
Remarkably sustained climbing of the highest quality singles this route out as one of the great sport climbs of the West Country.

Avon Somerset

North Devon

Culm Coast

Inland Cornwall

Atlantic Coast

West Penwith

The Lizard

Inland Devon

Torbay

Dorset

Catching some late afternoon sun close to the top of the multi-pitch sport climb *Castles Made of Sand* (6c) - *opposite* - at Cheddar Gorge.

Avon Somerset | North Devon | Culm Coast | Inland Cornwall | Atlantic Coast | West Penwith | The Lizard | Inland Devon | Torbay | Dorset

Avon Somerset

North Devon

Culm Coast

Inland Cornwall

Atlantic Coast

West Penwith

The Lizard

Inland Devon

Torbay

Dorset

Craig Eley carefully taking on the precarious crux of *Nose Decay* (E4 6a) - *page 122* - at Screda Point on the Culm Coast.

Avon Somerset

North Devon

Culm Coast

Inland Cornwall

Atlantic Coast

West Penwith

The Lizard

Inland Devon

Torbay

Dorset

The North Devon climbing experience - away from the culm coast that dips away into Cornwall - encompasses two phenomenal sea-cliff destinations. Both Baggy Point and Lundy Island are traditional venues that offer some of the most thrilling climbing to be found in the UK. Although, on a clear day one can be seen easily from the other, their geology and climbing style are completely different. The rock on Lundy Island is granite and the climbs are mainly steep multi-pitch crack-lines or super sustained slabs and walls. Baggy Point, on the other hand, is made up of compact sandstone slabs that are covered in well-travelled climbs, the majority of them being single-pitch. The ambience of the two is also at opposing ends of the spectrum the solitude and cosy isolation of Lundy being a very different experience to that of the buzzing day and night life of Croyde Bay's surf scene.

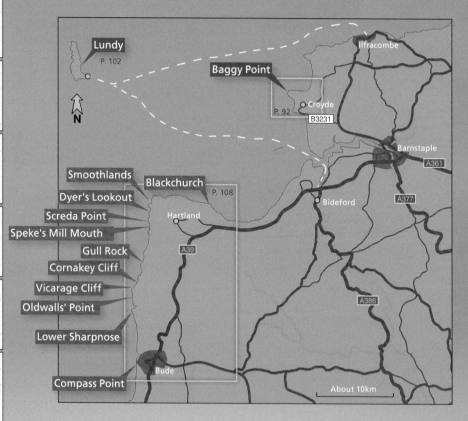

Lundy
P. 102

N

Baggy Point

P. 92

Croyde

B3231

Ilfracombe

Barnstaple

A361

A377

Bideford

Smoothlands

Blackchurch
P. 108

Dyer's Lookout

Hartland

Screda Point

Speke's Mill Mouth

A39

Gull Rock

Cornakey Cliff

Vicarage Cliff

Oldwalls' Point

A386

Lower Sharpnose

Compass Point

Bude

About 10km

Lundy island from the mainland.

Avon Somerset

North Devon

Culm Coast

Inland Cornwall

Atlantic Coast

West Penwith

The Lizard

Inland Devon

Torbay

Dorset

Rob Jordan enjoys some perfect conditions on the immaculate
Formula One (HVS 5a) - *page 104* - Landing Craft Bay, Lundy.

	No star	⚝1	⚝2	⚝3
Mod to S	-	2	1	2
HS to HVS	-	6	4	2
E1 to E3	-	1	4	1
E4 and up	-	-	2	-

The jutting prows of Baggy Point have for many decades been the traditional venue for high quality slab climbing in the West Country. The slabs are composed of excellent, compact sandstone which is cut by numerous thin cracks and overlaps that conveniently provide many of the routes with good protection.

Access

A seasonal bird restriction is in place on the whole of Long Rock Slab from March 15th to June 30th. A sign and stakes are usually in place.

Approach   Area map page 90

Take the B3231 from Barnstaple to Braunton and then on to the surfers' paradise of Croyde Bay. Follow the narrow road into the village and pick up the brown tourist signs to Baggy Point. Follow the signs for about a mile until the road ends at a National Trust car park (payment). From the car park take the coast path (clearly signed) to Baggy Point following the left branch where it splits. The walk takes around 20 minutes and arrives above The Promontory, with excellent views of Long Rock Slab, Slab Cove and in the distance, Scrattling Zawn.

Map labels: N · Long Rock Slab · Scrattling Zawn · Slab Cove · The Promontory · GPS 51.134984 -4.242070 · P · Croyde · About 1km · Surf Beach · B3231

Tides

All the cliffs are tidal, although careful planning will normally mean that something is accessible with calm sea conditions. The Promontory is only accessible during the period between low and mid tide. The same is true of the ledges at the foot of Long Rock Slab, although between *Undercracker* and *Urizen* they are usually accessible for much longer. Slab Cove and Scrattling Zawn are only inaccessible at high water.

Conditions

All the crags are exposed to the wind and rain. The crags have a sunny aspect and dry very quickly after rainfall. There is little seepage. Vegetation on the upper parts of the harder routes on Long Rock Slab has encroached in recent times.

Photo labels: Slab Cove · Long Rock Slab

Side tabs: Avon Somerset · North Devon · Culm Coast · Inland Cornwall · Atlantic Coast · West Penwith · The Lizard · Inland Devon · Torbay · Dorset

Avon Somerset

North Devon

Culm Coast

Inland Cornwall

Atlantic Coast

West Penwith

The Lizard

Inland Devon

Torbay

Dorset

Rich White picking his way up the final section of *Slip it in Quick* (E3 5c) - *page 96* - one of many long and technical single-pitch routes on Long Rock Slab at Baggy Point.

1 Chouinard's Yard 1 . . . . 🔆 🖼 ⬜ **HVS 5a**
The central line on the lower face makes for a spicy outing.
40m. Follow the faint crack up the centre of the slab.
FA. Dave Johnston, Alan Baker 10.4.1971

2 Scrattling Crack . . . . . . 🔆 🖼 ⬜ **VDiff**
The wide central corner-crack is a popular and very traditional
outing, being one of the earliest climbs to be accomplished on a
British sea-cliff. Start at the base of the boot-wide crack.
40m. The corner-crack is sustained all the way and needs plenty
of big gear.
FA. Tom Longstaff 1898

3 Moonshot . . . . 🔆 ⬜ **Diff**
The equally fine looking corner is an impressive feature, however
the climb is not as good as its near neighbour. Start at the base
of the corner.
43m. The easy-angled corner is very straightforward.
FA. Pete Biven, John Fowler, Pat Littlejohn 24.12.1968

Scrattling Zawn
A tranquil little section of Baggy Point with
one very popular climb.
Access - There are no restrictions on this
section of crag.
Approach - Abseil down the large corner
of *Moonshot* from stakes.
Tides - The base of *Scrattling Crack* is
only under water at high tide, but can be
wave-washed at lower tides in rough seas.
Conditions - The cliff is in full sun from
midday. The rock can be greasy if damp.

| From mid morning | 25 min | Tidal | Abseil in |

Approach path

Descent by abseil
from twin stakes

A

③

②

①

Avon Somerset · North Devon · Culm Coast · Inland Cornwall · Atlantic Coast · West Penwith · The Lizard · Inland Devon · Torbay · Dorset

4 Dream Lover . . . . . HVS 5b

A nicely sustained climb that is worth seeking out, especially if the rest of the slab is busy. Start 9m left of the full-height corner of *Doors of Perception* at the base of a diagonal crack that cuts across the slab beneath the overhangs.

30m. From the start of the diagonal crack, take a direct line up the slab via a thinner crack-line to the overhangs. Pull through the overhangs and take the sustained crack in the slab above to clean ledges.

FA. Pete O'Sullivan, Brian Rossiter 21.1.1979

5 Pickpocket . . . . HVS 5b

Intriguing moves and good protection ensure the popularity of this pitch. Start 8m left of the full-height corner of *Doors of Perception* at a narrow corner that leads to the overhang.

45m. Climb the narrow corner easily to the overhangs. Step right to a very slim corner and make a perplexing move to a big pocket up on the right just above the overhang. Stand in the pocket and reach a left-leaning break above that is followed to a point where it is possible to access a line of weakness running back rightwards to the top. If the upper wall is vegetated, move left to ledges at the end of the left-leaning break and scramble up the ridge to the belay. *Photo on page 99.*

FA. Ben Wintringham, Marion Wintringham 15.11.1969

6 Doors of Perception E1 5b

The full-height corner in the centre of the slab provides a superb and very sustained climb that requires good bridging technique. Start at the base of the left-hand of two corners that lead up to the base of the main line.

44m. Climb the left-hand corner easily to the overhang at the base of the corner and pull up into it. Sustained and technical moves gain an easing at mid-height. The upper section of the corner provides more great climbing.

FA. Ben Wintringham, J.Browne 15.3.1970 (Via the start of Twinkletoes).
FA. Chris King, Nigel Gifford 22.7.1976 (Direct Start previously aided).

Long Rock Slab

Although the routes here have some runout sections, the protection is normally reliable - as is the rock quality.

Access - A restriction due to nesting birds is in place from March 15th to June 30th inclusive.

Approach - Walk around the cliff edge on a narrow path until above the main face. A steep descent scramble to the top of the crag is best protected with a rope (stake in place). Abseil down the corner of *Urizen* to large sea-level ledges. The ledges can also be accessed at low tide across the rocks and beach from Slab Cove.

Tides - In calm seas the ledges close to the base of *Urizen* are above high water, but in a swell they are wave-washed.

Conditions - The routes dry quickly and it can get hot. Some of the harder lines are becoming vegetated in their upper reaches.

Access - A bird ban is in effect on this face between March 15th and June 30th.

Scrattling Zawn

Abseil from stake

Alternative finish

Twinkletoes - page 96

Urizen - page 96

Ledges

Low-tide approach from Slab Cove

Avon Somerset | North Devon | Culm Coast | Inland Cornwall | Atlantic Coast | West Penwith | The Lizard | Inland Devon | Torbay | Dorset

Avon Somerset

North Devon

Culm Coast

Inland Cornwall

Atlantic Coast

West Penwith

The Lizard

Inland Devon

Torbay

Dorset

⑦ Twinkletoes . . . . . . VS 4c
Start at the base of the right-hand of two corners that lead up to
the base of the main corner-line of *Doors of Perception*.
47m. Climb the corner to an overhang and swing up right to
a small left-facing corner with a very thin crack in the back.
A tricky move up this gains a ledge on the right. Take a good
thin crack on the right to a large flake and move up into a slim
corner on its right. Follow the shallow corner and right-trending
ramp-line to the top passing a detached block with care.
*FA. Ben Wintringham, Marion Wintringham, Alan Baker, Dave Johnston
18.10.1969*

⑧ Inferno E5 6a
A fine, fingery upper section that takes on the extremely blank-
looking area of slab to the left of the *Twinkletoes* ramp-line. Start
at the base of the right-hand of two corners that lead up to the
base of the main corner-line of *Doors of Perception*.
40m. Climb the corner to an overhang and swing up right to a
small left-facing corner. Move up this to a ledge on the right (this
lower section is common with *Twinkletoes*). Head up left to the
overlap below the blank sheet and a peg 2m above it. Difficult
climbing past the peg to a finger slot is followed by more hard
moves to another peg. One more fingery sequence moving out right
and up leads to a good horizontal break. Move left and finish easily.
*FA. Pete Bull, Nick Tetley 1985 (1pt)
FFA. Chris Nicholson 1986*

⑨ No Sweat E1 5c
A direct line that takes in some quite testing ground. Start below
a very thin crack-system in the wall to the left of *Undercracker*.
40m. Climb up the thin crack-system and continue directly to
the base of the ramp-line of *Twinkletoes* and *Undercracker*.
Follow the thin crack in the left wall to finish.

⑩ Undercracker E1 5a
Fairly bold but enjoyable climbing up the curving flakeline on the
left-hand side of the bald slab left of *Urizen's* corner. Start below
the left side of a flat pillar of rock with a very small wedged
block in it at 7m.
44m. Climb up the left side of the pillar to the small wedged
block and a good ledge just above. Traverse left along a break,
then move up to a narrow ramp-line. Follow this up right as it
steepens to form a corner, peg, and continue up the left curving
overlap to join the finish of *Twinkletoes*.
FA. Pat Littlejohn, P.Tower, Pete Thexton 20.3.1974

⑪ Slip It In Quick E3 5c
Intricate and very sustained slab climbing with reasonable
protection, despite appearances from below. Can suffer from an
excess of vegetation at times. Start as for *Undercracker*.
46m. Climb to the good ledge above the wedged block as for
Undercracker. Head up and rightwards to a good break and then
climb left and up to a good vegetated horizontal break. Climb
up the left side of a shallow arch feature to another horizontal
break and good nuts above. Move up rightwards to yet another
horizontal break and traverse this left to beneath a short thin
crack. Take this to the top. *Photo on page 93*.
FA. Steve Bell, Damion Carroll 18.11.1979

⑫ Terrapin E3 5b
A memorable and adventurous tour of the main section of
Long Rock Slab. Although protection is sound, the runouts
are thought-provoking. Start 3m right of the shallow pillar of
Undercracker at a very thin crack.
46m. Take the thin crack to a larger left-leaning crack that leads
to the pillar. Gain a small ledge on the top right side of the pillar
and move up left to a good break. Step left and up to a good
vegetated horizontal break (as for *Slip it in Quick*) and traverse
right to a peg. Climb up flakes to a horizontal break and then
pursue a bold line rightwards up positive finger flakes to another
vegetated horizontal break. Move right to a thin crack just right
of a very slight corner and take this to finish with good gear.
FA. Pat Littlejohn, Paul Buttrick, Dave Garner 16.5.1976

⑬ Soft Touch E4 6a
A direct and very intense climb up the blank section of wall to
the left of the long crack of *Lost Horizon*. There are a number of
difficult passages. Start 1m left of *Lost Horizon*.
41m. Climb up left to an overlap and move past it via thin
moves to a horizontal crack with a small jammed block on the
right. Move up left to a peg (and good small wire) in a thin
crack and make fingery moves to a horizontal break. Continue
more easily up to another break then move right and climb with
difficulty up to a ledge in the upper break. Step left and finish up
a thin crack, as for *Terrapin*.
*FA. Ben Wintringham, Marion Wintringham, Alan Baker 5.9.1976 (1pt)
FFA. A.Sharp*

⑭ Lost Horizon . . . . VS 5a
One of the best VSs in Devon. Start at the continuous crack-
system just left of the corner of *Urizen*.
42m. Follow the long, well-protected and sustained crack-
system without deviation, but lots of grinning.
FA. Ben Wintringham, Marion Wintringham 31.1.1970

⑮ Urizen . . . . VS 4c
The right-hand corner of the slab is a great line and very popular.
Start directly beneath the corner.
42m. Take the corner all the way with plentiful protection and
some vegetation as height is gained.
FA. Tony Willmott, Mike Spring, Dave Edwards 8.9.1969

⑯ Shangri-La . . . . S 4a
A classic. The arete to the right of *Urizen* is one of the finest
routes at Baggy Point and, as a consequence, sees a lot of
traffic. Start at the foot of the corner of *Urizen*.
43m. Move up slightly and climb right, around the arete past a
small corner to a crack-line in the face. Follow the line of cracks
and large holds right of the arete to the top.
FA. Ben Wintringham, Marion Wintringham, Alan Baker, Dave Johnston 1.3.1970

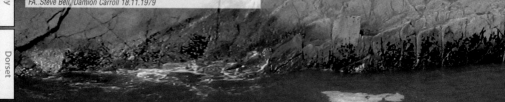

Access - A bird ban is in effect on this face between March 15th and June 30th.

From mid morning | 25 min | Tidal | Abseil in

Approach - stake in place for abseil/handrail rope as the path is steep and eroded

Scrattling Crack - page 94

Doors of Perception - page 95

Ledges

Low tide approach from Slab Cove

Avon Somerset

North Devon

Culm Coast

Inland Cornwall

Atlantic Coast

West Penwith

The Lizard

Inland Devon

Torbay

Dorset

1 Heart of the Sun   E2 5c

A massive, steep slab shoots skywards from the boulder beach of Slab Cove and presents an irresistible challenge. The cliff suffers from intermittent rockfall and the route has altered considerably over the years, and unfortunately the top pitch is now much poorer than it was. The first pitch requires a large rack of wires. Start to the left of the lower overhangs at a thin crack.

1) 5c, 50m. Climb to and through the lower overlaps with difficulty and move up right to gain a thin crack (this first section has also been climbed starting in the small corner just to the right at a similar grade). Follow the thin crack past a bulge and on up to a horizontal break. Move right and then climb up rightwards to the start of a thin crack-system. Superbly-sustained climbing up this gains a hanging belay at a horizontal break.

2) 5a, 50m. Climb up the right-leaning diagonal crack a little way to a thin break which is climbed up leftwards to below a long, loose and grassy groove at the left end of a diagonal overlap (belay possible). Climb the right arete of the groove and finish with care.

2a) 5c, 50m. A harder, but loose and serious finish is possible by continuing up the diagonal crack to just short of the vegetated corner, from where a very loose and serious traverse left under the diagonal overlap can be made to join the finish as described.

FAA. Tony Willmott, Mike Spring 19.10.1969
FFA. Arnis Strapcans, Chris King 2.1977 (The start and finish has changed over time)

Slab Cove

Slab Cove's huge sheet of overlapping slabs and grassy corners soars above its tiny boulder-beach. The one continuous section of clean rock is the setting for the main attraction of *Heart of the Sun*.

Approach - From the main path above The Promontory, pick up a vague path that winds its way down the slopes to the Cove.

Access - A restriction due to nesting birds is in place from March 15th to June 30th inclusive.

Tides - The base of the climb is only inaccessible around high tide or in very heavy seas.

Conditions - The climb gets plenty of sun and is sheltered. The route has changed on both the first and second pitches due to rockfall over the years and may still undergo periodic modifications.

Harder and very loose finish

Alternative start up small corner

1

Low tide approach possible to Long Rock Slab

From approach path

Avon Somerset

North Devon

Culm Coast

Inland Cornwall

Atlantic Coast

West Penwith

The Lizard

Inland Devon

Torbay

Dorset

Katherine Schirrmacher on the upper section of the technical, but well-protected *Pickpocket* (HVS 5b) - *page 95* - on Long Rock Slab at Baggy Point. Photo: Dave Pickford

The Promontory

The Promontory is a massive sheet of generally excellent rock, although its upper reaches are vegetated and slightly loose. The routes have sustained, well-protected and technical first pitches, although the upper easier pitches are less well protected and require caution.

Approach - All the routes, apart from *Kinkyboots*, are only accessible at lowish tides and during calm seas. The boulder beach is best reached by abseiling or downclimbing (Diff) the ridge to the right of the *Ben* and *Marion* slab.

Tides - The base of the slab is accessible for 2 hours (less at the seaward side) either side of low water except in rough seas.

Conditions - The slab is very exposed to the wind and rain but dries quickly. It is also a suntrap.

① **Freddie** . . . . ☼❶ 🧗🪝 ◻️◻️◻️◻️ **HS 4b**
The most testing of the four lines described on this section of the cliff. High in the grade. Start at the base of the easy-angled arete on the left side of the main slab.
37m. Move up the arete for 5m and transfer to cracks in the slab on the right. Follow the right-trending cracks all the way to the top passing a very thin section at two-thirds height.
FA. I.Bentley, N.Tritton 15.9.1976

② **Ben** . . . . ☼❶ 🪝◻️◻️◻️ **S 4a**
A superb pitch which follows the continuous line of right-leaning cracks up the best section of the slab. Start at a crack-line 5m right of the left edge of the slab.
40m. Follow the crack in its entirety with the main difficulties located in its upper half. Good gear.
FA. Ben Wintringham, Marion Wintringham 14.2.1970

③ **Marion** . . . . ☼❷ 🪝◻️◻️◻️ **HS 4a**
The sister route to *Ben* is an equally fine experience with the same combination of sustained climbing and good gear. Low in the grade. Start just left of the lowest section of the ledge.
38m. Climb the crack rightwards to the left of a square-cut overlap at 8m.
FA. Ben Wintringham, Marion Wintringham 14.2.1970

④ **In Her Eyes** . . . . ☼❶ 🧗◻️◻️◻️ **S 4a**
Steady climbing gains a thought-provoking final few metres. Start at the far right crack that begins on the higher section of the ledge. High in the grade.
35m. Follow the crack to a good small-nut slot below the final section of the slab, which is climbed on spaced but positive holds.
FA. D.Godfrey, G.Croft 19.10.1969

⑤ **Kinkyboots** . . . . ☼❶ ❘🧗◻️◻️ **VS 4c**
The first few moves are a Baggy legend, but unfortunately the upper pitch lets the route down. The first pitch provides an excellent alternative to the first pitch of *Midnight Cowboy*, should the tide be in. Start by abseiling or downclimbing the descent ridge to a small ledge, about 12m above the base of the zawn. Opposite is a small flat spike that touches the edge of the overhanging zawn wall.
1) 4c, 20m. Not a pitch for the short! Fall across the zawn to reach the spike and pull across on good holds. Move steeply up to the edge of the slab and pull around onto it. Move right and slightly upwards to a peg before traversing 7m right, either high or low, to a stance on a small sloping reddy/brown ledge. Belay on good wires.
2) 4b, 34m. Reverse the traverse back left to the peg, and climb up above it heading for a square-cut flake with an old thread. Before reaching the flake, move leftwards on the best rock and then take the cleanest line above with care to a stake belay.
FA. Dave Johnston, Ben Wintringham 19.10.1969

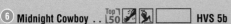

⑥ Midnight Cowboy .. [Top 50] 🗻 HVS 5b

The finest route on the The Promontory following the mid-height diagonal overlap via sustained and intricate climbing. If the tide is in the main pitch can be gained using the excellent first pitch of *Kinkyboots*. Start 4m right of the arete at the base of the slab.

1) 4c, 19m. Climb up left easily to a thin crack just left of a narrow corner. Follow the cracks to a small, sloping stance on a reddy/brown ledge. Belay on good wires.

2) 5b, 20m. Move up and right, above the overlap, for 3m and then make a tricky move back down right to good holds beneath it. Traverse right to a small flake on the slab before moving up to and following the overlap right until it breaks horizontally right. Climb the crack for 4m to a small stance. Belay on good wires.

3) 4b, 28m. Follow the crack until vegetated ground is reached. Pick a way up this with care. Belay on a stake if in place or walk back over the broad ridge and belay on the friction of the rope on the grass (which is considerable) as there are no other belays.

FA. Ben Wintringham, Marion Wintringham 15.11.1969

⑦ Long Rock Eliminate 🗻 HVS 5a

A good direct line right up the middle of the slab. Start 4m right of the arete as for *Midnight Cowboy*.

1) 5a, 19m. Climb directly up thin cracks to the apex of the first overlap at 8m. Continue up twin thin cracks above before moving up left to the reddy/brown sloping stance of *Midnight Cowboy*. Belay on good wires.

2) 4c, 35m. Move up rightwards through the overlap as for *Midnight Cowboy* and up to a small overlap. Take the thin line slightly rightwards until the rock becomes broken and vegetated. Finish slightly leftwards with care. Stake belay.

FA. Dave Johnston, Alan Baker 11.4.1971

⑧ Sexilegs .... 🗻 HVS 5b

Lots of great climbing on the first pitch. The route described is slightly different to that in other guidebooks taking in a better stance and line. Start at the left end of the low overhang at the base of the slab, 8m right of the arete.

1) 5b, 23m. Move through the overhang at a notch and climb the widest of the thin cracks to a thin horizontal break. Go left along this to the base of a right-facing corner and climb it to an overlap. Move left to a flake and take this until it is possible to move left once again across the main overlap with difficulty. Downclimb leftwards to the stance of *Midnight Cowboy*.

2) 4c, 34m. Move up rightwards above the overlap to a smaller overlap and horizontal break. Climb the thin diagonal crack leftwards to broken ground and finish up the cleanest line with care. Stake belays on the left and right.

FA. Ben Wintringham, Marion Wintringham 26.10.1969

Abseil descent or downclimb (Diff)

Ben Area

Avon Somerset | North Devon | Culm Coast | Inland Cornwall | Atlantic Coast | West Penwith | The Lizard | Inland Devon | Torbay | Dorset

	No star	⚐	⚐⚐	⚐⚐⚐
Mod to S	-	-	3	-
HS to HVS	-	-	7	6
E1 to E3	-	-	4	11
E4 and up	-	-	-	9

Lundy island almost appears to float on the surface of the sea off of the North Devon coast. Its steep granite cliffs and exposed, flat top are often visible from the mainland during fine weather. A visit to Lundy to sample its climbs is something a little bit special, not just because it holds some of the UK's greatest sea-cliff climbs, but also due

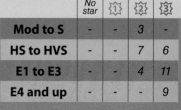

to its ambience; the island is car-free and for the most part unmodernised. Only a selection of Lundy's best and most popular routes are listed in this guidebook, the number of routes and complex access making the definitive rock climbing guide a necessary item for those contemplating a visit (Climbers' Club 2007 - www.climbers-club.co.uk - cover right). Much of the climbing on the island is fairly serious, the descents require care and the remoteness of the walls and zawns create a certain ambiance. However, these features all contribute to the appeal of the Lundy experience. All of the routes are trad, with both single and multi-pitch routes on excellent granite, most commonly approached by abseil. Lack of traffic on some cliffs, plus loose rock and vegetation at the very top of many of the cliffs, mean that care is required when topping-out, and a little gardening maybe also be necessary.

Getting to and staying on Lundy   See area map on page 90

Travelling to and choosing where to stay on Lundy require a considerable amount of forward planning. All the accommodation on the island is administered by The Landmark Trust (www.landmarktrust.org.uk) with around 20 options, ranging from small cottages to large barns and houses, along with a basic campsite. All of this accommodation, including the campsite, is in heavy demand and booking over a year in advance is needed to secure places on the island even at less popular times. Wild camping is illegal. Travel to and from the island is via boat (The HMS Oldenburg) which sails from Ilfracombe and/or Bideford on Devon's north coast, depending on tides. The costs for both the accommodation and the crossing are very reasonable. Food and other supplies are available from an excellent shop on the island, and meals and coffee are supplied all day at the pub - The Marisco Tavern - Lundy's social centre. Payment on a 'tab' can be made at both the shop and The Marisco Tavern and paid for by credit card at the end of a stay.

Restriction Due to Nesting Birds

There are huge numbers of nesting sites on Lundy and realistically a visit for climbers is only an option outside the main restricted period from April 1st to July 31st inclusive.

Tides and Conditions

The tidal range on Lundy is great and a good number of its cliffs are not accessible from mid to high tide. However, access to plenty of non-tidal routes is such that little time needs to be wasted waiting for lower tides. The majority of the best cliffs face westwards, and get little protection from high seas or poor weather.

Avon Somerset | North Devon | Culm Coast | Inland Cornwall | Atlantic Coast | West Penwith | The Lizard | Inland Devon | Torbay

The North Light

N

About 0.5 mile

Arch Zawn

The Diamond

The Devil's Slide

Threequarter Wall

Grand Falls Zawn

Deep Zawn

The Devil's Chimney

Halfway Wall

Flying Buttress

Landing Craft Bay

Quarter Wall

Sunset Promontory

The Old Light

Harbour

Shop and
Pub

The South Light

The Devil's Limekiln

Avon Somerset

North Devon

Culm Coast

Inland Cornwall

Atlantic Coast

West Penwith

The Lizard

Inland Devon

Torbay

Dorset

Mark Warnett making the best of the last sun of the day on
Double Diamond (HVS 5b) - *page 104* - Flying Buttress, Lundy.

Avon Somerset

North Devon

Culm Coast

Inland Cornwall

Atlantic Coast

West Penwith

The Lizard

Inland Devon

Torbay

Dorset

❶ The Flying Buttress . . . .   **Mod**
One of the best introductions for those taking their first steps on the lower grade Lundy classics. Easy access and very steady climbing amongst spectacular rock scenery.
FA. Pete Biven, Cliff Fishwick, A.Goodwin 8.1962

❷ Battery Rib . . . .   **VDiff**
Not far from *The Flying Buttress* and another good objective for a first foray into the lower-grade lines.
FA. Brain Martindale, T.Wright 2.5.1965

❸ Integrity. . . . .   **S**
Although time consuming and difficult to access, the small sea-stack of Needle Rock contains a handful of good pitches including this little gem.
FA. D.Brown, P.Bingham, J.Gill, J.Gaskill 29.3.1967

❹ The Devil's Slide . . . . .   Top 50   **HS 4a**
One of the UK's most notable sea-cliff features and also one of its greatest slabs. Can be climbed on a day visit by fast teams.
FA. Keith Lawder, Jimmy Logan 6.1961

❺ Horseman's Route . . . .   **HS 4b**
Two rewarding pitches, the second of which ventures out across the top of the exposed upper section of Flying Buttress.
FA. Frank McBratney, P.Gwilliam 9.1964

❻ The Black Hand . . .   **VS 4c**
The companion line to *Eclipse* but completely different in style being a steep and well-protected corner-crack.
FA. Keith Darbyshire, Ian Duckworth, Andy McFarlane 31.3.1972

❼ Albion . . . .   **VS 4c**
The main pitch follows THE corner-line that bounds the left-hand side of the Devil's Slide and is Lundy's finest VS pitch.
FA. Pete Biven, Viv Stevenson, Cliff Fishwick 15.4.1963

❽ The Devil's Chimney . . .   **VS 4c**
A remote and quite tough climb that gains the summit of the chimney itself, a large stack just metres from the mainland.
FA. Robin Shaw, Jimmy Logan 6.1961

❾ Shamrock . . . .   **VS 4c**
Three pitches of varied crack-climbing located in Landing Craft Bay - a popular and often sheltered cove with easy access.
FA. Terry Thompson, Bob Moulton, Paul de Mengel 17.3.1972

❿ Diamond Solitaire . . . . .   **VS 4c**
A much-photographed climb that has a difficult corner-crack on its first pitch and a lovely open face pitch to finish.
FA. Frank McBratney, Brain Martindale 5.5.1965

⓫ Road Runner . . . . .   **VS 4c**
A tough crack-pitch loaded with good gear and holds - if you can jam. Finishes at an abseil point.
FA. Graham Gilbert, Pat Littlejohn, Bob Moulton, 9.9.1972

⓬ Eclipse . . . .   **VS 4b**
An increasingly exposed two pitch climb that reaches a climax on its final arete. A long and exposed approach via 2 abseils.
FA. Frank Cannings, Arni Strapcans, Steve Berry 18.4.1976

⓭ Double Diamond. . . . . .   **HVS 5b**
The direct on the original classic of *Diamond Solitaire* has some difficult moves to get started. *Photo on page 103.*
FA. Simon Whalley, Gary Gibson 23.7.1984

⓮ Immaculate Slab . .   **HVS 5a**
A beautifully-located pitch that follows the left-hand side of a colourfully streaked slab.
FA. FA. Pete Thexton, Ken Wilson 15.4.1974

⓯ Formula One . . . .   **HVS 5a**
A long narrow cornerline that is one of the most coveted and finest single-pitch HVSs in the West Country. *Photo on page 91.*
FA. Pat Littlejohn, Bob Moulton, Graham Gilbert 6.9.1972

⓰ American Beauty . .   **HVS 5a**
Tremendous positions and lots of great climbing are the outstanding attributes of this long multi-pitch line.
FA. Pat Littlejohn, Dave Garner 31.3.1975

⓱ Headline **E1 5b**
Brilliant climbing in a charming zawn. Although the start is quite stiff the climbing gradually eases and the protection is good.
FA. Frank Cannings, John Kingston 19.4.1973

⓲ Fifth Appendage . . .   **E1 5b**
A highly acclaimed route with two excellent pitches, the first being the toughest. Best approached by abseil.
FA. Andy McFarlane, Ian Duckworth 18.4.1973

⓳ Satan's Slip **E1 5a**
Heart-in-mouth slab shuffling up the bald section of The Devil's Slide. Low in the technical grade but with very spaced gear.
FA. Paul Fatti, D.Ward 29.3.1970

⓴ The Ocean **E1 5b**
A massively long and serious route that has a very fine top pitch. Not the normal Lundy experience but the route is popular.
FA. Doug Kerr, C.Gilbert, S.Wilkie 13.8.1986

㉑ The Indy 500 . . . .   **E1 5b**
A full rope length of crack-climbing gives one of Lundy's finest and most coveted routes.
FA. Gary Gibson and others 21.7.1984

㉒ Dark Power **E1 5b**
An wild and imposing two pitch zawn climb best left for a calm and sunny evening.
FA. Roger Hughes, Leigh McGinley 2.8.1978

㉓ Redspeed **E2 5c**
Although a little awkward to access, the route itself is worth it - a technical wall and groove up the backside of the Devil's Slide.
FA. Roger Hughes, Leigh McGinley 3.8.1978

㉔ Slip Tide **E2 5b**
Another Landing Craft Bay favourite that outwits the steep stuff via some technical and runout manoeuvres.
FA. Gary Gibson, M.Brown 26.7.1981

㉕ Stop Press **E2 5c**
A much harder companion to *Headline* but equally memorable, featuring some steep and then technical climbing.
FA. Frank Cannings, John Kingston 21.4.1973 (1pt)

26 Destiny E2 5b
A magnificent, well-protected crack-pitch set high above the sea.
FA. Pat Littlejohn, Gus Morton. 2.4.1972

27 Quatermass E2 5c
An atmospheric 3 pitch journey into and out of Deep Zawn with a smattering of loose rock and vegetation.
FA. Keith Darbyshire, Hugh Clarke 16.4.1973 (some aid)
FFA. Ray Evans 10.1974

28 The Promised Land . E3 6a
A stunning multi-pitch line that forces its way through some huge overhangs on its initial pitch.
FA. Pat Littlejohn, Keith Darbyshire 16.4.1974

29 Wolfman Jack E3 5c
A two pitch thriller of a crack-climb with a sting at the start! However the crux is reserved for the finish.
FA. Pete Thexton, Ken Wilson 13.4.1974 (4pts)
FFA. Rowland Edwards 8.1979

30 Matt Black E3 5c
A reliable, well-protected proposition, although the bold start has put many off.
FA. Gary Gibson, Matt Ward, Adam Hudson, Simon Whalley 21.7.1984

31 The Great Divide E3 5b
A huge crack-line is the reward for some jiggery pokery that is needed to reach its base.
FA. Frank Cannings, Arni Strapcans 14.4.1977

32 Milky Way E4 6a
Tucked away in a deep narrow zawn is this stunning crack-line.
FA. Lyndsay Foulkes, Mick Learoyd, Roy Thomas 8.8.1986

33 Mal de Mer E4 6a
A modern favourite on the Parthenos; a very modern cliff.
FA. Matt Ward, Gary Gibson 3.8.1987

34 Cithaeron E4 6a
Brilliant, steep climbing on one of the Island's best hard cliffs.
FA. Gary Gibson, Matt Ward 27.7.1984

35 Antiworlds E5 6a
A multi-pitch zawn experience that rises from the confines of Deep Zawn itself.
FA. Pat Littlejohn, Bob Moulton, 11.9.1972 (4pt)
FFA. Matt Carr, Brian Molyneux 5.8.1989

36 Cullinan E5
The modern take on Flying Buttress moving out onto the very edge of its wing.
FA. Pat Littlejohn, Nick White 6.5.1989

37 Olympica E5
A bold wall climb on one of Lundy's most eye-catching cliffs.
FA. Pat Littlejohn, Chris King 28.8.1977

38 Supernova E5
Another Deep Zawn masterpiece up a system of thin cracks.
FA. Pat Littlejohn, Gus Morton. 20.4.1973 (3pts)
FFA. Steve Boyden, Paul Harrison 7.1980

39 A Widespread Ocean of Fear
. . . . E5
The classic of The Diamond, and one of the West Country's best hard routes.
FA. Gary Gibson, Derek Bettlestone 22.7.1981

40 Watching the Ocean E6
The central line on The Diamond. A very technical and bold climb of great quality.
FA. Gary Gibson, Hazel Gibson 1.8.1989

One of the West Country's finest sea-cliff features - The Devil's Slide.

Avon Somerset

North Devon

Culm Coast

Inland Cornwall

Atlantic Coast

West Penwith

The Lizard

Inland Devon

Torbay

Dorset

Culm Coast

Avon Somerset

North Devon

Culm Coast

Inland Cornwall

Atlantic Coast

West Penwith

The Lizard

Inland Devon

Torbay

Dorset

Avon Somerset

North Devon

Culm Coast

Inland Cornwall

Atlantic Coast

West Penwith

The Lizard

Inland Devon

Torbay

Dorset

Rich Mayfield eyeing up the steep finishing moves of *Pacemaker* (E5 6a)
- *page 142* - on the south face of the Middle Fin at Lower Sharpnose Point.

The multitude of jagged culm-fins that push out into the sea along this remarkable section of coastline are a geological wonder that provides the raw materials for some extremely fine sea-cliff climbing. The rock, in climbing terms, defies an easy overall assessment; its various guises range from iron-hard uniform sheets to huge skyscraping walls, buttresses and slabs of amorphous structure and composition. Reliable rock and good protection are not a given and the majority of the climbs, whilst not unduly runout or loose, require a steady approach. The odd patch of vegetation will be encountered. Nevertheless the Culm Coast is an enchanting place to climb with superb beaches next to many of the cliffs, remote villages with fabulous pubs and above all a good chance that, even at the height of the summer holidays, you may well have your chosen cliff to yourself - along with the adjacent beach.

Avon Somerset

North Devon

Culm Coast

Inland Cornwall

Atlantic Coast

West Penwith

The Lizard

Inland Devon

Torbay

Dorset

N

Smoothlands

Blackchurch

Titchberry

Dyer's Lookout

Page 114

Stoke

Hartland

Screda Point

Page 110

B3248

Speke's Mill Mouth

Page 120

Welcombe

Gull Rock

Cornakey Cliff

Page 124

Vicarage Cliff

Morwenstow

A39

Oldwalls' Point

Page 130

Page 136

Lower Sharpnose

Stibb

Kilkhampton

B3254

Page 144

Compass Point

Bude

A3072

About 5km

Avon Somerset

North Devon

Culm Coast

Inland Cornwall

Atlantic Coast

West Penwith

The Lizard

Inland Devon

Torbay

Dorset

One of the greatest sheets of culm at Oldwalls' Point holds the rarely climbed *Matchless* (E1 5b) - *page 134* - Marti Hallet mid crux but with a lot of climbing to go.

	No star	⛨1	⛨2	⛨3
Mod to S	-	-	-	-
HS to HVS	1	1	-	-
E1 to E3	-	2	1	2
E4 and up	-	-	1	-

The brooding nature of Blackchurch's northerly aspect, a green tinge of vegetation and soaring multi-pitch lines of less-than-perfect rock will repulse most and work as a magnetic draw to a few. In contrast the foreshore pinnacle of Blackchurch Rock itself is a haven of solid rock on its seaward face and is home to some classic pitches that should not be missed.

Approach   Also see main map on page 108

From the A39 Bude - Bideford road, take the B3248 to Hartland and turn right after a mile, signed to Hartland Point and Lighthouse. After a further 3/4 of a mile, turn right, signposted to Brownsham, and follow these signs to a small National Trust car park at Brownsham Farm. Walk out of the car park, turn left and pick up a bridlepath to Mill Mouth which passes farm buildings and leads to a track. Follow the track carefully down a wooded valley. Where the bridlepath heads steeply rightwards uphill, carry straight on along the track until it bears left over a small stream, then turn left onto another track that leads down to Mill Mouth (25 minutes).

N

Blackchurch Main Cliff

Blackchurch Rock

Brownsham Farm → P

GPS 51.007599 -4.444917

Hartland

B3248

About 1km

A39

Tides

The base of the climbs on Blackchurch Rock are only accessible for 3 hours either side of low tide and the starts need a little time to dry out. Blackchurch Main Cliff itself is only slightly tidal at its far left-hand end.

Conditions

All the routes on Blackchurch Rock are very clean, and dry quickly after rain, although during wet periods the cracks do seep. Blackchurch Rock faces northwest and receives sun only on summer evenings, and it is also very exposed to wind and rain. Blackchurch itself also receives very little sun and can take a long time to dry due to the amount of vegetation present on the crag.

Blackchurch Rock

Blackchurch Main Cliff

Nearing the final few metres of the immaculate *Sacre Coeur* (E2 5c) - *page 113* - at Blackchurch Rock. Climber: Alastair Smith. Photo: Dave Pickford.

Avon Somerset

North Devon

Culm Coast

Inland Cornwall

Atlantic Coast

West Penwith

The Lizard

Inland Devon

Torbay

Dorset

Avon Somerset · North Devon · Culm Coast · Inland Cornwall · Atlantic Coast · West Penwith · The Lizard · Inland Devon · Torbay · Dorset

❶ The Verger.... E1 5a

A big, committing climb right up the middle of the cliff finishing on the arete of the huge central slab. A very serious climb even when clean and dry. Start just left of the massive rubble heap, below a widening crack.

1) 4c, 20m. Move up over steep grass to the base of the crack. Climb the crack, which is thin to start, to a stance on the left at a large ledge.

2) 4c, 16m. Poor rock. Climb the corner on the left and work back right to a stance on a ledge next to the arete.

3) 5a, 45m. Move right, around the arete, to a vertical crack and take this to its end. Move up the wall above until it is possible to traverse leftwards to the arete. Climb the long slabby edge of the arete with little protection to the top. A serious pitch.

FA. Keith Darbyshire, Paul Buttrick 14.8.1974

❷ Loose Woman E1 5b

The most popular line on the Main Cliff offers some good, well-protected climbing on its first two pitches, but the final pitch requires care. Start at a long crack that sprouts from the apex of the massive rubble heap.

1) 4c, 20m. Take the clean-cut, widening crack-system to a ledge and belay on the left.

2) 5b, 16m. Climb steeply up into the corner on the right and then through the overhang with difficulty to better holds and a stance on a ledge above.

3) 17m. Move up the steep corner left of the edge of the slab for 5m and place some gear before stepping right onto the slab and climbing up this with care to the top.

FAA. Bill Chevrest, Ian Duckworth 4.1969
FFA. Keith Darbyshire 9.1974

❸ The Archtemper E3 5b

The soaring corner-line on the right side of the face is a serious climb that requires lots of large gear on its top pitch, plus nerve and skill to deal with the rock and vegetation on the first. Start at an awkward stance directly beneath the corner reached via a scramble up a grassy ramp and chimney.

1) 5b, 26m. Pass a low bulge, peg, and continue to another bulge at 12m. Move around the bulge and climb the corner above past a peg to two more pegs. Continue up the corner passing a useful large cam-notch to a stance and belay where the corner lies back. Old pegs, nut and large cams.

2) 5a, 22m. The corner now starts to overhang but is well protected with large cams and nuts. A recent rockfall has left some loose material just before the top.

FA. Pat Littlejohn, Graham Skerrat 30.3.1970

❹ Godspell E5 6a

The blank wall right of *Archtempter's* corner is a stunning pitch on good rock throughout. Approach as for *Archtempter*.

48m. Climb just right of the arete to a thin crack and good nuts. Move up right to a peg and continue rightwards to a smooth light coloured patch of rock and twin pegs. Head back up left to another peg and then make a couple of moves left onto the arete. Follow the arete with no protection to a good peg after 10m. Move rightwards to a thin crack and follow this until a wider crack on the left can be gained. Climb the crack to a prickly exit.

FA. Pete Whillance, Dave Armstrong 9.8.1978 (climbed in 2 pitches)

Not much sun · 25 min · Seepage · Multi-pitch

Descent

Scramble up rubble cone to stance

Scramble up chimney to awkward stance

Blackchurch Rock

Blackchurch

The two areas of Blackchurch offer contrasting climbing.
Approach - Walk along the beach to the base of the crag from Mill Mouth.
Descent - Walk off down a steep path to Mill Mouth.

An eye-catching, unique formation lying on the foreshore in front of the main cliff is Blackchurch Rock. The dark seaward-facing slab of excellent rock is split by some very thin cracks.

⑤ Rite of Spring . . . . 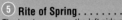 **VS 4c**
The inset corner on the left side of the slab. Start at the base of the corner by a rock pool.
30m. A steep barnacle-encrusted start is best attempted in dry conditions. Above, clean rock and good gear arrive and lead to the final section up the edge of the rock.
FA. Pat Littlejohn et al. 8.2.1970

⑥ Sacre Coeur **E2 5c**
A majestic pitch of flawless quality. Take lots of wires. Start beneath the disjointed crack-system on the left side of the slab.
30m. Move up to the widening of the crack at the overlap. Just above the overlap, make a long step left into another good crack. Follow this, and where it fades, move right to a thin crack and follow this to the top. Sustained. *Photo on page 111.*
FA. Pat Littlejohn, Hugh Clarke 20.5.1974

⑦ Jamaican Dub **E3 6a**
The thinner line of cracks on the right-hand side of the slab is the equal of its better known neighbour. Start 5m right of the start of *Sacre Coeur* at a thin crack.
30m. Take the crack to a small overlap. Move up and follow thin technical cracks with difficulty to a better crack. Continue up this crack and finish up another to gain the summit of the rock.
FA. Pete O'Sullivan, P.Bingham, J.Thompson 11.7.1981

⑧ Notre Dame . . . . **VS 4b**
The jagged right edge of the slab provides an airy and impressive pitch. Start close to the arete on the reverse side of the slab.
30m. Move up steeply rightwards on good, but barnacle-encrusted holds and then pull up to gain the arete. Follow the stepped arete until a crack on the left near the top can be climbed to the summit.
FA. Keith Darbyshire, Dave Garner 1974

Avon Somerset | North Devon | Culm Coast | Inland Cornwall | Atlantic Coast | West Penwith | The Lizard | Inland Devon | Torbay | Dorset

Descent

Start of *Notre Dame* on reverse side of slab

	No star	☆	☆☆	☆☆☆
Mod to S	-	-	-	-
HS to HVS	-	-	1	-
E1 to E3	-	1	2	-
E4 and up	-	-	-	4

Both Smoothlands and Dyer's Lookout are extremely impressive sheets of culm, and the climbs on them represent some of the hardest and most demanding, quality routes on the coast. The climbs see little traffic due to a combination of restricted tidal access and difficulty, although all remain clean apart from the slab taken by *Hellbound* at Smoothlands that may need a brush-up before an ascent.

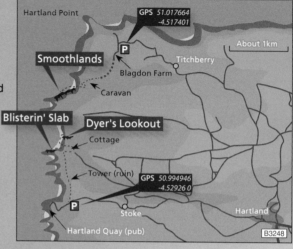

Approach   See area map page 108

Smoothlands - from the A39 Bude - Bideford road, follow signs to Hartland and pick up signs for Hartland Point and lighthouse. Follow these signs through narrow lanes to a toll booth (fee) before the road drops down to the lighthouse itself. Just beyond the toll booth take a track on the left and park immediately at one of two spots on the left. Walk down the track past Blagdon Farm and continue down to the beach. Boulder-hop left along the beach to the crag (25 minutes).

Dyer's Lookout - From the A39 Bude - Bideford road, follow signs to Hartland and then on to the village of Stoke. From Stoke, take the road to Hartland Quay. Just before the road drops down to the quay is a toll booth (fee in summer). For Dyer's Lookout and the Blisterin' Barnacle Slab, park at the toll booth and follow the coast path north, past a ruined tower, and down to a cottage and the beach (15 minutes). Dyer's Lookout is the huge fin rising from the beach on the right and the Blisterin' Barnacle Slab is the largest of the pinnacles on the left looking out to sea.

Tides

Smoothlands is only accessible during the period between low and mid tide. Dyer's Lookout is only inaccessible for a short time at high water. The ledges below the Blisterin' Barnacle Slab are only accessible during the period between low and mid tide, and only in calm seas.

Condtions

All the crags share a northerly aspect but do receive sun in the evening during the summer months. The faces dry quite quickly but some seepage can be a problem at Smoothlands. The Blisterin' Barnacle Slab is very exposed to wind and sea spray, and takes time to dry out.

Dyer's Lookout   The Blisterin' Barnacle Slab

Side tabs (left margin): Avon Somerset | North Devon | Culm Coast | Inland Cornwall | Atlantic Coast | West Penwith | The Lizard | Inland Devon | Torbay | Dorset

The author avoiding a soaking on the dark culm slab of *Jazz Discharge Party Hat* (E1 5b)
- *page 119* - on the Blisterin' Barnacle Slab at Dyer's Lookout. Photo: Carrie Hill

Avon Somerset | North Devon | **Culm Coast** | Inland Cornwall | Atlantic Coast | West Penwith | The Lizard | Inland Devon | Torbay | Dorset

❶ Creeping Flesh . . . . 　　　　 **E5 6b**

The long line of weakness on the left of the face is a very difficult but high quality climb that is high in the grade. Start on a raised ledge left of the largest arching overhang.

46m. Climb a thin crack and slab to meet the left-trending thin crack-line at a peg and better gear. Follow the line all the way, passing two pegs at two-thirds height where the most difficult climbing is encountered. The top section of rock, past a final peg is slightly loose.

FA. Ken Palmer, Pete Saunders 8.1989

❷ Hellbound . . . . 　　　　 **E6 6b**

The huge blank-looking, steep slab above the arching overhangs is the spectacular setting for this bold and very thin climb. High in the grade. The route sees very few ascents and may need to be cleaned before an attempt. Stakes in the steep grass slope above the slab may need replacing. Start as for *Creeping Flesh,* just to the left of the largest arching overhang.

1) 6b, 34m. Climb *Creeping Flesh* for 8m and then continue in the same line to a peg above on positive shallow pockets. Move up a thin seam to a small nut-placement and make hard moves up and right to a thin crack. Take the thin crack to a final difficult sequence of moves to reach a narrow belay ledge. Peg belays.

2) 6a, 20m. Above is a peg, climb very boldly to this and continue on the same line to the top.

FA. Ken Palmer, Andy Grieve 30.4.1990

The Great Slab

Smoothlands' Great Slab is a formidable blank sheet of culm that forms the left side of a huge dome-shaped cliff. The location is sublime and the climbs are some of the coast's finest and hardest.

Approach - From the beach, boulder-hop across the tidal foreshore to the base of the slab. If making an abseil-approach, follow the coast path until below the dome-shaped backside of the cliff and walk steeply to stakes in the grass directly above the slab.

Tides - The base of The Great Slab is approached along a tidal section of foreshore that is accessible for 3 hours either side of low water. However, in calm weather the base of the climbs are above the high-water level and can be reach directly by abseil from above.

Descent - Descend down the steep, grass-slope to the right (facing out) and pick up the coast path which leads back to the approach path and the beach.

Conditions - The slab sees little sun except in summer when it receives plenty from around 5pm onwards.

Descent

Evening | 25 min | Tidal

Dave Pickford at the halfway point of *The Earthsea Trilogy Part 1* (E6 6b) - *page 118* - on the gravity defying wall of culm at Dyer's Lookout Photo: Grant Farquhar

Avon Somerset

North Devon

Culm Coast

Inland Cornwall

Atlantic Coast

West Penwith

The Lizard

Inland Devon

Torbay

Dorset

Avon Somerset

North Devon

Culm Coast

Inland Cornwall

Atlantic Coast

West Penwith

The Lizard

Inland Devon

Torbay

Dorset

Main Cliff

An incredibly smooth fin of Culm that dominates the beach and provides the canvas for two of the coast's most impressive routes. The crag and its routes have undergone a number of major structural changes over recent decades due to rockfall, but the routes now seem to be as stable as they are going to get.

Approach - Walk along the beach to the base of the crag.

Tides - The base of the crag is covered at high tide. During heavy seas the base will be inaccessible for longer.

Descent - Walk off the back of the cliff and back down to the beach.

Conditions - The face is well drained and is not vegetated, therefore it dries very quickly after rainfall. Although normally in the shade, the face does get the sun from early evening during the summer months.

❶ The Walk of Life Top 50   **E9 6c**

The central section of the main wall at Dyer's Lookout is a truly amazing sheet of impenetrable-looking culm. Its ascent is the latest instalment in a long history of attempts on the line. Start in the centre of the wall.

48m. Climb the initial overlaps to gain the base of the smooth hanging slab. Move up this via a series of very thin, powerful and precarious moves, to good holds and the first reasonable protection at 15m. Continue on spaced thin breaks for 10m until the first and only good gear at a wide slot (Friend 2), climb past the slot to join and follow a hairline crack to the top of the wall passing several more difficult sections of climbing.

FA. James Pearson 6.2008. The upper section of the route was originally climbed as Dyer Straits, E8 6b, FA. Ian Vickers 3.8.1998

❷ The Earthsea Trilogy Part 1

....   **E6 6b**

A very tough culm testpiece that wends its way up the exposed edge of the architecturally stunning seaward fin of the main cliff. The cliff is constantly on the move and has recently suffered yet another rockfall to the landward side of the route. Start just to the left of the toe of the fin.

50m. Climb 8m to a peg at the start of a thin left-slanting crack and take it to a ledge on the arete. Pull left into a crack on the face - pegs - and follow the crack until it is possible to move back right onto the arete. Follow the arete to a peg on the left. Move up and out left onto the wall before tricky climbing leads back right in an exposed position to reach a peg high up near the arete, follow the arete to finish. The final section of the line is often dirty and a better finish is to step back down after clipping the final peg and follow a thin, sustained crack leftwards to meet up with the final section of *Walk of Life*. Photo on page 117.

FA. Nick White, Dave Thomas 24.7.1989

To the Blisterin' Barnacle Slab →

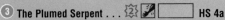

3 The Plumed Serpent . . . **HS 4a**
A hard-won but rewarding pitch that follows the bending line of cracks on the left-hand side of the slab. Start at low tide at the far left end of the narrow, sloping lower ledge.
25m. Climb the slab leftwards to the base of the cracks and follow them to the top.
FA. Pete O'Sullivan, B.Adams 1979

4 Jazz Discharge Party Hat
. . . . **E1 5b**
An impressive pitch on great rock and with very sustained climbing, although the protection is less than comforting. Start at a thin right-trending crack below a tiny vertical corner at 10m.
23m. Make thin moves up the crack to an easing. Follow the line of intermittent thin cracks 3m right of the tiny vertical corner to the top. *Photo on page 115.*
FA. M.Miller, R.Jones, I.Hamilton 1982

5 Blisterin' Barnacle . **E2 5b**
Culm slab climbing at its finest but again with limited protection in its lower reaches. Start right of the thin crack of *Jazz Discharge Party Hat* below a thin crack in the upper section of the slab.
23m. Pursue a line up the bold slab to better protection and holds at a thin seam. Move up this and step left to the upper crack and follow this pleasantly to the top.
FA. Pete O'Sullivan, B.Adams 5.1979

The Blisterin' Slab
The steep offshore slab is seamed with thin cracks and benefits from superb solid rock and a handful of good pitches, however finding good climbing conditions needs careful planning.
Approach - Boulder-hop out to the slab and scramble up to its summit and down the other side to access the small ledges beneath the face.
Tides - The ledges at the base of the face are only accessible from low to mid tide and only in calm seas.
Descent - Scramble back down to the ledges.
Conditions - There is no shelter from the wind or sea spray but the face gets the evening sun in the summer. The slab can remain damp at times and ideally a visit should be made at low tide on summer evenings in calm conditions.

6 Not Blisterin' Barnacle
. . . . **E2 5b**
A similar experience to *Blisterin' Barnacle*. Start to the left of the slab's right arete.
23m. Follow a bold line up the slab to meet a thin crack midway. Follow this to the crest and move left along the top of the slab to finish.
FA. D.Garrett, H.Sharp 30.7 1982

Descent

	No star	☆	☆☆	☆☆☆
Mod to S	-	-	-	-
HS to HVS	-	4	-	-
E1 to E3	-	2	3	1
E4 and up	-	-	1	-

The jagged promontory of Screda Point and the retiring non-tidal wall at Speke's Mill Mouth offer up some fine pitches on excellent culm. The climbs are off-vertical, but have a feel somewhere between slab and wall climbing. Protection in the main is spaced and the difficulties on most of the routes technical and sustained; a good supply of small wires is a must. The coastal scenery is outstanding and the approach, via the isolated car park at the Hartland Quay Hotel and its associated Wreckers' Inn adds to the rather special ambience of the coast and its history hereabouts.

Approach   See area map on page 108

From the A39 Bideford - Bude road, follow signs to the village of Hartland and then onto the hamlet of Stoke. Follow signs to Hartland Quay and park in one of the car parks near the Hotel. In summer a toll is charged to drive the last section of the road down to the quay.

Screda Point - The crags are easily viewed from the Hotel car park and can be approached across the boulder beach or via the coastal path and dropping down to the grassy plateau above the landward crags where an abseil from the many stakes accesses the base of the cliff (5 minutes).

Speke's Mill Mouth - Follow the coast path southwards which contours around most of the big hilltops to a final drop down to a grassy flat area above Speke's Mill Mouth beach. The crag is set back from the beach next to a narrow waterfall (25 minutes).

Tides

Screda Point - The base of the landward cliff is accessible for 3 hours either side of low water. The outer pinnacles are only accessible for an hour or so either side of low water in calm seas.
Speke's Mill Mouth - This cliff is not tidal.

Conditions

Screda Point - The faces get plenty of sun from mid afternoon and dry quickly, although a wet streak on the landward crag needs a dry spell to disappear.
Speke's Mill Mouth - The face receives little sun but is usually dry from spring to autumn. It is sheltered from the wind, but if the waterfall is in spate, spray can be a problem. The face is cool in hot weather.

Avon Somerset | North Devon | Culm Coast | Inland Cornwall | Atlantic Coast | West Penwith | The Lizard | Inland Devon | Torbay | Dorset

Map: Hartland Quay, N, P, Screda Point, Toll booth, Stoke, GPS 50.994375 -4.534103, Speke's Mill Mouth, About 1km

Main Cliff — Pinnacles

❶ Pressure Drop

········ ③ **E3 5c**

A classy, sustained pitch in an idyllic setting. The route follows the sheer-looking, blank wall to the right of the picturesque waterfall. Start on boulders in the stream at the base of the line.

32m. Climb the line of thin cracks to small ledges and continue past a peg to another small ledge midway up the wall. The upper section of the crack gradually steepens but the holds get bigger and better.

FA. Pete O'Sullivan, M.Doyle, I.Thomas 23.6.1984

Not much sun | 25 min | Sheltered

Speke's Mill Mouth

A lovely little section of cliff set well back from the sea and a useful escape from the sun in hot weather.

Approach - From the flat grassy area well above the beach scramble down to the stream directly underneath the cliff.

Descent - Walk off left across the stream and back down to the base of the cliff.

The sheltered dell of Speke's Mill Mouth is the setting for the crack-climb of *Pressure Drop* (E3 5c) - *this page* - a good place to escape high seas and or tides. Photo: Dave Johnson

Avon Somerset | North Devon | Culm Coast | Inland Cornwall | Atlantic Coast | West Penwith | The Lizard | Inland Devon | Torbay | Dorset

Avon Somerset
North Devon
Culm Coast
Inland Cornwall
Atlantic Coast
West Penwith
The Lizard
Inland Devon
Torbay
Dorset

Screda Point

A very reliable venue that has a good number of easily accessible single-pitch routes that are somewhere between slab and wall climbs. The rock is generally excellent but protection is spaced and the climbing sustained. Take lots of small wires.

Approach - From the car park at Hartland Quay the climbs are easily viewed and can be reached via the beach 3 hours either side of low tide or by walking along the cliff-top path and descending to the grassy field on top of the crag from where an abseil (many stakes in place) gains the base of the climbs.

Tides - The base of the main slab is accessible for three hours either side of low tide whilst the outer pinnacles are only accessible for a shorter period around low water itself and in very calm sea conditions.

Conditions - The routes dry very quickly but are unclimbable when wet. There is no shelter from the rain.

❶ Half Life . . . . . 　　　　　　　 E3 5c
The smooth left-hand side of the slabby wall provides the blank canvas for this intricate and bold pitch. The protection is very spaced. Start 6m right of the left edge of the slab on the left-hand side of an alcove.
26m. Pull through the low bulge onto the slab and move up to good holds. Now head up leftwards past intermittent cracks and finish via a move right and up on the best holds.
FA. Pete O'Sullivan, Chris Gibson 15.3.1980

❷ Nose Decay . . . 　　　　　　　 E4 6a
A fine, hard and very bold line. Start 6m right of the left edge of the slab on the left-hand side of an alcove, as for *Half Life*.
25m. Pull through the bulge and move up to good holds as for *Half Life*. Above is a lone peg, climb to and past the peg via a very tough move and proceed to the top with little in the way of protection. *Photo on page 88.*
FA. M.Millar, R.Jones 1982

❸ Lucky Streak . . 　　　　　　　 E1 5b
In the centre of the crag is a dark streak that is a seepage line during wet spells. *Lucky Streak* takes the thin crack in the streaks upper half. Start midway along the base of the crag at the right end of a low alcove.
25m. Move up to good holds and climb the wall with poor protection to meet the thin crack that starts halfway up the middle of the dark streak. Follow this to the top.
FA. Pete Bull, Clarke Alston 30.5.1989

❹ Lord Lucan is Missing
. . . . 　　　　　　　 E2 5c
The continuous thin crack-line just to the right of the dark streak has a hard move close to the end of the pitch. Start below the thin crack.
25m. Follow the thin crack in its entirety to an unexpectedly tricky move close to the top.
FA. J.Wyatt 1988

❺ One in Every Port . . 　　　　　 E1 5b
An excellent climb typical of the style on this slabby wall. Start below a line of left-slanting parallel thin cracks.
26m. Follow the line of the parallel cracks all the way to the top.
FA. Dick Swindon, Pete O'Sullivan, Renny Croft 20.4.1982

❻ Tourist Trap . . . 　　　　　　　 E1 5b
A great pitch that passes the small round hole high on the right-hand side of the face. Start 5m left of the right arete of the slabby wall. High in the grade.
26m. Climb up slightly right towards the arete and then move up to a crack that leads to the hole. From the hole a leftwards-trending line has a couple of small nut placements that protect the technical moves to the top.
FA. Pete O'Sullivan, Roger Mear 28.4.1979

Many belay stakes

Tidal approach across beach

7 Chien Lunatique . . . 🔆 ✏️ 🐾 ⬜ **HVS 4c**
The right-hand arete is a popular introduction to the crag. Start just left of the base of the arete. *Photo this page.*
26m. Climb good cracks to ledges on the arete. From the upper ledge boldly climb the arete on its left side to a crack and follow this to finish.
FA. Pete O'Sullivan, Renny Croft 29.4.1980

50m to the right are some triangular pinnacles that are accessible at low tide.

8 Föhn . . . . 🔆 ✏️ 💗 ⬜ **HS 4a**
The face of the inner pinnacle is far less tidal than its offshore near neighbour. Start below the summit of the pinnacle.
20m. Climb straight up the middle of the pinnacle's main face to an awkward belay. Sparsely protected, but technically easy.
FA. Roger Mear, Pete O'Sullivan 29.4.1979

9 Sea Breeze . . . . 🔆 ✏️ ⬜ **HS 4a**
The inset slab on the left-hand side of the seaward pinnacle is a good but hard to access pitch. Start below the inset slab.
26m. The left side of the slab has good gear and pleasant climbing at the grade.
FA. Roger Mear, Pete O'Sullivan 28.4.1979

10 The Needle Direct. . 🔆 ✏️ 🐾 ⬜ **VS 4b**
The front face of the seaward pinnacle is well positioned, but access to the start is quickly cut off. Start at the base of the face.
26m. Follow the slab direct up the middle to the top.
FA. Iain Peters, A.Clarke 4.1974

Lewis Blight on *Chien Lunatique* (HVS 4c) - *this page* - at Screda Point.

Downclimb

Downclimb

	No star	☆	☆☆	☆☆☆
Mod to S	-	-	-	-
HS to HVS	1	2	4	-
E1 to E3	-	2	3	-
E4 and up	-	-	-	1

Both Gull Rock and Cornakey Cliff are superb examples of what climbing on the Culm Coast is all about, ranging from serious, multi-pitch slabs to smooth single-pitches of finely weathered, off-vertical culm. The setting of the cliffs is remote and combined with the delights of the surfing beach at Welcombe Mouth and the Rectory Tearooms at Morwenstow, it offers a great starting point for exploring the area and getting used to the style of climbing.

Approach   See area map on page 108
Gull Rock - From the A39 Bideford - Bude road, take the minor road signed to Welcombe. Follow the signs for Welcombe and then for Welcombe Mouth. The last 1/2 mile is on a narrow track that ends at a car park above the beach at Welcombe Mouth. Gull Rock is the elongated headland easily seen to the south of the beach (the climbing is on the far side). Boulder-hop along the base of the cliffs towards the headland and pass through a large gap between the mainland crag and the detached sea stack. The main face is the largest slab on the mainland promontory whilst the narrow wall of *Booby Prize* is above the beach just left of a waterfall (25 minutes).

Cornakey Cliff - From the A39 Bideford - Bude road, take the minor road signed to Morwenstow. At Morwenstow park at the car park next to the Rectory Tearooms and Church. Take a footpath down through the graveyard, through some buildings and then over a small stream. Follow the path uphill a little way and then take a path on the left that heads out along the edge of a field to join the coast path on top of Henna Cliff. Head right (north) on the coast path and in a short distance the huge cliff of Cornakey comes into view. Walk to the top of the crag and then go through a gate in the fence a little further on. Drop down easy but at times rocky and thorny ground to a derelict hut at the end of the promontory and scramble down to the base of the cliff using a fixed rope (25 minutes).

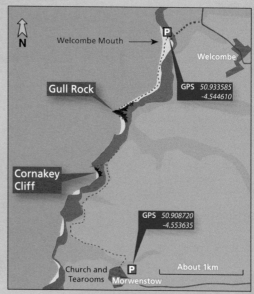

Tides
Gull Rock - The climbs are accessible for around 3 hours either side of low tide. Outside of this period the access between the main cliff and the sea stack of Gull Rock is cut off.
Cornakey Cliff - The cliff is only accessible for 3 hours either side of low water, although the beach is only wave-washed in very rough seas.

Conditions
Gull Rock - The main cliff is a suntrap and dries almost instantly. The *Booby Prize* wall receives no sun and is affected by spay from the waterfall.
Cornakey Cliff - Although a very serious cliff, Cornakey Cliff has a sunny aspect and dries quickly. The slabs will become unclimbable in rain.

Avon Somerset | North Devon | Culm Coast | Inland Cornwall | Atlantic Coast | West Penwith | The Lizard | Inland Devon | Torbay | Dorset

Avon Somerset

North Devon

Culm Coast

Inland Cornwall

Atlantic Coast

West Penwith

The Lizard

Inland Devon

Torbay

Dorset

Rob Byrom and Caz Neely clocking up some early season mileage on *Solid Air* (VS 4b) - *page 126* - at Gull Rock on the Culm Coast.

1 Seaward Edge . . . . **HS 4a**
The crack and left arete of the slab give a good introduction to the delights of the main slab. Start just right of the arete.
24m. Follow the crack to meet the arete midway and follow it to the top in a superb position.

2 Shivering Timbers . . . . **VS 4b**
A lovely pitch on good rock and with reliable protection - low in the grade. Start around 5m right of the arete at a crack that leads to a small square notch in an overlap.
23m. Climb the crack past an overlap and continue up the thinner crack above to join the arete just below the top. Finish up the arete as for *Seaward Edge*.
FA. Chris Nicholson, Andy Gallagher 5.1.1980

3 Solid Air . . . . **VS 4b**
One of the best single-pitches at the grade on the Culm Coast. Good protection from wires. Start around 8m right of the arete below a small quartz patch. *Photo on page 125 and cover.*
23m. Climb up a thin crack-line to the quartz patch and continue to a small ledge above. Finish up the wall and cracks, keeping just left of a large patch of vegetation.
FA. Steve Chadwick 18.2.1973

4 Argonaut Direct . . . . . . **HVS 4c**
A rather serious pitch, that is poorly protected and technically harder than the two VSs on the slab to its left. Start at a very thin seam right of the quartz patch of *Solid Air*.
23m. Move up the seam and then climb up and slightly right to a narrow ledge. Climb up to another thin ledge and follow the thin cracks and wall directly to the top.
FA. Pat Littlejohn, John Fowler 20.7.1968

5 Crazy Streak **E1 5a**
Excellent rock and climbing but with spaced protection. Start left of a thin crack that runs up to meet two rusty pegs in the centre of the slab - *Oiseaux*.
22m. Climb directly up the blank slab, which gradually increases in difficulty, to finish directly below the abseil point. There are a couple of good wire placements along the way that need a bit of searching out.
FA. Iain Peters, Gordon Jenkin 28.6.1981

6 Oiseaux **E1 5b**
The central line of the slab is an excellent climb that has just about adequate protection as long as care is taken to seek it out. Start in the centre of the slab below rusty twin pegs at mid-height.
23m. Follow a thin crack on good holds, slightly rightwards, to the twin pegs. Step right and climb the sustained upper wall on shallow dishes and thin seams to the top.
FA. Brian Wilkinson, Lionel Petherick 28.6.1981

7 Walking on the Moon . . . . . **HVS 5a**
Gradually increasing difficulties and varied climbing mark out this route as one of Gull Rock's finest. Start around 7m left of the narrow corner at the right side of the slab.
23m. Move up onto foot ledges and take a diagonal line rightwards on positive holds until a move left gains a standing position on a thin flake and foothold, twin pegs. Good sustained moves directly above the pegs lead to the top.
FA. Chris Nicholson, Andy Gallagher 5.1.1980

8 Lead Boots **E1 5b**
Good slab moves and a hard top section but with dubious protection from pegs. Start 3m left of the narrow corner at the right side of the slab below a quartz patch.
21m. Climb direct past the quartz patch to the twin pegs high on the face and pass these with difficulty to finish.
FA. Pate O'Sullivan, S.Deeming, S.Cooper 7.1983

All cliff-top belays are best backed up on the abseil anchors

Lots of sun | 25 min | Tidal

Avon Somerset | North Devon | Culm Coast | Inland Cornwall | Atlantic Coast | West Penwith | The Lizard | Inland Devon | Torbay | Dorset

Gull Rock

The Main Slab is a smooth sheet of low-angled culm set in a sunny position that offers a good selection of routes from Hard Severe to E2. The one hard route is unique, and worth a walk over to inspect its delights.

Approach - Boulder-hop through the gap between the mainland promontory and Gull Rock itself. *Booby Prize* is next to the waterfall that cascades onto the beach.

Tides - The climbs are accessible for around 3 hours either side of low water.

Descent - Abseil from the top of the slab.

Conditions - The Main Slab faces south and gets lots of sun but is exposed to wind and rain. The narrow wall of *Booby Prize* faces north.

100m to the right of the main slab is another clean sheet of rock.

⑨ Haile Selassie . . . . ⌁ 🗡️🖊️ ☐ **E2 5c**
Set apart from the main slab is this popular hairline crack. Start below the thin crack that starts at the top of a low, ground level cut-out in the slab.

21m. Take the thin crack in its entirety to the top. Belays left and right. To descend walk along the top of the crag to the abseil point above the main section of the slab; or scramble down steep, grassy ground directly behind the belay and walk back around the base of the crag as for the approach.
FA. Iain Peters, Pete O'Sullivan 13.4.1984

On the back wall of the beach is a waterfall, just to its left is a narrow wall of culm that is worth looking at, even if the climb is not attempted.

⑩ Booby Prize . . . . ⌁ 🗡️ ☐ **E6 6b**
The 'boob'-covered leaning wall gives a unique climb. Start in the middle of the narrow wall.

27m. Climb with difficulty to the first of 3 titanium pegs that mark out the line. Increasingly pumpy moves past the upper pegs end at a final wall of large pebbles. Move right to finish. An alternative start can be made from the arete on the right of the initial wall.
FA. Andy Grieve 8.8.1994

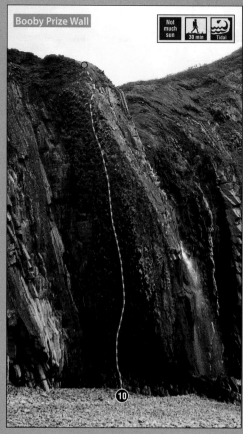

Booby Prize Wall

Approach
Main Slab
Waterfall and *Booby Prize*

Cornakey Cliff

Cornakey Cliff is composed of a series of overlapping slabs of generally poor rock. The situation is serious and the rock on the main attraction of the crag, *Wrecker's Slab*, needs an experienced leader for it to be climbed in relative safety. The two shorter climbs are on good rock and are excellent pitches in their own right.

Approach - From the very top of the crag walk north for a little way to a gate in the fence line. Go through the gate and drop down the broad, easy-angled but thorny and rocky-ridge above the crag to a derelict wooden hut. Just beyond the hut is an in situ rope that aids a scramble down to the base of the cliff.

Tides - The base of the cliff is accessible for around three hours either side of low water.

Conditions - The cliff receives plenty of sun and is fairly well sheltered, although the climbs become wet very quickly in the rain.

❶ Stormy Weather . . . . . . 🎴 HVS 5a

A cracking pitch that should not be passed by. Good rock, good protection and some excellent jamming. Start 6m right of the edge of the wall, at the base of a left leading diagonal break.

27m. Follow the diagonal break to a small ledge on the left arete of the wall. Work back rightwards across the wall and stand on a good hold. Jam away up the cracks, finishing up the middle of a trio of cracks in the steep final wall. The vegetation in the cracks at the top does not get in the way of the climbing. Stake belay 5m up the slope below a large block.

FA. Pete O'Sullivan, K.Tole 3.6.1984

❷ Sunday, Bloody Sunday 🎴 E2 5c

The pencil-thin crack in the upper reaches of the wall right of *Stormy Weather* is a worthy companion on equally good rock. Start 8m right of the edge of the wall.

27m. Climb easily to a right-trending break at 4m and then move up leftwards to a very shallow ramp and some gear. Make a tricky move left from the ramp to arrive at a good flat hold (on *Stormy Weather*). Step right to below the pencil-thin crack and climb this, via a hard starting sequence, to the top. Stake belay 5m up the slope below a large block.

FA. Pete O'Sullivan, K.Tole 3.6.1984

❸ Wreckers' Slab . 🎴 VS 4b

One of the longest, most alluring and serious VS climbs in the West Country, *Wrecker's Slab* is nevertheless the most attempted of its genre on the coast. The huge, slim slab rising from the beach on the far right-hand side of the cliff has very little in the way of technical difficulty but should not be underestimated as the rock is poor, protection spaced and the situations very serious. Start at the base of the slab just right of the overhangs. *Photo opposite.*

1) 4a, 35m. Make a couple of tricky moves to easier ground and work out leftwards along an easy-angled section of slab to the arete. Climb a loose corner groove just right of the arete to a good peg and then move up and right on more loose rock to a footledge stance and peg belays plus good nut belays 5m above.

2) 4b, 45m. Climb directly to the overlaps and pull through them onto the slab above. Climb the slab to a belay at a pillar on a grass terrace.

3) 4a, 45m. Climb up past the pillar to the easy-angled upper wall and follow this on its left side to the top of the slab and belay. A short scramble along a ridge is needed to finish.

FA. Tom Patey, John 'Zeke' Deacon, Keith Lawder 1959

Approach down broad ridge

Gull Rock

Derelict hut

Descent rope (handline)

Stake belay under block

Avon Somerset | North Devon | Culm Coast | Inland Cornwall | Atlantic Coast | West Penwith | The Lizard | Inland Devon | Torbay | Dorset

Avon Somerset

North Devon

Culm Coast

Inland Cornwall

Atlantic Coast

West Penwith

The Lizard

Inland Devon

Torbay

Dorset

Darren Russell following the serious first pitch of the huge slab expedition *Wrecker's Slab* (VS 4b) - *opposite* - at Cornakey Cliff.

	No star	🏵	🏵🏵	🏵🏵🏵
Mod to S	-	-	2	-
HS to HVS	-	2	3	1
E1 to E3	-	-	1	2
E4 and up	-	-	-	-

Vicarage Cliff is a charming crag with a superb collection of fine easier pitches that are both well protected and on some of the best rock on the Culm Coast. The setting of the cliff next to a deserted beach could not be better and has appeal for all, from those looking to cut their teeth on some of the best Severes on the coast to harder climbers seeking a rest from some of the serious business found elsewhere on the culm.
Oldwalls' Point holds one of the least trodden bits of classic culm, in the guise of a huge high-angled slab split by numerous thin finger-cracks. Well worth seeking out by local and visitor alike.

Approach   See area map on page 108

Vicarage Cliff - from the A39 Bude - Bideford road, follow signs to the village of Morwenstow and park next to the Rectory Tearooms and church. Take the track/path that gains the coastal footpath at the cliff edge and then head left passing the small curiosity of Hawker's Hut and continue along the coast path dropping down a long way to just before a stream. Locate a steep vague path that drops down towards the beach over the edge of the cliff. A rope is often in place but a stake is in place for attaching a handrail. Walk along the beach to the cliff (30 minutes).
Oldwalls' Point - from the A39 Bude - Bideford road, follow signs to the village of Morwenstow. Before Morwenstow at the village of Shop, follow signs for Coombe Valley and at a crossroads take the road to Stanbury Mouth. Just past Stanbury Farm are two small car parks. From the lower car park take a footpath down a rough lane on the left that eventually drops down to the beach at Stanbury Mouth. Boulder-hop northwards along the beach past a headland with a good looking crack-line in a slab to the next headland and the crag (40 minutes).

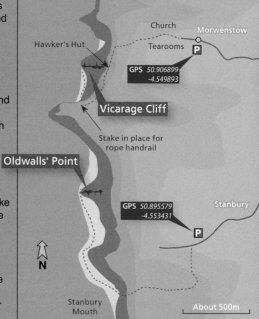

Tides

Vicarage Cliff is tidal and the routes can only be accessed for 3 hours either side of low tide.
Oldwalls' Point is also tidal and can only be accessed for 3 hours either side of low tide.

Conditions

Vicarage Cliff is very exposed to wind and rain, although the routes dry rapidly. The climbs all face due south and receive no shade. **Oldwalls' Point** faces north and gets very little sun. It is also vegetated in its upper reaches.

Sunstruck (VS 4c) - *page 132* - at Vicarage Cliff.

Avon Somerset

North Devon

Culm Coast

Inland Cornwall

Atlantic Coast

West Penwith

The Lizard

Inland Devon

Torbay

Dorset

Culm at its very best. Bruce Woodley inching his way up the sustained *Harpoon* (E2 5b) - *page 133* - on Vicarage Cliff, the Culm Coast.

Vicarage Cliff

Vicarage Cliff is one of the most pleasant and least serious of the Culm Coast's crags. Its relatively straight-forward approach, superb rock and climbing are equally matched by its tremendous location both next to the sea and near the Rectory Tearooms.

Approach - All of the climbs are easily reached along the base of the face from low to mid tide.

Descent - There are a number of good abseil/lower-off points spread along the top of the cliff that can be easily gained from all the routes described. It is also possible to descend the far side of the crag and then scramble back around the end of the promontory.

Tides - The climbs are accessible for the period between low and mid tide.

Conditions - The climbs dry very quickly after rainfall but are very exposed to the elements. The crag is a suntrap.

① **Pandora. . . . .** 🏕️ 🪓 🪓 ▭ **VS 4b**
A testing pitch on the far left of the promontory that samples some surprisingly diverse territory. Start at some raised ledges at the seaward end of the promontory.
20m. Move up easily to just below an elongated protruding blob and then make some difficult moves leftwards up a finger-crack to a small overhang. Move left around the overhang into a narrow corner; make a move up and then quit this rightwards onto the right-hand face which leads quickly to the top.
FA. Pete O'Sullivan, Martin Dunning, Don Sargeant 13.1.1985

② **Sunstruck . . . .** 🏕️① 🪓 🪓 ▭ **VS 4c**
Continually interesting moves on good rock. Start as for *Pandora* at some raised ledges. *Photo on page 130.*
21m. Move up rightwards to stand on an elongated blob, runner. Climb the thin crack-line steeply through a bulge and then with more ease up the final wall.
FA. Brian Wilkinson, P. Wilcox 29.11.1989

③ **Little Dribbler. . . . .** 🏕️② 🪓 🪓 ▭ **HVS 5a**
Good sustained climbing up a continous thin crack-system. Start just to the right of some raised ledges at the seaward end of the promontory.
21m. Move easily up a stepped corner and stand on a blob. Sustained moves up the thin crack-system and through the overlap gain the easier upper wall.
FA. Pete O'Sullivan, Martin Dunning, R.Cope 3.2.1985

④ **Box of Delights. . . .** 🏕️③ 🪓 🪓 ▭ **HS 4b**
Just as the name suggests a whole lot of beautiful climbing on superb rock. One of the best Hard Severes on the Culm Coast. Start at a thin line of weakness below the highest point of the overlap.
21m. Make a difficult move to leave the ground before heading up leftwards to gain and use cracks that lead to the overlap at its highest point. Pull through at the apex and take the easier crack in the wall above to the top.
FA. Pete O'Sullivan, Martin Dunning 4.1.1985

Descent is by abseil
from various rock spikes
on the cliff-top

⑤ Joi de Vivre . . . . **HVS 5a**
An eliminate but worthwhile pitch that shares some holds and gear with *Box of Delights*. Start as for *Box of Delights*.
21m. Make the first few moves on *Box of Delights* and continue up the continuation crack to the overlap. Move left and make a difficult move through the overlap with little for the feet. Continue up the cracks above to the top.
FA. Brian Wilkinson, P. Wilcox 28.4.1990

⑥ Tombstone . . . . **S 4a**
Excellent climbing at the grade taking a central line up the the middle of the wall. Start at a line of weakness below the lowest point of the overlap in the centre of the wall.
21m. Move up pleasant cracks and edges to the overlap and make an awkward move through it at a wide notch. The upper cracks are less taxing.
FA. C.Stripp, Dave Hillebrandt 30.3.1986

⑦ Sol . . . . **S 3c**
Another fine pitch that is the easiest on the wall. Start just right of the lowest point of the overlap.
21m. Move up ledges and cracks to the overlap and overcome it on good holds. Climb up the crack-system above to gain the top.
FA. Brian Wilkinson, P. Wilcox 28.12.1989

⑧ Wellington's Stand . . . . **VS 4b**
The right-hand crack-system continues the theme of excellence. Start at a slight bulge with a good jug above it.
21m. Pull onto the wall using the jug and continue to the overlap. Pull through the overlap and take the long crack to finish.
FA. R.Cope, Martin Dunning, Pete O'Sullivan 3.2.1985

The huge precariously balanced block in the middle of the crag is flanked on its right by a high-angled slab of blank looking culm taken by the following route.

⑨ Harpoon **E2 5b**
An intimidating pitch on compact rock. The gear is spaced and only just adequate. Take plenty of small wires. Start on a raised ledge just right of the arete. *Photo on page 131.*
22m. Climb the sustained wall right of the arete to better small holds that lead left to the arete itself and a spike runner. Progress to the overlap above, step up, and move left, past a peg, to the base of a very shallow depression. Sustained climbing past a couple of good small nut placements gains another peg. Pass this on the right and push on to the top not far above.
FA. Brian Wilkinson, P. Wilcox 27.12.1989

Avon Somerset · North Devon · Culm Coast · Inland Cornwall · Atlantic Coast · West Penwith · The Lizard · Inland Devon · Torbay · Dorset

Oldwalls' Point

The north face of Oldwalls' Point is an impressive sweep of blank looking dark culm. The two climbs described take on the wall at its highest point, and are very sustained undertakings. Although the upper sections of the lines are vegetated, the bulk of the good climbing is very clean.

Approach - Walk north along the boulder beach from Stanbury Mouth past one headland to the second one (40 minutes).

Tides - The base of the cliff is tidal, but it is accessible for a good 3 hours either side of low tide, leaving plenty of time to accomplish ascents of the routes.

Descent - Abseil from anchors on the wide ridge where the routes finish. The abseil points are slings around large blocks and may need backing-up or replacing.

Conditions - The face receives little sun and the start of *More than a Match* takes a while to dry out once the tide has gone out. The climbs are not sheltered from rain.

❶ More than a Match

....   **E3 5c**

One of the best pitches on the Culm Coast. A hard start through the guarding overhangs contrasts with a series of thin cracks up the centre of the face above. Start just right of two left-slanting gashes in the overhangs at the base of the face. *Opposite.*

50m. Climb steeply up leftwards and make a powerful move past a small square-cut notch in the lip to a rest above. Take the thin crack above to where it divides and follow the technical right-hand branch to an easing at a shallow shattered pocket. Follow the crack above to a vegetated final few metres.

FA. Martin Crocker 27.4.1996 (roped solo)

❷ Matchless **E1 5b**

A legendary Culm Coast line that just about stays free enough of vegetation in its upper third to retain its status. The climbing is extremely sustained and the positions are fly-on-the-wall like. Start below the thin crack-system that shoots up to a stuck-on pancake of rock high up near the right arete. *Photo on page 109.*

50m. Gain a ledge at 3m from the right. From the left end of the ledge, climb the thin crack, past a peg, to better holds and gear. Continue up the crack before stepping right to another crack just below the pancake. Pass the pancake on its left side and continue directly up the wall on good, but spaced holds to the top. The original finish stepped right onto the top of the pancake and finished up the arete. Both finishes are vegetated.

FA. Iain Peters, P.Freeman 3.7.1979

Abseil from blocks on ridge with care

A

Not much sun   40 min   Tidal

① ②

Avon Somerset

North Devon

Culm Coast

Inland Cornwall

Atlantic Coast

West Penwith

The Lizard

Inland Devon

Torbay

Dorset

Having negotiated the powerful start, Toby Keep sets himself up for the contrasting upper wall on the Culm Coast masterpiece *More than a Match* (E3 5c) - *opposite* - at the towering Oldwalls' Point.

	No star	⚜	⚜	⚜
Mod to S	-	-	-	-
HS to HVS	-	2	-	1
E1 to E3	1	-	4	3
E4 and up	1	1	3	5

The Lizard · **Inland Devon** · **Torbay** · **Dorset** · **West Penwith** · **Atlantic Coast** · **Inland Cornwall** · **Culm Coast** · **North Devon** · **Avon Somerset**

Wafer-thin and defying the onslaught of wind and sea, the three massive fins of rock that poke out from the coastline at Lower Sharpnose Point provide some of the UK's most spectacular rock climbs. The routes span the grades from HVS to E8 and all share the magnificent combination of exposure and great positions that make a visit to Lower Sharpnose a memorable experience. The rock is on the whole well supplied with good holds and gear, although a high level of fitness is required in order to hang on and place it. The majority of the lines follow discontinuous thin crack-lines up the blank-looking faces of the fins apart from the classic easier corner-lines. Some of the lines have in situ equipment in the form of pegs which should always be backed-up if possible and a good rack of cams will be found very useful. The faces of the fins allow for climbing in the sun and shade throughout the day and also may give shelter from the wind.

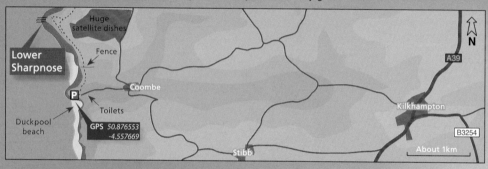

Approach   See area map on page 108

From the A39 just south of Kilkhampton, follow signs to Stibb and then Coombe Valley. Follow the road all the way down the Coombe Valley to the car park next to the sea and lovely beach at Duckpool. Take the coast path north steeply up the hill and as it flattens out the crag can be seen in the distance. Follow the coast path all the way to the headland (just before the satellite station) and drop down leftwards until a rock tower can be seen on the cliff edge – this is the summit of the Middle Fin. A good path winds down the slope to the right (looking out) of the tower and ends on the top of the North Fin. Either abseil in from here or locate a vague path on the north side of the slope and scramble carefully down to the base of the north face of the North Fin (35 mins)

Conditions and Tides

All the climbs are accessible for around 3 hours either side of low tide. At higher tide states movement between the fins is cut off. However, those climbs on the landward end between the North and Middle Fins (*Out of the Blue, Lunakod* etc.) can be climbed in calm seas at most tide states. These lines are easily accessed at higher tides by abseiling down the line of *Out of the Blue* from the top of the North Fin.

North Fin

Middle Fin

Climber on *Misery Goat* (E2 5b) - page 138

Avon Somerset

North Devon

Culm Coast

Inland Cornwall

Atlantic Coast

West Penwith

The Lizard

Inland Devon

Torbay

Dorset

Joe Bawden enjoying some late summer sun on *Crooked Mile* (E3 5c) - *page 139* - at the unique Lower Sharpnose fins on the wild Culm Coast.

North Fin - North Face

A sheer, black and very blank-looking wall that sees no sun and as a consequence is the most intimidating of the cliff's walls. The climbing is spectacular, although the gear availability and rock quality are variable.

Approach - The wall is the first encountered on the scramble down.

Tides - The base of the wall is accessible for a minimum of 3 hours either side of low water in calm seas.

Descent - Walk off of the top of the fin.

Conditions - The wall can be damp and cold and in these conditions the base of the face does not dry out.

❶ The Devonian E5 6a
A hard pitch up the very centre of the face. Start in the centre of the wall below a thin left-trending crack.
35m. Climb up to the crack and follow it with difficulty to an easing where it terminates at the bottom of a quartz-flecked right-leading ramp. Move up the ramp to a peg and climb the fingery wall above past another peg to the top.
FA. Steve Monks, Jane Wilkinson 18.5.1987

❷ Mascon E1 5a
Sustained and strenuous crack-climbing in an outrageous position. Start at a crack-system 3m left of the seaward arete.
30m. Follow the crack-system to a large ledge and an optional belay. Make a tricky traverse left from the ledge across the face to a long vertical crack. Follow the widening crack all the way to the top taking care with a couple of rickety holds.
FA. Pat Littlejohn, Hugh Clarke 27.8.1972

Not much sun | 35 min | Tidal

The south side of the fin offers fantastic routes and all-day sun.

❸ Misery Goat E2 5b
An impressive wall-climb that is endowed with good holds. Start below the upper end of a low, left-trending crack in the centre of the wall.
28m. Climb steeply through the lower bulge via a horizontal crack at 3m to better holds on the wall above. Continue to a left-trending crack and take the wall above it rightwards to a peg. Trend left up the easier wall to the large break of *The Smile* and finish up the thin finger-cracks above (as for *The Smile*).
FA. Clarke Alston, Nick White 23.8.1987

❹ Last Laugh E2 5c
A good line on good rock with a testing but well-protected crux. Start on a boulder at the base of a low, left-trending crack in centre of the wall.
30m. Follow the crack left to its end and move up to a narrow ledge. Climb the slim corner above and traverse left to the base of a small staggered corner. Follow the technical corner and steep flake above to a final short wall and the top.
FA. Steve Bell, Rowland Perriment 25.4.1981

❺ Diamond Smiles E3 5c
Brilliant wall-climbing on excellent rock. Start in the centre of the wall at a boulder below a wide horizontal crack at 3m.
30m. From the wide crack move onto the wall above via a pocket up and right. Follow the wall on good holds to the wide mid-height break of *The Smile*. Traverse the wide break left for 5m to below an old ring-peg in the upper wall. Climb the fingery wall past the peg to the top.
FA. Chris Nicholson, Nick White 16.8.1984

6 Crooked Mile . . . . 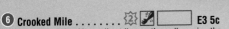 **E3 5c**
Another great pitch taking a direct line up the wall passing the break of *The Smile*. Start 4m right of the boulder at the start of *Diamond Smiles*. *Photo on page 137.*
30m. Move up the wall to a good nut-placement in a pocket at 4m and continue to the wide break of *The Smile*. Move left and follow a faint line of weakness rightwards up the vertical wall to another diagonal break. Move left along the break to a brown stained widening of the break and take the left leading crack above it to the top.
FA. Mick Hardwick, Pat Littlejohn 15.5.1986

7 Wraith . . . . 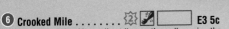 **E4 6a**
Enjoyable, well-protected wall climbing. Start at a thin line that leads up to the break of *The Smile*.
25m. Climb the thin line direct to the break of *The Smile* and move up to a good horizontal crack. Climb the fine wall above past two pegs to the top.
FA. Nick White, Clarke Alston 23.8.1987

8 The Smile **E1 5a**
A fabulous route that follows the sweeping, wide break across the face of the fin and is topped off by a well-positioned thin crack. Start at a vague line of holds that lead up to the break.
42m. Climb up the wall to the left-slanting break. Follow the break all the way to a broken niche and climb up the wall above via a thin crack to the top.
FA. Pat Littlejohn, Steve Jones 3.4.1971

9 Out of the Blue **E2 5b**
A really good and mighty popular pitch that requires care in its lower reaches. Start below a short crack in a bulge and shallow scoop.
24m. Climb boldly up the crack and scoop to a good hold and some gear above. Continue on well-spaced but positive holds to a steep finishing sequence.
FA. Keith Marsden, Andy March 27.7.1980

10 Sea Green **E4 5c**
A similar but harder climb to its neighbour *Out of the Blue*. Start between the crack in the bulge of *Out of the Blue* and the corner that defines the right side of the wall.
24m. Climb boldly up the wall to better holds and gear. Follow a series of reasonable holds up the sustained upper wall to the top.
FA. Richard Harrison, Keith Marsden 6.1987

North Fin - South Face
A fabulous wall of jug-infested culm that provides some of the most inspiring single-pitch climbs on the coast. The protection possibilities and the rock quality are generally good and climbing is possible for a longer length of time than on the other faces if the abseil approach is utilised.
Approach - Scramble down to the boulder beach and around the end of the fin to the base of the wall. Alternatively abseil to the base of the wall from the landward end of the fin.
Tides - The base of the wall is accessible for a minimum of 3 hours either side of low water in calm seas.
Descent - Walk off of the top of the fin.
Conditions - Quick drying, sunny and not prone to seepage, although the base needs a little time to dry once the sea has receded.

Middle Fin - North Face

An impressive sweep of culm that is cut by a couple of tall corner-cracks which are the lines for two of Sharpnose's great HVSs pitches. The rock is not as solid as it first appears and needs careful handling in places, although protection is normally at hand.

Approach - Scramble down to the boulder beach and around the end of the North Fin to the base of the wall. Alternatively abseil to the boulder beach at the base of the wall from the landward end of the North Fin.

Tides - The base of the wall is accessible for a minimum of 3 hours either side of low water in calm seas and far longer if the abseil approach is taken.

Descent - There are fixed abseil points at various locations on the top of the fin. The climb out along the ridge to the top of the cliff is unstable.

Conditions - The face sees no sun but dries fairly quickly, although the base needs time to dry out once the tide has gone out.

❶ Spoils of War E4 5c

A huge pitch that incorporates some fine climbing, although not without some loose rock in its mid section. Start at a thin crack in the dark crevasse on the landward side of the face.

45m. Climb the thin cracks up the bulging lower wall to an easing at 15m. Continue up the face-crack passing a loose section to better climbing and rock where the crack starts to thin.

FA. Steve Bell, Pete O'Sullivan 12.4.1986

❷ Lunakhod . . . . HVS 5a

One of the Culm Coast's greatest lines - both intimidating and sustained. A good number of cams is needed. Start below the steepening corner on the left of the face. *Photo opposite.*

42m. Follow the corner past an awkward initial section to below the smooth-walled upper corner. Climb the sustained corner-crack to the small upper overhang, pull over this to reach the top just above.

FA. Keith Darbyshire, Pat Littlejohn 30.4.1971

❸ Clawtrack . . . . HVS 4c

The wide crack/flake system on the left side of the face is a good climb that requires a lot of large cams and/or nuts. Start at the base of a ramp that rises leftwards to the flake-line.

40m. Climb up the ramp to the flake/crack-line and follow it all the way to the top via some strenuous and committing moves.

FA. Pat Littlejohn, Keith Darbyshire 4.1971

Not much sun | 35 min | Tidal

Avon Somerset

North Devon

Culm Coast

Inland Cornwall

Atlantic Coast

West Penwith

The Lizard

Inland Devon

Torbay

Dorset

Mark Glaister bridging up the magnificent corner of *Lunakod* (HVS 5a) - *opposite* - on the north face of the Middle Fin at Lower Sharpnose. Photo: Bridget Collier.

Avon Somerset | North Devon | Culm Coast | Inland Cornwall | Atlantic Coast | West Penwith | The Lizard | Inland Devon | Torbay | Dorset

Middle Fin - South Face

One of the UK's most impressive sections of cliff with a number of memorable extreme lines. The climbing is sustained and the holds are generally good, nevertheless some of the rock is not quite as good as it looks and the pegs are now showing their age, although alternative protection is often available.

Approach - Scramble down to the boulder beach and walk around the ends of the North and Middle Fins to the base of the face. Alternatively abseil in from the top of the North Fin.

Tides - The base of the wall is accessible for a minimum of 3 hours either side of low water in calm seas. Remember that you need to get back off the top of the fin back to the boulder beach after doing a route.

Descent - There are fixed abseil points at various locations on the top of the fin. The climb out along the ridge to the top of the cliff is very unstable.

Conditions - Quick drying, very sunny and not prone to seepage, although the base needs a little time to dry once the sea has receded.

Lots of sun | 35 min | Tidal

❶ Break On Through **E4 5c**
An immaculate pitch on the best rock that Sharpnose has to offer. Start at a low ledge a few metres right of the arete. Low in the grade. *Photo on page 3.*
23m. From the right-hand end of the ledge, make a series of technical moves up a thin crack on the right to better holds. Continue up the wall via another crack to a quartz break that heads diagonally left to the top. Follow this line boldly to the top.
FA. Pat Littlejohn, P.Amphlett 24.4.1986

❷ Pacemaker . . . . Top 50 **E5 6a**
An outstanding wall-climb that rates as one of the best pitches in the West Country. Start at the base of a right to left diagonal line of quartz cracks. *Photo on page 106.*
26m. Climb the diagonal cracks until it is possible to move up the wall to another left-trending crack. Follow the crack left until below a thin crack-line that heads up back right. Climb the thin cracks, peg, to a break and another peg before finishing steeply leftwards along the break.
FA. Pat Littlejohn, Mick Hardwick 16.5.1986

❸ Fay . . . . Top 50 **E4 5c**

A stunning, pumpy wall climb that fires up the face on generally-good holds. The pegs on the route are fast deteriorating but alternative gear options are available. Start at the base of a right to left diagonal line of quartz cracks.

30m. Move up the cracks and then head diagonally right across the wall on good holds to another left-trending line of quartz cracks, good spike runner above. Climb the cracks to a wider section and follow this to below some thin cracks that head up the wall. Climb the wall and thin cracks, past pegs, to a short thin crack that heads slightly right to a break. Follow the break left to a niche and the top just above.

FA. Pat Littlejohn, Mick Hardwick 15.5.1986

❹ Coronary Country **E6 6b**

A high grade testpiece of the Culm Coast that combines some technical and fingery climbing in its mid-section, with a tiring and not overly-geared upper wall. Start at a left-trending crack which leads to the good spike runner low on *Fay*.

32m. Gain the spike on *Fay* and follow the wall on the right to another diagonal break. Move left along the break for 3m to below a blank wall with pegs in it. Hard climbing to and past the pegs gains a quartz break. Move up to another break and follow this left a little way before heading up the final wall to the top.

FA. Steve Monks, Jane Wilkinson 17.5.1987

❺ The Monk's Satanic Verses
. . . . Top 50 **E8 6c**

Another quality climb that takes on one of the blankest-looking sections of wall on the face and has a particularly hard sequence at mid-height in a runout situation. Start at the base of a left-trending crack as for *Coronary Country*.

32m. Climb up the wall directly above the base of the diagonal crack to a break at 10m. Above the break is a discontinuous series of thin cracks and seams. Climb these - low gear - to a crux sequence to just below the next prominent diagonal break. Follow the steep wall above to the top, easier but serious.

FA. Mark Edwards, Rowland Edwards 5.1989

There is one further route that deserves a mention. It is on the North Face of the South Fin. The approach and tides are as for the Middle Fin - South Face. It is north-facing and doesn't get much sun. The huge fractured face to the left of the line described is generally loose in its upper half.

❻ Dulcima . . . . **HVS 5a**

The soaring, slim corner-crack-line towards the seaward end of the South Fin is a good climb that is worth seeking out.

30m. Climb the sustained corner-crack to the top.

FA. Pat Littlejohn, Keith Darbyshire 7.4.1973

Not much sun | 35 min | Tidal

	No star	☆	☆☆	☆☆☆
Mod to S	-	2	-	-
HS to HVS	-	2	1	-
E1 to E3	-	-	-	1
E4 and up	-	-	-	-

The overlapping slabs that dominate the jutting prow of Compass Point have been climbed on since the early days of exploration on the Culm Coast. The cliff's close proximity to the large beach at Bude, the quality of its routes and the quick-drying nature of the rock mean that Compass Point is one of the coast's most popular venues. All of the climbs described are on the friendly side of vertical, very sustained, and on Compass Point's best rock which, although generally solid, does need some care as the top of the ridge is approached. The ridge on which the climbs finish has seen periods of instability over the years but less so in recent times.

Approach Area map page 108

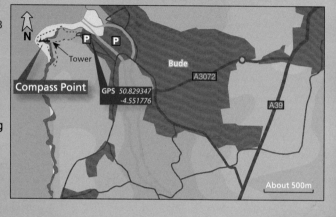

From the A39 take any major road signed for Bude. On entering the town turn left at the first major junction signed to Widemouth and Lynstone (not the Town Centre). Follow this road a short way, crossing over a river and canal and turn right at the Falcon Inn. Take the road signed to the Breakwater and park on the right as the canal comes into view (alternative parking is available at busy times – see map). Walk along the road by the side of the canal and before reaching the lock gates, follow the coast path up left and onward to the Compass Tower directly above the cliff. Walk a further 200m and descend a steep but easy path to the beach below the cliff (10 mins). Alternatively, for around 2 hours either side of low water, the cliff can be accessed from the beach beyond the canal by walking around the point itself.

Conditions and Tides

The crag is tidal but some of the routes are accessible for a greater length of time than many on the coast. The landward climbs are only inaccessible for a couple of hours around high water in calm conditions, however those further out towards the point are only accessible for 3 hours either side of low water. The cliff faces south so receives plenty of sunshine and dries very quickly.

Avon Somerset
North Devon
Culm Coast
Inland Cornwall
Atlantic Coast
West Penwith
The Lizard
Inland Devon
Torbay
Dorset

Approaching the final section of the
sustained slab on *Tydomin* (HVS 4c) - *page
146* - at Compass Point on the Culm Coast.

❶ Westerlation . . . . S 4a

A well-positioned pitch on good rock and with a spectacular finish along the crest of the North Ridge. Start at the third jammed-boulder in from the mouth of the narrow zawn between the South and North Ridges. *Photo opposite.*

1) 4a, 20m. Move straight up the wall to meet a short crack on the right and then move up to the larger right-trending crack above. Move right along the crack and climb direct to the top of the fin and belay.

2) -, 40m. Scramble along the ridge to its high point and then either continue to the tower or abseil from metal stakes.

FA. Keith Darbyshire, Hugh Clarke 6.5.1973

❷ The South Ridge . . . . . . Diff

A very pleasant 'Alpine style' outing that traverses the crest of the point from its seaward end to the Compass Tower. Start at the toe of the ridge on the south side of the narrow zawn at the end of the point.

1) -, 25m. Follow the easy-angled stepped ridge to a ledge and belay at a boulder bridge.

2) -, 30m. Continue along the narrowing ridge to a high point and just beyond belay on stakes.

3) -, 70m. Move along the easy but exposed and slightly loose ridge to the Tower.

FA. 1930s

❸ Sugar Magnolia . . . . . . HVS 5a

A neat little pitch. Start at a thin crack just left of a larger left-leaning crack.

16m. Climb the thin crack and then head left along a narrow ramp above the overlap to finish on the ridge. Descend easily down the South Ridge.

FA. Keith Darbyshire, Dave Garner 1974

Lots of sun | 10 min | Tidal

Compass Point

A Culm Coast favourite that provides a choice selection of very good routes which are easily accessed and on reasonably good, quick-drying rock.

Approach - From the Compass Tower walk a further 200m along the cliff-top path and take a steep but straightforward path down to the beach and walk along this a short way to the base of the cliff. The cliff may also be accessed from the beach at Bude but this approach is tidal.

Descent - Walk back down to the beach from the Tower or abseil from stakes midway along the ridge.

❹ Tydomin . . . . HVS 4c

A spectacular pitch on good rock and good holds all the way, with enough protection from wires to keep the flutter factor manageable. Start beneath the amazing narrow wall of culm in the centre of the cliff. *Photo on page 145.*

25m. Climb the heavily pock-marked wall just to the right of the arete, past a small spike runner at 8m (on the arete) to where it forks left. Continue up the face on the right past good but spaced gear to the top. Low in the technical grade.

FA. Keith Darbyshire, A.Clark 1974

Metal stakes

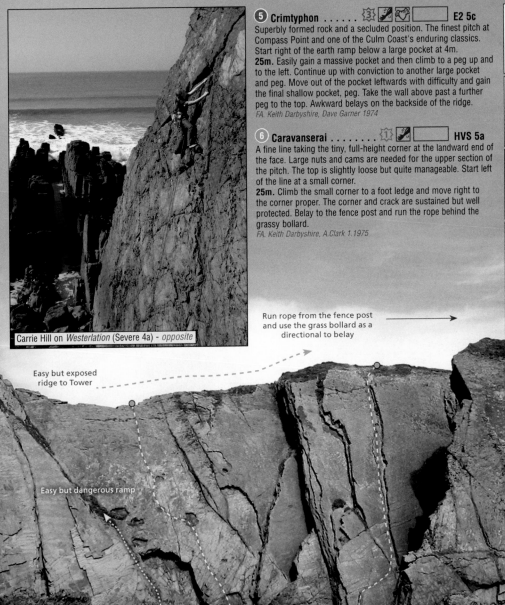

⑤ Crimtyphon . . . . . . ⬚🗝️📷 ☐ **E2 5c**

Superbly formed rock and a secluded position. The finest pitch at Compass Point and one of the Culm Coast's enduring classics. Start right of the earth ramp below a large pocket at 4m.

25m. Easily gain a massive pocket and then climb to a peg up and to the left. Continue up with conviction to another large pocket and peg. Move out of the pocket leftwards with difficulty and gain the final shallow pocket, peg. Take the wall above past a further peg to the top. Awkward belays on the backside of the ridge.

FA. Keith Darbyshire, Dave Garner 1974

⑥ Caravanserai . . . . ⬚🗝️ ☐ **HVS 5a**

A fine line taking the tiny, full-height corner at the landward end of the face. Large nuts and cams are needed for the upper section of the pitch. The top is slightly loose but quite manageable. Start left of the line at a small corner.

25m. Climb the small corner to a foot ledge and move right to the corner proper. The corner and crack are sustained but well protected. Belay to the fence post and run the rope behind the grassy bollard.

FA. Keith Darbyshire, A.Clark 1.1975

Run rope from the fence post and use the grass bollard as a directional to belay ⟶

Easy but exposed ridge to Tower

Easy but dangerous ramp

Carrie Hill on *Westerlation* (Severe 4a) - *opposite*

Avon Somerset | North Devon | Culm Coast | Inland Cornwall | Atlantic Coast | West Penwith | The Lizard | Inland Devon | Torbay | Dorset

Avon Somerset | North Devon | Culm Coast | Inland Cornwall | Atlantic Coast | West Penwith | The Lizard | Inland Devon | Torbay | Dorset

Inland Cornwall

Avon Somerset

North Devon

Culm Coast

Inland Cornwall

Atlantic Coast

West Penwith

The Lizard

Inland Devon

Torbay

Dorset

Setting out on the crux second pitch of the technical *Eyefull Tower* (E2 6a) - *page 156* - at Cheesewring Quarry, Cornwall.

Avon Somerset

North Devon

Culm Coast

Inland Cornwall

Atlantic Coast

West Penwith

The Lizard

Inland Devon

Torbay

Dorset

Cornwall's picturesque frame of rock, sea and sand is a stark contrast to its interior landscape of barren moorland and extensive network of low-lying wooded valleys, often scarred by the remains of its mining heritage. Scattered over the interior is a small number of surprising venues that range from large abandoned quarries to small 'tors' that have provided locals with good sport over the decades, and some of which are well worth a look from the visiting climber. The style of the climbing available in the area ranges from some very traditional lower-grade lines in out-of-the-way places up on Bodmin Moor to high-standard trad and sport climbs.

The Hurlers standing stones, Bodmin Moor.

Avon Somerset

North Devon

Culm Coast

Inland Cornwall

Atlantic Coast

West Penwith

The Lizard

Inland Devon

Torbay

Dorset

The steep finishing moves of *Warrior* (6c) - *page 157* - on the smooth
granite of Cheesewring Quarry high up on Bodmin Moor, Inland Cornwall.

	No star	1 star	2 star	3 star
Mod to S	-	1	-	-
HS to HVS	-	5	2	-
E1 to E3	-	1	3	2
E4 and up	-	1	1	2

Carved out of the compact granite of Bodmin Moor, Cheesewring Quarry has for decades been one of Cornish climbing's forcing grounds. Its development has kept up with the grades of nearby Devon's sport climbs and has provided a good spread of tough trad pitches that compliment those of Cornwall's sea-cliffs. The strange gravity-defying Cheesewring itself peers down over the edge of the quarry, taking in the view of the walls that for the first time visitor can be a bit of a revelation, being both extensive and up to around 30m in height. The style of the climbing is often very specific, the nature of the quarried rock giving little in the way of intermediate holds that might take the sting out of the moves. As a consequence the climbing feels tougher that on the natural granite in the region. Nevertheless, the climbs are excellent and the spread of both trad and sport climbs is such that most tastes will be catered for.

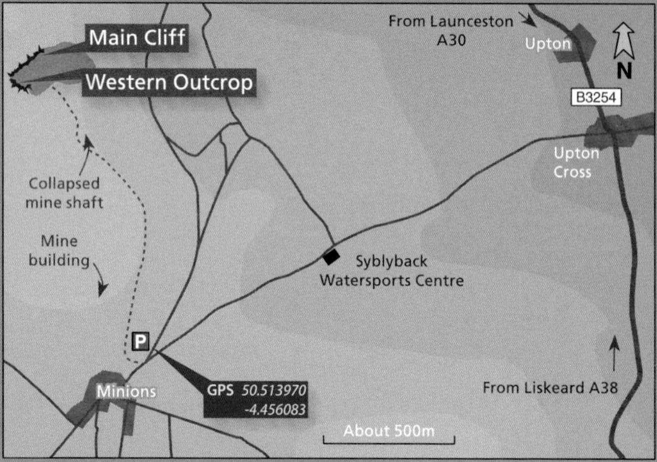
Main Cliff
Western Outcrop
From Launceston A30
Upton
N
B3254
Upton Cross
Collapsed mine shaft
Mine building
Syblyback Watersports Centre
P
Minions
GPS 50.513970 -4.456083
From Liskeard A38
About 500m

Approach

Area map on page 150

From either the A30 to the north of Bodmin Moor or the A38 to its south, various country roads lead up onto the moor and the hamlet of Minions from where the parking at the start of the approach is easily located just to the north east. From the car park walk along a track northwards taking a deviation to pass a collapsed mine shaft to reach the quarry entrance.

Access

The quarry is owned by the Duchy of Cornwall and, although there are signs and fences around the perimeter of the quarry, climbing has gone on for decades without problems. However, permission to climb should be obtained from the Duchy (01579 343194) although this is very rarely undertaken.

Conditions

The quarry is very exposed and set at an altitude of 350m. Even though it has a sunny aspect a visit should only be planned in good warm weather. Seepage can occur after wet weather but the faces dry quickly.

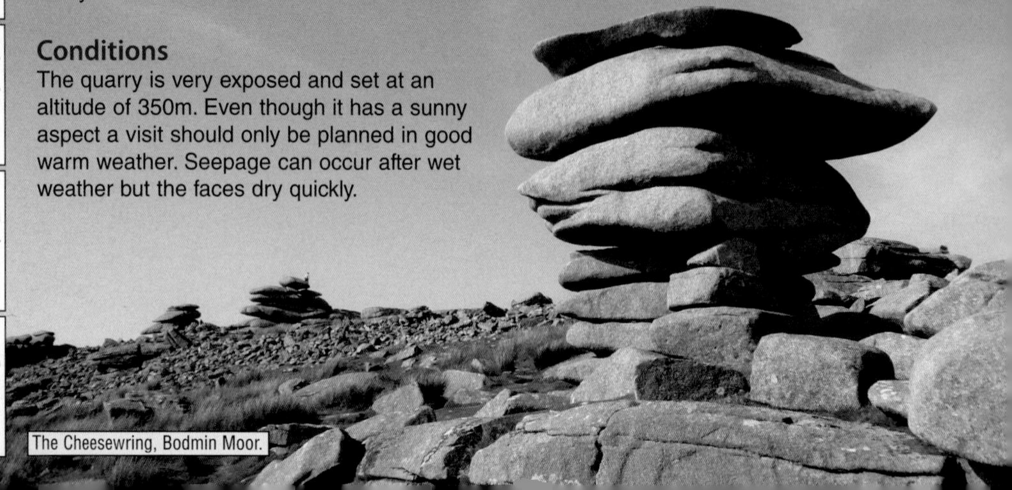

The Cheesewring, Bodmin Moor.

Avon Somerset

North Devon

Culm Coast

Inland Cornwall

Atlantic Coast

West Penwith

The Lizard

Inland Devon

Torbay

Dorset

Ken Palmer on the highly technical *Psychokiller* (7c+) - *page 156* - at the Main Wall of Cheesewring Quarry, Bodmin Moor, Inland Cornwall.

Western Outcrop

A compact wall of excellent rock with a small selection of good lines, some bold and some very fingery. This section of the quarry also gets the morning sun and is sheltered from westerly winds.

Approach - From the quarry entrance head leftwards over boulders to the base of the wall.

Descent - Walk left (looking out) a short distance along the cliff edge to the descent gully.

Conditions - The wall is sheltered and dries quickly, although some moss build up can occur over the winter months.

❶ Double Agent . . **7a+**
The blank, mottled wall is taken centrally by this exquisite little climb. Start 4m left of the corner.
12m. Move up slightly right to the middle of the wall, step right and then climb direct to a final fingery pull.
FA. Andy Grieve 1993

❷ Agent Provocateur . **7b**
The counter line to *Double Agent* has a very hard sequence in its upper half. Start 2m to the left of the corner.
12m. Climb past a small overlap just to the left of the corner and step left to join *Double Agent*. Make a long move up and left to a good hold before stepping back right to tackle the final fingery wall.
FA. Ken Palmer, Nick Hancock, Andy Grieve 9.9.1986

❸ Potential Energy . . . **6c+**
The easiest way up the wall is another great little route but still no pushover. Start 4m left of the corner as for *Double Agent*.
12m. Climb the mottled wall as for *Double Agent* to join up with *Agent Provocateur*. Follow *Agent Provocateur* to its good hold and then break left up the final wall to finish.
FA. Sean Hawken 5.7.1993

❹ Trouble with Lichen. **E3 6a**
The blind corner on the right-hand side of the wall provides an engrossing exercise on the smallest of holds. Protection is from micro wires. Start below the corner on the right-hand side of the wall.
12m. Increasingly tricky moves up the corner gain the final blank section which is overcome via a precarious move to a good jug.
FAA. Martin Dunning, Tim Mason 23.2.1975
FFA. Andy Grieve 19.4.1985

❺ Central Route . . . . . **VS 4c**
The wide, central depression in the next bay is a good but serious line on very good rock, although large amounts of moss can build up on the upper ledges. Start below the central depression.
13m. Move easily left to below a thin finger-crack and climb this with difficulty to a ledge below the upper right-trending line of ledges. Follow these carefully to the top, this section is unprotected.
FA. Peter Stanier, Toni Carver 10.7.1971

❻ Direct Route . . . . **VS 4a**
The easy-angled staggered ridge on the right-hand side of the wall is a fine feature but completely devoid of protection. Start 2m to the right of the arete.
14m. Move left up ledges to join the arete. Follow the arete delicately all the way to the top on flat holds.
FA. Toni Carver 8.1964

Descent

Main Wall - Left

The left-hand end of the massive back wall of the quarry is plastered with corners and long horizontal ledges that are connected by blank leaning walls. The climbs are all multi-pitch and on good rock, although protection is spaced in places.

Approach - From the quarry entrance walk across boulders to the base of the cliff.

Descent - Walk right (looking out) to the descent gully.

Conditions - The cliff is clean but does suffer from seepage and can take a while to dry out. The face gets plenty of sun but is exposed to the elements.

7 The Purple Revrac . . . . **HS 4b**

A well-travelled little route tucked away on the far left of the Main Cliff. Start at a large rectangular block on the boulder slope.
1) 4b, 9m. Climb up ledges and small corners to a belay ledge on the left. Escapable and slighty vegetated.
2) 4b, 10m. The steep but short-lived corner provides the meat of the route.
FA. Peter Stanier, John Burley 3.8.1969

8 Rampage **7b**

One of Cheesewring Quarry's best and hardest offerings on superb rock. Start directly below the left-hand end of the rightward sloping ramp in the middle of the striped overhanging wall.
1) 7b, 21m. Move up the wall to the ramp and head out right across this before climbing up and left into, then up, a groove to its end. Belay on a ledge just above.
2) 7a+, 9m. Climb up to and through the large overhang above the belay, and finish up the headwall.
FA. Andy Grieve, Steve Golly 9.1993

9 Simanon Direct . . . . . **HVS 4c**

The long standing Cheesewring classic. A serious route that requires good judgement and a cool head. The route seeps for long periods after rainfall, although the alternative direct variation on the second pitch does dry a little quicker but it is no less serious. Start at a large quarry-ring at the very base of the crag.
1) 4b, 10m. Climb up leftwards to a long chain which is used for protection but not as a means of ascent! Belay at the rock ring holding the chain.
2) 4c, 13m. Climb up onto a ledge and then step up to another ledge on the right below a leaning wall. Traverse out right along the ledge to a groove and a good small nut-placement. Move up the groove to good holds, and then traverse back left along a large vegetated ramp to its end and move up to a large belay ledge. Very bold.
2a) E1 5a, 8m. A variation takes the direct line to the second stance past a poor peg, also bold.
3) 4b, 12m. Move rightwards to the base of a line that cuts back left and up a diagonal crack to the top in a fine position.
FA. Toni Carver, Richard Grose 9.9.1967

Lots of sun | 13 min

Descent

7

8

9

Main Wall - Centre

The middle section of the Main Wall is the centrepiece of Cheesewring Quarry. The rock and climbing is superb and the lines are striking.

Approach - From the quarry entrance walk across boulders to the base of the cliff.

Descent - Walk off either to the left or right.

Conditions - The cliff gets plenty of sun and dries quickly, although wet streaks do appear at times. The face very exposed to wind and rain.

❶ Eyefull Tower . . . . ▨▨ ▨ [ ] E2 6a

Cheesewring's most popular extreme that takes on the quarry wall at its highest point and incorporates plenty of good moves and a well-positioned final pitch. Start at a short right-angled corner to the right of a low bouldering wall. *Photo on page 148*.

1) 5a, 22m. Climb the corner and then a crack on the right to its end and a small shot-hole nut placement just above. Traverse left to a grassy ledge and iron-spike runner, climb the corner above to a stance and belay on another iron spike.

2) 6a, 17m. Move up leftwards from the belay and climb through bulges, peg, to a ledge below a smooth right-leaning groove. Climb the difficult groove, bolt, to a good shot-hole thread and continue up the pleasant wall to finish.

FA. Toni Carver, Richard Grose, Peter Stanier (2pts) 24.3.1967
FFA. Nick Hancock 8.3.1986

❷ High Noon/Mauritius ▨▨ ▨ ▨ [ ] E3 6a

Spectacular and bold climbing up the impressive nose and headwall in the centre of the crag. Start in the corner below the right-hand side of a pinnacle known as 'The Wizard's Hat'.

1) 5b, 27m. Move up to the crack on the right side of the pinnacle and climb to its top. Follow ledges rightwards to a bolt, and move up to a hand-ledge directly above it. Mantle onto the ledge and step out toward the arete before moving up to the overhang and good wires. Climb the wall and crack on the left side of the arete to a stance. Bolts and nut belay.

2) 6a, 12m. Move out right onto the exposed hanging groove and climb it, bolts, to its end, bolt, where some fingery moves lead directly to the top. The original finish went direct at E4 6a but the gear is now old.

FA. High Noon. Toni Carver, Richard Grose (1pt) 16.4.1967
FFA. High Noon. Ken Palmer 8.3.1986
FA. (Mauritius) Ken Palmer 1989

❸ Psychokiller . . . . . . ▨▨ ▨ ▨ [ ] 7c+

A precise and well-carved line on immaculate rock. One of the better pitches of its type in the UK. Start on a high ledge at the back of the steep bay below a triangular niche at 15m. *Photo on page 153*.

22m. Long, and then technical moves up the initial wall lead to a precarious position below the niche. Udge into the niche and exit left with difficulty to a lower-off 4m higher.

FA. Steve Mayers 1988

Over on the right-hand end of the quarry is a wide section of wall with yet more good multi-pitch climbs on mostly good rock.

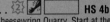

④ Warrior **6c**

A sport route with a traditional feel about it. Start just below a thin crack that becomes a groove higher up. *Photo on page 151.*
18m. Move up and devise a method of attaining the ledge up on the left. Mantle onto the ledge and take the wall and steepening grooves above past a wobbly hold to a lower-off.
FAA. Len Benstead, Steve Chadwick 14.3.1970
FFA. Andy Grieve 4.11.1988

⑤ Khyber Wall **E2 5c**

A wildly positioned final pitch. The first two pitches can be wet, and under these conditions it is better to abseil to the large belay ledge at the start of the top pitch. Start at a wide crack in the short wall at the base of the arete.
1) 4a, 11m. Climb the wide crack and continue to a grassy ledge with a huge iron ring and belay.
2) 4b,11m. Unprotected. Move up left on sloping hand-ledges, past a loose block, to a large block and belay ledge below the corner just left of the arete.
3) 5c, 12m. Make a series of long moves past 2 bolts to the small overhang, peg. Pull out left to a good crack and make one last reach past a peg for the top.
FAA. Len Benstead, Denis Morrod 21.3.1970
FFA. Andy Grieve 19.9.1986

⑥ Juliet's Balcony . . . . . . **HVS 5a**

Airy climbing featuring a runout wall and a tricky crux. Start at an area of easy-angled water-washed ledges.
1) 9m. Climb easily up sloping ledges to a long grassy ledge and block-belay on the left.
2) 5a, 22m. From the block, move up slightly left to a thin right-slanting flake-crack. Climb this to its end and then climb the bold wall above to below an overlap with twin pegs on the right. Move right past the pegs and make a tricky move up onto a ledge, 'The Balcony'. A couple of steep moves on good holds gain the top.
FA. Toni Carver, Steve Bramble 12.2.1967

⑦ Peter . . . . **VDiff**

A popular climb on good rock and with a variety of moves and situations. Start at a ramp that rises up to a narrow vertical corner.
1) 16m. Move rightwards up the ramp to the narrow corner. Climb the corner with difficulty and continue above it to a ledge, and belay at a large block.
2) 16m. Walk right along the ledge to its end and make some steep moves up to easier ground. Traverse left a few metres and then finish direct past a threadable borehole on the lip of the wall.
FA. Toni Carver, Peter Stanier 8.1964

⑧ Figuzzi . . . . **HS 4b**

The best route at the grade in Cheesewring Quarry. Start at the base of the ramp as for *Peter.*
1) 4b, 15m. Follow the ramp and corners as for *Peter* to just before its belay ledge. Step left and then up before traversing left to a stance with two pegs and nut belays.
2) 4b, 10m. Move left and climb a corner-crack until level with an overhang on the left. Move under the overhang and climb straight up to finish.

⑨ Star Fox . . . . **HVS 5a**

A rather odd route that features two disjointed, bouldery pitches, but is quite challenging and popular nevertheless. Start at a sickle-shaped corner.
1) 5a, 8m. Climb the sickle-shaped groove by some balancy and technical moves to a narrow ledge. Move up to the next ledge and belay on *Peter.*
2) 5a, 11m. Move right and climb the wall on good hidden holds to easier ground.
FA. Toni Carver, Peter Stanier 9.8.1969

Descent - - - →

Avon Somerset

North Devon

Culm Coast

Inland Cornwall

Atlantic Coast

West Penwith

The Lizard

Inland Devon

Torbay

Dorset

Avon Somerset
North Devon
Culm Coast
Inland Cornwall
Atlantic Coast
West Penwith
The Lizard
Inland Devon
Torbay
Dorset

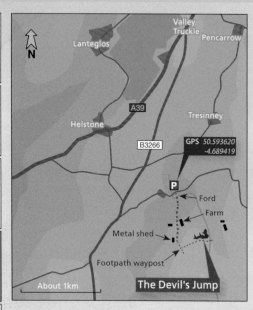

The Devil's Jump

Tucked away on a rarely visited bit of Bodmin Moor is this small but interesting outcrop. Although not by any stretch of the imagination a major destination the climb and its surroundings are well worth a diversion if passing by.

Approach   See area map on page 150

From Camelford, follow the A39 west and turn left onto the B3266 to Bodmin. Take the second turning left (not signposted) and follow the narrow lane down to a river, and a short distance on, a ford and parking for two cars on the right. Walk across the ford footbridge and go up a lane past Henon Farm to a metal clad shed on the right. Continue up a path where the lane narrows to a footpath waypost. Go through a gap in the wall on the left then head out across open ground to eventually end up above a river valley. The top of The Devil's Jump is visible just below the edge of the valley below two dead trees.

Conditions

The lower section of The Devil's Jump is mossy and needs dry conditions.

Bridge across gap

Downclimb

Descent path

❶ South East Climb

. . . . . ❄ ✂ ☐   **VDiff**

One of Bodmin Moor's earliest rock climbs. The crag is set in glorious countryside, and provides a good couple of hours entertainment. Start below the wide corner-crack at the base of the buttress.

1) 12m. Climb the wide crack and its mossy left wall to a good stance. Dry conditions needed.

2) 12m. Move up and then right above an overhang to below an exposed corner. Climb the corner to the top. To descend - cross the gap and downclimb the short landward wall to the ground.

FA: Donald Romanis, Bertrand Jerram 1921

	No star	☼	☼☼	☼☼☼
Mod to S	-	2	1	-
HS to HVS	-	2	2	-
E1 to E3	-	1	-	-
E4 and up	-	-	1	-

Roche Rock has a long standing folklore attributed to it, and was among the first crags in the West Country to be explored and have its climbs recorded. The climbs have stood the test of time; and today still give many their first climbing experience. The geology of Roche Rock is scroal - a mix of quartz and felspar set in tourmaline that looks like granite, and like granite is a joy to handle and climb on.

Approach   See area map on page 150

From the A30, 7 miles west of Bodmin (the Victoria Interchange), take the exit signed for Roche. Follow the signs to Roche and in the middle of the village, carry straight on to the edge of the village and take a left turn signed to Bugle. 100m down this road is a layby on the right from where the crags are easily viewed. Walk across open ground to the crag (1 min).

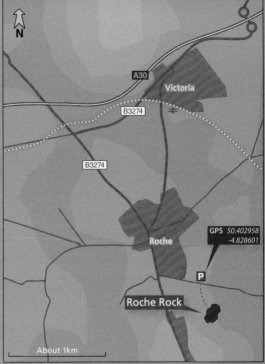

Access

Roche Rock is a SSSI and the ruined chapel a protected monument. An information board states that climbing is not allowed. However, climbing has gone on unhindered for many decades. Absolutely no gardening or climbing on the ruined chapel should be undertaken.

Conditions

The cliff is exposed to wind and rain and can be cold on its northern face. The South Face dries very quickly and gets plenty of sun.

Avon Somerset · North Devon · Culm Coast · Inland Cornwall · Atlantic Coast · West Penwith · The Lizard · Inland Devon · Torbay · Dorset

Avon Somerset

North Devon

Culm Coast

Inland Cornwall

Atlantic Coast

West Penwith

The Lizard

Inland Devon

Torbay

Dorset

1 Tregagle's Buttress . . . . HS 4b

An exquisite little climb on fine holds and in an open position. Start just left of the arete on a raised ledge.

9m. Climb the steep wall just left of the arete on good holds to a spike. Finish up the short wall above.

FA. Donald Romanis, Bertrand Jerram 1921

2 Tregagle's Crack . . . . . . S 4a

Well-protected but tough crack-climbing. Start below the fist size crack in the buttress on the left of the face.

10m. The crack can be laced with good gear but the ascent is still a good test of jamming especially the first few metres.

FA. Donald Romanis, Bertrand Jerram 1921

3 Corner and Staircase. . . Diff

A very popular climb that provides a rewarding way up the crag and into the ruined tower. Start below the wide corner-crack.

20m. Climb the corner and then move out above the right wall past a small patch of gorse to a crack that leads back left to a point where a finish can be made between two summit blocks.

FA. Donald Romanis, Bertrand Jerram 1921

Lots of sun | 1 min

4 The Lord Falmouth E1 5b

The squat slab to the right of the crack of *Corner and Staircase* is a micro-classic friction problem. Start below the thin right curving seam.

20m. Move up to the seam and climb the slab just on its left to meet a wide horizontal break. Reach a jutting ledge in the bulging wall above and finish direct.

FA. Toni Carver 5.1997

5 Porky . . . . VS 4c

Roche Rock's finest climb. Start at a wide crack which curves to the left at mid-height.

20m. Climb the crack to a corner where the rock steepens. Bridge up the corner and pull steeply up right, using good holds into a niche. Move up the crack on the right to easier ground and finish leftwards.

FA. Bob Lambourne, Martin Dunning 27.6.1974

Descent

Descent

Avon Somerset
North Devon
Culm Coast
Inland Cornwall
Atlantic Coast
West Penwith
The Lizard
Inland Devon
Torbay
Dorset

Roche Rock

The unmistakable profile of the main Roche formation provides some good climbs on tremendous rock.

Access - Absolutely no climbing on the monument walls. No gardening as this is a SSSI.

Approach - The two faces are less than a minute apart via an easy path.

Descent - Use steps and fixed ladders to descend through the ruins of the chapel.

Not much sun | 1 min

---

6 Moping Owl . . . . ⭐ ✏ ▭ **VS 4c**

An interesting link-up. Start as for *Porky* at its wide crack.

21m. Climb the crack to meet up with *The Lord Falmouth* on the left and move up to its jutting ledge. Hand traverse the ledge right and swing along good holds, past the niche of *Porky,* to a ledge on the arete. Finish direct via some arete hugging moves.

FA. Geoff Sutton 1955

7 South East Buttress . ⭐ 🧗 ✏ ▭ **VDiff**

A fairly tricky climb that follows an impressive line loosely based on the right-hand arete of the face. Start at a small pinnacle close to the arete.

18m. Stand on the pinnacle and make some tricky moves up the wall to stand on a ledge on the arete. Climb on good holds around and up the left side of the arete to the top.

FA. Donald Romanis, Bertrand Jerram 1921

8 God Forbid . . . . ⭐ 🆎 ▭ **E4 6b**

The steep crack and arete that overlook the parking give a major undertaking. Start below the severely-overhanging crack.

18m. Climb the steep crack via a pocket to a difficult exit below the upper arete. Finish up the arete.

FA. Andy Grieve, Sean Hawken 14.10.1994

9 Shorty's Folly . . . . . ⭐ ✏ 🗺 ▭ **HVS 4c**

A bold and exciting climb on superb holds that requires a confident approach. Start at the toe of a ramp below the steep pocketed wall.

18m. Climb up the ramp for a few metres and then swing up onto the wall on a good pocket and use the crack on the left, close to the arete, to move up to more good holds at mid-height. Finish steeply up the central crack-line on yet more good holds.

FA. A.Stringer, J.Williams 15.5.1971

Avon Somerset

North Devon

Culm Coast

Inland Cornwall

Atlantic Coast

West Penwith

The Lizard

Inland Devon

Torbay

Dorset

The Atlantic Coast

Max Dutson catches perfect summer evening conditions for an ascent of the impeccable main pitch of *Black Magic* (E5 6a) - *page 175* - on the Great Wall at Pentire Head. Photo: Grant Farquhar

Avon Somerset

North Devon

Culm Coast

Inland Cornwall

Atlantic Coast

West Penwith

The Lizard

Inland Devon

Torbay

Dorset

Cornwall's Atlantic Coast is a rugged yet enchanting series of coves, beaches and huge cliffs all fronting onto the relentless swell of the sea hereabouts. The watchword for the climber embarking on virtually all the routes on this section of coastline is adventure! The climbs described are a small sample of the total number of routes recorded on this coast, and although they are amongst the most popular and travelled it would still be an uncommon event to be stuck in a queue at the start of any of them. The combination of length, difficulty, seriousness and variable rock quality guarantees that these routes are at the top of the tree when it comes to commitment. With an eye on these factors it comes

as no surprise that the West Country's most seminal climber, Pat Littlejohn, was instrumental in the development of the major high standard lines on this coast with the 'Big Three' of *Darkinbad the Brightdayler*, *Il Duce* and *America* - all initially climbed in 1972/73 - the high point of the coast's history. Such is the intimidating nature of the climbs that the innovation of modern equipment and training has done little to blunt the reputations of most of these routes.

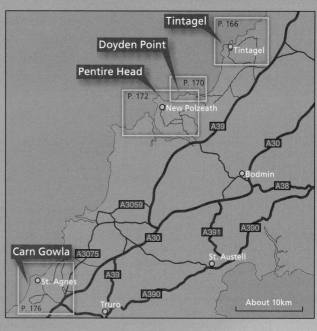

Getting Around

All of the cliffs are on beautiful and wild headlands, although they are only short walks from the nearest car parks. Most of the parking is close to typically Cornish fishing coves such as St Agnes and Port Quin. All of the parking is accessed from various minor roads that are signed from either the A30 or the A39 - *the Atlantic Highway*.

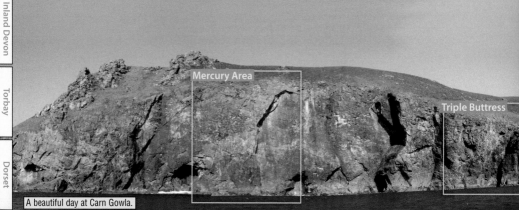

A beautiful day at Carn Gowla.

Avon Somerset

North Devon

Culm Coast

Inland Cornwall

Atlantic Coast

West Penwith

The Lizard

Inland Devon

Torbay

Dorset

Nolan Smyth finishing the traverse of the big corner on the 4th pitch of *Journey to Ixtlan* (HVS 4c)- *page 182* - with the massive corner-line of *Mercury Direct* (E2 5b) - *page 181* - in the background. Carn Gowla. Cornwall. Photo: Pete Saunders

	No star	⟨1⟩	⟨2⟩	⟨3⟩
Mod to S	-	-	-	-
HS to HVS	-	-	-	-
E1 to E3	-	-	-	-
E4 and up	-	-	1	2

The island of Tintagel - purportedly the site of Camelot in Arthurian legend - is a formidable sight when viewed from the mainland, but for the climber it keeps its prime cliffs well hidden. In fact the business end of the island - the 'dolomitic wall' of High Cliff - can only be viewed in full from the sea. The routes included in this guidebook are the most popular on High Cliff, however this is a relative term as even the famous *Il Duce* sees very few ascents each year. All of the climbs are multi-pitch adventures that, for those capable of climbing them, will not disappoint. The routes are very serious and even though only a few metres from the normally tourist-packed summit of the island, the isolation of the climbs should not be underestimated.

Access

The island is managed by English Heritage. The BMC have negotiated an access agreement as follows. If you wish to climb at Tintagel you must first write to English Heritage, Room 225, 25 Saville Row, London W1X 2BT (enclose a SAE for a quick reply). You should get a response about access to routes and sensitive areas.

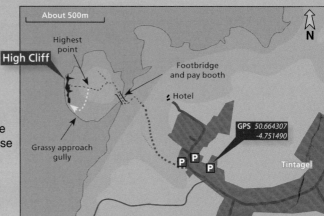

Approach   See area map on page 164

From the A39 Wadebridge to Bude road, follow signs to Tintagel (actually a large village on the mainland). There are numerous car parks from which the island itself is well sign-posted. Follow the footpath down to the entrance where a fee is payable (c.£5.00 per person). Cross to the island via a wooden bridge and walk to the highest point of the island from where the descent to the start of the climbs is described (20 minutes).

Tides and Conditions

The base of the cliff drops straight into the sea but the traverse to the starting points of the climbs is non-tidal, although affected by moderate or heavy seas. There is no shelter from either sun, wind or rain. Seepage is unlikely to be a problem during the spring through to autumn period.

Avon Somerset | North Devon | Culm Coast | Inland Cornwall | Atlantic Coast | West Penwith | The Lizard | Inland Devon | Torbay | Dorset

Avon Somerset

North Devon

Culm Coast

Inland Cornwall

Atlantic Coast

West Penwith

The Lizard

Inland Devon

Torbay

Dorset

Dave Turnbull moving around the initial bulge on the third pitch of *Il Duce* (E5 6a) - *page 168* - on the towering High Cliff at Tintagel. Photo: Nick Hancock

Sidebar tabs (left margin): Avon Somerset · North Devon · Culm Coast · Inland Cornwall · **Atlantic Coast** · West Penwith · The Lizard · Inland Devon · Torbay · Dorset

High Cliff

Tintagel's High Cliff is an extremely intimidating crag that rises straight out of the sea, and is impossible to view in detail from the land. The three climbs described are all big and serious adventures, that involve multiple pitches of hard climbing on rock of variable quality.

Access - Permission to climb must be sought prior to a visit (see page 166).

Approach - From the highest point on the island, walk down a steep grassy gully on the left (looking out to sea). Near the base, contour back right where easy scrambling gains a gearing-up spot above a rock ramp that dips away down to the sea.

Tides - The large platform and the traverse to it are non-tidal, although they will be wave-washed in moderate or heavy seas.

❶ Vagabond E4 5c

A very sustained and imposing line that weaves its way up the wall left of the corner of *Il Duce*. Start at the bottom of the rocky ramp that slopes seawards below the gearing-up spot.
1) 5a, 35m. Traverse left to a protruding ledge and continue around an arete to a large platform beneath roofs and the main corner.
2) 5c, 20m. From the left end of the ledge, follow a chimney/groove through the overhangs until it pinches out. Climb diagonally rightwards to a narrow ledge, then move back up and left to a ledge and belay.
3) 5c, 20m. Climb up rightwards on compact rock, heading for the prominent overlap. Follow this until it closes, and make tricky moves up to a ledge. Follow this rightwards, past an overlap to a belay.
4) 5a, 10m. The corner above leads to a bulge, where moves on the bulging rib to the right gain ledges leading rightwards to a stance on *Il Duce*.
5) 4c, 24m. Climb the crack in the right wall of the corner for 10m then step back left and follow the groove to a roof. Move rightwards easily but on deteriorating rock until a fault-line leads up to the top.
FA. Mick Fowler, Mike Morrison 26.5.1978

❷ Il Duce .... Top 50   E5 6a

The central corner that rises from the overhung ledge at the base of High Cliff is a stunning line. Technically reasonable but the commitment required earns it the grade. The nature of the climbing and the situation is very serious and this is not a place to get into trouble. Start at the bottom of the rocky ramp that slopes seawards below the gearing-up spot. *Photo on page 167.*
1) 5a, 20m. Traverse left to a protruding ledge and continue around an arete to a large platform beneath roofs and the main corner as for *Vagabond*.
2) 6a, 20m. From the right-hand side of the large platform, climb the right-hand of two converging cracks past a short, hard section to better holds beneath the roof. Committing moves leftwards gain a precarious rest in a chimney on the lip of the roof. Move up this and its left wall to a small stance.
3) 5c, 20m. Climb the main corner, moving left around a bulge, to a good ledge and belay.
4) 4c, 24m. Climb the crack in the right wall of the corner for 10m then step back left and follow the groove to a roof. Move rightwards easily but on deteriorating rock until a fault-line leads up to the top.
FA. Pat Littlejohn, Keith Darbyshire 23.4.1972
FFA. Tom Jones, Roger Hughes 1980

❸ King's Arete E4 5c

Steep climbing in great positions on *Il Duce's* right arete. The climbing becomes easier but the rock deteriorates in quality as height is gained. Start at the bottom of the rocky ramp that slopes seaward below the gearing-up spot.
1) 5a, 10m. Traverse left and take a belay on a protruding ledge.
2) 5c, 40m. Climb straight up to a small ledge at 7m using positive holds but with minimal gear. Move diagonally left to the arete and ascend it to a narrow ledge. Move rightwards along the ledge (possible belay) then diagonally back left to the arete again. Follow this to a short steep crack on the right which leads to a belay in a niche.
3) 5b, 30m. Climb steeply on good holds to the right then move back left towards the arete and continue up to reach an easy traverse-line (junction with *Il Duce*). Follow this rightwards to a fault-line that leads up to the top.
FA. Andy Meyers, Mick Fowler 3.7.1982

Highest point on Island

Approach down wide grassy gully

Gearing-up spot

Approach ramp

Access - Permission must be sought before climbing.

Afternoon | 20 min | Multi-pitch

Avon Somerset

North Devon

Culm Coast

Inland Cornwall

Atlantic Coast

West Penwith

The Lizard

Inland Devon

Torbay

Dorset

① ② ③

Approach ramp

	No star	💢	💢💢	💢💢💢
Mod to S	-	-	-	-
HS to HVS	-	-	1	-
E1 to E3	-	1	-	1
E4 and up	-	-	1	-

Doyden Point is a friendly cliff that enjoys a sunny outlook with a choice of good routes to keep most content for an afternoon. It is only a short distance from the quaint fishing village of Port Isaac and the surf beaches of Polzeath.

Approach   See area map on page 164

Take the B3314 off of the A39 either at Camelford or Wadebridge dependent on the direction of approach. Follow signs off of the B3314 for Port Quin and follow a narrow lane to the tiny fishing hamlet and park in the National Trust car park.

Tides

The base of Doyden Point is not tidal but is to be avoided in heavy seas.

Conditions

Doyden Point enjoys a sunny westerly aspect and dries very quickly.

Side tabs: Avon Somerset · North Devon · Culm Coast · Inland Cornwall · Atlantic Coast · West Penwith · The Lizard · Inland Devon · Torbay · Dorset

Pentire Head Great Wall

Doyden Point

Port Quin

GPS 50.588903 -4.866815

N

Pentireglaze

New Polzeath

Polzeath

About 2km

B3314

Climbers enjoying a perfect summer's day on *Caprice (VS 4c) - opposite -* Doyden Point.

❶ Flying Circus E2 5c

The left-hand arete is a tempting prospect that is also reasonably tame for the grade. Start at the left end of the sloping ledge under the arete.
27m. Move up left to a niche and step up and left before traversing right below the arete to a small ledge at the bottom of a groove. From a short distance up the groove move left to the arete and climb thin cracks to a small ledge on the left. Make some tricky moves up the rib and finish up the arete.
FA. Iain Peters, Ken Hosie 26.4.1986

❷ Caprice . . . . VS 4c

A perfect introduction to the delights of the cliff and a very worthwhile goal in its own right. Start at the upper end of the ramp below a slab with some quartz patches. *Photo opposite.*
27m. Move up onto the slab and go left to a small corner. At the top of the small corner step out left onto the slab and climb the slim diagonal crack left, stepping up above it midway, to finish at a ledge around the arete.
FA. Pat Littlejohn, Steve Jones 26.10.1971

❸ Lotus E1 5b

Despite its modest height this route packs in some excellent climbing in increasingly exposed positions. Start at the top of the ramp below the large corner in the centre of the crag.
1) 5b, 30m. Climb the corner, which soon becomes strenuous. At the top of the second bulge, join the diagonal crack on the steep right wall and follow this to a slab. Climb the slab to its end at a bulge. Move around this, high or low, to nut belays.
2) 4c, 15m. Make a tricky move to the right around a rib and onto a small slab. Follow this up to a ledge beneath a short steep wall. Move over this and belay on an old iron ring.
FA. Pat Littlejohn, Iain Peters 26.6.1977

Doyden Point

Approach - Walk out of the car park and go left and up the steep road, past a hairpin, and then take a path on the right over a wall. Ahead is a distinct folly on the left-hand of a twin topped headland. Doyden Cliff is on the opposite side of the right-hand summit. An easy path contours to the top of the crag (10 minutes). Abseil direct down the main corner to sloping ledges below the wall.

❹ Yogic Flyer E5 6a

The steep wall crossed by *Lotus*. Start at the top of the ramp as for *Lotus*.
35m. Move up the corner to the first overhang. Traverse right to below a short crack and climb the steep wall to join *Lotus* at the end of its traverse across the wall. Move left 2m and climb the steep and exposed wall on 'pancake' holds to the top taking care with some loose rock on the finishing moves.
FA. Dave Henderson, Martin Crocker 8.4.1995

Abseil approach

Afternoon | 10 min | Abseil in

	No star	⚐1	⚐2	⚐3
Mod to S	-	-	-	-
HS to HVS	-	-	-	-
E1 to E3	-	-	-	-
E4 and up	1	-	1	4

Pentire Head's Great Wall is without a shadow of a doubt one of the UK's finest cliffs and for many years has been a beacon for those intent on picking off its exquisite lines. In recent times the aid peg on the second pitch of the legendary *Eroica* has rusted away and will possibly not be replaced. Pentire Head is conveniently located near the fishing village of Port Isaac and the surf beaches of Polzeath.

Approach
Take the B3314 off of the A39 either at Camelford or Wadebridge dependent on the direction of approach. Take signs off of the B3314 for Polzeath and New Polzeath and then a minor road to Pentireglaze. At the hamlet of Pentireglaze go along a track to Pentire Farm (NT). Park at the Farm (small fee).

Tides
The base of the Great Wall is not tidal but in a very heavy sea waves do reach its base.

Conditions
The Great Wall is quite sheltered but only sees the evening sun in the summer and therefore can take time to dry out after wet weather.

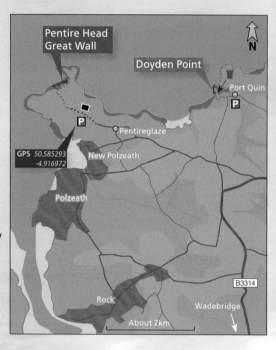

Pentire Head Great Wall
Doyden Point
Port Quin
Pentireglaze
GPS 50.585293 -4.916972
New Polzeath
Polzeath
Rock
Wadebridge
B3314
About 2km
N

Great Wall

Side tabs: Avon Somerset | North Devon | Culm Coast | Inland Cornwall | Atlantic Coast | West Penwith | The Lizard | Inland Devon | Torbay | Dorset

Avon Somerset

North Devon

Culm Coast

Inland Cornwall

Atlantic Coast

West Penwith

The Lizard

Inland Devon

Torbay

Dorset

Steve Ramsden (leading) and Alex Mason on the second pitch of the legendary *Eroica* (E4 6a) - *page 175* - The Great Wall, Pentire Head. Photo: Adrian Berry

The Great Wall

This huge vertical wall, capped by steep slim corners gives unrivalled rock quality, climbing and atmosphere.
Approach - Follow the path/track out of the left side of the farmyard and take this following the direction of Pentire Point (not The Rumps). Follow the path to the cliff-top coast path and turn right. Walk 100m and the top of the Great Wall is on the left. Descend down easy grass and slabs starting 70m to the right (facing out) of the summit of the Great Wall.

Avon Somerset

North Devon

Culm Coast

Inland Cornwall

Atlantic Coast

West Penwith

The Lizard

Inland Devon

Torbay

Dorset

① Eroica . . . . 🔲 🔲 **E4 6a**

One of the UK's most illustrious sea-cliff challenges, following a spectacular line of flake-cracks up the lower portion of the Great Wall and finishing up the narrow central corner. The second pitch was for many years climbed with a peg for aid at 5b but this has now gone. Start below a small corner at the base of the left side of the wall. *Photo on page 173.*

1) 5a, 30m. Move steeply up the corner, which eases as it trends left to a triangular niche. Move right and take cracks to a rest below double overhangs. Undercut wildly left between the overhangs and continue up the wide crack to a stance at its top.

2) 6a, 12m. Climb the corner/groove above to its end before traversing rightwards to a stance at the base of a corner.

3) 5b, 20m. Climb the corner, which is technical and sustained in its lower half to an obvious exit on the right at its end.
FA. Pat Littlejohn, Gus Morton 11.4.1971
FFA. Pete Livesey, Jill Lawrence 1975

② Black Magic . . . . . . 🔲 🔲 🔲 **E5 6a**

A wonderful route tracing a sustained path up the Great Wall on immaculate rock. Take lots of small wires. Start 5m right of *Eroica* at a short high-angled slab beneath a thin crack-system. *Photo on page 162.*

1) 6a, 46m. Step up onto the high-angled slab and move up left to the thin cracks. Climb the thin crack-system to two short left to right-leaning cracks - peg. Move up the wall rightwards past a distinct white quartz patch and enter the very slim left-facing corner above. Follow the corner to a tricky exit onto easier-angled rock. Work up the slabby, lichen splashed wall to a stance beneath a leaning corner.

2) 5c, 20m. Climb the corner and steep flake to an easier exit.
FA. Steve Monks, Jane Wilkinson 27.5.1987

③ Darkinbad the Brightdayler

. . . . Top 🔲 🔲 🔲 **E5 6a**

Phenomenal climbing on both pitches mark this route out as one of Britain's best. Although the start is bold the meat of the difficult climbing is reasonably protected. Start on huge boulders 7m right of *Eroica* at a vague line of weakness below the left side of a narrow ledge at 8m.

1) 6a, 48m. Step up off a boulder onto the wall and climb boldly to the left end of a ledge at 8m. Climb the wall via cracks to a flake and follow it leftwards to a peg in two short left to right-leaning cracks. Traverse left for 4m and make fingery moves up to the line of overhangs above. Follow a steep flake and crack diagonally rightwards to its end and climb the thin crack in the wall above with difficulty to the second stance of *Eroica*.

2) 5c, 22m. Traverse left into the base of the next corner and climb to where it starts to overhang. Make forceful moves up the steep section to an easing as the corner kicks back. Finish up the wall above.
FA. Pat Littlejohn, Ian Duckworth 25.4.1972
FFA. Ron Fawcett, Pete Gomersall 1976

④ Wall of Spirits . 🔲 🔲 🔲 🔲 **E8 6b**

The spooky headwall that looms above *Black Magic* is the Atlantic Coast's hardest and boldest lead to date. Start as for *Black Magic* at its short slab.

1) 6a, 45m. Follow *Black Magic* until just beyond its distinct white quartz patch. Take the faint line of weakness that swoops out left into the centre of the shield. When directly below a small overlap, climb direct, making bold moves through the overlap to gain the ramp leading left to the *Black Magic* stance. A fine pitch.

2) 6b, 40m. Move out left along a shelf until directly below a crystal pocket in the centre of the wall. Tricky, bold climbing gains the pocket (crucial friend 2.5 - the only gear before the crux). Move up right on crimps to gain a poor rest. Now follow a line of holds back left, heading towards the arete, until a very bold crux sequence enables a standing position on the arete to be gained. Move up to better holds and gear, and follow the much easier groove system to the top.
FA. Dave Pickford, Mike Robertson 9.2004 Pitch 2 (headpointed)
FA. Dave Pickford, Sarah Garnett 6.2006 Pitch 1

⑤ Siren's Cry . . . . 🔲 🔲 **E6 6a**

Stunning rock but very serious climbing that is reliant on the ageing pegs. Start on a huge boulder left of the big corner on the right-hand side of the Great Wall.

1) 6a, 40m. Pull onto the easy-angled wall and head for a protruding peg. Traverse left below this, thin tape on low spike, to and up a shallow rising rampline to a point beneath twin pegs. Make thin, bold moves up to the pegs and continue up the fingery wall above them for 5m to better holds and some wires. Move on up the still steep wall to another peg. Climb an easier shallow groove to a good jug, and move right to a corner and climb it to a stance on ledges.

2) 5c, 30m. Climb leftwards to meet the top pitch of *Black Magic* and finish up this.
FA. Richard 'Nipper' Harrison 8.1983

Belay stakes

Approach

Avon Somerset | North Devon | Culm Coast | Inland Cornwall | Atlantic Coast | West Penwith | The Lizard | Inland Devon | Torbay | Dorset

	No star	☆	☆☆	☆☆☆
Mod to S	-	1	-	-
HS to HVS	-	-	2	-
E1 to E3	-	-	5	2
E4 and up	-	-	1	3

The massive cliffs that fringe the bleak St Agnes Head, south of the tranquil fishing village of St Agnes, are some of the most impressive but least ventured upon in the West Country. The various buttresses and walls collectively known as Carn Gowla reach their highest around the headland, and are serious cliffs that drop straight into the relentless Atlantic swell. The climbs described here are some of the better travelled at Carn Gowla, although it is rare to see another party on the cliffs. The approaches to, and the abseils themselves, need to be carefully executed with due regard to the prevailing sea conditions. These considerations combined with the isolation and at times unsettling rock quality means that Carn Gowla will not appeal to all. However, for climbers looking for adventure on a grand scale this is a cliff that is unlikely to disappoint, and if caught on a calm summer's afternoon, or a wild spring day, will be a spot not to be forgotten.

Approach   Area map on page 164

From the A30, 4 miles east of Redruth, take the B3277 to St Agnes. Shortly after entering St Agnes, turn left at a mini roundabout signed to Beacon. Follow this road which eventually bends right at a sign for Beacon Drive and continue along the road as it climbs up to open land. In the far distance, on the left, is a coastguard lookout. A minor road on the left leads out to this but there is no signpost, although it is fairly easy to locate. Follow the minor road out to the coastguard lookout and parking for the various approaches to each cliff.

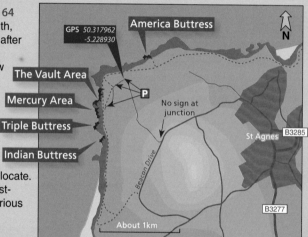

Tides

Access to all the cliffs is tide dependent and in moderate or heavy seas the cliffs here are best left alone. In calm seas and with little swell many of the routes can be accessed even at high tide.

Conditions

Seepage on the cliffs can be persistent and the climbs will at certain times remain damp, however many of the cliffs do get plenty of sun. The rock becomes very slippery when wet.

The Black Walls

America Buttress

Avon Somerset

North Devon

Culm Coast

Inland Cornwall

Atlantic Coast

West Penwith

The Lizard

Inland Devon

Torbay

Dorset

Midway up the final pitch of the austere *America* (E4 5c) - *page 178* - at Carn Gowla. Climber Tim Emmett. Photo: Ian Parnell

① America . . . . [Top 50] E4 5c

A towering, adventurous route that combines diverse climbing with a serious situation. Dry conditions are essential. The base is reached via abseil or, in calm sea conditions, at low tide via a sea-level traverse. Start on sea level ledges at the left edge of the lower wall below a corner. *Photo on page 177.*

1) 5b, 26m. Climb leftwards, easy but serious, to an old peg on the left. Traverse right two metres and climb a short, bold wall to reach the safety of a niche. Follow the awkward, wide crack above to its end at a stance and spike belay.

2) 5b, 40m. A poorly protected pitch. Move up the slab to where it starts to steepen and move left towards its edge. Climb up and pass a blanker section on the right, to reach a dodgy flake. Move left, back towards the arete, and follow the slab to a stance below the upper buttress.

3) 5c, 25m. Climb up a groove on the left and enter a corner above it. Move up a short way and traverse the steep wall on the right, around an arete, to a steep corner that is climbed to a ledge and a large bird's nest. Move left and climb very steep ground to a ledge. Follow the thin crack above it to the top.

FA. Pat Littlejohn, Keith Darbyshire 16.7.1973

② Guernica E6 6a

An awe-inspiring route whose main pitch climbs the central section of the severely-overhanging upper buttress. Start as for pitch 1 of *America*; or at the stance at the top of its first pitch if the tide or sea conditions do not allow access to the base.

1) 5b, 26m. Pitch 1 of *America*.

2) 5c, 35m. Move rightwards and climb up the slab to meet the corner formed with the steep upper buttress. Climb the slab to the left of the corner and continue to a stance at a crack on the left side of a large block.

3) 6a, 24m. Move up the slab for 3m and climb the wall to a flat handhold. Traverse right to a large block on the edge of an overhang and ascend a thin crack and shallow groove above to a peg and a shake-out on the right. Committing moves up the overhanging wall leftwards lead to flake holds that are traversed steeply right to a large sloping ledge and belay.

4) 5b, 20m. Move steeply left to a huge niche. From here, traverse left until it is possible to gain a corner above that leads to the top.

FA. Pat Littlejohn, Hugh Clarke 16.5.1982 (1pt)
FFA. Pat Littlejohn 4.1987

③ Mausoleum E2 5b

The huge open-book corner to the right of the upper part of *America* is a good pitch, although it is prone to seepage and can be vegetated. This is the final pitch of the original line that started at sea-level. Start by abseiling to the base of the corner.

30m. Ascend the corner to a ledge and then less strenuously to an overhang. Move out left to a ledge and using good holds above a bulge, pull through it and continue to the top.

FA. Keith Darbyshire, Pat Littlejohn 29.4.1973

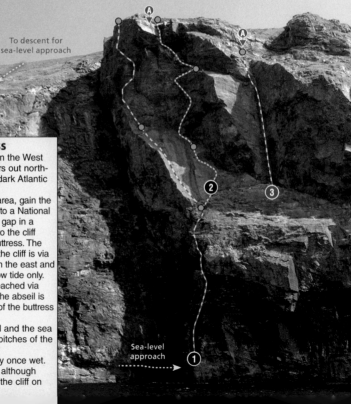

To descent for
sea-level approach

Sea-level
approach

America Buttress

One of the most intimidating cliffs in the West Country, the America Buttress peers out northwards over the normally turbulent dark Atlantic and is not a place to take lightly.

Approach - From the first parking area, gain the coast path and walk right for 300m to a National Trust sign for Newdowns Head at a gap in a wall. Follow the wall for 50m down to the cliff edge and the very summit of the buttress. The traditional approach to the base of the cliff is via a committing sea-level traverse from the east and requires a Tyrolean across a gap, low tide only. However, the base is most easily reached via a massive abseil on joined ropes. The abseil is from a stake 5m left of the very tip of the buttress and is free to the central slab.

Tides - The base of the cliff is tidal and the sea is often rough, however the upper pitches of the routes can be reached by abseil.

Conditions - The cliff is slow to dry once wet. The face receives virtually no sun, although it does creep around onto parts of the cliff on summer's evenings.

Avon Somerset | North Devon | Culm Coast | Inland Cornwall | Atlantic Coast | West Penwith | The Lizard | Inland Devon | Torbay | Dorset

④ Supernatural . . . . VS 4b

A long crack-line in a very impressive, smooth-looking wall. Start at a hanging stance at the start of the crack. There used to be a ledge at this point but it has now been reported to have fallen off.
30m. Climb the interesting crack all the way back to the top, taking care with loose ground on the finish.
FA. Keith Darbyshire, Hugh Clarke, Pat Littlejohn 4.1973

⑤ Phantasm E4 6a

This impressive pitch takes the long crack-line immediately right of *Supernatural*. Abseil in as for *Supernatural* but go past the hanging stance to arrive at the base of the crack at a patch of luminous green seaweed that can be seen from above. Start at this point.
40m. Follow the crack all the way until it ends at a jug, traverse horizontally left to finish on the final moves of *Supernatural*.
FA. Martin Haycock, James Forbes 21.06.2005

⑥ A Sack Full of Clowns . . E1 5b

A relatively popular corner pitch that takes some time to dry out. An atmospheric climb that has good gear and rock. Start by abseiling down the line to a small sea level ledge and belay.
35m. Climb steeply to a ledge. Continue up the fine corner finishing to the left of the top overhang.
FA. David Hope, Tony Penning, Roger Lanchbury, Pete Creswell 20.9.1987

The Black Walls

A series of shorter, but still very steep walls and buttresses that extend towards St Agnes Head from America Buttress. The cliff is extremely intimidating and drops straight into the sea.

Approach - From the summit of the America buttress, the top of the Black Walls are 100m back towards St Agnes Head and are approached via abseil points in the steep grass slope above.

Tides - The base of the cliff is tidal and the sea is often rough which will restrict access to the base of the routes.

Conditions - The cliff is slow to dry once wet. The face receives sun only on the longest of summer evenings. The finishes of the climbs are loose and need care both in ascent and descent.

← America Buttress summit, 300m

Avon Somerset | North Devon | Culm Coast | Inland Cornwall | Atlantic Coast | West Penwith | The Lizard | Inland Devon | Torbay | Dorset

The Vault Wall

A huge hulk of a cliff that leans out seaward and is flanked on the left by some equally large walls (The Red Walls) and on the right by a huge slab (The Teflon Slab). The Vault Wall is a large and serious cliff on which good conditions are hard to come by.

Approach - Drive past the coastguard lookout and park in the very last parking area. Looking out to sea from the parking area, two small rocky promontories can be seen with an old sewage pipe just visible between them on the cliff edge. The Vault Wall is to the right of the right-hand promontory. From the right-hand promontory a huge slab can be seen, the abseil approach is from nuts and cams in a small bluff of rock on top of the steep wall above the slab. The abseil is 90m from where a traverse left (looking in) gains the start of *The Tomb*.

Tides - The base of the cliff is slightly tidal but access is restricted in moderate or heavy seas.

Conditions - The Vault Wall is badly affected by seepage and a long period of dry weather is needed for it to come into condition. The wall doesn't see a great deal of sun.

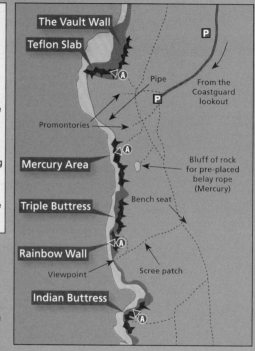

❶ The Tomb .... 🎲③ 📷 ⬜ **E4 5c**

Although unlikely to become a popular route in its current incarnation, the line remains one of the West Country's most audacious - crossing the Vault Wall from left to right. Start at a right-trending ramp left of the central gash of the vault itself.

1) 4c, 24m. Climb the ramp and move up a small corner at its top before traversing left to the end of the overhang above. Move up to a belay on the slab.

2) 5c, 20m. Ascend to the right-hand corner of the slab, move right and up through the overhang to a stance and belay. This pitch used to have a peg for protection on the hard move through the overhang and was graded at E2/3 with this in place.

3) 5b, 50m. Traverse into the massive corner on the right (The Vault). Climb up a short distance and then move right onto a small slab. Follow the slab right to a big flake and ascend this to a ledge, go right to a thin crack and take this to the finishing slabs. Follow the slabs rightwards to finish at the abseil point.

FA. Rowland Perriment, Richard Broomhead 1974

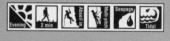

Teflon Slab

The Vault

❶

2 Mercury Direct . . . . [Top 50] E2 5b

The arching corner is a magnificent line and is climbed in two very long and sustained pitches. Some big cams and nuts are needed to protect the first pitch. Start at the base of the corner.

1) 5a, 42m. Ascend the corner until it starts to steepen and widen. Climb the wide crack to a flake from where easier climbing gains a big ledge on the left and a belay.

2) 5b, 50m. Climb the corner and its subsidiary to its end. Traverse right across the slab on small holds stepping down at a steepening to a pillar of compact red rock and better holds. Move up to small ledges (the site of an old belay) and continue for 5m before stepping right to a weakness in the overhang above. Climb up this and the easy groove above to the top.

2a) 4c, 50m. An easier but poorer finish moves left around the arete from the belay ledge and then climbs up the wall above the edge of the arete on big, but at times dubious, holds to a grassy final 10m.

FA. Pat Littlejohn, Steve Jones 1974 (Finishing up the wall left of the upper corner). FA. (Pitch 2 as described) Rowland Edwards and others 8.1979

Mercury Area

An enormous, intimidating cliff on which is one of the West Country's greatest lines. The rock is good but the climb has a very remote and serious feel about it even though it lurks only a short distance from the car park.

Approach - Drive past the coastguard lookout and park in the very last parking area. Looking out to sea from the parking area, two small rocky promontories can be seen with an old sewage pipe just visible between them on the cliff edge below. From the left-hand promontory a small outcrop of rock can be seen down the slope about 70m to the left (looking out); this is directly above the line of *Mercury* and where a fixed rope for the belay should be run down to the cliff edge. The approach to the base of *Mercury* is by an abseil of around 110m (joined ropes) from a thread and nut anchors in a bluff of rock above the cliff edge which is reached by walking down the slope to the left of the left-hand promontory (see topo). The bluff of rock is above a large boulder on the cliff edge. Abseil down the face to the arete of *Mercury's* corner and move around it into the corner at the point of its belay at the top of the first pitch. Either continue abseiling (if rope long enough) down to a ledge at its base or another ledge 10m higher if the sea is threatening. Those with shorter ropes will need to belay at the top of the first pitch and make another abseil.

Tides - The ledge at the base of the route is virtually non-tidal, although it is wave-washed in moderate or high seas even at low tide.

Conditions - The upper corner of *Mercury* suffers from seepage and takes time to dry out.

Promontories

Sewage pipe

Pre-place rope from this outcrop to cliff edge for final belay

Line of alternative finish

(A)

Boulder on cliff edge

Approximate line of abseil

Higher belay ledge if lower ledges are sea washed

Sidebar tabs: Avon Somerset · North Devon · Culm Coast · Inland Cornwall · Atlantic Coast · West Penwith · The Lizard · Inland Devon · Torbay · Dorset

Avon Somerset | North Devon | Culm Coast | Inland Cornwall | Atlantic Coast | West Penwith | The Lizard | Inland Devon | Torbay | Dorset

① Journey to Ixtlan... HVS 4c
A very spectacular and exposed traverse of the Triple Buttress that has the benefit of being non-tidal and a good distance above the sea at all times. However, the situations are serious and the rock needs careful handling with regard to both the climbing and the setting up of belays. Take plenty of slings for tying-off bollards, spikes and threads. Start above a ramp on the landward side of the descent to the top of C Buttress. *Photo on page 165.*
1) 22m. Downclimb the easy ramp to a ledge and belay.
2) 4c, 21m. Move down the ramp for a further 5m then climb leftwards up the wall until level with the belay. Move up again before traversing left steeply to the arete and a belay just beyond.
3) 4c, 20m. Step down and move across grooves to a corner. Descend the wall left to an exposed stance and belay on the arete.
4) 4c, 40m. A wild-looking pitch for both leader and second. Traverse into the corner and traverse left across its opposite wall above an overhang to an arete. Move up the arete for 6m to a stance and belay.
5) 4c, 25m. Move up and climb leftwards to reach and climb a diagonal line across the wall until steeper moves lead to a position just before a big corner. Finish straight up via the left-hand side of a block. Stake belay.
FA. Rowland Perriment, C.Owen 2.9.1978

② Looking for a Rainbow..... S 4a
A good introduction to this section of the cliff that takes on the open corner/chimney on the left flank of C Buttress. Start at the left end of the sea level belay ledges below the leaning pink wall.
34m. Move left to below the corner/chimney line. Good climbing up this ends at a big ledge from where a short wall on the right is climbed to easier ground that runs up to the summit of the buttress.
FA. David Hope, A.Camm 27.5.1990

Coast path from parking ➔

Triple Buttress
A series of shallow buttresses (named A, B and C Buttress) and corners make up this unusual section of cliff, which is one of the more popular due to its accessible routes and less-restrictive tidal access. The routes still have an air of seriousness about them, the protection can be awkward to arrange and poorer sections of rock should be anticipated.

Approach (See map on page 180) - Approach as for Mercury Area up to the two promontories. From the left-hand promontory, walk south along the coast path to a bench seat. Follow a faint path directly down the slope towards the sea to a scree patch. Ahead can be seen a rocky ledge on the cliff edge, this is a good spot to view the Triple Buttress and Indian Buttress. To access the top of Triple Buttress walk back up the slope a little and traverse the slope north for 60m until the top of C Buttress comes into view down to the left. To access the ledges at the base of C Buttress, abseil down the wall directly.
Tides - The ledges at the base of C Buttress are not tidal in calm seas. *Journey to Ixtlan* is non-tidal.
Conditions - The walls dry quickly after rain. The base of C Buttress is sea washed in moderate seas.

③ Rainbow Games... E2 5b
A fine pitch. The leaning pink wall that fronts C Buttress has a couple of thin, vertical crack-lines that split the lower smooth section of the wall. Start below the left-hand thin crack.
33m. Climb the thin crack and where it fades continue up the buttress above on good but fragile holds.
FA. David Hope, A.Camm 27.5.1990

④ Four for Texas....... E2 5b
The right-hand thin crack in the pink wall is another good pitch in a similar mold to *Rainbow Games*. Start below the crack.
33m. Climb the thin lower wall to better holds and a thread. Continue carefully up the middle of the wall on good holds.
FA. Tony Penning, Roger Lanchbury, Pete Cresswell, David Hope 20.9.1987

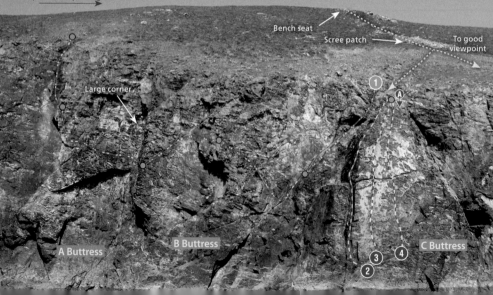

Bench seat / Scree patch / To good viewpoint / Large corner / A Buttress / B Buttress / C Buttress

⑤ Alex of Gowla..... 🏁2 ✒️🥾 ☐ **E1 5b**
A very good pitch on sound rock and with reliable protection.
Start at a spike belay on a ledge at the base of the corner-line.
38m. Climb the corner to the large roof at 30m. Traverse right
below the roof and pull into the groove on its right. Follow the
groove to the top.
FA. Tony Penning, Roger Lanchbury, Pete Cresswell, David Hope 19.6.1988

⑥ Indian Country .... 🏁 ✒️ ☐ **E2 5b**
The wall between *Alex of Gowla* and the deep chimney. Start at
the left end of the ledges at the base of the deep chimney.
37m. Climb a steep corner and continue to a line of overhangs.
Traverse right and down before crossing a gap below a crack.
Ascend slabby grooves leftwards to finish.
FA. Tony Penning, Roger Lanchbury, Pete Cresswell, David Hope 19.6.1988

Indian Buttress

At the southern end of the Carn Gowla crags is this
buttress of good rock with one very good corner climb.
Approach (See map on page 180) - Approach as for
Mercury Area up to the two promontories. From the left-
hand promontory, walk south along the coast path, past a
bench seat, and take a subsidiary path that drops down
right towards the sea. As the path levels out head down
the slope to the cliff edge and good ledges on top of the
buttress. Abseil from various anchors on the loose slope
to sea level ledges.
Tides - The ledges at the base of the lines are not
covered at high water in very calm conditions.
Conditions - The cliff has a northerly aspect and takes
time to dry.

Good gearing-up spot

Deep chimney

West Penwith

Avon Somerset
North Devon
Culm Coast
Inland Cornwall
Atlantic Coast
West Penwith
The Lizard
Inland Devon
Torbay
Dorset

John Warner nearing the end of the second pitch of
Pendulum Chimney (Severe 4b) - *page 260* - at Chair Ladder.

Avon Somerset

North Devon

Culm Coast

Inland Cornwall

Atlantic Coast

West Penwith

The Lizard

Inland Devon

Torbay

Dorset

Paul Cox sets out on the atmospheric *Sensible Shoes* (VS 4c)
- *page 197* - on the dark greenstone of Robin's Rocks, West Penwith

West Penwith is the traditional home of climbing in the West Country, its great rock, beautiful coastal scenery and 'End of the Land' atmosphere blend together to form a world-class trad climbing destination. Although the majority of the climbs are on the coast's famed granite sea-cliffs, the neighbouring killas slate and greenstone offer equally good routes that add much to the caché of the area. With kindly weather, a day doesn't get much better than a cooling dip in the sea and a trip to the pub after a light toasting on some of the best sea-cliff climbs anywhere.

Getting Around

Most of the paths to the cliffs are approached from either villages or remote parking spots. Nearly all of the car parks are reached on narrow country lanes that can become congested at busy times. It is also worth noting that the popular parking spots fill up quickly at peak holiday times.

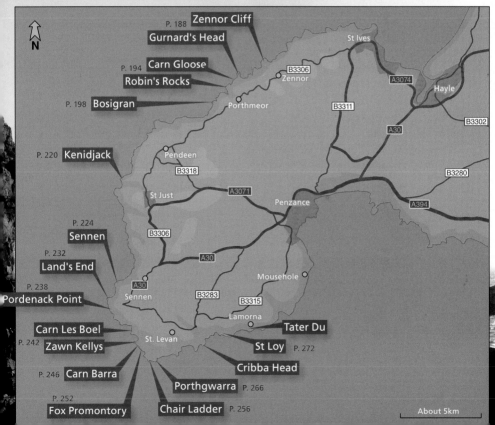

Avon Somerset

North Devon

Culm Coast

Inland Cornwall

Atlantic Coast

West Penwith

The Lizard

Inland Devon

Torbay

Avon Somerset | North Devon | Culm Coast | Inland Cornwall | Atlantic Coast | West Penwith | The Lizard | Inland Devon | Torbay | Dorset

Zennor Crag is a small but useful crag being located well above the sea away from any tide problems. It has a couple of good mid-grade routes which are worth stopping by for, especially if the weather is a bit rough.

Approach   See main area map on page 187

Take the B3306 St Ives - Pendeen road and turn off into the hamlet of Zennor and park on the road or in the car park. Walk between the pub and church and pick up a track that cuts back left behind the pub and then heads out towards the coast. Where the track ends at a house entrance continue on a footpath that meets up with the coast path. Turn right and follow the coast path to a rocky summit with a memorial plaque. From the memorial plaque, descend to the left (facing out) down to a grassy-ledge below the wall.

Conditions

The crag gets plenty of sun and is fast-drying. It can be climbable when the cliffs nearer the sea are being battered by the wind and waves. The rock can become a bit green and fuzzy early in the season.

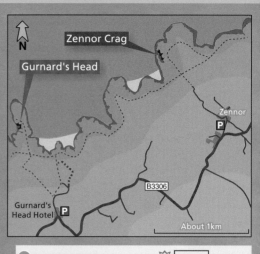

① **Rosebud in June** . . . . ⚄ ☐   **HVS 5a**
Sustained and pleasant climbing with a well-positioned top crack. The first 9m are not well-protected. Start at a good nut belay just right of a narrow chimney. *Photo opposite.*
26m. Move up a flake-crack and take the wall above to a move right into a triangular niche. Climb to the next horizontal break, step left, and follow the delightful face-crack to the top.
FA. Toni Carver, R.Nadin 3.6.1973

② **The Royal Forester** . . . . ⚄ ☐   **VS 4c**
Steep and varied climbing with good protection. Start at the base of a clean, narrow corner.
26m. Climb the narrow corner to the overhang and layback steeply up rightwards to good holds. Follow a finger-crack left to its end and step onto a ledge on the right. Move up and left to the bottom of a final corner that leads to the top.
FA. Toni Carver, P.Turner 29.4.1973

Approach

Avon Somerset

North Devon

Culm Coast

Inland Cornwall

Atlantic Coast

West Penwith

The Lizard

Inland Devon

Torbay

Dorset

Lee Proctor escaping some heavy seas on *Rosebud in June* (HVS 5a) - *opposite* - at Zennor.

190   **Gurnard's Head**

	No star	⭐	⭐⭐	⭐⭐⭐
Mod to S	-	-	-	-
HS to HVS	-	-	-	1
E1 to E3	-	1	2	1
E4 and up	-	-	1	-

A superbly-located zawn of vertigo-inducing steepness, whose black walls plunge straight into the sea at the bottom of the wide zawn. The climbs are very intimidating and require good judgment of conditions to be enjoyed to the full.

Approach   See main area map on page 187

Take the B3306 St Ives - Pendeen road to the Gurnard's Head Hotel and park on the verge opposite the Hotel. Walk down the lane to the right of the Hotel, past cottages, and follow a signed footpath towards the coast, taking the higher, left-hand path where it splits. Gurnard's Head is the large, rocky headland directly ahead. Right Angle cliff is easily located on the left, at the beginning of the headland.

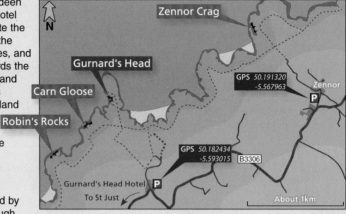

Tides

Most of the climbs are affected by both tide and sea state. Although it is possible to do *Right Angle* at high tide if the sea is calm, all the other lines require a low tide and calm sea-conditions.

Conditions

The rock is generally excellent, and has good friction when dry. However, the routes are susceptible to persistent greasiness and are therefore best attempted in the sun or after long dry-periods. The zawn is generally west facing, which means that best conditions will normally be found from mid-afternoon onwards.

Right Angle Zawn

Avon Somerset · North Devon · Culm Coast · Inland Cornwall · Atlantic Coast · West Penwith · The Lizard · Inland Devon · Torbay · Dorset

Avon Somerset

North Devon

Culm Coast

Inland Cornwall

Atlantic Coast

West Penwith

The Lizard

Inland Devon

Torbay

Dorset

Barney Carver on the adventurous *Behemoth* (E2 5c)
- *page 192* - Right Angle Zawn. Photo: Tobi Carver UE Images.

① Right Angle ...... [Top 50] HS 4b

A true classic of its grade, which follows an almost unbelievable path into, and out of territory that looks as though it should be reserved for far more extreme climbs. Start on ledges level with an orange, lichen-covered ledge (this is the belay ledge at the end of the first pitch) as viewed from the easy, rocky-ground that runs down the right side of the zawn. *Photo on page 41.*

1) 13m. Traverse horizontally rightwards past a bay to a good stance on the orange ledge.

2) 4b, 22m. Continue the traverse rightwards for a further 12m, then descend the steep wall and corner to a point just above the high-water mark. Move right to a stance and belay. This pitch requires careful route-finding, and is much trickier if damp.

2a) 4b, 18m. An inferior variation on the second pitch continues the traverse, below a long, narrow overhang, all the way to meet the base of the corner above the cave, and a restricted stance. This variation is less affected by sea conditions.

3) 4a, 38m. Take the wall above the stance to meet the corner at the overhang. Follow the corner in a breathtaking position, all the way to the top.

FA. Iain Peters, J.Bember 26.8.1966

| From mid morning | 15 min | Multi-pitch |

② Behemoth E2 5c

The eye-catching rightward exit from the sea-level cave of the back wall is rarely attempted. The often-greasy first pitch has been the scene of a few epics. Start in the cave, which can be gained by an abseil or via an awkward traverse from *Right Angle*. *Photo on page 191.*

1) 5c, 16m. From the ledge, climb two steep, offset corners (aid, if at all damp) and pull out rightwards onto the open face to an awkward, hanging belay.

2) 5a, 17m. Climb the wall rightwards to the left-leaning corner/groove-line, and follow this to a protruding ledge and belay.

3) 10m. Finish up the corner.

FA. Pat Littlejohn, Steve Jones 30.8.1969 (2pts)

Approach

Avon Somerset · North Devon · Culm Coast · Inland Cornwall · Atlantic Coast · West Penwith · The Lizard · Inland Devon · Torbay · Dorset

3 Mastodon E3 5c

A great route with fly-on-the wall style situations on a subtle right-to-left line across the sheer back wall of the zawn. The start is often damp, and care is needed in setting up a solid belay at the end of the first pitch. If the sea is rough or the tide high, it is usual to abseil to the first stance and do only the top two pitches. Start from a belay at the base of *Shark*.

1) 5b, 22m. From the belay, climb up left to a niche at the base of a crack in the wall left of *Shark's* corner. Immediately traverse left to another niche in a crack. Climb the crack to a move leftwards and a tiny stance and hanging belay.

2) 5c, 18m. Move left and up to the base of a thin crack via an awkward move. Climb the thin crack. At its end, traverse rightwards to a stance in the left-leaning corner.

3) 5c, 10m. The steep crack-line above the stance provides a pumpy climax.

FA. Rowland Edwards, Sam Salmon 3.9.1978

4 Black Magic. E2 5b

The long, thin crack-line in the black wall, left of the long corner of *Shark* is a fine, sustained pitch on very good rock. The route can be slippery if damp. Start on ledges at the bottom of the *Shark* corner.

34m. Climb up leftwards to a niche at the base of the crack. Follow the crack-line past a flat spike to the left leading crack/ groove of *Behemoth*, and finish up the steep crack above.

FA. Rowland Edwards, Sam Salmon 2.10.1978

Right Angle Zawn

The awe-inspiring zawn can be easily viewed from both sides (with a bit of careful scrambling).

Approach - For *Right Angle,* walk and scramble very easily to the start down the right-hand side of the zawn (when looking out). For *Behemoth* abseil down the final pitch of *Right Angle.* For *Mastodon, Black Magic* and *Shark,* it is best to abseil down the corner of *Shark.*

5 Shark E1 5b

The long, dark, right-angled corner that defines the right-hand side of the back wall is a good, but again condition-dependent climb. Well protected. Start at the base of the corner.

32m. Climb the impressive corner and exit up the wall on the right to finish.

FA. Pat Littlejohn, Steve Jones 29.8.1969

6 Tropospheric Scatter E4 5c

The thin crack-system in the wall to the right of *Shark's* bounding arete is a sustained exercise that features a long move at two thirds height. Start at a steep crack just right of the arete.

32m. Climb the crack to an overhang, and pass it on the right. Move up rightwards to another overhang, manoeuvre through this via a big reach to gain a tiny ledge. Move left and finish up a thin crack.

FA. Rowland Edwards, Sam Salmon 2.10.1978

Avon Somerset · North Devon · Culm Coast · Inland Cornwall · Atlantic Coast · West Penwith · The Lizard · Inland Devon · Torbay · Dorset

	No star			
Mod to S	-	-	-	-
HS to HVS	-	-	-	1
E1 to E3	-	-	-	1
E4 and up	-	-	-	-

The dark greenstone headlands of Carn Gloose and Robin's Rocks have some intimidating west-facing cliffs that have two brilliant rising traverses on them. The cliffs need good conditions that are best found on calm and sunny afternoons. Both crags can be easily combined with a visit to Gurnard's Head.

Approach   See main area map on page 187

Take the B3306 St Ives - Pendeen road to the Gurnard's Head Hotel and park on the verge opposite the Hotel. Walk down the lane to the right of the Hotel past cottages and follow a signed footpath towards the coast taking the higher left-hand path where it splits. Follow the path to where it meets the coast path (Gurnard's Head is directly ahead) and turn left. Carn Gloose is the large rocky ridge 500m west. Robin's Rocks is located on the next headland west of Carn Gloose and is reached by continuing along the coast path to a stile in a stone wall. 150m past the stile, a good small path heads right to the headland itself. Walk down to the headland and cross a massive chasm via a convenient boulder bridge to the top of the buttress.

N

Gurnard's Head

Carn Gloose

Robin's Rocks

Zennor

GPS 50.182434
-5.593015 B3306

Gurnard's Head Hotel P

To St Just

About 1km

Tides

Neither of the climbs are tidal, although both will require careful judgement in anything other than benign sea conditions.

Conditions

The climbs are on generally excellent rock that has good friction when dry. The climbs are prone to greasiness and are therefore best attempted in the sun or after long dry periods.

Carn Gloose

Gurnard's Head

Avon Somerset | North Devon | Culm Coast | Inland Cornwall | Atlantic Coast | West Penwith | The Lizard | Inland Devon | Torbay | Dorset

Avon Somerset

North Devon

Culm Coast

Inland Cornwall

Atlantic Coast

West Penwith

The Lizard

Inland Devon

Torbay

Dorset

Alan James enjoying the steep finish of the third pitch of *Astral Stroll* (E1 5b) - *page 196* - at Carn Gloose.

① Astral Stroll . . . . Top 50 | E1 5b

Astounding positions and superb climbing combine to give one of the region's great climbs. The route follows a severely overhung diagonal line across the cliff, starting at sea level on the tip of the headland. The positions are serious for both leader and second and in anything but good, dry conditions the climbing on the third pitch can feel insecure. Calm sea conditions are essential if the route is attempted at high tide. Start on a sea-level ledge at the tip of the headland. *Photo on page 195.*

1) 4b, 20m. Climb around the headland onto the west face just above the high-tide mark. Move up a small slab before moving right below a little overhang and up again to a stance on a slab at the base of a left-leaning corner.

1a) 4c, 20m. An alternative first pitch, if the tide is very high, is to climb up and then traverse a steep pocketed wall right to a good ledge on the edge of the west face, before traversing down and right to the stance.

2) 5b, 10m. Move right and down via a difficult move (back rope for second) and traverse right, either high or low, to a stance at a wide crack in the corner.

2a) 5b, 20m. An alternative high-level version of the previous pitch is possible, for conditions when the sea is a bit choppy.

3) 5b, 20m. A wild pitch. Move up to the roof and then move down slightly before heading out across the steep wall and up to regain the roof. Continue right beneath the roof, passing a protruding fin of rock, to gain a steep hanging slab. Cross this, and a small corner, before making a steep move up to better holds, small spike. Move right and swing down to a stance on a projecting foot ledge.

4) 5a, 18m. Pull through the small overhang to the base of the large right-trending corner and move out right and up onto the wall to a small ledge. Finish up the wall. Belay well back. A scramble up the cracks on the left regains the ridge.

FA. Rowland Edwards, Charlie Bryan 31.3.80

Scramble exit

Large ledge
40m above sea

High variation
first pitch (4c)

Robin's Rocks

A compact, isolated buttress that has bags of atmosphere. The approach and traversing nature of the route described calls for a competent team as a fall by the leader or second could end in space above the sea. This is a useful non-tidal line that can also be approached via a pleasant walk from Bosigran.

Approach - Continue along the coast path past Carn Gloose towards the next headland. 150m past a stile in a stone wall, a good small path heads right to the headland itself and Robin's Rocks. Walk down to the headland and cross a massive chasm via a convenient boulder bridge to the top of the buttress.

Afternoon 25 min

② **Sensible Shoes . . .** **VS 4c**
A fine mini-adventure that requires competence from both leader and second. A chance to sample the ambience of *Astral Stroll* at a lesser level of difficulty. Start by abseiling 5m down a crack in a corner to a foothold stance next to an undercut slab on the right. *Photo on page 186*.
30m. Move onto the slab and make a difficult move up and out right onto the next slab, crux. Traverse right and then move under an overhang and across a bottomless corner to another slab. Move rightwards up the slab to the edge of the chasm. Climb the arete and left-slanting groove to the top.
FA. Pete O'Sullivan, Cathy Woodhead 25.9.1978

Chasm

Avon Somerset | North Devon | Culm Coast | Inland Cornwall | Atlantic Coast | West Penwith | The Lizard | Inland Devon | Torbay | Dorset

	No star	☆1☆	☆2☆	☆3☆
Mod to S	-	3	6	2
HS to HVS	-	1	6	4
E1 to E3	-	1	5	5
E4 and up	-	-	-	1

Bosigran is where many climbers get their first taste of Cornish granite and is perhaps the West Country's best known sea cliff. Bosigran's reputation for superb routes on perfect rock has been widely publicised and the cliff has been at the heart of developments on Cornwall's granite throughout the decades since its first climbs were established early in the 20th century. The position of the cliff is majestic, projecting out into the sea above a remote and rocky cove, and for the most part its base is high above the sea. The cliffs elevation makes it a reliable venue to get something done if the tides are not ideal for accessing other cliffs, or the sea is rough. The routes are simply stunning, predominantly multi-pitch and will interest those looking for long, lower and mid-grade climbs.

Approach   See main area map on page 187

Take the B3306 St Ives - Pendeen road to the prominent ruined mine buildings of Carn Galver and park in the National Trust car park adjacent to them. Follow the path that heads seaward, initially through bushes and then fields, and over a couple of granite stiles. The path from Carn Galver mine meets the coast path at some remains of old buildings (5 minutes). From this viewpoint, the jagged crest of Commando Ridge is easily seen to the left and the outline of the emerging Bosigran Main Cliff is ahead. Details of the approaches to each of the various areas are given at the start of their respective sections.

Tides

Bosigran Main Cliff is completely non-tidal except for the Lower Cliff. The Lower Cliff is non-tidal in calm seas, but in heavy seas great care must be exercised as the base becomes sea-washed.

Conditions

The conditions at Bosigran are, on the whole, a delight and you can often climb here when other crags are 'out' due to tides or rough seas. The Main Cliff gets the afternoon sun, and dries pretty quickly after rain. Seepage does occur after prolonged rainfall and the rock can be very slick in the morning, before the sun has crept around. There is little shelter from sun, wind or rain though if required.

Side tabs: Avon Somerset | North Devon | Culm Coast | Inland Cornwall | Atlantic Coast | West Penwith | The Lizard | Inland Devon | Torbay | Dorset

Carn Galver mine ruins

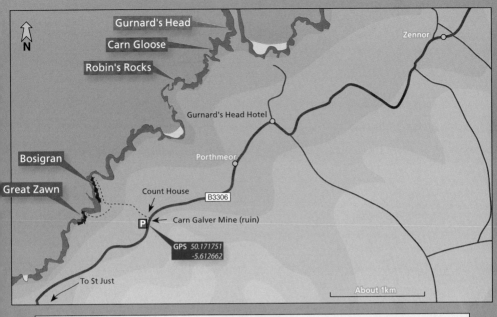

Avon Somerset · North Devon · Culm Coast · Inland Cornwall · Atlantic Coast · West Penwith · The Lizard · Inland Devon · Torbay · Dorset

Main Cliff

The Main Cliff at Bosigran is complex in its layout but access along its base is fairly straightforward.

Approach - From the point where the approach path from the parking reaches the coast path, walk straight ahead over rocky ground until the path becomes more distinct and exposed once under the cliff itself.

Descent - There are three normal descent routes which are shown on the overview below.

Avon Somerset | North Devon | Culm Coast | Inland Cornwall | Atlantic Coast | West Penwith | The Lizard | Inland Devon | Torbay | Dorset

① Ochre Slab Route II. . . . S 4a

Delightful climbing on fabulous rock. One of the better Severes at Bosigran. Start on a high, flat ledge left of *Black Slab*.

1) 4a, 23m. Move up a corner on the left side of the slab and swing out left at the overhang on big holds. Climb up to a small overlap and move right and up onto the slab that leads up to the large overhang. Move right to belay.

2) 4a, 9m. Make some fingery moves up the wall left of the large overhang and follow cracks leftwards to finish.

② Ochre Slab Route I . HVS 5a

A popular and rewarding climb that consists of two totally contrasting pitches; the first technical and the second super steep. Start on a high flat ledge left of *Black Slab*.

1) 4c, 24m. Pull onto the slab. Climb rightwards to its edge and move up to where it meets the steep wall above. Make technical moves up and right to a black vein and follow this more easily, moving right after 5m, to a belay below the overhanging corner at the right-hand end of the large overhang.

2) 5a, 8m. Climb the overhanging corner, perplexing but well-protected, and pull over the lip on massive holds to easier ground. A wild pitch.

FA. Trevor Peck, Peter Biven 3.1956

③ Black Slab . . . . Diff

A beautifully-situated first pitch that takes on the left edge of the prominent black slab in the centre of the cliff. Start directly below a large spike at 8m.

1) 26m. Climb up cracks on the right side of the large spike and stand on its top. Pull onto the base of the black slab and climb it on plentiful holds just to the right of the blunt arete. Belay below the right-hand end of the large overhang.

2) 17m. Traverse the foot ledge beneath the large overhang leftwards to a grassy bay and finish up the wide, easy-angled gully.

FA. Colin Kirkus, P.Fallows 3.8.1938

Lower Cliff

Approach - Follow the path under the Main Cliff until just beyond the difficult step-down where a narrow path forks off the main path, down and left to the base of the lower cliff.

Descent - A wide, low-angled gully runs down to the left (facing out) of the Lower Cliff. Either downclimb or abseil down this to pick up the approach path, or walk along the top of the Main Cliff all the way to the descents at its far end.

Tides - The base of the cliff is not tidal but care must be taken during heavy seas.

Conditions - The Lower Cliff is generally more exposed to the wind than the other sections of the Main Cliff.

④ Ding . . . . VS 4c

Deceptively steep climbing with some exciting moments. Start at the base of a dark right to left-trending vein of rock with a small grassy hollow in it at 7m.

1) 4c, 22m. Climb up from the vein to gain the overhang capped recess just right of a short right-facing corner. Pull up past the overhang's right end and climb flakes and cracks to a ledge and belay next to a big pinnacle.

2) 4b, 20m. Move up cracks on the left of the pinnacle before breaking out left and continuing on up through the final overhangs.

FA. John Deacon, B.Grey, Mike Banks 14.4.1957

⑤ Dong. . . . . S 4b

A pleasant route with some good climbing on its top two pitches. Start below a small left-facing corner on the first section of cliff reached on the approach.

1) 10m. Move up past a large block to the small left-facing corner and climb it to a grass fringed ledge and belay.

2) 4a, 11m. Just above the right-hand end of the overhang above, make an exposed traverse left, before climbing the steep wall to a ledge and belay on the right side of a large pinnacle.

3) 4b, 18m. Climb up the wide crack to the top of the pinnacle and gain a ledge above it by a cramped mantleshelf move. Move right and up to finish.

FA. Mike Banks, B.Grey, John Deacon 14.4.1957

Descent (Sea Gully)

Approach

Avon Somerset

North Devon

Culm Coast

Inland Cornwall

Atlantic Coast

West Penwith

The Lizard

Inland Devon

Torbay

Dorset

Paul Cox pauses prior to tackling the crux crack of *Thin Wall Special* (E1 5b) - *page 206* - on the Main Cliff at Bosigran.

Avon Somerset
North Devon
Culm Coast
Inland Cornwall
Atlantic Coast
West Penwith
The Lizard
Inland Devon
Torbay
Dorset

Kafoozalem Area

A fabulous, secluded bay of immaculate rock architecture and the prime spot at Bosigran for single-pitch extremes. The routes take strong lines that are much steeper than they appear.

Approach - Follow the path below the Main Cliff past the difficult step-down and continue until the path climbs up a short way into a lovely flat bay with a large grassy base.

Descent - Walk off down to the left and descend Sea Gully via a downclimb or abseil back to the base of the climbs.

Tides - The area is non-tidal.

Conditions - This section of crag is a real suntrap and can become extremely hot once the sun has come around onto it. The climbs can retain dampness and also seep after prolonged rainfall.

❶ The Armchair . . **HVS 5a**

The huge left-leaning corner is a fantastic line. The initial wall is hard and committing. Start on a block at the left side of a black wall that leads up into the base of the corner.

36m. From the block, step onto the black wall and climb it on diminishing holds to eventually enter the base of the main corner. Climb the excellent corner-line all the way to an easing near the top and finish up the steep black corner on good holds. This pitch can easily be split at a good stance (the 'Armchair') midway up the main corner.

FA. John Smoker 3.8.1958

❷ Beaker Route . . . . **HVS 5a**

Sections of good climbing on a snaking line up the slab to the left of the corner of *The Armchair*. Start at a layback crack directly under the corner of *The Armchair*.

1) 5a, 14m. Climb the layback crack with conviction and make tricky moves left and up into the base of the corner. Traverse left to ledges and belay.

2) 4c, 15m. Climb the slabby wall leftwards, and then up to a belay on a grassy ledge.

3) 4a, 15m. Traverse 10m rightwards to a steep black corner and finish up this on good holds.

FA. Hamish Nichol, R.Brooke 5.1955

❸ Kafoozalem . . . . . . Top 50 **E3 6a**

Immaculate climbing on golden rock taking a thin crack up the middle of the central shield. Start at a small corner right of the main faultline of *The Armchair*.

38m. Climb the small, technical corner to the bulges and hand traverse up right to beneath the crack-line. Enter the crack from the right with difficulty and make sustained moves up it until a weakness on the left runs up left to a grassy ledge. Climb the still tricky layback crack above the ledge to the top.

FAA. Frank Cannings, P. Badcock 28.6.1964
FFA. Jim Moran, D.Banks 27.6.1977

❹ Evil Eye **E5 6b**

High standard climbing centred on the narrow tapering corner right of *Kafoozalem's* crack-line. Start at a huge spike of rock.

35m. Gain a flat ledge under a severely overhanging corner from either the left or right and climb it to a junction with *Kafoozalem*. Climb the narrow corner to its end and pull right with difficulty to less steep ground. Move up to an overhang, pull around this and take the wall above to a ledge and finish leftwards.

FA. Pat Littlejohn, Chris King 16.6.1978

Descent

Routes 4 - 6 on facing page

5 **Raven Wall** E3 5c
The large, overhanging corner is one of Bosigran's most coveted Extreme testpieces. It stays damp a lot longer than most of the other routes. Start 5m right of the large spike at a corner.
36m. Climb the corner to an overhang and pass it on the left. Move up to the main corner and make technical moves up it to an overhang. Steep climbing past the overhang is rewarded by better holds on the right wall that enable a swing right out onto the arete and a rest. Move back into the corner and follow it to its end and the top just above. *Photo on page 22*.
FAA. John Deacon, Rawdon Goodier 19.9.1955
FFA. Pat Littlejohn 1977

6 **Grendel** E2 5c
Raven Wall's smaller twin is also a fine climb, and like many of the lines hereabouts is far steeper and longer than first appearances might suggest. Start 5m right of the large spike as for *Raven Wall*.
36m. Climb the corner to the overhang and take the crack on its right up to the base of the steep leaning corner. Make tenuous moves up the slabby left wall of the corner to its top and swing right to a ledge. Move left and finish up the black vein above.
FAA. Mike McDermottt, Iain Peters 30.6.1966
FFA. Pat Littlejohn, Frank Cannings 5.1971

7 **Patience** E3 5c
A good route that rises to a climax in its upper corner. Start at a wide chimney at the right-hand end of the ledge.
36m. Climb the chimney and then move out onto its left wall. Work up leftwards to join the right-trending crack-line. Climb the crack-line to its end below a steep groove. Make some hard moves to enter and move up the groove. Easier ground above leads to the top.
FAA. Trevor Peck, Barrie Biven 15.6.1957
FFA. Pat Littlejohn, Charles Wand-Tetley 8.1970

Avon Somerset
North Devon
Culm Coast
Inland Cornwall
Atlantic Coast
West Penwith
The Lizard
Inland Devon
Torbay
Dorset

Avon Somerset

North Devon

Culm Coast

Inland Cornwall

Atlantic Coast

West Penwith

The Lizard

Inland Devon

Torbay

Dorset

Suicide Wall Area

The massive, black streaked wall left of the main face's upper overhangs is split by some prominent horizontal breaks. Linking these breaks are some of Cornwall's best and most popular multi-pitch routes.

Approach - Follow the path under the main cliff until it drops down below the wall to reach the top of the awkward step-down in the path.

Descent - Walk to descents on the left or right.

Tides - The area is non-tidal.

Conditions - This section of crag is very exposed and catches the wind.

Awkward step in path

1

2

3

4

5

6

7

① Zig Zag . . . . VS 4c

A steep and strong line that links some prominent features on the left-hand side of the main cliff. Start a short distance left of the awkward step-down in the path, right of a black corner.
1) 4b, 10m. Climb the wall and cracks just right of the black corner's right arete to a belay at a huge spike. A good steep pitch on positive holds. The black corner itself is an alternative at 4c.
2) 4c, 23m. Move up the blocks to a ledge, step right and climb a steep black vein to a ledge on the right below a large overhang.
3) 4c, 26m. From the left end of the ledge climb up left of the overhang and move up to a crack that runs back rightwards. Near the top of the crack make a final puzzling move to easier ground that leads left to the top.
FA. Jim Cortlandt-Simpson, R.G Higgins, Keith Lawder 9.1948

② Autumn Flakes . . . . HS 4b

Energetic lower moves lead the way to a superbly airy top pitch that requires careful route finding. Start just right of the awkward step-down in the path at a left-slanting hand-crack.
1) 4a, 8m. Nip up the crack to a large grassy ledge with a big flake on it.
2) 4a, 20m. Strenuously climb the flake and pull onto another ledge. More flakes lead up and rightwards before a step right gains a small foot-ledge and various belays at the top of the reddish rake and just beneath a long black vein and weakness that runs up leftward. This is just above the larger ledge of the *Nameless* belay at the top of its first pitch.
3) 4b, 28m. Move up above the black diagonal vein to a good runner and step leftwards with feet just above the vein to an easing in a scoop. Finish via much easier climbing along the diagonal break.
FA. Rawdon Goodier, P.Henry 3.9.1955

③ Paragon. . . . . HVS 5a

A popular, intricate and sustained climb that visits some of the trickier sections of the crag bypassed by the well-trodden VSs. Start below a series of narrow corners just left of a huge flake at the base of the wall.
1) 5a, 26m. Move up cracks to a ledge and make a committing move up right into another small corner. Climb this, and its continuation to a belay at the junction with the red band of rock that crosses the face.
2) 4c, 23m. Traverse right for around 8m to a steep groove. Climb the groove past a black stained hole and an overlap just above to a flake that leads left under an overhang to a slabby bay and a belay at its left-hand side.
3) 5a, 12m. Move back right to the bottom of a wide, rounded flake-crack. Climb the crack strenuously to where it eases and move right to a belay below a leaning corner.
4) 5a, 15m. Climb the leaning corner which is hard but well-protected, to a welcome jug on the left. The top is not far above.
FA. Peter Biven, Trevor Peck 24.5.1956

④ Nameless . . . . VS 4c

A memorable climb, its two upper pitches especially containing some great climbing. They are split by an exposed belay. Start at the base of the reddish left-slanting rake.
1) 26m. Climb pleasantly up the rake to a small ledge where it steepens.
2) 4b, 12m. Step up and then pull up right on good holds to a small slanting overhang and make a tricky move past it to a good ledge. Move up the wall into a slabby bay and traverse left to good wire belays in a crack. A great stance.
3) 4c, 20m. Climb the technical crack and corner above to finish.
FA. Dennis Kemp, Nea Morin 2.5.1953

⑤ Beowolf. E2 5c

A shy classic that features some precarious, technical groove climbing on immaculate rock. Start at the base of the reddish left-slanting rake.
1) 4c, 29m. Follow the reddish rake for a few metres before branching up right to enter the base of a large overhang niche. Climb up the back of the niche and make a trying traverse right to easier ground and block-belays. An awkward pitch.
2) 5c, 20m. Traverse left along the top of the overhung niche past a back streak and pull into a slim groove. Climb the technical groove past a peg to a ledge and then make more hard moves left and up another groove to a belay ledge.
3) 5c, 20m. From the left-hand end of the belay ledge climb leftwards with difficulty to easier-angled ground and finish up cracks and grooves.
FA. Peter Biven, Trevor Peck 3.6.1966
FFA Phil Gordon 1960's

⑥ Suicide Wall E1 5c

A legendary Cornish classic that traces an exposed line across the blankest section of Bosigran's Main Face. Start at an easy-angled line of weakness that runs up rightwards to beneath a black wall known as the Coal Face.
1) 25m. Follow the weakness to a belay under the Coal Face.
2) 4b, 14m. Move up the corner right of the Coal Face to the start of a thin diagonal crack that runs up left across the Coal Face. Climb the crack to a large block on the arete and belay - the Pedestal stance.
3) 5a, 15m. Follow flakes leftwards across the wall above the Pedestal and move up to a wide break and good cams. Traverse the break left a short way until it is possible to gain a small ledge and belay below a smooth groove.
4) 5c, 9m. Some very hard but well-protected moves start the groove which then eases just before a belay ledge is reached a short distance above.
5) 4b, 15m. Move up the leaning corner above the belay for a few metres before swinging rightwards on good holds out of the corner to easier climbing and the top. Climbing the leaning corner directly is the strenuous top pitch of *Paragon* 5a.
FA. Peter Biven, Trevor Peck, Barrie Biven 8.8.1955

⑦ The Ghost E3 5b

Wildly exposed moves in an outrageous location mark out the top pitch of this intimidating line. Start at an easy-angled line of weakness that runs up rightwards to beneath a black wall known as the Coal Face.
1) 5a, 30m. Follow the line of weakness rightwards for around 10m until a direct line can be taken past a groove, ledge and corner to a stance on the arete at a large block – the Pedestal stance. The left arete of 'The Coal Face' can also be climbed to the stance and belay, at the same grade.
2) 5b, 28m. Climb up a thin crack in the Coal Face to the first overhangs. Traverse left and move up a groove to a slab that leads to below the upper overhangs. Make committing and very exposed moves out rightwards past an old peg to a sudden easing and a stance above.
3) 10m. The easy wall above to the top.
FAA. Peter Biven, Trevor Peck 26.8.1956
FFA. Ed Drummond, Tom Proctor 20.4.1973

Avon Somerset | North Devon | Culm Coast | Inland Cornwall | Atlantic Coast | West Penwith | The Lizard | Inland Devon | Torbay | Dorset

Avon Somerset · North Devon · Culm Coast · Inland Cornwall · Atlantic Coast · West Penwith · The Lizard · Inland Devon · Torbay · Dorset

Bow Wall Area

The centrepiece of Bosigran is packed with classics to suit most tastes and abilities. This section of the crag and its neighbour, the Suicide Wall Area have the rare accolade of being host to routes in Classic, Hard and Extreme Rock.

Approach - Follow the path below the Main Cliff past the low-angled arete of *Alison Rib* to below the section of the Main Cliff that at first appears to be a huge arete. The leaning golden brown wall of *Bow Wall* is on the left and to its right are the lines of *Doorpost* and *Little Brown Jug*.

Descent - Walk off to the right (facing in) and descend either the steep Simon Gully that leads down between the Anvil Chorus and Alison Rib areas and splits midway down and requires some tricky and exposed scrambling, or walk further along the cliff-top and descend easier slopes beyond the Alison Rib Area.

Tides - The area is non-tidal.

Conditions - The climbs can retain dampness and seep after prolonged rainfall.

❶ Bow Wall . . . . [Top 50] E2 5b

Bosigran's most celebrated Extreme, and one of its most exciting. Start by scrambling up a corner and crack to a stance under the leaning light brown wall.

1) 5b, 26m. Follow a line of surprisingly good holds out rightwards across the impressive wall to a small spike. Continue up a crack, past a horizontal crack with what looks like a pancake of rock sandwiched in it, to a traverse-line slightly higher. Strenuous moves rightwards lead immediately into more technical ground that gains a cramped slab under an overhang. Move right and pull through the overhang to a belay just above.

2) 5b, 26m. Make an exposed traverse left along the lip of the overhang to meet a diagonal break that leads more easily back rightwards to the top of the crag.

FA. Joe Brown 7.1957

❷ Doorpost . . . . [Top 50] HS 4b

The major Bosigran classic that combines superb rock, climbing and position in about equal measures. Start at a broken corner below the leaning brown wall capped with overhangs.

1) 4a, 27m. Scramble up the broken corner past a block to a point at which a diagonal break leads up rightwards under the leaning brown wall. Follow the diagonal break all the way to a belay on a ledge at its end. This pitch can seep after rain.

2) 4b, 15m. Climb twin cracks on the left, at first using the left one and then the right to another good ledge and belay.

3) 4a, 25m. Move out left and follow cracks and huge holds up the left wall of the corner, finishing just left of the capping overhangs.

FA. Barrie Biven, Trevor Peck, Pete Biven 7.8.1955

❸ Thin Wall Special E1 5b

A popular Extreme, which has a particularly attractive first pitch that is often climbed in its own right. Start below a diagonal black seam at a finger ledge above a low horizontal break. *Photo on page 201.*

1) 5b, 26m. Move up to, and stand on the finger ledge. Follow the thin line leftwards up to a small overhang and continue up the technical crack to an easing below the steep wall above. Follow the diagonal line rightwards to a belay on a ledge.

2) 11m. Continue up easily to a good ledge and belay below the huge upper corner.

3) 5a, 28m. Climb the corner all the way to the capping roofs and exit right via some very spectacular moves.

FA. Pete Biven, Trevor Peck 26.5.1956 (1pt)

❹ Little Brown Jug . . . VS 5a

An exquisite climb that culminates in a breathtaking finale at the very top of the crag. Start just right of a low, overhung niche.

1) 4b, 22m. Take the line of left-trending flakes to a small corner groove and climb this to a ledge and good belay. The pitch can be climbed direct, passing the overhung niche on its right at HVS 5a.

2) 4a, 14m. On the right is a blank-looking slab, climb the slab rightwards on good small holds to a huge flake. Scramble behind it to a good ledge and belay on its opposite side.

3) 5a, 30m. Move up big ledges to where the rock steepens. Climb steep cracks heading for a black stain in an overlap above. Pull over the overlap, peg, and then step left before climbing up slightly right to easier territory. Layback up the exposed, leaning cracks in the headwall to finish.

FA. Pete Biven, Barrie Biven 21.8.1955

❺ Visions of Johanna E1 5b

A much-talked-about first pitch is followed by easier but still worthwhile climbing. E1 if you don't fall off! Start just to the left of the right edge of the wall.

1) 5b, 23m. Climb to below a small overhang and make a couple of committing moves up to, and then past it on the right (small wires). Continue directly up the lovely wall to a belay on a good ledge next to a huge flake.

2) 5a, 35m. Move up big ledges to where the rock steepens. Climb steep cracks heading for a black stain in an overlap above. Pull over the overlap, peg, and then step left. Move leftwards once again up a slab to the base of a chimney. Climb the chimney exiting onto easy ground, the top is not far above.

FA. Mark Springett, Frank Cannings, Pete Biven 13.4.1968

The Coal
Face

①

Suicide Wall –
previous page

Approach scramble

②   ③   ④   ⑤

Avon Somerset

North Devon

Culm Coast

Inland Cornwall

Atlantic Coast

West Penwith

The Lizard

Inland Devon

Torbay

Dorset

Afternoon 10 min

Descent

Little Brown Jug - previous page

6

7

8

9

10

❻ Doorway .... S 4a

A huge corner high up on the face provides the meat of this varied line that has both technical and strenuous sections. Start at a small left-trending ramp 3m left of a corner groove.
1) 4a, 22m. Follow the ramp past an overhanging section to a stance and belay on a good ledge next to a massive flake.
2) 10m. Scramble left behind the massive flake and continue traversing to a stance on a ledge below the huge corner.
3) 4a, 28m. Climb up slightly left to below the corner proper and follow it past an awkward section to the roof. Traverse left to clear the roof and finish easily.
FA. Jim Simpson, W.Hutchinson 1949

❼ Venusberg ...... VS 4c

Disjointed but technically one of the more testing VSs at Bosigran and also slightly runout on its main pitch. Start at the base of the low-angled corner groove.
1) 4a, 11m. Move up the corner until a flake-crack on the right wall can be gained. Climb the flake-crack to a mantleshelf next to a thorny bush and a good belay below a pinnacle just above.
2) 4b, 12m. Chimney up the left side of the pinnacle and from its top move left to a narrow slanting corner. Technical moves up this quickly lead to a large belay ledge.
3) 6m. Walk left along a narrow grassy ledge to a belay below a thin black seam.
4) 4c, 13m. Climb up to the base of the black seam. Hard moves followed by a short runout are rewarded with a rest out to the left before some awkward moves up and right gain a restricted belay in a corner under a roof.
5) 4b, 9m. Move up the corner and pass the roof with dificulty before a black vein on the left can be used to finish.
FA. Pete Biven, Cliff Fishwick 30.4.1961

❽ Anvil Chorus .... VS 4c

A string of superb and intense pitches make up for the rather wandering line. High in the grade. Start at a thin line of weakness in the wall just right of the low-angled corner groove.
1) 4b, 10m. Climb the wall and thin cracks directly to a tricky exit onto a large belay ledge next to a thorny bush.
2) 4b, 12m. Take a good crack in a corner to a roof at its top and pull around this on the right to another good belay ledge.
3) 6m. Walk left along a narrow grassy ledge to a belay below a thin black seam, as for *Venusburg.*
4) 4c, 18m. Move up right to the base of a steep corner and climb this with difficulty to a horizontal break that can be followed rightwards across the wall to a belay on its edge.
5) 4b, 8m. Move up left to a break and climb the thin crack above to finish.
FA. Pete Biven, Trevor Peck, Barrie Biven 19.5.1956

Anvil Chorus Area

A very popular section of the Main Cliff that has a handful of long and testing climbs that, although slightly wandering, are nevertheless packed with a vast amount of brilliant and exposed climbing. The majority of the climbs have accommodating belay ledges.
Approach - Follow the path below the Main Cliff past the low-angled arete of *Alison Rib* to below the first section of the Main Cliff proper. The most obvious feature at the base of the crag is a low-angled left-slanting corner groove up which *Venusburg* starts.
Descent - Walk off to the right and descend either the steep gully that leads down between the Anvil Chorus and Alison Rib areas which splits midway down and requires some tricky and exposed scrambling, or walk further along the cliff-top and descend easier slopes beyond the Alison Rib Area.
Tides - The area is non-tidal.
Conditions - The climbs can retain dampness and seep after prolonged rainfall.

❾ Ledge Climb .... HVD

A complex line, varied climbing and increasingly exposed positions combine to give Bosigran its best VDiff. Start at a wide crack.
1) 16m. Climb the well-protected but awkward crack to a good ledge and belay.
2) 22m. Traverse easily left and then up and leftwards to a steep wall. Climb the wall to a good ledge and belay directly under a flared chimney.
3) 35m. Enter the chimney with difficulty and follow it until a long, gently rising ledge can be viewed on the left. Follow the ledge in a very exposed position to easy rocks and the top. This pitch can be split at the end of the chimney.
FA. Arthur Andrews, Elise Andrews 1905

❿ Andrew .... S 4a

Well positioned, although escapable climbing that takes on the full-height of the main face. The top pitch has been upgraded to Severe from its traditional grade of HVD. Start just to the right of a boot-wide crack.
1) 15m. Climb the slab just right of the crack to some big flakes. Climb these to a belay ledge that runs rightwards into Simon Gully.
2) 14m. Traverse right to a crack 1m left of the gully and climb this, and its left wall, to slabby ground. The awkward corner left of the crack can also be climbed, but is harder. Climb leftwards to a belay platform on the arete.
3) 10m. Above is an arete with a crack on its left. Gain the crack from the right, tricky, and follow it to below the leaning wall and arete above. Move right, around the base of the arete and up to a stance at the base of a steep chimney/corner.
4) 4a,13m. A wild pitch. Bridge up the steep corner/chimney which eases after 5m. Continue on better holds to easier ground and the top.
FA. Pete Biven, Trevor Peck, J.Andrew 13.9.1958

Avon Somerset | North Devon | Culm Coast | Inland Cornwall | Atlantic Coast | West Penwith | The Lizard | Inland Devon | Torbay | Dorset

Alison Rib Area

The first section of the Main Cliff is home to a handful of very popular climbs in the lower grades. The rock is off-vertical but at times the gear is a little spaced.

Approach - Follow the approach path to the Main Cliff past some boulders to arrive at the base of the low-angled arete of *Alison Rib*.

Descent - The easiest and safest way to descend is by walking off to the right (facing in) from all the routes (including the second pitch of *Alison Rib*) and descend the slope back to the approach path. The descent to the left requires some exposed scrambling.

Tides - The area is non-tidal.

Conditions - The climbs can retain dampness and seep after prolonged rainfall.

❶ Big Top . . . . VDiff

An easily-missed pitch that is well worth seeking out. Start at a crack on the front of the buttress just right of some ivy.

25m. Climb the crack and continue up a thinner one on the right to below the overhang - the 'Big Top'. Move right below it and climb a ramp to easy ground and a belay. There are a number of possible variations on the lower section of the route.

FA. Cliff Fishwick, Trevor Peck 31.5.1958

❷ Oread . . . . HVD

Technical climbing up a broad rib that is furnished with good but spaced protection. Start at the base of a low-angled rib just left of the open corner of *In-Between*.

33m. Climb the rib to a steeper wall at 9m, make a fingery pull up the wall to better holds and continue to a sloping ledge. Quit the ledge via cracks on the left and proceed more easily to the top.

FA. P.Jaynes, E.Byne 5.8.1955

❸ In-Between . . . . VDiff

An excellent line with plenty of good moves. Start at the base of the open corner 4m left of *Alison Rib*.

33m. Bridge up the corner to an overhang at 16m. Move left and then back right above the overhang to a ledge. Move awkwardly up a crack on the left to another ledge and then work back rightwards to join and follow *Alison Rib* to finish.

FA. Pete Biven, R.Woodman, Cliff Fishwick 12.10.1963

❹ Kate . . . . VDiff

Intimidating, but in practice a steady and rewarding pitch that provides a good alternative start to *Alison Rib*. Start just to the right of the open corner of *In-Between* at a low hanging rib of knobbly rock.

33m. Climb the hanging rib of knobbly rock - starting on its left or right - to the base of a steep wall at 8m. Climb the wall using a good crack to an easing at its top. Move up to an open groove and follow this pleasantly to join up with *Alison Rib* which is followed to the top.

FA. Cliff Fishwick, R.Mavin 9.3.1963

❺ Alison Rib . . . . Diff

The often-occupied low-angled arete of exquisite granite is the best introduction to the easier routes at Bosigran. Start at the base of the arete.

1) 22m. Climb up the steep right-hand side of the arete on generous holds for 5m and then, as the angle eases, step left on to the arete itself and follow it to a stance and spike belay.

2) 18m. Continue up the arete to a terrace and various belays.

3) 19m. Move to the back of the bay and climb steep cracks to the top.

FA. Donald Romanis 1923

Ledge Climb
- previous pag

Afternoon | 10 min

Descent

Descent

Descent

Descent

Descent

Avon Somerset
North Devon
Culm Coast
Inland Cornwall
Atlantic Coast
West Penwith
The Lizard
Inland Devon
Torbay
Dorset

	No star	⚜	⚜	⚜
Mod to S	-	-	-	1
HS to HVS	-	-	1	-
E1 to E3	-	-	2	2
E4 and up	-	-	-	2

The alpine-like jagged arete of Bosigran Ridge, which dominates the foreground of the view from Bosigran itself, is a classic Cornish expedition. The ridge's setting, diverse climbing and length mark it out as one of the region's most famous climbs and should not be missed. In contrast to the open aspect of Bosigran Ridge is the deeply-incised dramatic gash of the Great Zawn, hidden only a short distance away from the ridge, but offering a very different experience in terms of both atmosphere and difficulty.

Approach   Area map page 199

Take the B3306 St Ives - Pendeen road to the prominent ruined mine buildings of Carn Galver and park in the National Trust car park. Follow the path that heads seaward, initially through bushes and then fields and over a couple of granite stiles. The path meets the coast path at some ruins. From this viewpoint the jagged crest of Bosigran Ridge is easily seen to the left. Cross the stream by the ruins and head across boggy ground to meet the ridge where a memorial plaque is bolted to the rock. This is the best place to gear up for

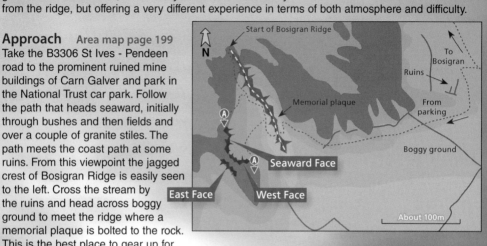

Bosigran Ridge and the starting point for the descent to the base of Bosigran Ridge and the Great Zawn. For both Bosigran Ridge and the Great Zawn, cross the ridge (up slope of the pinnacle with the memorial plaque) via a scramble to meet a narrow path on its opposite side. The descent and approaches are described in the relevant sections from this point.

Tides

The start of Bosigran Ridge is only accessible at lowish tides and in calm conditions. Great Zawn is a non-tidal venue, although in rough seas the base of the routes at the zawn's mouth will become wave-washed.

Conditions

Bosigran Ridge dries very quickly and is exposed to any sun that is going. Parts of the outer edges of the Great Zawn see the sun in the afternoon but the inner confines see little sun and take time to dry out after rain. In heavy seas the bases of both Bosigran Ridge and Great Zawn are wave-washed.

Avon Somerset | North Devon | Culm Coast | Inland Cornwall | Atlantic Coast | West Penwith | The Lizard | Inland Devon | Torbay | Dorset

Avon Somerset

North Devon

Culm Coast

Inland Cornwall

Atlantic Coast

West Penwith

The Lizard

Inland Devon

Torbay

Dorset

Ashley Lewis poised above the crux-roof of the magnificent
The Dream/Liberator (E3 6a) - *page 217* - in the atmospheric
Great Zawn at Bosigran. Photo: Virgil Scott

Avon Somerset
North Devon
Culm Coast
Inland Cornwall
Atlantic Coast
West Penwith
The Lizard
Inland Devon
Torbay
Dorset

Bosigran Ridge

The majestic, serrated *Bosigran Ridge* (often called *Commando Ridge*) is one of the longest routes in the West Country, that combines sustained climbing with great rock, airy positions and expansive views.

Approach - Just before the ruined building remains on the approach from the parking, head left towards the ridge across some boggy ground and gain a gearing-up ledge just up and left from a memorial plaque on the face of the ridge itself. Cross the ridge at the col via a short downclimb on its opposite side and follow a path down hill next to the ridge until steeper ground requires a steep downclimb or abseil from insitu slings. Continue down to sea level ledges and traverse smooth rock and ledges around the base of the ridge to a belay ledge.

Tides - The base of the ridge is only reachable at lowish tides and in calm conditions. Great care must be taken to judge whether it is safe to traverse around the base of the ridge to the start.

Conditions - The climb dries quickly and the ridge itself gets the sun all day. The ridge is very exposed to the wind.

Passing through the gap at the end of the 4th pitch of *Bosigran Ridge* (VDiff) - *opposite* .

Point at which the ridge is crossed on the descent

Memorial plaque

Perched block

Avon Somerset | North Devon | Culm Coast | Inland Cornwall | Atlantic Coast | West Penwith | The Lizard | Inland Devon | Torbay | Dorset

1 Bosigran Ridge ...... Top 50   VDiff

Continuously excellent climbing, brilliant rock, exhilarating situations and a stunning location make this the very best VDiff in the West Country. Although protection is always at hand, the exposure, sections of downclimbing and the traversing nature of the route call for all party members to be competent at the grade. Slings are very useful. Start at a belay ledge just before the arete.

1) 25m. Move left around the arete to a ramp above the zawn. Move along to a corner at the end of the ramp. Climb the wall on its left on good holds, left and then back slightly right, to beneath a vertical crack. Climb the crack on superb holds to a belay on the ridge.

Neb

Chimney and 3rd belay hidden

2) 10m. Move along the easy-angled ridge to a belay at the base of an open corner that forms a chimney at its top.

3) 18m. Climb the corner and chimney to a belay under a protruding neb.

4) 16m. Move up left to beneath the neb, and then make a traverse left through a large gap and climb down to a belay at a col.

5) 17m. Move up the ridge to where it steepens and move left to a traverse line. Follow the traverse line for about 5m and then climb a short corner up onto the ridge. Move along the ridge to a belay on its summit.

6) 30m. Downclimb a corner on the right of the ridge (when looking up the ridge) and then scramble along easy ground to a belay in the next col.

7) 25m. Move up the ridge to a perched block and traverse the foot ledge on its right. Descend awkwardly to a belay in the col.

8) 20m. Make a tricky move onto the right side of the pinnacle (this is the large pinnacle with the memorial plaque on it). Climb the face and ridge all the way to finish at the point where the ridge is crossed at the start of the descent.

9) VS 4b (optional). Another pitch is possible but is much tougher than the rest of the climb.

FA. Arthur Andrews, Elise Andrews 1902
FA. Pitch 1 J.B.Bretland, Arthur Andrews 1905

① **Variety Show** . . . . HVS 5a

A fine and friendly introduction to the delights of the Great Zawn, having plenty of atmosphere and outstanding climbing on its first pitch. Start right of the abseil approach at a narrow corner/groove that leads to a thin crack-line in the smooth wall.

1) 5a, 32m. Climb to, and then up the difficult corner/groove to better holds in the crack. Climb the crack to a move right into a small corner, and climb past a horizontal break to a stance.

2) 4b, 25m. Head up right to below a steep corner and climb this to finish on easier ground. Some loose blocks.

FAA. Trevor Peck, Barrie Biven, Cliff Fishwick 25.5.1958
FFA. Pat Littlejohn, Frank Cannings 23.5.1970

② **Green Cormorant Face**. . E2 5c

The front of the Seaward Face is taken centrally by this well-positioned and popular line. Start by negotiating 'The Crevasse' and then traversing 7m to a stance in a small corner.
Photo on page 4.

1) 5a, 20m. Move up steeply leftwards through a small overhang to a flake in the wall above and then on up to a horizontal break. From the horizontal break climb up either on the left or right to a good belay ledge.

2) 5c, 10m. Above the stance is a corner with a thin black crack in its right wall. Gain the crack, either direct, or from a ledge on the left, and climb it to a ledge and belay.

2a) E3 6a, 10m. A good variation up the corner to the left.

3) 4a, 20m. Finish up the groove and broken ground above.
FAA. John Deacon, Mike Banks 21.4.1957
FFA. Frank Cannings, Pat Littlejohn 12.9.1969 (1pt)

Bosigran Ridge

'The Crevasse' jump

Large platform

Sloping ledge

The Seaward Face

A stunning sweep of immaculate granite in a phenomenal setting and with climbing to do it justice.

Approach - Cross Bosigran Ridge and descend the path for around 100m until easy ground on the left can be crossed to a viewpoint of the face. Abseil 15m from here to a large platform. For all routes apart from *Variety Show*, the wide Crevasse must be negotiated via a jump or downclimb.

Tides - Non-tidal but wave-washed in rough seas.

Conditions - The face dries quickly in the afternoon sun.

Avon Somerset | North Devon | Culm Coast | Inland Cornwall | Atlantic Coast | West Penwith | The Lizard | Inland Devon | Torbay | Dorset

❸ Deja Vu . . . . ⬚⬚⬚⬚ **E4 5c**

The upper, thin blank wall of the Seaward Face is overcome by this airy, sweeping line located directly above the narrow strip of blue water at the bed of the zawn. Start by negotiating 'The Crevasse' and then traversing 7m to a stance in a small corner.

1) 5b, 22m. Traverse right, around the arete into another corner and then up a few metres, from where a rising traverse left, back around the arete and across the wall leads to a break. Climb the short corner above to a good belay ledge.

2) 5c, 30m. Traverse right from the belay to below a steep high-angled slab and climb this boldly to an easing at a left-trending shallow ramp-line. Follow this to the overhang above and move to its left end before working back right again above it to cracks that lead to the top.

FA. Henry Barber, Frank Cannings 5.1974

❹ The Dream/Liberator ⬚⬚ **E3 6a**

One of the region's greatest climbs that wends its way up the sensational arete dividing the Seaward and West Faces of the Great Zawn. The climbing is at the very upper limit of the grade. Start by negotiating 'The Crevasse' and then traversing right 7m to a stance in a small corner. *Photo on page 213.*

1) 5a, 9m. Traverse right, around the arete into another corner and ascend this to a stance just above.

2) 6a, 23m. Climb up the corner and then swing right at a horizontal break to below a right-leaning groove. Make some tricky moves up its right wall to below an overhang and pull leftwards through it, hard, to a thin crack in the wall above it. Follow the shallow ramp-line up the wall to a break, and traverse this right,past a peg, to a hanging stance on a foot-ledge just around the arete. The belays are hard to find but there is a good large cam in the crack above the stance.

3) 5c, 32m. Climb the steep cracks and narrowing small corner above until a sensational traverse right, below an overhang, can be made into the base of a long corner and thin crack. Follow this and the continuation groove to the top.

FAA. (The Dream) M.Gulliard, R.Wilson 12.1968
FFA. (The Dream) Pete Livesey 6.1976
FA. (Liberator) Frank Cannings, Pat Littlejohn 24/25.5.1970
FFA. (Liberator) Ron Fawcett, Pete Livesey 4.1976

The next route takes a line up the oppressive, overhang-strewn leaning wall that is taken centrally by a magnificent line of cracks. The base is non-tidal. See the next page for the approach and conditions.

❺ The West Face ⬚⬚⬚ **E5 6b**

The central line of cracks and overhangs gives a stunning line and a powerful, difficult trip up the Great Zawn's most impressive wall. Start on boulders below a corner-crack in the centre of the face.

1) 5c, 20m. Move up the wall and pull through the overhang into the corner-crack. Climb the crack to an overhang and move up right to a stance and belay below the main overhangs.

2) 6b, 23m. Move left to a smooth-walled groove. Climb the difficult groove, peg, to the overhangs and follow the cracks and corners strenuously up through the stepped overhangs to a belay above the difficulties.

3) 12m. Straightforward ground leads to the top.

FFA. Pete Livesey, Jill Lawrence 1975 (1pt)

Avon Somerset | North Devon | Culm Coast | Inland Cornwall | Atlantic Coast | West Penwith | The Lizard | Inland Devon | Torbay | Dorset

Avon Somerset

North Devon

Culm Coast

Inland Cornwall

Atlantic Coast

West Penwith

The Lizard

Inland Devon

Torbay

Dorset

East and Upper West Face

The East Face of Great Zawn is an imposing, dark wall that is not easily viewed from most angles. However, the one route described is a fine climb that is not to be underestimated, being strenuous, technical and slightly bold. A perfect route for a hot summer's day. The Upper West Face has one relatively popular line that is less steep than others in the Great Zawn.

Approach - Cross Bosigran Ridge and descend 50m down the path before breaking left over heather covered rocks to a short step down a corner that gains a grassy gearing-up ledge high above the zawn. Where the ledge narrows is a good rock spike from which an abseil can be made into the zawn. The base of the zawn is composed of grass, unstable rock and earth. Care should be taken when moving over this ground to the base of the climbs.

Tides - The base of the zawn is non-tidal in calm sea conditions.

Conditions - The East Face receives very little sun and can take a long time to dry out. There is usually no real path back to the gearing-up ledge. The upper half of *Desolation Row* gets sun from late morning but the base sees very little sun so can remain damp after rainfall.

❶ Xanadu **E2 5b**

The east facing wall of Great Zawn is carved by an eye-catching left curving corner, which provides the line for this tremendous route. The climbing is remarkably diverse but the line takes some time to dry out. Start below the corner-line on boulders at the mouth of the zawn.

1) 5b, 25m. Climb the corner which is steep and sustained, but takes plenty of gear, to a stance under an overhang.

2) 5b, 20m. Move up and then work leftwards below the overhangs until it is possible to move up to the overhangs from where more leftward traversing gains a belay below a wide crack in the overhang above. A slightly bold and technical pitch.

3) 5b, 10m. Pull up steeply through the overhang and get stuck into the wide crack which is thankfully not too long. A large cam is useful on this pitch. A vague climbers' path sometimes leads through bracken around the head of the zawn back to the top of the abseil and the gearing-up ledge.

FA. Pat Littlejohn, Ian Duckworth 4.1970

This section of the zawn bed, reached via abseil, is very unstable and slippery in damp conditions

Avon Somerset

North Devon

Culm Coast

Inland Cornwall

Atlantic Coast

West Penwith

The Lizard

Inland Devon

Torbay

Dorset

①

To the mouth of the zawn and the lower West Face

②

❷ Desolation Row   **E2 5b**

A prized pitch that is very sustained but can be adequately protected by a very large number of small wires. Take extra quickdraws. Start near the left edge of the Upper West Face where a shallow groove is capped by a small overhang.

40m. Enter the groove from the right and climb to a small overhang. At the small overhang move up and left around the arete. Climb past the right end of a huge roof and then move right with difficulty to join cracks which are followed all the way to the top. Move up steep grass to find a belay.

FA. Frank Cannings, Pat Littlejohn 14.9.1969

	No star	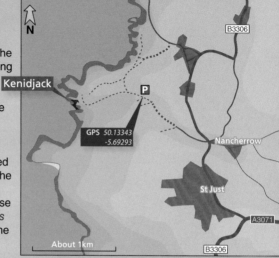 ☆	☆☆	☆☆☆
Mod to S	-	-	-	-
HS to HVS	-	2	-	1
E1 to E3	-	1	1	1
E4 and up	-	-	-	-

Kenidjack's Main Cliff is an impressive sweep of killas slate that glows a golden brown in the sun and has a number of fine and challenging wall climbs that pick their way up the subtly featured face. The rock on the whole is good, although protection is not always close at hand. The base of the crag is sunny, sheltered and non-tidal, making it a good place to head for in windy weather.

Approach   Area map on page 187

From St Just, drive north 0.3 miles to Nancherrow and, at the bottom of a dip in the road, turn left onto a narrow road. Drive along the road until it becomes unsurfaced - ignoring left turns - continue until a slight hill is encountered and a parking bay on the right. Park here (or carefully a little further on). Walk up the track and take the left fork at a junction. Follow the track and footpath until it rounds a bend and two small quarried bays mark the start of the descent. Below the second quarried bay is a rocky ridge which is a good place to gear up. To reach the base of the cliff, abseil down the corner of *Gneiss Gnome* or from a rounded boulder above the finish of *Saxon* (see topo on next page).

GPS 50.13343 -5.69293

Kenidjack

Nancherrow

St Just

About 1km

Tides

The base of the crag is non-tidal, although in extremely rough seas it could become wave-washed.

Conditions

The cliff is very sheltered and gets plenty of sun. It does seep after prolonged rainfall.

Kenidjack

Avon Somerset

North Devon

Culm Coast

Inland Cornwall

Atlantic Coast

West Penwith

The Lizard

Inland Devon

Torbay

Dorset

Inching up the fine wall of *Rock Dancer* (E1 5b) - *page 223* - at Kenidjack, West Penwith. Photo: Dave Johnson.

Kenidjack

Kenidjack is an impressive wall of quartz-flecked killas slate. The cliff has a number of sustained wall climbs on its central section that looks very smooth when viewed from above or below.

Approach - From the gearing-up spot, either scramble carefully down to a notch midway down the side of the cliff and abseil to the bottom of the cliff, or alternatively abseil from a large rounded boulder above the main wall (see topo).

Emma Medara starting out on the classic *Saxon* (HVS 5a) - *opposite*.

1 Gneiss Gnome . . . .   **HS 4a**
The right-leaning corner gives an interesting climb up a strong line. Gulls nest here early in the season. Start at a crack which leads up to the corner proper.
26m. Climb the crack to the overhanging corner and climb it to a belay on the left at a shoulder.
FA. Keith Darbyshire, Pat Littlejohn, 31.12.1971

2 In the Gallery . . . .   **HVS 5a**
A worthwhile pitch that is high in the grade. Start below a very thin crack right of the start of *Gneiss Gnome*.
34m. Climb the crack past a quartz band to a ledge and flake. Move off of the flake and follow a seam and slab to meet a horizontal finger-crack. Finish up the left margin of the slab above and move right to a ledge and flake belay. Scramble off left.
FA. Rowland Edwards, Mark Edwards 20.4.1979

3 Rock Dancer **E1 5b**
An excellent, sustained wall-pitch with good but spaced protection. It is at the upper end of the E1 grade. Start 6m left of the house-sized boulder and just right of a narrow corner above the low overhang.
36m. Make some hard moves through the low overhang to reach the diagonal break. Step left and climb the wall directly to the right end of a short left-slanting hand-ledge. Move up onto it and from its left end move up the wall past wires to a horizontal finger-crack. Finish direct to a flake belay and scramble off left.
FA. Rowland Edwards, Mark Edwards 17.4.1979

4 Saxon . . . .   **HVS 5a**
A tremendous climb that follows a subtle line of weakness up the smooth looking main face. The climb is both intimidating and amenable in equal measures. Start next to the house sized boulder.
36m. Boulder up to the break (either using the crack between the boulder and the wall, or the wall just to the left of the boulder). Move along the break to a niche. Carry on leftwards up a crack until moves straight up gain good holds at the start of a shallow left leading depression. Follow this until a move up reaches a horizontal finger-crack. Move right and climb direct to a flake belay. Scramble off left.
FA. Pat Littlejohn, Steve Jones 31.3.1974
FA. (Direct Finish) Rowland Edwards 2.4.1979

5 The Shield **E1 5a**
A swerving line that finishes boldly up the headwall of the cliff. Start on the huge boulder that rests against the base of the right-hand side of the crag.
1) 4c, 23m. Move up the wall to a horizontal break and climb leftwards along a crack to an area of quartz. Move up to the corner and follow it to a stance and belay below an overhang.
2) 5a, 18m. Move rightwards to clear the overhang and gain the headwall. Move up rightwards towards the corner of *Thane* before climbing back slightly left and boldly ascending the wall to the top.
FA. Pat Littlejohn, Keith Darbyshire 31.12.1971

6 Thane **E1 5b**
An intimidating line which gains the hanging corner in the centre of the cliff. Start on the huge boulder that rests against the base of the right-hand side of the crag.
42m. Climb up the quartz-flecked wall to a small overlap, and just beyond a left-trending groove line. Move left to steep rock below the corner. Climb through the steep rock just left of the corner then move into the corner and climb it to the top.
FA. Pat Littlejohn, Steve Jones 31.3.1974

Avon Somerset | North Devon | Culm Coast | Inland Cornwall | Atlantic Coast | West Penwith | The Lizard | Inland Devon | Torbay | Dorset

Lots of sun | 20 min | Abseil in | Sheltered

Approach scramble
to abseil point

Scramble out
from belay

Huge boulder

Avon Somerset
North Devon
Culm Coast
Inland Cornwall
Atlantic Coast
West Penwith
The Lizard
Inland Devon
Torbay
Dorset

	No star	☼1	☼2	☼3
Mod to S	-	5	5	-
HS to HVS	-	4	12	1
E1 to E3	-	-	4	1
E4 and up	-	-	1	1

The squat, blunt nose of black and golden granite that protects the village of Sennen from the worst of the Atlantic weather is one of Cornwall's best-loved climbing venues. Although not particularly high, the quality of the climbing, the location of the crag and the impeccable quality of the granite combine to provide a crag for all, including non-climbing mates who are just here to sunbathe. Sennen also has the advantages of being virtually non-tidal, only a quick stroll from the parking and within easy walking distance of a fantastic beach. The climbing itself is generally well-protected, vertical crack-climbing interspersed with some serious face climbs.

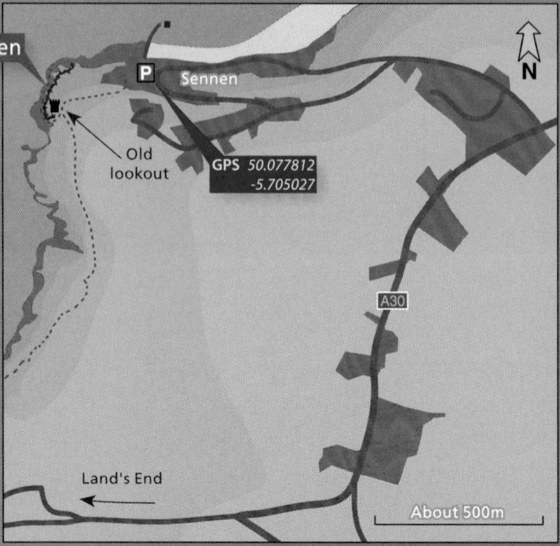

Approach   Area map on page 187

Drive down into Sennen village and along the front to a car park at the end of the narrowing road (payment). From the public toilet at the far end of the car park, pick up the coast path and follow it a small distance up hill and then out to the old coastguard hut that is situated right on top of the crag. There are a number of options for gaining the base of the cliff but the most straightforward on first visit is to descend the gully with a large chockstone a short way down. The gully starts just to the left of the landward side of the old coastguard hut. A worn, narrow path heads rightwards to wide rock-ledges just above sea level as the gully opens out. Above these ledges is the Terrace Cracks Area. The other areas are easily reached by scrambling up and along rock steps and ledges that run along the base of the whole length of the cliff.

Tides

The cliff's only tidal section is the Black Zawn, which is sea-washed at high tides. However, the base of the crag is prone to being wave-washed in rough seas and is very dangerous during these periods.

Conditions

The crag gets plenty of afternoon sun, although the Terrace Cracks Area gets the sun from midday. Conditions can be greasy in the morning before the sun creeps around, and the cliff is exposed to wind and rain, though the crag dries very quickly.

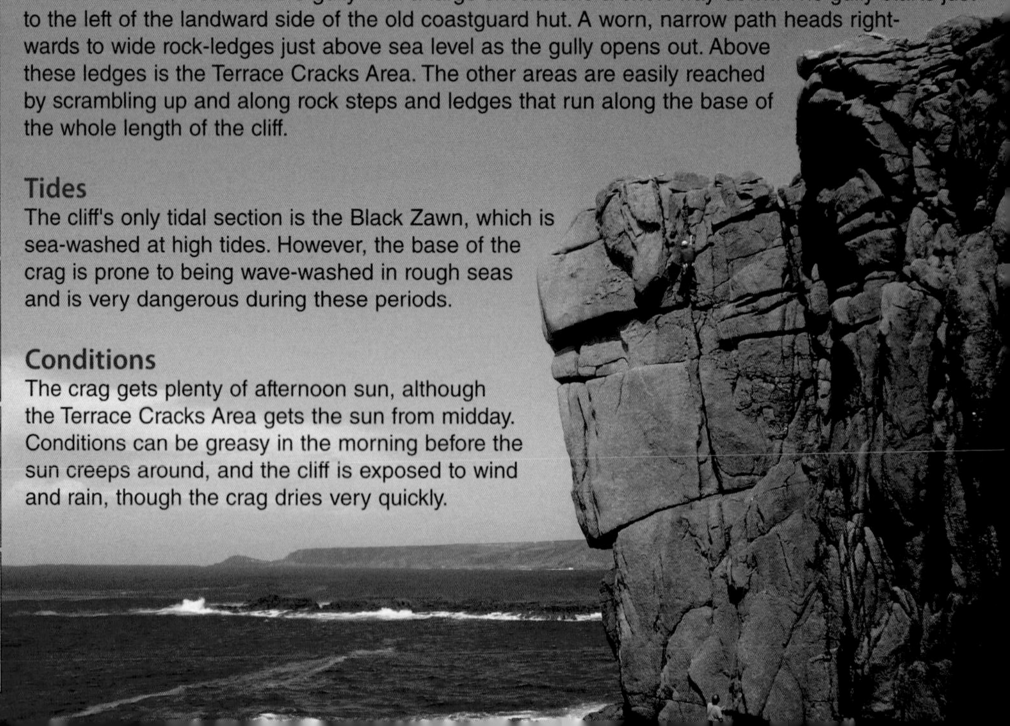

Avon Somerset

North Devon

Culm Coast

Inland Cornwall

Atlantic Coast

West Penwith

The Lizard

Inland Devon

Torbay

Dorset

Alison Martindale committed to the layback flakes
of *Samson Arete* (E2 6a) - *page 226* - Sennen.

Black Zawn and Demo Route Area

The imposing nose and cracked wall that bracket Black Zawn are Sennen's most impressive buttresses, whilst the featured wall to the right has a number of the area's best easier lines.

Approach - Walk and scramble to wide platforms below the buttresses. The Black Zawn is very dangerous during heavy seas.

Descent - Scramble or abseil back down to the platform.

Tides - The lower wall in Black Zawn is tidal.

Conditions - The climbs around Black Zawn can remain damp as they see little sun.

1 Delilah **E2 5b**
Delightful and well protected but a touch strenuous. Start below a thin crack left of the wide 'forked lightning' central crack.
15m. Climb the V-groove and crack which eases as height is gained.
FFA. Mike White 1973, previously aided.

2 Zig Zag . . . . **HVS 5a**
The steep, 'forked lightning' crack. Start below the crack.
18m. Move up ledges to beneath the crack and then climb it with conviction.
FA. Mike Banks 10.7.1955

3 Tears of a Clown **E6 6b**
The blank wall right of *Zig Zag* is a fine piece of wall climbing. Start below a large square-cut niche.
20m. Move up into the niche and, from its left side, pull up onto the wall and then traverse out right to the blunt arete. Move up until a thin horizontal break leads back left to below thin cracks. Climb the cracks with difficulty to the final overhang and pull over it to finish.
FA. Mark Edwards 7.1986. Climbed via a slightly different line at E7.

4 Slippery Slab . . . . . **VS 5a**
When dry, the thin crack in the upper slab of Black Zawn's right wall is a must. Start at the back of the zawn.
22m. Pull up onto easy rock and climb to the smooth corner left of the slab. Place a high runner in the smooth corner and then descend to a point level with an open groove at the base of the slab. Make a perplexing step right across the groove to the slab and climb a tiny corner to a small ledge halfway up the slab. Finish up the still tricky crack above.
FA. Pete Biven, Trevor Peck, W.Bacon 31.7.1955

Afternoon | 12 min | Tidal

5 Genge's Groove . . . . . . **HVS 5a**
Although unbalanced, this is a memorable struggle from which few escape unmarked. Start at a crack above a gap in the ledge.
26m. Burly crack manoeuvres ease at the midway point. Follow the natural line of steep cracks above to finish.
FA. Joe Barry 1947

6 A Swift Flight of Fancy **E3 6a**
A wild and exciting line that is much steeper than first impressions suggest. Start at a thin left-slanting crack.
26m. Difficult moves up the crack soon ease from where less steep ground gains a break. Move right and climb a crack up a black streak to another horizontal crack. Traverse the break right for 4m and make a long stretch for a ledge above it. Finish up the crack above the ledge.
FA. Rowland Edwards, Mark Edwards 25.4.1984

7 Samson Arete **E2 6a**
Great climbing on a finely sculptured line. Start at a thin crack just to the left of the base of the arete.
21m. Move up the crack and pull up right into another that ends at a break below an overhang. Layback up the steep rounded flakes above to an easing and continue to beneath the large overhang. Traverse right and pull over on good holds and finish up the short wall.
FA. Rowland Edwards, I.Pomfret 7.1974. Given HVS for years!

8 Demolition **E6 6a**
A pulse-enhancing and memorable pitch that features an extremely runout crux. Start just right of the arete below some thin cracks.
21m. Gain and climb the cracks to the first horizontal break. Move up the wall to a small flake from where a stiff rock-over gains a thin seam up to the left and the second break just above. Pull through the overhang and step right to finish up the steep prow on good holds.
FA. Mark Edwards, Ian Blake 8.1985

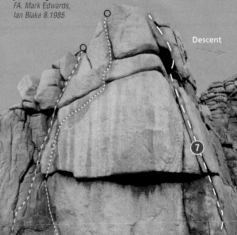

Descent

⑨ Demo Route . . . . . . `Top 50` HS 4b
A Sennen classic which is very photogenic. Start at a right-leading flake right of the arete. *Photo on page 423.*
1) 4b, 12m. Climb the flake to the base of a chimney/crack. Take the precarious chimney/crack via some initially insecure moves to a good ledge and belay.
2) 4b, 7m. Move up to the right-hand side of the overhanging nose above and then undercut left to good holds and pull up to easier ground and the top just above.
FA. Joe Barry 1943

⑩ Intermediate Route . . . . `1` S 4a
A tricksome start gains easier but delightful ground above. Start at a sloping ledge that is just above a low overhang.
1) 4a, 13m. Gain the sloping ledge and then work up rightwards on flakes to a ledge. Follow a vein of rock diagonally left to a ledge and belay.
2) 6m. Take the corner and cracks above to the top.
FA. Commando Cliff Assault Wing c.1940s

⑪ Corner Climb . . . . `2` VDiff
An engaging climb with lots of good moves and gear. Start beneath the corner.
20m. Climb the corner and then head left to a ledge at mid-height. Finish up the corner and cracks above the ledge.
FA. Commando Cliff Assault Wing c.1940s

⑫ Civvy Route . . . . . . `2` HS 4b
A good combination of pitches, the first a sustained crack and the second requiring a bit of a grunt. Start just right of the corner.
1) 4b, 13m. Climb the steep crack to an easing and then continue up the widening continuation to a ledge and belay on the right.
2) 4b, 9m. Move up left past the wide crack to a flake and climb left onto it. Make a steep couple of pulls straight up to easier ground and the top.
FA. Commando Cliff Assault Wing c.1940s

⑬ Letterbox . . . . `2` HS 4b
A much-attempted climb that features a tough series of moves to leave the belay ledge at the start of the second pitch. Start below a steep, thin corner-crack above a rock-pool.
1) 4a, 13m. Move up to the steep corner-crack and climb it until easier moves up less steep cracks gain a large ledge and belay.
2) 4b, 9m. Make some bouldery moves up just left of the overhang to a ledge above it. Finish up cracks heading left to the top of the buttress.
FA. Commando Cliff Assault Wing c.1940s

To the right is the deep Griptight Gully (Mod)*.*

⑭ Banana Flake . . . . . `2` VDiff
A great climb at the top end of the grade. Start just to the right of the base of the right-hand of two slim, clean-cut corners.
1) 12m. Move up left to the right-hand slim corner and follow it with difficulty to a large ledge and belay.
2) 10m. Climb the vertical crack at the back of the belay ledge to a ledge just below the top, and make a steep move up and over the bulge to finish.
FA. Commando Cliff Assault Wing c.1940s

⑮ The Arete . . . . `2` VS 4b
Varied and spectacular climbing on, for the majority of the route, big holds. Start right of the twin grooves on *Banana Flake*.
25m. Climb up to a wall and small juggy ridge, then cross an easy rake - on *Main Face Climb* - and gain a sloping ledge at the base of a right-facing corner. Climb the corner to a ledge and then move right and climb steeply on jugs stepping right near the top.
FA. Viv Stevenson, P.Stevenson 1.8.1961

⑯ Main Face Climb . . . . . `1` Diff
At popular initiation to the delights of Sennen with steady climbing and plenty of protection. Start at the base of a left-trending line of weakness that ends at a mid-height ledge.
1) 13m. Move up to the left-trending line of weakness and follow this on good holds to a large ledge and belay.
2) 10m. The corner-crack at the rear of the ledge has holds aplenty.
FA. Commando Cliff Assault Wing c.1940s

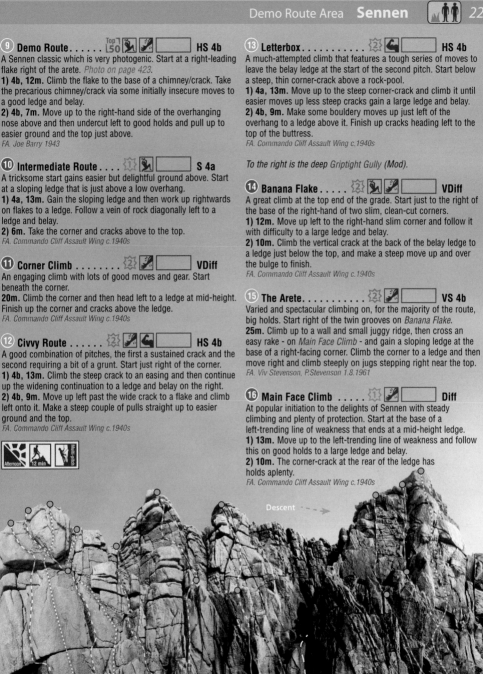

Descent - - - ->

Griptight Gully (Mod)

Avon Somerset
North Devon
Culm Coast
Inland Cornwall
Atlantic Coast
West Penwith
The Lizard
Inland Devon
Torbay
Dorset

Staircase and Dexter Areas

A convenient section of the cliff with a good selection of climbs in the lower and mid-grades. Take care in high seas as the ledge can become unexpectedly wave-washed.

Approach - Walk and scramble to wide platforms below the buttresses.

Descent - Scramble or abseil back down to the platform.

Tides - Non-tidal.

Conditions - The climbs can be damp before the sun has come onto them.

① Black Slab . . . . VDiff

A long and varied line whose name refers to the starting slab. Start at the low black slab that has a wide crack on its left.

1) 12m. Using a combination of the thinner crack on the slab and the wide crack, climb to the easier-angled section below a steep chimney. Make a couple of moves up the chimney from where good holds allow a step left onto a good ledge and belay next to a large spike. It is possible to climb the initial slab on the right using a diagonal crack for the feet at about the same grade.

2) 12m. Climb the cracks above the spike to a ledge, move right and finish up a left leading corner-line.

FA. Commando Cliff Assault Wing c.1940s

② No Name . . . . HVD

A good but testing line. Start at slim corner-crack on the right of the black slab.

22m. Climb the slim corner-crack to a ledge. Make some tricky moves up right to another crack and follow this to the top.

FA. Commando Cliff Assault Wing c.1940s

③ Staircase . . . . Diff

A fabulous pitch that follows a narrow strip of black, hold-infested rock. Start below a corner with a black left wall.

22m. Gain and climb the narrow off-vertical wall of black rock on great holds and continue in the same line above to the top.

FA. Commando Cliff Assault Wing c.1940s

④ Overhanging Corner . . . VS 4c

A good but awkward climb that does remain wet for a while after rain. Start below the wide, right-slanting crack.

22m. Move up cracks to below the corner proper. Climb the wide crack to an awkward exit onto a sloping ledge and continue up the still-tricky continuation crack above to the top.

FA. John Deacon, Rawdon Goodier 9.9.1955

⑤ Africa Route . . . . VS 5a

A testing line that features a bouldery initial wall and a contrasting final crack. Start below small flakes in the low wall.

19m. Boulder up to, and past the flakes to a ledge. Climb left up easy-angled rock to the base of a crack and the tiny 'Africa' shaped flake on the left. Climb the crack and steeper leftward continuation to a ledge and belay. Scramble off to the left.

FA. R.Flemming 10.1955

⑥ Double Overhang . . . . . VS 4c

An enjoyably steep romp on good holds for the most part. Start at a shallow crack-system on the right-hand side of the low wall.

19m. Climb the line of cracks to a ledge, then move left and climb steeply on huge holds to an easing. Step left to a crack and finish up this via a couple of awkward moves.

FA. Commando Cliff Assault Wing c.1940s

Descent

(7) Dexter . . . . VS 5a

A fine pitch that has a reachy exit - high in the grade. Start just left of the corner that drops down from the upper approach-ledge.
20m. Climb the wall to a widening crack and follow this on excellent holds to a point level with a wide flake-crack on the right wall. Swing out right along the flake to below a black blob on the wall above. Step up onto the blob and make a crucial stretch for a good hold on the finishing ledge. Scramble off right.
FA. J.Kinnaird 1954

(8) Dextrose . . . . HVS 5a

A worthwhile variation on *Dexter*. Start as for *Dexter* just left of the corner that drops down from the upper approach-ledge.
21m. Climb the wall to a widening crack and follow this on excellent holds for a few metres until level with a line of weakness on the right wall. Move out right along the line of weakness and, from where it fades, reach right to a rounded shallow crack. Take the flake above leftwards to the finish of *Dexter*.
FA. Viv Stevenson, G.Wilson 12.11.1962

(9) Sinner's Route . . . . . . Mod

A naughty little number that has some surprisingly-good climbing, though the route is all too brief. Start at the edge of the ledge, before the short downclimb to the main platform.
1) 15m. Climb either of the cracks which converge at 5m. Continue up the series of right-trending cracks to a huge ledge and belay.
2) 9m. Move right along the ledge to an easy broken corner and finish up this.
FA. Commando Cliff Assault Wing c.1940s

*Demo Route
page 226*

Demo Route page 226

Afternoon | 12 min

Avon Somerset | North Devon | Culm Coast | Inland Cornwall | Atlantic Coast | West Penwith | The Lizard | Inland Devon | Torbay | Dorset

Avon Somerset | North Devon | Culm Coast | Inland Cornwall | Atlantic Coast | West Penwith | The Lizard | Inland Devon | Torbay | Dorset

Golva Area

A steep wall of cracks set high above the sea. This is a great place for those searching for some excellent jamming pitches.

Approach - Walk and scramble to boulders below the buttresses. The Golva Area is slightly up and to the right of the scramble along the base of the cliff.

Descent - Scramble back down to the platform.

Tides - Non-tidal.

Conditions - The climbs dry very quickly but this wall can be particularly hot in warm weather and the cracks become slippery.

① Junior's Route . . . . **Diff**
A popular first pitch. Start at a slightly raised ledge at the left end of the platform at the base of the Golva Wall.
1) 14m. Climb the well-protected, left leading crack and its continuation to a huge ledge.
2) 9m. Walk left to the middle of the huge ledge and finish up the easiest line.
FA. Commando Cliff Assault Wing c.1940s

② Senior's Route . . . . **Diff**
A fabulous line and one of Sennen's best pitches at the grade. Start at the left end of the platform.
25m. Climb the narrow corner/groove that has a black mottled left wall all the way to the top.
FA. Commando Cliff Assault Wing c.1940s

③ Monday Face . . . . **VS 4b**
Steep and juggy wall-climbing that requires a confident approach. Start at a small pinnacle of rock that sits flush to the face at the left end of the platform.
18m. Move up onto the pinnacle, step right and climb the hold plastered steep wall to a ledge. Finish up the corner and wall to its left.
FA. Commando Cliff Assault Wing c.1940s

④ Vertical Crack . . . . **VS 4c**
A good introduction to Cornish granite cracks, being well-protected but requiring a subtle balance between caution and action. Start at the corner-crack.
18m. Climb the sustained crack that eases with height gained.
FA. Joe Barry 1943

⑤ Gillian **E3 5c**
Enthralling wall-climbing, tempered by the need for careful gear placement. Start just left of the thin crack of *Golva*.
18m. Climb the thin left-slanting crack and then move up to a pocket. Continue slightly right and up to the first large horizontal break. Finish up the cracks and breaks.
FA. Rowland Edwards, Mark Edwards 8.1977

⑥ Golva **E2 5c**
Sennen's most coveted crack-pitch is a test of technique and determination. Start below the long finger-to-hand-crack.
19m. Follow the crack-line all the way to the top.
FA. Rowland Edwards, Mark Edwards 8.1976

Descent

⑦ Dolphin Cracks . . . . . . **HVS 5a**

A classic crack-fest that follows the intimidating wide vertical crack on the left side of the face and the exposed corner to the left of the huge capping roof. Start on ledges below the wide corner-crack.

1) 5a, 10m. Move up to below the crack and bridge and layback up it, past a useful chockstone, to a large belay ledge.

2) 4c, 18m. Climb the knobbly curving crack in the less steep face above to below the corner-crack to the left of the huge roof. Pull steeply up into the corner and follow it all the way to the top. An exposed pitch.

FA. T.Genge 1947 (pitch 1)
FA. John Deacon, Rawdon Goodier 9.9.1955 (pitch 2)

⑧ Terrace Cracks . . . .   **HVS 5a**

A popular crack-climb and nearly always out of the clutches of the sea. Start on a high ledge at its left end below a thin crack.

1) 5a, 19m. Climb the thin crack and then step left to another, which quickly leads to a good ledge. Climb a left leading flake-crack and then work back up right to a stance and belay next to a gully.

2) 4c, 14m. Move up the gully to below an overhanging V-shaped corner. On its left wall is a series of thin undercut cracks, climb these to the top.

FA. Rowland Edwards, Mark Edwards 6.1976

Terrace Cracks Area

The tallest section of the cliff at Sennen, and the first to get the sun. The routes described follow cracks of all shapes and sizes, are multi-pitch and dry quickly.

Approach - Walk and scramble to boulders below the buttresses.
Descent - Scramble back down to the platform.
Tides - Non-tidal.
Conditions - The climbs dry very quickly.

⑨ Hayloft . . . . **VS 4c**

An entertaining series of short pitches, the second being bold and the final pitch a rarity! Start on a high ledge below a crack that leads up to an acute right-trending corner.

1) 11m. Climb the crack and acute corner to a belay on a large ledge.

2) 4b, 10m. A poorly-protected pitch. Follow a shallow crack, just to the left of an arete, to a black blob. Stand on the blob and make a precise step up onto the slab above, which quickly leads to a big ledge and belay.

3) 4a, 10m. Across the gully on the right is a crack. Climb the crack to a ledge and then another short, wide crack to a large ledge and belay on the right.

4) 4c, 10m. Traverse left to an undercut corner and make an awkward move up into a chimney above and slightly right. Squeeze up the chimney to finish.

FA. Commando Cliff Assault Wing c.1940s

Avon Somerset · North Devon · Culm Coast · Inland Cornwall · Atlantic Coast · West Penwith · The Lizard · Inland Devon · Torbay · Dorset

	No star	⛺ 1	⛺ 2	⛺ 3
Mod to S	-	2	-	1
HS to HVS	-	1	-	-
E1 to E3	-	1	1	1
E4 and up	-	-	5	-

Although only a stone's throw from the bustling tourist attractions that cap Land's End, the cliffs and climbs are well hidden from the gaze of the masses and retain an air of seriousness that is out of proportion to their location and height. The scenery is extremely beautiful and many of the climbs follow eye-catching lines, however, the rock quality is not the same as that found on the other more popular cliffs nearby, being grittier and lichenous. Escape could be awkward if failure on a line forces a retreat once the tide has crept back in or the sea conditions deteriorate.

Approach

Area map on page 187

Follow signs to Land's End and park in the main car park (payment but there is also an agreement to allow climbers to park for free, ask at the entrance).

Cormorant Promontory and World's End Face - Walk out of the right-hand corner of the car park (when facing out to sea) and follow a paved track to the First and Last House. From the viewing area in front of the house, walk down the slope until the distinctive profile of the Cormorant Promontory can be seen on the right. Continue down to the top of the cliff and locate a broken corner that becomes a narrow chimney lower down; this is the line of the abseil. Abseil to a large ledge from where the World's End Face climbs are accessed. For access to the Cormorant Promontory, continue the abseil to the sea-level ledges from where the base of the Cormorant Promontory can be reached via boulders in the bed of the zawn.

Longships Zawn - Walk to the front of the Hotel and locate the right-hand of two small round booths. Walk down the slope until the top of the zawn is reached from where an abseil gains a rock platform at the base of the zawn.

Hotel Buttress - Walk to the front of the Hotel and locate the left-hand of two small round booths. Walk down the slope slightly left and then back rightwards to the base of the cliff.

Tides

Cormorant Promontory is only accessible for 3 hours either side of low water in calm seas. The World's End Face is not tidal but can be wave-washed in rough seas. Longships Zawn is only accessible for 3 hours either side of low water in calm conditions but is badly affected by even moderately rough sea conditions. Hotel Buttress is accessible at all tide states and is only inaccessible in very rough seas.

Conditions

All the cliffs get plenty of sun and are usually at their best in the afternoon when they have dried out as they can be damp in the morning. The cliffs are very exposed to wind and rain.

Avon Somerset

North Devon

Culm Coast

Inland Cornwall

Atlantic Coast

West Penwith

The Lizard

Inland Devon

Torbay

Dorset

Midway up the taxing corner of *The Cormorant's Bill* (E1 5b)
- *page 234* - Cormorant Promontory, Land's End. Photo: Sam Mayfield

❶ Cormorant Slab ...... S 4a

Stunning positions in a remote-feeling location make this a relatively popular line. Start on the tip of the promontory at a narrow left-facing corner.

26m. Climb the corner to a sloping ledge on the left where it fades. Move right and climb a crack to the top of the promontory and belay. Scramble off along the crest of the promontory.

FA. Derek Holroyd, Alan Blackshaw, John Deacon 1957

❷ The Cormorant's Bill E1 5b

A memorable climb of sustained interest that follows the appealing corner just right of the tip of the promontory. Start on high ledges below a large ledge at the base of the corner itself. *Photo on page 233.*

26m. Mantleshelf onto the large ledge below the corner. Climb the sustained corner via jamming and bridging to an easing below an overhang. Pass the overhang with a big pull on good holds out to the left and finish more easily. Belay on the tip of the promontory. Scramble off along the crest of the promontory.

FA. John Deacon, Cliff Fishwick 29.8.1971

❸ The Last Dance ... E4 6b

A very good, but difficult pitch that will need a clean if it has not seen any traffic. Start on high ledges below a large ledge at the base of a corner as for *Cormorant's Bill*.

26m. Follow the corner of *Cormorant's Bill* for 6m until it is possible to move rightwards to the arete below a small groove. Move up the groove and rightwards onto the arete. Move left and up past the overlap above and follow the slab and arete past a peg to the top. Scramble off along the crest of the promontory.

FA. Rowland Edwards, Mark Edwards 1985

❹ Johnstone's Route .... S 4a

An adventurous excursion that should not be undertaken in the nesting season as the ledges are guano covered and home to numerous birds. Start at the base of an intrusion of black and pink rock below the massive corner.

1) 4a, 9m. Climb steeply up right and then back left to a belay on large ledges below the corner.

2) 4a, 19m. Climb a corner to the right of the main corner to a point where moves left gain the main corner, follow this to the top. Scramble off along the crest of the promontory.

FA. John Deacon, Derek Holroyd 1957

❺ Day Tripper E4 6a

A tremendous pitch when clean, that takes on a thin crack-system up the impressive hanging wall at the back of the zawn. The last 8m is on poor rock and it is advisable to pre-place a rope down this section. Start under the large overhang at the base of the wall.

1) 6a, 38m. Take the steep wall to the overhang and move up into the equally-steep groove on the right. Exit the groove at its top, moving out left to the base of the wall and less-steep ground. Climb to a wide horizontal break, move right and climb a crack to another wide horizontal break. Move up to a tiny triangular ledge and climb a crack and follow this to a ledge, sustained. Belay on pre-placed rope.

2) 8m. Either abseil off, or aid out on the rope with care.

FA. Rowland Edwards, Mark Edwards 4.4.1981

Pre-place rope for final 8m

Scramble off

Approach

❻ World's End E1 5a

An intimidating and pumpy pitch with a bold start. Start under the low overhang at the right end of the ledge.
23m. Move up to the overhang and then left under it to gain a diagonal break on the wall. Follow the break leftwards to a vertical seam and follow this to the top.
FA. John Deacon, Derek Holroyd, A.Day 1957

❼ Zawn Face Route . . . . HVS 4c

An unusual route that gains the exposed side wall of the zawn via a cramped crawl. Start at the right-hand end of the ledge.
1) 17m. Crawl under the overhang and climb a groove to easier ground that leads left to a ledge and belay.
2) 10m. Finish up the cracks above.
FA. Derek Holroyd, John Deacon 1957

Cormorant Promontory and World's End Face

This section of cliff has a more serious feel about it than might be expected. The rock is generally good but can be gritty in places.
Approach - Abseil to the zawn bed and cross boulders to the climbs on the promontory. A higher ledge passed on the abseil to the zawn bed gives access to the World's End Face.
Tides - The zawn bed is only accessible for 3 hours either side of low tide. The ledges below the World's End Face are non-tidal.
Conditions - The climbs are fairly exposed and at times can be a little dirty.

Line of abseil

②

Continue abseil to lower ledge for approach to Cormorant Promontory

Ⓐ

⑥ ⑦

Crawl under overhang

Avon Somerset · North Devon · Culm Coast · Inland Cornwall · Atlantic Coast · West Penwith · The Lizard · Inland Devon · Torbay · Dorset

Avon Somerset

North Devon

Culm Coast

Inland Cornwall

Atlantic Coast

West Penwith

The Lizard

Inland Devon

Torbay

Dorset

❶ Pyjamarama **E4 6b**
A difficult pitch. Start at a crack left of the overhangs or at higher tides, by abseiling to a ledge at 7m.
23m. Climb the crack to a ledge at 7m, easy to this point. Climb the leaning crack in the pillar on the left past a peg. The start is thin and a very small cam is useful.
FA. Mark Edwards, Rowland Edwards 10.3.1986

❷ Antenna **E4 5c**
A good variation on *Longships Wall*. Start at a thin crack on the right side of the square-cut overhangs.
27m. Climb the difficult thin crack for 8m. Traverse left to just above the upper overhang and then finish directly up the wall.
FA. Pat Littlejohn, Iain Peters 6.1977

❸ Longships Wall **E3 6a**
A great single-pitch that follows an intermittent crack-line up the centre of the wall. Start at a thin crack on the right side of the square-cut overhangs as for *Antenna*.
25m. The crack is very hard work to start.
FA. Pat Littlejohn, Iain Peters 6.1977

❹ New Editions **E4 6b**
The groove that bounds the right-hand side of the wall is a difficult, but excellent pitch. Start below the groove.
25m. Gain the groove with difficulty and climb to a peg. Continue up the sustained groove to the capping roof and finish on the left, or with more difficulty by moving right and pulling through the overhang.
FA. Rowland Edwards, Mark Edwards 20.3.1986

Longships Zawn
A compact wall that has a number of difficult climbs set in a magnificent location.
Approach - Abseil down the line of *Longships Wall* to the smooth ledge at the base of the wall.
Tides - The ledge at the base of the climbs is only accessible for around 3 hours either side of low water in calm seas.
Conditions - The wall gets plenty of sun and dries quickly.

| Lots of sun | 5 min | Multi-pitch | Tidal |

Atlantic Ocean Wall (E5 6b)

❺ Land's End Long Climb . `Top 50` 🖊 ☐ **VDiff**

A fabulous route that is packed with plenty of interesting pitches and spectacular situations. The climb also benefits from being well above the clutches of the tide during calm and moderate seas. Some of the pitches are serious for both leader and second and care is needed with protection. Start at a wide crack at the base of the buttress.

1) 16m. Climb the wide crack and its continuation above a wide break to a large ledge. Belay at its back, below a corner-crack.

2) 9m. The 'Elbow Crack'. Climb the fine, well-protected corner-crack to a belay next to a tilted block that forms a slab.

3) 15m. Climb the centre of the slab to its top. Drop down, cross a wide gap and move up to belay below a short wall with a crack in it.

4) 6m. Climb the short wall via cracks to a good ledge and belay.

5) 12m. Move right to the base of a wide chimney and bridge up this until it is possible to transfer to the landward wall of the chimney. Climb the wall until a final pull up right gains a good belay.

6) 10m. Move down and across to a wall that must be traversed right via a short but precarious move into the base of a large gully and belay.

7) 10m. Traverse right again around a rib to a ledge and then climb the short steep cracks to another good ledge and belay below a lichen-covered wall - 'The Green Face'.

8) 7m. 'The Green Face'. Climb the steep lichen-covered wall above the stance to the top via a left-trending weakness. A tough pitch at the grade.

FA. Royal Marines 1946

Hotel Buttress

Directly below the Land's End Hotel is a striking ridge that drops down to sea level. The ridge is made up of a jumble of walls, huge stacked boulders and pinnacles.

Approach - From the left-hand round booth (looking out to sea) at the front of the Land's End Hotel drop down easy slopes slightly to the left and then scramble easily down and slightly right to the base of the buttress.

Descent - Same as the approach.

Tides - The base of the climb is non-tidal in calm and moderate seas.

Conditions - The climb dries rapidly and gets plenty of sun. However, it is very exposed to the elements.

The Green Face

The 'Elbow Crack' pitch

Middle pitches are hidden

Lots of sun | 5 min

Descent

❺

	No star	⚹	⚹⚹	⚹⚹⚹
Mod to S	-	2	-	-
HS to HVS	-	3	1	-
E1 to E3	1	-	1	-
E4 and up	-	-	-	2

Pordenack Point is a convenient and tranquil series of buttresses that hosts a fine line up of pitches across the grades. The outlook is beautiful, and the extensive set of flat ledges under the cliff gives the area a less serious feel than others nearby. The rock is excellent on the routes described and the climbs are longer than first impressions may suggest.

Approach   See main area map on page 187

Follow signs to Land's End and park in the main car park (payment but there is also an agreement to allow climbers to park for free, ask at the entrance). Pordenack Point is the first headland to the south of Land's End. Pick up the coast path that heads southward from the car park (the left-hand corner when facing out to sea). Follow the coast path past the childrens' animal farm and on to the top of the headland. From the tip of the headland, drop down a grassy gully on the left (facing out to sea). About 50m down the gully, a weakness can be found in the right wall and this becomes 'the squeeze' - a narrow defile that leads to a trough. Scramble easily down to the base of the cliff from here. Alternatively, just after 'the squeeze', set up an abseil to descend directly to the base of the cliff.

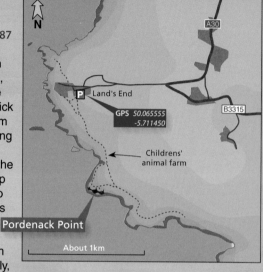

Tides

The base of the cliff is only accessible for 3 hours either side of low water and in calm sea conditions. However, at neap tides, and in calm weather, the base is non-tidal for the climbs described. During rough seas access is not possible even at low tide.

Conditions

The cliffs dry very quickly and get plenty of sun but are very exposed to westerly winds. There is no shelter from rain.

Avon Somerset | North Devon | Culm Coast | Inland Cornwall | Atlantic Coast | West Penwith | The Lizard | Inland Devon | Torbay | Dorset

Avon Somerset

North Devon

Culm Coast

Inland Cornwall

Atlantic Coast

West Penwith

The Lizard

Inland Devon

Torbay

Dorset

Midway up the well-named *Immaculate Arete* (E4 6a) - *page 241* - at Pordenack Point. Climber Dave Henderson.

Pordenack Point

A superb cliff that has both fine climbs and a very appealing ambience.

Approach - From the exit of 'the squeeze', either scramble down the rake and follow ledges back left to below the climbs, or abseil directly to the base of the cliff.

1 Economist's Climb ....   VDiff

A long and interesting outing that requires a steady lead on the first pitch. Start at the base of the distinctive red-coloured dike on the left side of the main buttress.

1) 17m. Follow the dike to a ledge and belay on the descent rake.
2) 14m. From the landward side of the rake, climb the left-hand groove to the short red wall and a belay on a large ledge above it.
3) 15m. Move rightwards easily over large blocks to belay below a steep white wall.
4) 10m. Climb the open groove on surprisingly good holds to the top.

2 Vietnamerica E1 5b

A tense little pitch that is now more serious following a rockfall. Start at a sentry box where a couple of blocks have disappeared.

21m. Move up into the sentry box and make some bold moves to and then up a thin crack in the wall above on crunchy rock to a finishing groove just before the top.

FA. Gary Gibson, Derek Beetlestone, M.Brown 22.7.1982

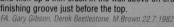

3 Zeke's Route ....   HS 4b

Varied and engaging climbing with a number of steep moves on good holds. Start on a large, flat ledge below a wide, rounded crack.

23m. Move up big ledges to below cracks in the left wall of the wide, rounded crack. Make an exhilarating layaway to gain a ledge and then follow cracks, short walls and ledges to a final stiff pull up into a narrow corner and then easier cracks that lead to the top.

FA. John Zeke' Deacon, Rawdon Goodier 4.7.1955

4 Stone Boom E2 5c

A popular climb with two contrasting pitches. Start on a large, flat ledge below a wide, rounded crack.

1) 5b, 17m. Climb the wide rounded crack to a horizontal crack in the right wall. Traverse the crack right to just past the arete and then move up the wall to a good ledge and belay.
2) 5c, 12m. Climb the thin and fingery corner above the ledge to the top. A good piece of climbing.

FA. Rowland Edwards, Roland Perriment 16.3.1980

5 Sea Fury ....   HVS 5b

A fairly fierce but well-protected crack-climb. Start just to the right of a deep chimney/crack.

30m. Climb the crack via some awkward moves to an overhang. Make some hard pulls over the overhang and get established in the continuation crack. Climb to a short corner-crack on the right and finish up this.

FA. Barrie Biven, Trevor Peck, Pete Biven 22.8.1955

Lots of sun | 15 min | Tidal

Approach/descent

Top pitches
not shown

❻ Immaculate Arete . . Top 50 ‖ E4 6a

A stunning line and one of West Penwith's best pitches. Start just right of the arete. *Photo on page 239.*

32m. Move up and left to a peg. Make gymnastic moves past the peg and up the wall to a break and thin flake on the right. Pull up and left past a thin crack to a reasonable horizontal break, from where another move brings better holds and a rest. Move right and climb the wall on great holds to a short corner and finish up this.
FA. Rowland Edwards, Mark Edwards, 10.1.1981. It originally started from the right.

❼ Cain . . . . ‖ E4 6a

A boldish start and an extended series of surprisingly difficult moves through the mid-height overhang are the highlights of this much-eyed line. Start below a thin crack 5m right of the arete.
32m. Climb just left of the thin crack to pass the low overhang and then move up steeply to the main overhang. Pull over this and follow the tricky right-leaning crack to the capping overhang. Finish up a crack on the wall right of the overhang.
FA Pat Littlejohn 1978. Start described is the original start to Immaculate Arete.

❽ Nothing Much. . . . . ‖ HVS 5b

A meandering but worthwhile and well-protected pitch. Start at a narrow corner below a bottomless groove under the mid-height overhang.
32m. Climb the corner, step left and move up the bottomless groove to the overhang. Move right with difficulty to clear the overhang and climb the crack and wall on the left to below the capping overhang. Join *Wrist Climb* to finish.
FA. D.Wiggett, A.Smythe 8.6.1965

❾ Friends . . . . ‖ VS 5a

A steep and direct line that has some interesting moves. Start at the base of the red stained corner.
1) 5a, 28m. Climb to the overhang and pass it using a crack. Continue up the steep cracks above to a ledge in the gully.
2) 4c, 18m. Move up onto a block and climb the steep wall above it to a ledge. Move left, and then climb to the summit of the pinnacle. Abseil off.
FA. Mark Edwards, S.Peplow 13.2.1981

❿ Wrist Climb . . . . ‖ HVD

A long outing that builds to an exciting and exposed finale. Start at the base of a red stained corner.
1) 30m. Climb up the red-stained corner until a traverse right leads to another corner. Climb the corner and head leftwards to a ledge and belay next to a gully.
2) 23m. Move down the gully until it is possible to make an exposed traverse left underneath the capping overhang and continue to a good ledge beneath a short corner (possible belay). The short corner is hard but well-protected and leads to a ledge and easier ground to finish.
FA. Rawdon Goodier, R.Shepton, R.Bisley 22.5.1955

Top pitch of
Friends not shown

Avon Somerset · North Devon · Culm Coast · Inland Cornwall · Atlantic Coast · West Penwith · The Lizard · Inland Devon · Torbay · Dorset

	No star	⭐	⭐⭐	⭐⭐⭐
Mod to S	-	-	-	-
HS to HVS	-	-	1	-
E1 to E3	-	-	-	1
E4 and up	-	-	1	2

Carn Les Boel and Zawn Kellys are remote cliffs that are often unoccupied. The climbing on both is on the steep side of vertical, although generally the protection is reasonable. The cliffs are positioned at either end of Pendower Cove - a magnificent arc of granite with a beautiful boulder-beach as its centrepiece, which is home to many playful seals.

Approach   See main area map on page 187

From the car park at Porthgwarra, take the road to the right, up the hill, then through a gate. At the first left bend, carry straight-on along a footpath. The path leads across open country and arrives at a distinctive wall made up of huge rocks. Cross the wall and continue along the coast path to the next headland (Carn Barra) where the respective approaches split.

Carn Les Boel - Continue on the coast path around the huge Pendower Cove to the next headland - Carn Les Boel. For *Excalibur*, walk out to the headland and just before it begins to narrow, drop down a steep, grassy gully on the left to a point where an abseil can be made to a good ledge at sea level. For the Paradise Wall, it is quickest to abseil from the top of the wall, direct to ledges at the base. The abseil takes a bit of finding, but once over the edge, the ledges at the base are easily seen. The Paradise Wall can also be reached by an easy traverse along ledges from the end of the first pitch of *Excalibur*.

Zawn Kellys - Continue along the coast path for a short distance. Zawn Kellys can be seen down to the left. The easiest access to the base is by abseil directly down the line of the climb described. The boulder-beach can also be reached by descending the grassy gully on the Carn Barra side of the zawn.

Tides

Carn Les Boel is non-tidal but it is not a good venue if the sea is rough. Zawn Kellys is tidal and can only be accessed for 3 hours either side of low water.

Conditions

Both cliffs dry quickly and get plenty of sun. Nesting birds can be problematic at Carn Les Boel.

(Map labels: B3315, Polgigga, Carn Les Boel, Pendower Cove, Zawn Kellys, Stone wall, Carn Barra, Fox Promontory, GPS 50.037979 -5.672920, Porthgwarra, Chair Ladder, Cafe, About 500m, Porthgwarra Buttress, Hella Point)

(Photo labels: Carn Les Boel, Zawn Kellys)

(Side tabs: Avon Somerset, North Devon, Culm Coast, Inland Cornwall, Atlantic Coast, West Penwith, The Lizard, Inland Devon, Torbay, Dorset)

Wilf Williamson moving across the initial wall of the little-travelled *Excalibur* (HVS 5a) - *page 245* - in the atmospheric chasm of Carn Les Boel.

Avon Somerset

North Devon

Culm Coast

Inland Cornwall

Atlantic Coast

West Penwith

The Lizard

Inland Devon

Torbay

Dorset

Avon Somerset

North Devon

Culm Coast

Inland Cornwall

Atlantic Coast

West Penwith

The Lizard

Inland Devon

Torbay

Dorset

Abseil for other lines on the wall

Ⓐ

Abseil for *Excalibur*

Ⓐ

Easy traverse

① ② ③ ④

Lots of sun | 25 min | Abseil in | Multi-pitch

Carn Les Boel

An intimidating arena that holds some of the area's best hard routes, on Paradise Wall. The location is sublime, and far less frequented than many of the other cliffs nearby. The narrow inlet between the cliff and Bosistow Island is a favourite haunt of seals.

Approach - For *Excalibur*, abseil down a gully to the right of the cliff (see topo) to good ledges at sea level. For routes on Paradise Wall itself abseil directly from the top of the crag to the starting ledges of the individual routes.

Tides - Non-tidal except in heavy seas.
Conditions - The cliff gets plenty of sun and dries quickly. Some of the rock can be gritty if the routes have not been climbed for sometime.

❶ Excalibur . . . .  HVS 5a

A splendid, little-travelled foray into beautiful surroundings. Great positions, rock and climbing make this route a must for those searching for some quiet on busy days. Birds usually nest on the stance at the top of the pinnacle between March and the end of June (do not climb the route during this period). Start from good ledges at the base of the approach abseil.
Photo on page 243.
1) 4b, 14m. Climb onto and then rightwards up the wall to a ledge, poor gear. Continue to a belay at the base of a large corner.
2) 5a, 20m. Climb the steep corner to its end on top of a pinnacle. Climb the steep wall above to finish.
FA. John Deacon, Derek Holroyd 1957

❷ Interspace E4 6a

Breathtaking climbing and positions are the main ingredients of this sustained pitch that fires up the left-hand side of Paradise Wall. Start on a ledge at the base of the left-hand corner.
40m. Take the corner direct to a point where it is possible to traverse rightwards across the steep wall on various breaks to a diagonal crack that leads into another, thinner crack. Climb this to a horizontal break and continue up another crack above to beneath a triangular shaped overhang. Finish by traversing left under the overhang and then up a corner to the top.
FA. Rowland Edwards, Mark Edwards 26.6.1982

❸ Burning Gold E4 6a

A powerful line with climbing to match. It follows the right-trending crack-line up the centre of the wall. Start on a ledge at the base of the left-hand corner.
1) 6a, 32m. Climb rightwards to a niche and pull up left to a groove. Climb the groove and long, pumpy crack to a belay below the upper overhang.
2) 6a, 14m. Move up the steep groove and make a hard move out left and up to less pressing territory and the top not far above.
FFA Pat Littlejohn, Chris King 21.5.1978

❹ Cool Diamonds E5 6b

A spectacularly-positioned top pitch that has a couple of very hard moves in its upper reaches. Start on a low ledge, 10m down and right (facing in) of the ledge at the base of the corner on the left-hand side of Paradise Wall.
1) 6a, 15m. Climb the wall to a good ledge. This pitch is easily avoided by a traverse to the belay from the ledge at the base of the left-hand corner of Paradise Wall.
2) 6b, 40m. Move up to a horizontal break and traverse right to a line of cracks near the arete. Climb the line of cracks, moving right below the first overhang to another crack-line. Powerful and technical climbing through the overhangs and up the headwall lead to the top.
FA. Rowland Edwards, Mark Edwards 30.6.1982

The next route is passed on the way to Carn Les Boel.

❺ American Dream E1 5b

A great route set in a beautiful cove. High in the grade. Start left of a massive chimney at a small corner.
40m. Climb the corner to a ledge. Move up slightly left and then rightwards to a prominent right-facing flake-crack. Climb the flake-crack past a small overhang and then on to below another overhang. Climb the steep left-hand crack above the overhang and its continuation to the top.
FA. Rowland Edwards, Charlie Bryan 30.3.1980

Zawn Kellys

A splendid cliff that can be easily combined with climbing at the nearby Carn Barra or Carn Les Boel.
Approach - Either abseil directly down the line or scramble down the grassy gully to the left of the zawn (facing out).
Tides - The base of the cliff can only be accessed for 3 hours either side of low water.
Conditions - The climb gets plenty of sun and dries quickly.

Avon Somerset | North Devon | Culm Coast | Inland Cornwall | Atlantic Coast | West Penwith | The Lizard | Inland Devon | Torbay | Dorset

Alternative low-tide approach across boulders from grassy gully

	No star	☆	☆☆	☆☆☆
Mod to S	-	2	1	-
HS to HVS	-	4	5	-
E1 to E3	-	3	4	2
E4 and up	-	-	1	2

Avon Somerset | North Devon | Culm Coast | Inland Cornwall | Atlantic Coast | West Penwith | The Lizard | Inland Devon | Torbay | Dorset

Carn Barra has a sunny aspect, high quality rock, classy climbs, easy access and little in the way of tidal constraints, making it a reliable and favoured venue. The routes are single-pitch and the grade coverage is good, although the very best climbs are in the E grades.

Approach   See main area map on page 187

From the car park at Porthgwarra, take the road to the right, up the hill and through a gate. At the first left bend, carry straight-on along a footpath. The path leads across open country and arrives at a distinctive wall made up of huge rocks. Cross the wall and continue for about 250m. Just before the headland of Carn Barra, a wide gully drops down to the cliff edge and the top of the Socket Wall Area. From here the cliff fans out to the left and right, and the top of each sector can be accessed by scrambling along the cliff edge to the various abseil access points.

Tides

The majority of the climbing described is essentially non-tidal during calm sea-conditions, and even during moderate seas the high starting ledges of the Central Wall and large platform below the Grand Plage wall offer a good deal of protection.

Conditions

Sunny, quick drying and often sheltered from the wind, Carn Barra is a reliable venue - although it can get extremely hot at times.

Map labels: B3315, Polgigga, Carn Les Boel, Pendower Cove, Zawn Kellys, Stone wall, Carn Barra, Fox Promontory, GPS 50.037979 -5.672920, Porthgwarra, P, Cafe, Chair Ladder, About 1km, Porthgwarra Buttress, Hella Point

Fox Promontory

A wild, early spring day on *Peel Crack* (HVD) - *page 249* - at Carn Barra.

Avon Somerset

North Devon

Culm Coast

Inland Cornwall

Atlantic Coast

West Penwith

The Lizard

Inland Devon

Torbay

Dorset

Sarah Burmester peeps over the change in angle to make the transition from steep to merely vertical on the brilliant *Grand Plage* (E3 6a) - *page 248* - Carn Barra. Photo: Ian Wilson

Grand Plage Area

Set above a large sea-level platform and protected from all but the heaviest of seas is this wall of excellent golden granite. The wall is cut by a number of corners and thin cracks that give sustained and technical pitches.

Approach - From the cliff edge at the base of the approach gully, walk right (looking out) along the narrow cliff-top path to an obvious bad step right on the edge of the cliff. Just before the bad step, abseil to the base of the crag. At low tide and in calm seas it is possible to scramble down to the base of the crag by crossing the bad step and then following a gully and ledge system down to the platform below the crag.

Tides - During calm seas this area is non-tidal but care should be taken in rougher conditions.

Conditions - Sunny and quick drying, this area is a reliable venue in unsettled weather but can be very hot when directly in the sun.

❶ Crack in the Sky . . . . . . 🖈🖈 ⬛ 　　 E1 5b

A striking line taking in the wide crack in the upper section of wall left of the corner, through which daylight can be seen! Start on a massive boulder directly beneath the corner.

27m. Climb up the corner for 5m and step left to a ledge, from which moves up and left gain a slab. Climb the steep wall above past a ledge to the base of the crack and follow this to the top.

FA. Rowland Edwards, Mark Edwards, Charlie Bryan 10.5.1980

❷ Mean Street . . . . 🖈🖈 🖈 　　 E4 6a

High quality, technical wall-climbing up the thin crack above the massive right-hand boulder. Start on top of the right-hand boulder.

30m. Pull up into the crack on the wall with difficulty and follow it to where it eases, then reach the break above. Move left and pull up steeply to a ledge and the top just above.

FA. Rowland Edwards, Mark Edwards 2.3.1984

❸ Sunny Corner Lane . 🖈🖈 🖈 🖈 　　 E3 5c

The acute corner and left-hand continuation is a superb line, and has climbing to match. Start on boulders below the corner.

30m. Climb the corner to the overhang where it splits. Move left and make a perplexing move up into the continuation corner. Follow the corner to the next overhang and pull up rightwards into a short, steep overhang-capped corner that is quitted on the right.

FA. Rowland Edwards, Mark Edwards 23.5.1980

❹ Grand Plage . . . . . . 🖈🖈 🖈 🖈 　　 E3 6a

The classic of the crag, and one of Cornwall's finest single-pitches. The difficulty of the start is influenced by the position of the huge boulder at the base of the wall, which moves around during very heavy seas! Start on the boulder. *Photo on page 247.*

30m. Pull onto the steep wall and move up to good wires. Make some hard moves to get established at the base of the easier-angled headwall above. Climb the sustained thin crack-line all the way to the top, or from midway up the headwall, move left to a small corner and finish up this.

FA. Rowland Edwards, Mark Edwards 23.5.1980

❺ Golden Brown. . 🖈🖈 🖈 🖈 👁 　　 E4 6a

A good, well-positioned right-hand finish to *Grand Plage* that is fairly runout but on reliable rock. Start as for *Grand Plage*.

31m. Climb *Grand Plage* past its crux to the base of the headwall. Follow the ramp on the right to a thin crack and take this to the top.

FA. Gary Gibson, Phil Gibson 1982

❻ Footless Madness . . . . . 🖈🖈 🔩 　　 E5 6b

A wild pitch up the steep, thin crack in the wall to the right of *Golden Brown*. Start as for *Grand Plage*.

28m. Climb up until it is possible to gain the thin, steep crack on the right. Follow the crack to a peg, and make hard moves past it, then push on to the top.

FA Mark Edwards, Rowland Edwards, R.Greaves 6.7.1985

Main gully approach ←

Easy scramble out

Abseil from blocks Ⓐ

Lots of sun · 20 min · Abseil in · Tidal

❼ Geireagle II E2 5b
A technical and sustained lead. Start below a line of grooves.
27m. Climb the grooves past a ledge to a steep finish.
FA. Rowland Edwards, Mark Edwards 24.5.1980

❽ Marisco Striptease E2 5b
A fun, steep pitch. Start at a wide corner groove.
27m. Climb the groove until level with a diagonal line in the wall
to the right. Swing up along the line to gain a ledge and then
finish up rightwards on easier ground.
FA. Paul Harrison, Steve Boyden 5.8.1984

❾ Socket Arete .... VS 4c
Short in stature, but not in interest. Start at the base of the blunt
arete with a heavily pock-marked right wall.
14m. Pull up onto the ledge just left of the arete proper, and
make some balancy moves up it to gain and climb a crack on its
right-hand side to the top.
FA. Rowland Edwards 1983

❿ Cumbelloe .... HS 4b
The centre of the pock-marked wall is high in the grade and very
sustained. As a consequence it feels a lot bigger than it looks.
Start under a handrail at 4m below the middle of the wall.
14m. Heave up to good holds on the handrail, step left and climb
the pock-marked wall and thin crack to the top.
FA. Rowland Edwards 1983

⓫ Socket Wall .... S 4b
A fine little climb that packs a mean punch low down. Start at the
right end of the overhangs at the base of the pock-marked wall.
14m. Make a steep pull up and left to good holds above the
overhang and then make another hard move to enter the base of a
small corner. Follow this more easily to the top.
FA. Rawdon Goodier, John Deacon, Mike Banks, J.Peel 29.6.1955

Socket Wall Area

Although not as impressive as the other sections of Carn
Barra, the Socket Wall provides some worthwhile easier
climbs that are very sheltered.
Approach - The Socket Wall Area lies directly below the
ledges at the base of the gully. The base of the climbs
are best reached by abseil from good block-belays on the
ledges.
Tides - The base of the cliff is non-tidal in calm or
moderate seas.
Conditions - Sunny and quick drying, this area is a
reliable venue in unsettled weather but can be very hot
when directly in the sun.

⓬ Glass Arete E3 5c
The tall arete that defines the right side of the wall is a striking
line. Start at the base of the arete.
20m. Climb the arete in its entirety.
FA. Rowland Edwards, Mark Edwards 1.9.1983

⓭ Sleazy Corner .... VDiff
The eye-catching wide corner-crack is deceptive both in style and
protection possibilities. Start at the base of the lower arete.
16m. Climb up the left side of the arete on good holds to a big
ledge and climb the wide crack at the back of the ledge to the top.

⓮ Peel Crack .... HVD
A magnificently-positioned climb. Start at a small corner below a
ledge and thin crack in the upper wall. *Photo on page 246.*
16m. Move up the corner to the ledge from where a technical
move starts the thin crack in the upper wall.
FA. F.Peel, R.Flemming, Rawdon Goodier 2.7.1955

Avon Somerset · North Devon · Culm Coast · Inland Cornwall · Atlantic Coast · West Penwith · The Lizard · Inland Devon · Torbay · Dorset

Lots of sun · 20 min · Abseil in

Central Wall

A popular wall of excellent rock that rises above a good ledge set well above the sea. The climbs are steep and well-protected, the majority of the lines following vertical cracks of various sizes.

Approach - From the bottom of the approach-gully, walk left (facing out) to a big, flat ledge with large boulders on it. Abseil from here to a wide, flat ledge.

Tides - The good, flat starting ledge is set well above the sea and is only sea-washed in very rough seas.

Conditions - The cliff is a suntrap, and dries very quickly, although some of the cracks do seep after prolonged rainfall. A good place to head for in strong northerly winds.

❶ Ra . . . . **HVS 5a**
The widening corner-crack, split by good ledges, gives a challenging pitch that would not feel out of place on a Grit Edge. Start on the left-hand side of the ledge beneath the widening crack.
17m. Follow the crack to the second ledge and prepare for battle with the tougher upper section that requires some large gear to protect it adequately.
FA. Paul de Mengle, C.Bartlett, B.Hocken 23.7.1972

❷ Illustrated Man **E2 5b**
An enjoyable exercise that follows the thin crack and small corner/groove in the arete right of *Ra*. Start as for *Ra*.
17m. Gain the first ledge on *Ra* and move right to, and climb a crack to the next break. Pull through the overhang into the small corner/groove from the left and finish up this.
FA. Rowland Edwards, Mark Edwards 23.10.1979

❸ Dialectics . . . . **HVS 5b**
An enticing and much-attempted pitch with good gear. Start below an open corner right of *Ra*.
18m. Move up to the crack in the blunt arete right of the corner, and climb this with difficulty to the large mid-height break. Pull up into the continuation crack and take this to the top. The lower section can also be climbed via the corner on the left or the wall to the right at about the same grade.
FFA. Rowland Edwards, Mark Edwards 5.1980

❹ Axis . . . . **VS 5a**
Fine sustained climbing up the left-facing corner-crack in the centre of the wall is preceded by a short, fingery start. Start at a weakness in the lower wall that leads to a ledge under the corner.
18m. Make a hard move to better holds and the ledge just above. Bridge and jam away up the steep corner-crack to the top.
FA. Andy McFarlane, Ian Duckworth, B.Hocken 30.8.1972

❺ Exodus . . . . **VS 5a**
Not quite as good as its nearby cousins but still very worthwhile. Start as for *Axis*.
20m. Climb the hard initial wall of *Axis* and its corner-crack to the mid-height horizontal break. Traverse the break right for 5m and pull up into a crack just left of a larger corner and crack just to the right. Follow the crack to finish just left of a boulder hanging over the top of the crag.
FA. Rowland Edwards, Mark Edwards 22.10.1979

Alternative E1 5c start.
Approached from the southern platform at low to mid-tide

6 Fourteen Fathoms. . . . . ⚙🧗 ☐ **E2 5c**
Surprisingly exposed and fingery climbing on the upper wall but with good gear. Low in the grade. Start as for *Axis*.
19m. Gain the ledge above *Axis's* initial fingery wall and climb the arete on the right to the mid-height break. Move right and pull up into a niche above the break. Reach good flake holds just above and left of the niche and using these step left and then up the wall on small holds via a little crack to the top.
FA. Gary Gibson 1982

7 Cruising for a Bruising. . ⚙ ✊ ☐ **E2 5c**
A gymnastic outing up the lower half of the wall, with a much easier finish. Start below the long, low roof at the right-hand side of the starting ledge, 2m right of a blank open groove.
19m. Make a move up left to a good incut and use another directly above to reach the horizontal break under the roof. Reach up right around the roof to good sidepulls and layback around the lip to get established on the wall. Climb the wall to the mid-height horizontal break and then work leftwards to a corner and easier finish.
FA. Paul Rogers, K.Rogers 6.1984

8 Niche Wall. . . . . . . ⚙🧗✏️ ☐ **HS 4b**
Varied climbing with a couple of teasing moves all on superb rock. Start where the lower right side of the X feature meets the platform.
25m. Climb the wall either directly or from the right to a ledge. The thin technical corner above gains another ledge from where a slabby wall leads right to finish.
FA. Rawdon Goodier, J.Lawton 7.7.1955

9 Sea Wolf . . . . ⚙ ☐ **HVS 4c**
The most direct line up the wall is very pleasant. Start at the base of the wall.
25m. Climb up the wall via some disjointed thin cracks to the right side of the ledge on *Niche Wall*. Follow the thin left curving crack above until it is possible to climb up to, and past a small niche to finish.
FA. Rowland Edwards 1983

10 Weasle . . . . ⚙✏️ ☐ **VS 4c**
A cracking pitch with excellent protection. Start at around low tide on a small ledge below an overhang-capped corner on the far right side of the wall.
27m. Climb the corner to the overhang and make a committing move around it to positive holds and a ledge just above. Make a move up the corner at the back of the ledge before moving left around the arete to finish up the obvious crack.
FA. Brian Wilkinson, G.Hollyman 16.4.1976

Southern Platform

The right-hand side of the wall above the spacious Southern Platform is a fine section of the crag and sees less traffic than the other areas of Carn Barra.
Approach - From the bottom of the approach gully, walk left (facing out) to the big ledge at the top of the Central Wall and then continue left via a scramble, at first up and then down to a boulder-strewn area on the cliff-top. From here either abseil straight down to the platform or downclimb short walls and ledges to the platform (Diff).
Tides - The right-hand end of the platform is tidal and is badly affected in heavy seas.
Conditions - The cliff is a suntrap and dries rapidly.

Approach from top of Central Wall

Line of downclimb

Avon Somerset
North Devon
Culm Coast
Inland Cornwall
Atlantic Coast
West Penwith
The Lizard
Inland Devon
Torbay
Dorset

	No star	⚀	⚁	⚂
Mod to S	-	-	-	-
HS to HVS	1	1	5	-
E1 to E3	-	-	-	-
E4 and up	-	-	-	-

Fox Promontory is composed of excellent vertical granite and, although tidal and less easily accessed than many of its neighbouring cliffs, it sees a steady trickle of visits. The climbs are all worthwhile, following good lines that are generally well-protected. The only drawback is the need for dry conditions on the North West Face, which are not frequently found. The location is magnificent, and the views from the cliff are breathtaking.

Approach   Area map on page 187

From the car park at Porthgwarra, take the road to the right up the hill, through a gate and, at the first left bend, carry straight on along a footpath. The path leads across open country and arrives at a distinctive wall made up of huge rocks. Cross the wall and after around 50m head left to the edge of the cliffs where the long jagged ridge of Fox Promontory is easily seen. Drop down to the start of the Promontory and scramble out along its ridge to a gearing-up spot about halfway along, just before some boulders perched on the top of the Promontory. To descend, scramble to the seaward end of the Promontory and abseil down the North West Face to ledges.

Tides

The base of the Promontory is only accessible for 3 hours either side of low water in calm seas. At high tide and in calm seas the higher ledges at the base of The Nose can be accessed by an abseil directly to them from the very tip of the Promontory.

Conditions

The Promontory is very exposed to the elements. The North West Face is prone to dampness and often needs the evening sun to dry it out and bring it into top condition. The Nose is a much sunnier spot and dries out very quickly.

Abseil down Northern Face (A)   Gearing-up spot

Avon Somerset

North Devon

Culm Coast

Inland Cornwall

Atlantic Coast

West Penwith

The Lizard

Inland Devon

Torbay

Dorset

Jonny Aylwin and John Warner checking out the second pitch of
The Whisker (VS 4c) - *page 255* - at the remote Fox Promontory.

The North West Face

A little-visited section of the coastline, that requires favourable tides and dry conditions however, when in condition, the cliff provides some fine pitches that have a remote feel about them. The rock is very slippery when wet.

Approach - The abseil from the top of the seaward end of the Promontory gains large ledges at the base of the North West Face from which the starts are easily reached.

Tides - All of the climbs on the north west face are tidal and are only accessible for around three hours either side of low water in calm seas.

Conditions - The North West Face needs to be dry for the routes to be climbed and this is often only possible once the sun has come onto them from late in the afternoon.

① The Huntsman . . . . **VS 5a**

The series of short thin cracks up the wall just right of where the ledge dips down provide a good exercise that eases in its upper section. Start below the cracks just before the ledge starts to fall away down to the left.

26m. Climb the cracks to easier climbing on the upper half of the pitch.
FA. Andy Gallagher, Brian Wilkinson 28.10.1978

② Reynard's Revenge . . . . **HS 4b**

A stout and strenuous pitch for the grade that stays wetter than the other lines hereabouts. Start at a wide crack-system with an overhang at 8m.

26m. Battle up the crack and over the overhang to a ledge a little higher. Finish up the chimney and easier ground above.
FA. P.Vaughan, E.Herbert 1.6.1966

③ Sunshine Cracks . . . . . . **HS 4b**

The best line on the North West Face. Start at the appealing crack-line 20m to the left of the edge of the face.

26m. Start up the initially wide section of crack to a ledge at 4m and then follow the corner-crack and chimney above to the top.
FA. John Deacon, Alan Blackshaw 20.5.1956

④ Reveille . . . . **HS 4b**

A memorable pitch that contains a good variety of moves. The start especially needs good dry conditions. Start 4m left of the right edge of the face at the base of a left-trending line of improving holds.

28m. Move up and leftwards along the line of improving holds to below a wide crack. Traverse left across the face to another widening crack/chimney and climb this line and the wall above to the top.
FA. John Deacon, Alan Blackshaw 5.1956

⑤ The Curtain Raiser . . . . **HVS 5a**

The thin quartz line in the face to the left of the arete provides the striking line of this route.

27m. Step onto the face and climb the quartz line to a very shallow niche. Above, a slight line of weakness leads right to a ledge and easier climbing up cracks to the top.
FA. Viv Stevenson, Denis Bateman, Don Brown 21.8.1963

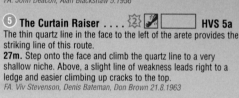

The Nose

Avon Somerset · North Devon · Culm Coast · Inland Cornwall · Atlantic Coast · West Penwith · The Lizard · Inland Devon · Torbay · Dorset

The Nose

The end of Fox Promontory juts out into the sea and has a sunnier aspect than the neighbouring north west face.

Approach - The abseil from the top of the seaward end of the promontory gains large ledges at the base of the North West Face, from which the starts of the climbs on The Nose are easily reached. At high tides in calm seas the ledges at the start of the climbs on The Nose can be reached by abseiling directly down the front face of The Nose.

Tides - The large ledges at the base of The Nose are only accessible for around 3 hours either side of low water in calm sea conditions. However, the higher starting ledges of the climbs are non-tidal in calm seas.

Conditions - The Nose gets lots of sun and the climbs dry quickly.

6 The Muzzle . . . . **HVS 5a**
The handsome corner in the front face of the Promontory. Start from a small ledge in a corner on the right side of the prow.
1) 13m. Climb the low-angled corner to its top and then move left and down to a good ledge and belay below the central corner.
2) 5a, 15m. Nip up the crack to below the final overhanging section which is climbed via a move out onto the left wall.
FA. Alan Blackshaw, John Deacon 20.5.1956

7 The Whisker . . . . **VS 4c**
A pleasant way up the front face of the Promontory. Start from a small ledge in a corner on the right side of the prow.
Photo on page 253.
1) 13m. Climb the low-angled corner to its top and then move left and down to a good ledge and belay below the central corner.
2) 4c, 16m. Move back right and take a slim ramp out to the arete and pull around it. Move up the right side of the arete, past a jutting block to finish up cracks.
FA. Viv Stevenson, Denis Bateman, Don Brown 21.8.1963

Lots of sun | 10 min | | Tidal

The Northern Face

High ledges

Avon Somerset | North Devon | Culm Coast | Inland Cornwall | Atlantic Coast | West Penwith | The Lizard | Inland Devon | Torbay | Dorset

	No star	⭐	⭐⭐	⭐⭐⭐
Mod to S	-	-	2	2
HS to HVS	-	-	4	4
E1 to E3	-	1	3	1
E4 and up	-	-	-	-

Chair Ladder is one of the UK's premier destinations for multi-pitch sea-cliff climbs. The rock, style of climbing and stupendous location are all unbeatable. All the climbs are worthwhile, and the harder routes are rarely busy. Perhaps the cliff's only flaw is that it can be a frustrating place to climb during high seas or when the tides are not conven- ient, although the non-tidal crags of Carn Barra and Porthgwarra Buttress are not far away.

Approach   See main area map on page 187

From the car park at Porthgwarra (fee), take the road to the right up the hill and through a gate. At the first left bend, carry on up the hill on the road to the coastguard lookout, which is directly above the highest section of Chair Ladder. On a first visit, the location of the three main descents (Zawn Rinny, Ash Can Gully and Pinnacle Gully) to the base of the cliff are not immediately obvious, and it is worth taking time to check which gully is which. When standing facing out to sea from the coastguard lookout, the top of Ash Can Gully is 20m to the left, whilst the top of Pinnacle Gully is about 70m to the left. Zawn Rinny is around 150m to the right. For 3 hours either side of low water the base of Chair Ladder is easily traversed (in calm seas) however, each descent has its own merits in accessing the various buttresses.

Zawn Rinny descent - For the Bulging Wall. From the top of Zawn Rinny, follow a path along its west rim (right looking out) and scramble down easy rocks to a huge boulder at the mouth of the zawn. Cross the boulder to the base of the Bulging Wall.

Ash Can Gully descent - Scramble easily down rock and grass to where the gully steepens. Either abseil from this point or downclimb moderate ground to sea level.

Pinnacle Gully descent - The best access for Bishop's Buttress and Terrier's Tooth. Descend the gully to the distinct pinnacle (the summit of *Terrier's Tooth*) and keep descending to the left of the pinnacle until the ground steepens. Either abseil from this point, or downclimb steep ground (at Diff) to the base of the cliff.

Coastguard Lookout

Pendulum Chimney

Bulging Wall

East Gully

Ⓐ

Scramble approach via Zawn Rinny

Zawn Rinny

Large boulder at mouth of zawn

Side tabs: Avon Somerset | North Devon | Culm Coast | Inland Cornwall | Atlantic Coast | West Penwith | The Lizard | Inland Devon | Torbay | Dorset

Tides

The base of Chair Ladder is only accessible for 3 hours either side of low water in calm seas. At higher tides the route *South Face Direct*, and the top 2 pitches of *Aerial* and *Terrier's Tooth* can be easily gained (see relevant section).

Conditions

Chair Ladder is very exposed to the elements and big seas. Great care is needed when traversing the base of the cliff. The rock dries quickly and the cliff gets plenty of sun, although the Bulging Wall section of the cliff stays in the shade longer than the other buttresses. Seagulls can pose problems during the nesting season.

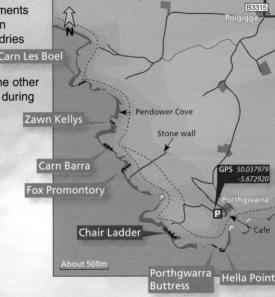

Avon Somerset · North Devon · Culm Coast · Inland Cornwall · Atlantic Coast · West Penwith · The Lizard · Inland Devon · Torbay · Dorset

Avon Somerset

North Devon

Culm Coast

Inland Cornwall

Atlantic Coast

West Penwith

The Lizard

Inland Devon

Torbay

Dorset

① Kittiwake .... HVS 5a

The first pitch is a fine outing. Start at the bottom of the slab, 6m left of the base of *Pegasus*' corner.

1) 5a, 30m. Climb directly up the slab to reach the base of the steep headwall. Pull up and gain a left-trending wide break and continue up the wall above on good holds to a small overhang. Pull through the small overhang and ascend directly to a stance and belay on a good ledge below a long chimney.

2) 30m. Climb the chimney and easier ground above to the top.

FA. J.Cooke 23.5.1968

② Seal Slab .... VS 4c

The meat of this climb is crack-climbing and only the start of the route lives up to its name. Start 6m left of the base of *Pegasus's* corner.

1) 4c, 30m. Climb a faint crack-line rightwards to join a large corner at 10m. Ascend the steepening corner with difficulty to its top and move right to a large ledge and belay.

2) 4b, 20m. Climb easy-angled rock to a crack in the steep wall above a right to left-slanting break. Climb the crack and its continuation to a wide break from where a short awkward section of wide crack above accesses a good ledge and belay.

3) 8m. Climb the easy corner on the left to the top.

FA. G.Smith, John Deacon 1955

③ Pegasus .... HS 4b

The enduring classic of the western end of Chair Ladder provides a long and diverse expedition. Start at a corner-crack in the centre of the bulging wall left of a deep seawater filled trench.

1) 4b, 32m. Climb the wide crack to its end and continue to an overhang above it. Pull over the overhang at a crack (easier on the right) and ascend a short, easy wall to a large ledge and belay.

2) 4a, 20m. Pull up onto a bubbly slab on the right and climb it to the base of a corner. Climb the corner and the enticing right curving continuation to a stance at its end.

3) 4b, 18m. Move back left and make a hard move up onto a ledge. Traverse left to gain another ledge and then step right and finish up a short slabby groove and wide crack.

FA. R.Handley, E.Philips 6.1952

From mid morning | 12 min | Tidal | Multi-pitch

Zawn Rinny

Approach

① ② ③ ④ ⑤

4 West Face Direct ... E2 5c

A series of short and intense pitches which provide some excellent sport. Start at a thin crack-line just right of the corner of *Pegasus*.
1) 5c, 20m. Climb the difficult, thin crack to an easing and then traverse left to a belay under an overhang.
2) 5b, 8m. Make strenuous moves through the bulging overhangs via cracks and gain a large ledge and belay.
3) 5a, 20m. Above the stance is a slab with a steep wall above it. Move up the slab to a blunt arete in the steep wall. Climb the arete to a good ledge on the right. Step up onto the slab on the left and climb it to a ledge and belay.
4) 4c, 15m. Climb through the overhang above and finish up cracks in the wall.
FA. Rowland Edwards, Mark Edwards, A.Sheerder 10.9.1980

5 Rake's Progress ..... VDiff

A long line that has a very traditional feel to it, and is a little dirty in places. Start at the toe of the ramp at the end of a seawater-filled trench.
1) 20m. Climb the intimidating right-trending ramp and crack to a good ledge and spike belay at its right-hand end (care is needed to protect the second on this pitch).
2) 12m. Ascend the large flake rightwards to its top and then work up the slab above it to a stance next to a large crack/corner.
3) 14m. Move right to a crack and climb it to a break. Step right to another wider crack and climb its left wall to a ledge and belay on blocks.
4) 10m. Climb a short crack to a horizontal break, traverse left to a ledge and finish up the corner-crack above it.
FA. R.Handley, A.Hallam, V.Phillips 27.6.1952

Bulging Wall

Set back slightly from Chair Ladder's other faces, the bulging wall is a high and well featured section of rock that has some excellent routes spread across it.
Approach - Descend to the base of the wall via the Zawn Rinny approach or alternatively scramble along the base of the cliff from any of the other descents.
Tides - The base of the wall is tidal and is only accessible for 3 hours either side of low water in calm sea conditions.
Conditions - The wall gets plenty of sun and dries quickly. Nesting birds can be a problem.

Ash Can Gully

South Face Direct - page 258

Avon Somerset · North Devon · Culm Coast · Inland Cornwall · Atlantic Coast · West Penwith · The Lizard · Inland Devon · Torbay · Dorset

Avon Somerset

North Devon

Culm Coast

Inland Cornwall

Atlantic Coast

West Penwith

The Lizard

Inland Devon

Torbay

Dorset

❶ Red Wall . . . . S 4a

Amazing positions on the second pitch make this a memorable route that luckily has a bark far worse than its bite! Start at the wide crack/gully beneath the red tower, a distinct feature of the left side of the buttress.

1) 12m. Climb up via the easiest line and belay on a ledge below the sheer red wall on the left.

2) 4a, 13m. An intimidating pitch. Climb the sheer red wall to the left on surprisingly good holds to a ledge.

3) 4a, 12m. Climb up to the summit of the buttress and make a stride across to a chimney on the left and follow it to a large ledge.

4) 4a, 17m. Take the line of cracks from the back of the ledge, that lead steeply at first, to easier ground and the top.

FA. Jim Courtlandt-Simpson, Eric Stones 1947

❷ Excelsior E1 5b

A long and varied line-up of steep pitches build to an exposed climax on the final headwall. Start left of the base of East Gully.

1) 4b, 13m. Climb three square-cut corners to a large ledge.

2) 5a, 15m. On the left of the ledge are two parallel rounded cracks. Take these steeply, and the crack above, to another good belay ledge.

3) 5a, 17m. Climb easily to another ledge in an overhung recess. Take the steep right hand corner to the overhang and pull right to an exposed ledge and belay.

4) 5b, 12m. Move right beneath the wall to a line of weakness and climb to a black streak. Climb the black streak on small holds to a break and make a final tricky sequence to pass it. The top is just above.

FA. Viv Stevenson, John Deacon 25.10.1959

❸ Pendulum Chimney . . . . S 4b

The classic of this buttress does not disappoint. The climbing is well-protected and can be climbed at highish tides during calm seas by making a straightforward abseil approach down East Gully and belaying on high ledges at the start of the first pitch. *Photo on page 184.*

1) 4a, 13m. Move up easily to the base of a wide crack. Take the crack that leads up left to a large belay ledge.

2) 4a, 12m. Move up to the V-chimney behind the stance and climb it before making a move right and up to a guano stained belay ledge.

3) 4a, 10m. Move right to a steep crack and climb to a belay ledge.

4) 4b, 12m. The wide crack/chimney above leads to a niche from which harder climbing accesses a ledge and belay.

5) 4a, 12m. Continue up short corners, past ledges, to the top of the cliff.

FA. J.Courtland-Simpson, Eric Stones 1947

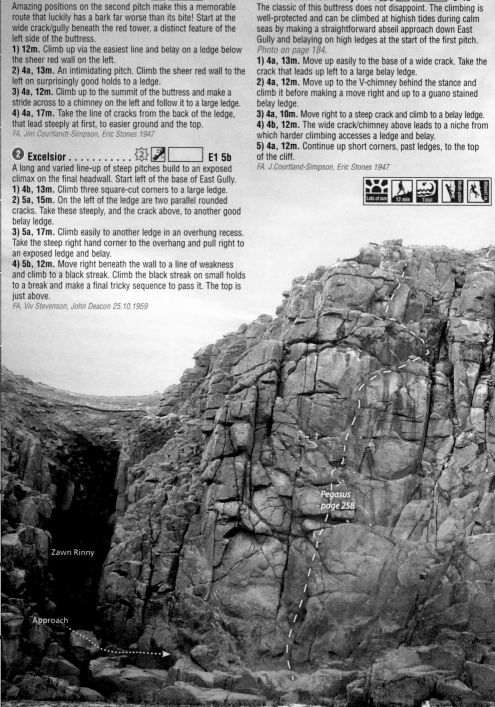

Lots of sun | 12 min | Tidal | Multi-pitch | Abseil in

Zawn Rinny

Approach

Pegasus - page 258

❹ South Face Direct . . . . . [Top 50] ▱ **VS 4c**

Beautiful climbing and positions mark out this route as one of West Penwith's most sought-after VSs. The route can be climbed at high tide during calm seas by making a straightforward abseil approach down East Gully and belaying on high ledges at the start of the first pitch. Start on a good ledge at a crack on the left wall of East Gully, around 10m up from the bottom of the crag.

1) 4a, 14m. Climb the crack to a belay ledge on the left. The ledge is just below where the crack thins.

2) 4c, 20m. Climb up the thin crack-system with difficulty, which soon eases, and continue up the crack to a large mushroom shaped blob. Use the blob to move right into a short corner and follow it to a stance on a good ledge.

3) 4c, 12m. Take the steep crack above, passing the last bulging section with difficulty. Move left to a stance and belay on a long ledge.

4) 4a, 13m. Move right and up behind a large perched block and follow cracks up a wall to the top of the buttress.

FA. Jim Courtlandt-Simpson, Eric Stones 1948

Pendulum Chimney

A tapering tower of walls, cracks and good ledges that gives the routes a good deal of diversity. The climbs are some of the longest on the coast and getting more than one route done is a challenge if the tides are awkward. However, the classic *South Face Direct* can be climbed at high tide by abseiling down East Gully to the start.

Approach - Descend to the base of the wall via the Ash Can Gully approach or alternatively scramble along the base of the cliff from any of the other descents.

Tides - The base of the wall is tidal and is only accessible for 3 hours either side of low water in calm sea conditions.

Conditions - The wall gets plenty of sun and dries quickly. Nesting birds can be a problem during the spring.

Scramble off of the back of the pinnacle down ledges and a wide crack

Ash Can Gully

High tide approach down East Gully

Ⓐ East Gully abseil

Approach

Avon Somerset | North Devon | Culm Coast | Inland Cornwall | Atlantic Coast | West Penwith | The Lizard | Inland Devon | Torbay | Dorset

Lots of sun | 12 min | Tidal | Multi-pitch | Abseil in

Pinnacle Gu

High-tide approach
from Ash Can Gully
(Sev)

Avon Somerset

North Devon

Culm Coast

Inland Cornwall

Atlantic Coast

West Penwith

The Lizard

Inland Devon

Torbay

Dorset

❶ Aerial . . . . 🔋 **VS 4c**

A perfectly-positioned middle pitch and less busy than some of the other lines in the area. The first stance at the start of the best climbing is easily reached at high tide by traversing across and down to it from the lower part of Ash Can Gully (Sev). Start at a thin crack right of the bottom of Ash Can Gully and just to the left of a small corner.

1) 4b, 12m. Climb the thin crack and work up rightwards to a ledge and belay next to an arete on the right.

2) 4c, 22m. Traverse right to double converging cracks and follow these to a good ledge. Take the crack on the left to the overhang and make a short, awkward traverse left beneath it before breaking through at a crack to gain a ledge. Climb the cracks and wall above to a belay.

3) 13m. From the right side of the ledge take the easiest line to the top.

FA. Trevor Peck, Pete Biven 25.5.1956

❷ Caliban . . . . 🔋 **E3 6a**

A testing thin crack up the smooth wall. Start below the thin crack.

1) 6a, 20m. Gain the crack and climb it past 2 old pegs to join *Aerial*. Continue to *Aerial's* second stance.

2) 13m. Finish as for *Aerial*.

FFA. Jon de Montjoye, A.Whitehouse 18.4.1981

❸ Flannel Avenue . . . 🔋 **HS 4b**

Space-walking stuff on its final pitch and with plenty of interesting climbing throughout. Quite tough at the grade. Start above the 'Suicide Pool' at a deep, narrowing chimney.

1) 4b, 24m. Bridge up the chimney and where it narrows move out onto its left rib. This point can also be gained by climbing the corner-crack right of the chimney to a ledge and then moving left. Move up and then step right to a ledge on the main buttress. Climb to a small stance at the left end of the roof that comes in from the right. This pitch can be split above the initial chimney.

2) 4a, 17m. Traverse rightwards above the lip of the overhang and follow cracks up the centre of the wall in a fantastic position until a leftward line can be followed to a big ledge and belay blocks.

3) 4b,11m. The line of steep thin cracks above the centre of the ledge provides an excellent but short lived finish.

FA. Royal Marines 1949

❹ Diocese . . . . 🔋 **VS 5a**

One of Cornwall's greatest VS routes. High in the grade and requiring a broad selection of techniques, the line follows the huge corner up the middle of Bishop's Buttress before making a memorable leftwards traverse to clear the huge roof. Start at a short crack just left of the corner-line.

1) 4c, 20m. Move up to a long ledge and then move right into the wide crack. Climb the slab and corner right of the wide crack (or the wide crack itself) to join up with the wide crack once again at 7m. Climb the widening crack awkwardly to a stance in the back of the crack beneath the roof.

2) 5a, 10m. Make a technical horizontal traverse left across the face and move up a little way to a stance where the overhang fades. (The crack that runs underneath the roof to the stance may also be climbed at around the same standard).

3) 4a, 15m. Climb cracks in the wall directly above the stance to a large ledge and block-belays.

4) 4b, 11m. The line of steep thin cracks above the centre of the ledge as for *Flannel Avenue*.

FA. M.Ridges, J.Lilly 1951

Wolf and Bishop's Buttress

The showpiece of Chair Ladder is Bishop's Buttress, its fine lines and superb rock making it one of West Penwith's most attractive venues. The slender, adjoining Wolf Buttress is climbed centrally by *Aerial*, whose main pitches can be accessed at high tide via a traverse from Ash Can Gully.

Approach - Descend via either Ash Can Gully or Pinnacle Gully.

Tides - The base of the wall is tidal and is only accessible for 3 hours either side of low water in calm sea conditions.

Conditions - The wall gets plenty of sun and dries quickly.

❺ The Spire. . . . . . . 🔋 **E3 5c**

The hairline crack in the rib to the right of *Diocese's* corner gives a fine pitch with a difficult initial wall. Start above a trench at the foot of the very thin crack.

1) 5c, 20m. Climb the thin, technical crack with difficulty to a ledge at 8m. Move left and follow the thin line up the wall right of the arete to a steep narrow corner. Follow the corner to a semi hanging stance just above.

2) 4c, 22m. Climb the cracks directly above the stance to a break and continue easily up cracks and blocks to ledges. Either belay here and then scramble off to the right or move left and continue easily for a further 15m to the top of the buttress.

FA. Pat Littlejohn, Toni Carver 4.7.1974

❻ Bishop's Rib. . . . . . 🔋 **E1 5b**

Engrossing and varied climbing up the right-hand side of the buttress. The initial slab is often damp and needs a little afternoon sun on it to dry it out. Start in the deep shady corner on the right side of the buttress.

1) 5b, 13m. Move up and traverse up leftwards across the slabby wall with spaced protection to a small ledge below a left-facing corner that rises to the stepped overhang. Make some difficult moves up the corner and pull over the overhang then continue to a stance just beneath the next overhang.

2) 5a, 20m. Climb the wall on the left to another overlap and traverse a crack steeply left until it is possible to pull up through yet another small overlap onto the wall. Climb the wall via the most obvious crack to a good ledge.

3) 20m. Climb easily up and left to the summit of the buttress.

FA. John Deacon, J.Oakes 1956 (accessed from Diocese)
FA.. Mike McDermott, R.Mellor, Denis Bateman 21.7.1963 (Line in its entirety)

❼ Bishop's Arete . . . . . . 🔋 **HVS 5a**

Although not one of the well known classics of Chair Ladder, this hybrid is a very worthwhile climb that travels across some of the best bits of Bishop's Buttress and finishes up its right arete in a very spectacular position. Start as for *Diocese*.

1) 4b, 14m. Follow *Diocese* to the point just before it rejoins the wide corner-crack and pull right around the arete and traverse to the first stance of *Bishop's Rib*.

2) 5a, 20m. Pull over the overhang and make hard moves up right onto, and up the arete to a wide break. Climb the arete using wide, flared cracks to a good ledge.

3) 20m. Climb easily up and left to the summit of the buttress.

FA. Rowland Edwards, Mark Edwards, Nick Wharton 18.10.1981

Avon Somerset | North Devon | Culm Coast | Inland Cornwall | Atlantic Coast | West Penwith | The Lizard | Inland Devon | Torbay | Dorset

Terrier's Tooth

One of Cornwall's great summits that is climbed on its front face by this superb route. The positions, rock and summit are magnificent. If the base of the route is inaccessible due to high water or rough seas, the stance at the end of the first pitch can be easily reached via a short traverse from the Pinnacle Gully descent.

Approach - Descend via Pinnacle Gully.

Tides - The base of the wall is tidal and is only accessible for 3 hours either side of low water in calm sea conditions.

Conditions - The pinnacle gets plenty of sun and dries quickly.

1 Terrier's Tooth . . . . Top 50 **VDiff**

A classic expedition up the seaward side of the large tooth-topped pinnacle, the summit of which can be seen in the lower reaches of Pinnacle Gully. There are two starts described the second being VS, a fine pitch but more difficult and serious than the rest of the climb. Start at the base of a steep and rounded vertical crack in the middle of the buttress.

1) 18m. From the base of the steep crack move up leftwards to a wide rounded crack in the corner on the left and follow this to a ledge. Move up the wall and crack leftwards to a good ledge and belay.

1a) VS 4b, 17m. Climb the tricky stepped vein in the wall 5m left of the steep rounded crack to a good small spike runner. Pull up to easier terrain and climb the wall just right of the arete to a good ledge and belay. *Photo opposite.*

2) 10m. Take the steep crack above the ledge on good holds to another ledge and belay.

3) 12m. Climb up the corner behind the stance and move right onto the front of the pinnacle, beneath a wide crack in the summit block. Move up into the crack and climb to the summit.

Descent - Either stay roped-up and downclimb the steep wall to the left (looking up the gully) at Diff standard, or abseil from a prominent spike on the landward side of the summit.

FA. J.Mallory, M.Roster 24.3.1940

FA. J.Barford, F.Feilden 25.8.1940 (Variation first pitch)

Avon Somerset

North Devon

Culm Coast

Inland Cornwall

Atlantic Coast

West Penwith

The Lizard

Inland Devon

Torbay

Dorset

Nearing the end of the variation first pitch of *Terrier's Tooth* (VS 4b) - *opposite* - at Chair Ladder. Climber John Warner.

	No star	☆	☆☆	☆☆☆
Mod to S	-	1	2	1
HS to HVS	1	2	1	-
E1 to E3	-	-	4	-
E4 and up	-	-	-	-

Close to the charming fishing cove of Porthgwarra and the perfectly proportioned beach at St. Levan, are a collection of cliffs that, although not of the same quality as nearby Chair Ladder, are well worth tracking down. The climbs on offer range from multi-pitch easier lines at Porthgwarra Buttress and Hella Point, to a handful of single-pitch, harder lines on the compact, steep faces of Vessacks West and St. Levan's Wall. All of these cliffs are in beautiful surroundings and are convenient for a bit of post climbing relaxation on the beach.

Approach   See main area map on page 187

Porthgwarra Buttress and Hella Point - From the car park at Porthgwarra (fee), walk back towards the cove and turn right onto the coast path. Follow the coast path, always taking the left turn until the pinnacle of Hella Point comes into view on the first headland (5 mins). Gear up here.

Vessacks West - From the car park at Porthgwarra (fee), walk back towards the cove, turn left and pick up signs for the coast path. Walk east on the coast path for around 1km to a distinct split in the path (note 50m prior to the split in the path the cliff can be viewed in profile). Take the right branch of the path for 100m and then turn right on a faint path that leads down to the top of the cliff (20 mins). Either abseil to the base or scramble down to the left (facing out).

St. Leven's Wall - Park at St. Leven (fee). Follow the footpath to the beach. From the left end of the beach (facing out) scramble over large boulders to the wall (12 mins).

Tides

All of the cliffs are tidal, the bases only being accessible for around 3 hours either side of low water in calm sea conditions. However, the bases of the cliffs become wave-washed in moderate seas.

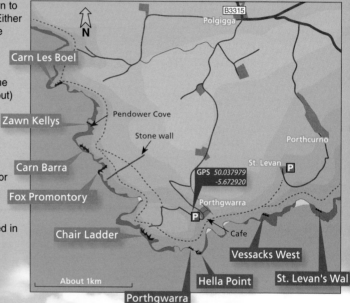

B3315
Polgigga
Carn Les Boel
N
Pendower Cove
Zawn Kellys
Stone wall
Porthcurno
Carn Barra
St. Levan
P
GPS 50.037979
-5.672920
Fox Promontory
Porthgwarra
P
Cafe
About 1km
Chair Ladder
Vessacks West
Hella Point
St. Levan's Wal
Porthgwarra
Buttress

Hella Point

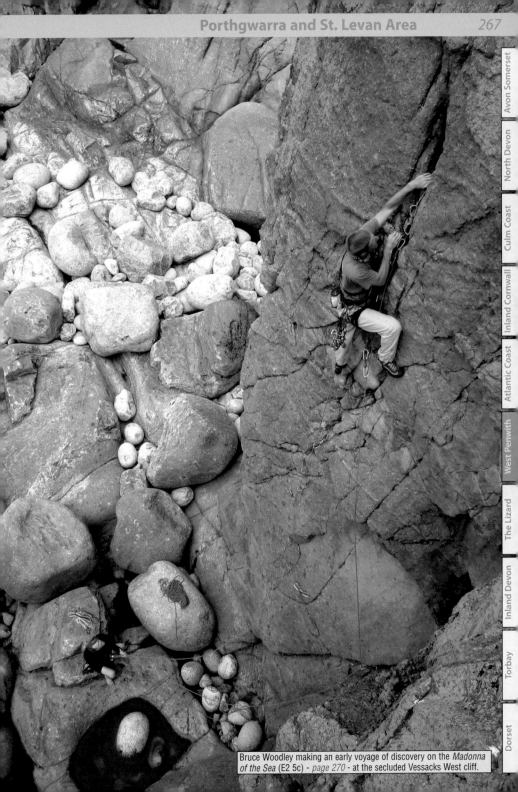

Avon Somerset

North Devon

Culm Coast

Inland Cornwall

Atlantic Coast

West Penwith

The Lizard

Inland Devon

Torbay

Dorset

Bruce Woodley making an early voyage of discovery on the *Madonna of the Sea* (E2 5c) - *page 270* - at the secluded Vessacks West cliff.

Porthgwarra Buttress

A large and heavily-featured buttress composed of superb rounded granite with a trio of worthwhile climbs that are quickly accessed, sunny and in a gorgeous setting.

Approach - Descend the large gully on the right (facing out) and scramble down boulders and ledges until a short traverse and descent of a corner is necessary to get to the base of *Porthgwarra Face* itself. A rope may be needed for this last section which is Mod standard. Alternatively abseil to the base from directly above the face.

Tides - The base of *Porthgwarra Face* is only accessible for 3 hours either side of low water.

Conditions - A sunny and sheltered cliff and a good option if waiting for tides at Chair Ladder or Hella Point.

❶ Porthgwarra Face . . . . . ☒ 🖉 ☐ VDiff

One of the earliest and very best rock climbs of its grade discovered on the peninsula. Although described in three pitches it is often accomplished in one. Start at some right-trending cracks and holds above the lower of the smooth ledges at the base of the face.

1) 17m. Take the good holds and cracks to a stance and belay.

3) 17m. Follow the crack to another good ledge below an overhang.

3) 8m. Move up under the overhang and traverse right to an easy finishing slope.

FA. Colin Kirkus, P.Fallows 7.8.1938

❷ Shawangunk . . . . ☒ 🖉 ☐ VS 4b

A long and varied pitch that has a couple of sections of gritty rock. Start on the high sloping ledge below the line. Good, low nut-belay.

32m. Move up to an overlap and then climb the serrated crack above it rightwards to a ledge. Step left to a short runnel and reach above this for a jug. Move up and then rightwards to the base of a long, easy chimney and follow this past two chockstones to the top.

FA. Mike Westmacott, Sally Westmacott, Roger Chorley 5.1966

❸ Porthgwarra Chimney . . ☒ 🖉 ☐ S 4a

The crack and chimney line on the right of the high, sloping ledge is a challenging but worthwhile pitch. Start on the high sloping ledge below the line. Good low nut on the left for a belay.

32m. Climb up and right into the line and move up to below where the crack widens and becomes rounded. Make some awkward moves to get started on the rounded section of the chimney before things ease towards the top.

FA. Wilfred Noyce 3.1956

Approach

Final section of the descent is Mod

Hella Point

The distinctive conical pinnacle of Hella Point is the centrepiece in a stunning setting and home to the excellent *Helluva Slab*, a good climb that compares with the those on nearby Chair Ladder.

Approach - Scramble down at first left and then back right (when facing the pinnacle) to boulders linking the mainland to the pinnacle. From the boulders, climb easily to a ledge just below the top of the pinnacle. Abseil down the far side of the pinnacle to a traverse line that leads to the start of *Helluva Slab*. The general line of the abseil is Diff standard and can be downclimbed

Tides - The base of *Helluva Slab* is accessible between low and mid tides, but not at all in heavy seas.

Conditions - Sunny on *Helluva Slab* and shady on *Sun Shadow*.

④ **Sun Shadow** . . . . 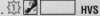 **HVS 5a**

A sustained route that ventures on to the shady landward face of the pinnacle. Start on a sea level ledge at the base of a narrow, west facing slab - *Helluva Slab*.

1) 5a, 22m. Climb the left side of the slab to a wide, horizontal break that leads left onto the landward-facing wall. Traverse left onto the face and climb a crack and flake to a good ledge and belay.

2) 4c, 16m. Step left from the ledge and climb the left-slanting line of cracks and grooves to the top.

FA. Rowland Edwards, Mark Edwards 30.7.1982

⑤ **Helluva Slab** . . . . **S 4a**

When viewed from the mainland, the long seaward edge of Hella Point is an irresistible line. The approach and the climb itself combine to provide a classic outing at the grade. Start on a small ledge below a slab at the base of the arete.

1) 4a, 17m. Climb the slab to a large ledge and belay.

2) 14m. Climb the chimney and move up over blocks to a good ledge and belay.

3) 4b, 12m. Boulder up the wall above the ledge and continue up a chimney to finish. Scramble off and reverse the approach back to the mainland.

FA. Cliff Fishwick, R.Fishwick 25.5.56

Porthgwarra Buttress

Abseil down seaward face, and traverse to the base of Helluva Slab

Vessacks West

A small but delightfully-located cliff that has a couple of very interesting lines, which are unlikely to be busy. The beach at St. Leven is only a matter of minutes away.

Approach - Abseil to the base of the cliff or scramble down to the left (looking out) and then walk back right to below the lines.

Tides - The cliff is tidal and is only accessible for around 3 hours either side of low water.

Conditions - The wall faces southwest but the corners have a more northerly aspect and the climbs are partly shaded until late afternoon.

❶ Madonna of the Waves . **E2 5c**

A shy, but very beautiful little route taking the steep, crack infested wall left of the corner with a large rock pool at its base. Well-protected and low in the grade. Start just left of the corner. *Photo on page 267.*

20m. Move up a right-slanting crack almost into the corner and then move left to a good hold. Climb up leftwards to the start of the cracks in the upper wall and climb these to finish up a small corner.

FA. Brian Wilkinson, Margaret Grapes 1.9.1996

❷ Saskia . . . . **HVS 5a**

A suitable partner to its alluring neighbour which tackles the corner-crack above the rock pool. The initial traverse above the rock pool that guards the base of the corner will provide much fun for onlookers! Start on the right-hand side of the rock pool.

20m. Traverse left just above the rock pool on smooth rock and enter the corner steeply. Climb the vertical corner which gradually eases to finish.

FA. Brian Wilkinson, Margaret Grapes 18.8.1996

Scramble approach

Large rock-pool

3 Bermuda Wall E3 5c
A very good single-pitch that takes a right-trending line of flakes across the wall. The start is bold. Start on a block at the beginning of the thin line in the lower wall.
18m. Make some fingery and bold moves off of the block to better holds. Climb the right-trending line more easily to the top.
FA. Martin Doyle, John Hooper 4.1983

4 Devil's Meridian . . . E2 5c
The central, thin crack is a very fine but hard won pitch. Well-protected. Start at the base of the crack.
16m. Climb the thin crack to join *Bermuda Wall* at its final moves.
FA. Andrew Trevorrow, Pete O'Sullivan 18.3.1984

5 Midnight Express . . E1 5b
The very thin crack and narrow corner on the right-hand side of the wall are superb, but at the very upper limit of the grade.
16m. Climb the hairline crack past a good hold and runner to the horizontal break. Finish up the still pressing narrow corner above.
Photo on page 11.
FA. Andrew Trevorrow, Des Hannigan 3.3.84

6 Geriatrics . . . . S 4a
A good warm-up and the easiest way up the wall. Start at the base of a right-slanting weakness.
17m. Climb the crack and ramp to mid-height before finishing up the black slab on the left.
FA. R.James, A.Skinner 20.8.1977

St. Leven's Wall
A short, tough wall of excellent rock that is very close to a magnificent beach. The climbs are all hard work at their respective grades but still very worthwhile. Although close to the beach, care is needed with the approach as the boulders quickly become wave-washed and in rough seas they can be dangerous to cross.
Approach - From the left end (looking out) of the beach boulder-hop along the foreshore to the base of the cliff. If caught out by the tide, climb out from the large ledge above the climbs and then scramble up to the headland and take the coast path back to the beach.
Descent - At around low water walk left (facing out) for around 50m and then downclimb to the base of the cliff, or abseil from various large blocks on top of the wall.
Tides - The base of the climbs are non-tidal but the approach is only possible for around 3 hours either side of low water.
Conditions - The wall gets plenty of sun from around midday and dries quickly.

Lots of sun | 12 min | Tidal

Avon Somerset | North Devon | Culm Coast | Inland Cornwall | Atlantic Coast | West Penwith | The Lizard | Inland Devon | Torbay | Dorset

	No star	☆	☆☆	☆☆☆
Mod to S	-	-	-	-
HS to HVS	1	1	1	1
E1 to E3	-	1	2	-
E4 and up	-	2	3	2

The section of coastline that runs east from the idyllic beach of Porthcurno to Lamorna Cove has three characterful crags dotted along its picturesque fringe. Cribba Head and St. Loy are composed of the finest granite and are home to some bold and difficult testpieces that follow jutting aretes and featureless slabs. In contrast, Tater Du is a large, dark greenstone cliff that hides one of the area's classic routes that requires crisp conditions and a benign sea as prerequisites for an ascent.

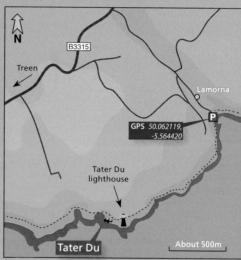

Approaches   See main area map on page 187

Cribba Head - From the B3315/B3283 St. Buryan to Land's End road, turn off to the village of Treen and park in its car park (fee). Walk out of the car park entrance and turn left. Walk along the road for 15m until a footpath to Logan Rock on the left is encountered (care needed to find this). Follow the footpath that heads off rightwards across fields from the initial track, and when at the coast path, turn left and walk towards the next headland. As the path crosses the headland, break right onto a narrow path through gorse, out to Cribba Head. Various paths and scrambling, either left or right (care required), gain the base of the face.

St. Loy - There is no short way to this cliff due to the lack of parking anywhere near the closest public footpaths. Park at Penberth where there are only a few parking places (or Treen if this is full). Follow the undulating coast path east for around 2km until the cliff becomes visible on the hillside ahead, high above the sea. Walk to a point directly above the crag and drop down to its top. If staying at the Treverven Campsite (no public parking), a shorter approach via a path from the campsite to the coast path is possible.

Tater Du - Park at Lamorna harbour car park (fee). Walk along the road past the cafe and out to a small quarry. Pick up the coastal path ahead, marked by yellow arrows, and follow this past one headland from where the Tater Du lighthouse comes into view. Continue along the coast path until directly above the lighthouse from where a steep concrete track leads directly down to the lighthouse. Go down the track to the unmanned lighthouse and walk right a short distance to the cliff-top.

Tater Du lighthouse.

Side tabs (left margin): Avon Somerset | North Devon | Culm Coast | Inland Cornwall | Atlantic Coast | West Penwith | The Lizard | Inland Devon | Torbay | Dorset

Tides

Both Cribba Head and St. Loy are non-tidal. Tater Du is tidal and is only accessible for 3 hours either side of low tide.

Conditions

Cribba Head and St. Loy are located well above the sea, have sunny aspects and dry very quickly. Tater Du can seep after wet weather and the rock is very slippery if damp. The base of the cliff is wave-washed in moderate seas even at low tide.

Midway up the fine corner-line of *Kernyck* (HS 4b) - *page 274* - Cribba Head. The super serious aretes of *Question Mark* (E9 6c) and *Pre-Marital Tension* (E8 6c) are on either side. Photo: Alex Ekins.

Avon Somerset | North Devon | Culm Coast | Inland Cornwall | Atlantic Coast | West Penwith | The Lizard | Inland Devon | Torbay | Dorset

Avon Somerset | North Devon | Culm Coast | Inland Cornwall | Atlantic Coast | West Penwith | The Lizard | Inland Devon | Torbay | Dorset

❶ Pass the Pigs E4 6a

The bow-shaped flared crack is a meaty and difficult line. Start just left of the arete.

19m. Pull up and climb to meet the crack as it widens. Follow the crack to where it fades and use a small hold to gain the wide break with difficulty. Finish up the rounded, wide crack. A good selection of medium to large cams are useful.
FA. Andy Grieve, Nick Hancock 30.12.1982

❷ Lovely, Lovely, Lovely E5 6b

The striking flake and arete provide an enticing, though difficult lead. Start below the arete.

20m. Pull up into the flake and follow it to its end. Make difficult moves up to the next flake and follow this rightwards to the wide, horizontal break, then step left and finish up the short wall.
FA. Nick Hancock, Andy Grieve, Graham Butler 2.9.1982

❸ Question Mark . . . E9 6c

The severely overhanging arete to the left of the deep, central corner is a fingery and extremely bold undertaking. Start at the base of the corner.

20m. Climb the steep, shallow flake-line to a horizontal edge at mid-height and some meager protection from a nut and sky hooks. Continue up the increasingly-difficult arete to an easing just below the top.
FA. Mark Edwards 1994 (headpointed)

❹ Kernyck . . . . HS 4b

The deep-set corner is a fine line and has climbing to match. Start below the corner. *Photo on page 273.*

20m. Climb the corner past a perched block to a rest. Increasingly-testing moves lead airily to the top.
FA. Mike McDermott, Denis Bateman 9.5.1965

❺ Boysen's Groove E3 5c

The slim curving corner is a battle from beginning to end. Start at the base of the tapering corner.

21m. Fight up the corner to an easing before finishing up the flake-crack above. Well protected.
FA. Martin Boysen, Alan Hubbard 1981

Cribba Head

The intimidating aretes, rounded cracks and deep corners found here are some of the hardest routes on the peninsula.

Approach - Descend awkward ground, care required, to the base of the crag.

Descent - Climb down the landward end of the summit ridge to a gully and then take the short easy gully on the east side of the cliff to a wide ledge that quickly gains the base of the climbs.

Conditions - The cliff gets plenty of sun and dries very quickly, although there is little shelter from wind or rain.

❻ Pre-Marital Tension

. . . . E8 6c

The jaw-dropping central arete is a masterpiece. Start at the base of the arete.

20m. Climb the left-hand side of the arete all the way to the top. Skyhooks protect the central section of the line.
FA. Nick Dixon, T.Reseigh 1990 (headpointed)

❼ Harder . . . . VS 4c

The shorter corner, right of *Pre-Marital Tension*.

17m. Climb the very steep corner and right wall to the top.
FA. Mike McDermott, Denis Bateman 9.5.1965

❽ Storms over Africa

. . . . E5 6a

A tight line which has a number of variations. Start just to the right of the arete.

15m. Climb the right wall of the arete to the base of a thin crack just to the right of the arete. Climb the thin crack and arete without recourse to the crack-system on the right for either gear or holds.
FA. Mark Edwards 1990

❾ Boysen's Cracks E2 5c

Another innocuous-looking crack that puts up a good fight. Start below the full-height crack-system on the narrow front face of the cliff.

15m. Climb the sustained thin cracks to the top. Well protected.
FA. Martin Boysen, Alan Hubbard 1981

Lots of sun | 15 min

Approach →

⑩ Chlorophyll Cluster .... 🔖 🖊️ ▢ E1 5b

Popular and well-protected climbing taking on the large flakes and cracks up the left side of the main wall. Well worth the walk and a good consolation should the other lines here prove too harsh. Start at the base of the main left to right line of weakness in the centre of the crag.

32m. Gain the excellent right-facing layback crack either from the easy line of weakness, or direct via a couple of moves up the wall just to the left. The layback crack ends at a good ledge and a possible belay. From the ledge, move left and climb up the steep twin cracks above a small overlap. The left-hand crack gradually widens to hand width as height is gained and this is followed until just below the top, where a step left and then up is required to finish. The hand-crack has some grass in it but this does not get in the way of the climbing. Thread belays in blocks well back.

FA. Phil Gordon 14.6.1970

⑪ The Baldest ...... 🔖 🖊️ ▢ E5 6a

Immaculate granite climbing and a stunning line is tempered by serious situations. Start as for *Chlorophyll Cluster*.

31m. Follow *Chlorophyll Cluster* up the layback flake to the possible belay ledge. Take the wide crack directly above to a point where moves out right and up on crystals gain an easing just above a small overlap and a small micro nut on the left. Move up the steep slab and then reach up left to a thin seam which widens to a crack higher up. Move up the seam on improving holds before stepping left to a final finger-crack. Thread belays in blocks well back.

FA. Pat Littlejohn, Steve Jones 7.4.1974

St. Loy

Remote and beautifully positioned well above the sea, the main face of St. Loy is a challenging, just off the vertical, wall of rounded granite. The climbing is superb but the protection on the harder lines is some of the worst and taking to the air is not recommended. Although the approach is a relatively long one, the scenery on view from the coast path is charming.

Approach - From the top of the crag, drop down to the grassy base of the wall on a good path that follows the right flank looking out.

Descent - As for the approach to the base of the wall.

Conditions - Its location, well above the sea, and its sunny aspect, make St. Loy a good option in cool weather or during high seas. There is little shelter from the rain and getting caught-out en-route after the long walk-in is not a pleasant thought.

⑫ Finesse .... 🔖 🖊️ ▢ E4 5c

A stiff first pitch contrasts with a death-defying unprotected second. Start below a thin, left-facing flake right of the main left to right weakness.

1) 5c, 17m. Make difficult fingery moves to gain and then leave the flake rightwards to eventually reach more substantial holds in a crack that comes in from the right. Continue with less difficulty up flakes and cracks to a narrow ledge and a high spike plus nut belays.

2) 5c, 16m. Unprotected. Follow the line of holds rightwards up the wall and then step up right onto scooped holds before making a heart-in-mouth friction move to better holds and easier ground above. Thread belays in blocks well back.

FA. Pat Littlejohn, Steve Jones 5.4.1974

Descent

Approach

Avon Somerset · North Devon · Culm Coast · Inland Cornwall · Atlantic Coast · West Penwith · The Lizard · Inland Devon · Torbay · Dorset

Lighthouse 100m

A Descent

Low-tide approach

Avon Somerset
North Devon
Culm Coast
Inland Cornwall
Atlantic Coast
West Penwith
The Lizard
Inland Devon
Torbay
Dorset

① Crow's Nest Ordinary . .   **HS 4b**

A good way up the cliff that gradually increases in exposure as height is gained. Start on the left side of the cliff at a ramp that runs up below the cliff.

1) 25m. From the ramp, climb up easily to a gangway that also runs up leftwards and ends at a steep corner. Follow the gangway until a break in its right wall allows a slab above to be gained. Climb the slab rightwards to a ledge and belay.

2) 4b, 28m. Climb leftwards up into a depression on the arete of the face below the upper overhangs. Traverse left around the arete on good holds and then make an airy stride left to below a final steep wall which is climbed on good holds to the top.
FA. Viv Stevenson, G.Wilson 6.11.1962

② Martell Slab . . . . . . Top 150   **VS 4c**

An often overlooked classic on a fine crag. The climbing and line are intricate and in its lower reaches on compact rock that requires crisp conditions. The first pitch is high in the grade. Start in the back of the recess at a short, thin corner-crack. *Photo on this page.*

1) 4c, 18m. Step up into the thin corner-crack from the right and climb it for a couple of metres before stepping onto the slab on the left. Move up to a niche and high runners. Bridge up to good hand holds above the niche and step left to a crack. Follow the crack until the slab on its left can be climbed to a fine ledge and belay.

2) 8m. Traverse rightwards on easy ground to a good ledge below a steep corner.

3) 4b, 17m. Climb the steep corner and then move left to another. Follow the corner to an overhang and pull leftwards on good holds to clear it before a short wall gains the top.
FA. John Deacon, Derek Holroyd 1957

Tater Du

An underrated cliff that proves to be an extensive and fairly intimidating spot. The rock is generally solid, although towards the top it becomes slightly unreliable and has a good covering of lichen.

Approach - Abseil to the base of the cliff.

Tides - The bottom of the cliff is tidal and is only accessible for 3 hours either side of low water. However, in anything but reasonably calm sea conditions the base is wave-washed even at low water.

Conditions - Seepage can be a problem and if at all damp the rock becomes frictionless.

Avon Somerset
North Devon
Culm Coast
Inland Cornwall
Atlantic Coast
West Penwith
The Lizard
Inland Devon
Torbay
Dorset

The first pitch of the outlying, and often overlooked classic *Martell Slab* (VS 4c) - *opposite* - Tater Du.

The Lizard

The slabs and walls of Pen Olver offer some great pitches in spectacular surroundings. James Aird and Lucy Hammond on *Blind Pew* (VDiff) - *page 292*

Dorset · Torbay · Inland Devon · The Lizard · West Penwith · Atlantic Coast · Inland Cornwall · Culm Coast · North Devon · Avon Somerset

The peninsula of the Lizard protrudes southward from the inland granite spine of western Cornwall and provides the region with yet another wild and intriguing set of sea-cliffs.
The rock varies from the fine-grained granite of Trewavas Head, to the dark and jagged amphibolite-faces of the cliffs clustered around the tip of the Lizard peninsula. In the main it is well weathered and seamed with cracks.
The climbing on the Lizard is not as extensive or as well-trodden as that of is near neighbour West Penwith, however, the cliffs and climbs provide a worthwhile alternative, and the beaches and scenery are spectacular. One of the Lizard's main attractions is its potential for providing some sheltered climbing during northerly gales; Trewavas and Pen Olver are well worth a look should Bosigran and Chair Ladder be too windy or the sea rough. Most of the climbs rarely see more than one or two parties in action, with the exception of Trewavas which has become a very popular little cliff.

Getting Around

Access to the parking spots, from where all the cliffs are approached is relatively straight-forward. The main roads from Penzance, St Ives and the Falmouth area quickly lead to Helston from where all the approach roads are easily located.

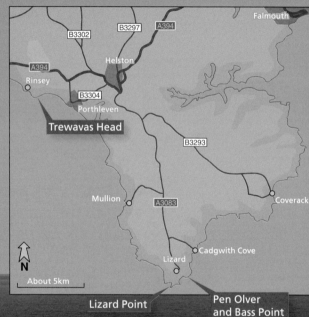

Pat Littlejohn on his own route *Lazarus* (E6 6b) - *page 295* - at Bass Point, Lizard Point.

Sidebar tabs: Avon Somerset | North Devon | Culm Coast | Inland Cornwall | Atlantic Coast | West Penwith | The Lizard | Inland Devon | Torbay | Dorset

Avon Somerset

North Devon

Culm Coast

Inland Cornwall

Atlantic Coast

West Penwith

The Lizard

Inland Devon

Torbay

Dorset

Tom Skelhon nearing the finish of the exposed *Mae West* (HVS 5a) - *page 289* - on the Hollywood Walls at Lizard Point.

	No star	☆	☆☆	☆☆☆
Mod to S	-	2	-	-
HS to HVS	-	2	2	-
E1 to E3	-	-	1	-
E4 and up	-	-	-	-

Trewavas Head is a small, granite crag that has a number of popular climbs, set high above the clutches of the sea. Although not strictly on the Lizard, its position, close to the town of Helston, puts it within easy striking distance of the routes further to the south. Trewavas Head is a reliable spot to search out if a gale is blowing from the north or the sea is too rough.

Approach   See main area map on page 280

From the A394 Penzance to Helston road, turn onto the minor road signed to Rinsey at the village of Ashton. Follow the signs to Rinsey hamlet and take a track to the National Trust car park. Follow the coast path down to an old mine building and take the path that gently climbs up hill (not the coast path). Follow the path which skirts walls and open ground past another cluster of old mine buildings until a short, steep section of crag can be seen on the right. A little further on, where the path crosses a wall, cut right to the top of the main crag. A path leads down the eastern side of the cliff to its base (20 minutes).

Tides

The cliff is on a vegetated slope well above the sea.

Conditions

Trewavas Head is very sheltered from north and westerly winds, however it does not offer the possibility of climbing in the rain.

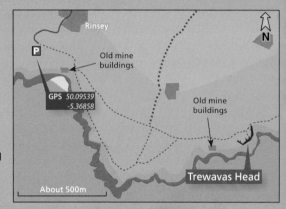

Pulling through the upper overhang of the finely positioned *West Wing* (E2 5c) - *page 284* - at Trewavas Head. Photo: Steve Watt

Avon Somerset | North Devon | Culm Coast | Inland Cornwall | Atlantic Coast | West Penwith | The Lizard | Inland Devon | Torbay | Dorset

Avon Somerset

North Devon

Culm Coast

Inland Cornwall

Atlantic Coast

West Penwith

The Lizard

Inland Devon

Torbay

Dorset

Paul Cox pulling through the crux of *Mascara* (VS 4c) - *page 285* - at Trewavas Head.

Trewavas Head

The section of Trewavas Head described here is the most significant and has a number of very rewarding single-pitch lines that are on very good steep granite.

Approach - From the summit of the buttress, a good but steep and narrow path leads down the eastern side of the walls to below the faces. An alternative descent is under the south face, see topo.

Descent - As for the approach.

① Mouseproof . . . . **S 4a**

A neat little line with a couple of balancy moves. Start below a wide corner/groove 10m down the alternative easy way down.

12m. Climb the corner to a ledge. Move up to a slab and step up onto it via a balancy move. Finish steeply up the arete.

FA. Sam Salmon, M.Crayton 2.9.1981

② Avalanche . . . . **VS 5a**

A well-protected pitch that builds to an exciting climax. Start at the base of a wide recess.

14m. Climb up the wide recess to the steep upper cracks. Climb the thin middle crack with assistance from its wider right-hand neighbour to the top.

FA. Les Williams, Denis Bateman 15.9.1974

③ West Wing **E2 5c**

A wildly exposed prow is preceded by a deceptively technical groove. Start below a groove on the seaward face just left of the rounded arete. *Photo on page 282.*

23m. Make a committing semi-mantel to get established at the base of the groove. Climb the technical groove to where it eases, then traverse a break rightwards to below an overhang on the edge of the exposed prow. Pull through the overhang and move up the short wall to the summit of the prow - belay advisable here. Step across the gap back onto the main crag and the top just above.

FA. Shane Ohly, M.Bell, G.Slade 19.1.1994

Alternative descent

④ Colomen . . . .  **HVS 4c**

An initially serious slabby wall gives way to a steep crack-system. Start at a left-slanting seam, right of the broad arete.

22m. Climb the seam past a ledge on the right, then make a committing move left to a good foothold in the shallow groove on the left, and a thread in the break above. Climb the gradually steepening line of cracks to the col between the prow and the main cliff. Finish up the wall and corner opposite the prow.

FA. Les Williams, Denis Bateman, P.Murray 1974

⑤ William's Chimney . 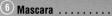 **HVS 5b**

Absorbing and varied climbing from beginning to end. Start at a slim corner directly below a narrow chimney in the upper wall.

20m. Climb the line of slim corners past a couple of difficult sections to the overhang. Step right and enter the narrow chimney which leads pleasantly to the top.

FA. Les Williams, Denis Bateman, P.Murray 7.9.1974

⑥ Mascara . . . . 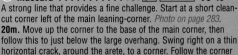 **VS 4c**

A strong line that provides a fine challenge. Start at a short clean-cut corner left of the main leaning-corner. *Photo on page 283.*

20m. Move up the corner to the base of the main corner, then follow this to just below the large overhang. Swing right on a thin horizontal crack, around the arete, to a corner. Follow the corner and cracks to a steep finish.

FA. S.Young, K.Peterson 6.7.1970

⑦ Joy . . . . **S 4a**

A well-travelled and well-protected line with plenty of interest and a low crux. Start directly below the left side of a low overhang.

20m. Gain a flake and use it to reach the overhang. Make some steep moves to pass it on the left and immediately pull back rightwards onto a ledge above it. Climb cracks that join up with the top of a narrow chimney and then continue up a crack and rounded breaks to the top.

FA. Les Williams, Denis Bateman, 21.4.1974

Main descent

Good gearing-up spot

Avon Somerset · North Devon · Culm Coast · Inland Cornwall · Atlantic Coast · West Penwith · The Lizard · Inland Devon · Torbay · Dorset

	No star	⭐	⭐⭐	⭐⭐⭐
Mod to S	2	6	1	-
HS to HVS	-	5	4	-
E1 to E3	-	2	-	3
E4 and up	-	-	2	1

The UK's most southerly point is a barren expanse of fields and common land fringed by some ferocious looking cliffs, stunning beaches and quaint fishing villages. On the tip of the Lizard is a cluster of steep black cliffs that, although not particularly high, have some wild pitches that are both challenging and charming. The rock is mainly solid, if slightly brittle on the routes described, and, although protection is generally available, it requires careful placement since some of the rock is a little fragile. Although traditionally viewed as an add-on to the climbing in West Penwith, the number and quality of the routes here make the Lizard worthy of a visit in its own right.

Approach   See main area map on page 258§

From Helston, follow the A3083 to Lizard village and park on the large village green in its centre.
Lizard Point - Follow the road signed to 'The most southerly point' down to the coast and pick up the coast path. Follow the coast path west (right looking out) until a small cliff-top bench is reached, this is directly above the Hollywood Walls and the next summit 100m further on is the top of Tower Buttress.
Pen Olver and Bass Point - From the parking on the village green follow a road east (Beacon Terrace), past Anne's Famous Pasty Shop to a right turn signed to 'The Housel Bay Hotel'. Follow signs to the Hotel and join the coast path just before the entrance Once on the coast path, turn left and follow it until the distinctive Lloyds' Signal building comes into view. At this point refer to the individual cliff approaches.

Tides

Tower Buttress is non-tidal but all the other cliffs are tidal to some extent.

Conditions

All of the cliffs are exposed to the elements. The bases of some of the tidal cliffs will become inaccessible in moderate seas even at low tide.

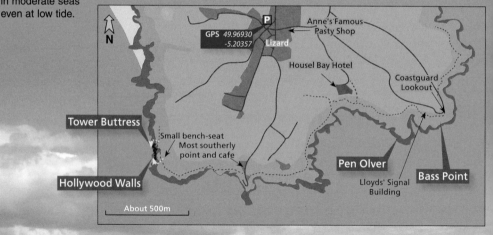

The UK mainland's most southerly point

Avon Somerset

North Devon

Culm Coast

Inland Cornwall

Atlantic Coast

West Penwith

The Lizard

Inland Devon

Torbay

Dorset

The best of The Lizard's rock, a big sea and sunshine on *The Goldrush* (HVS 4c) - *page 288* - Hollywood Walls at Lizard Point. Photo: Anna Rayner

Coastguard Cliff - Tower Buttress

An extensive buttress with one relatively popular route that wends its way under and around some very big overhangs. The route has the advantage of being non-tidal.

Approach - Locate Tower Buttress which is 100m to the west of the cliff-top bench on the coast path above the Hollywood Walls. Scramble down the slabs, walls and corners to the west of the top of the buttress to non-tidal slabs below a huge overhang.

Tides - Non-tidal.

Conditions - The rock may retain some dampness.

① Sirius . . . . 🔆 ⚒ ▢ **HS 4b**

An exposed journey that winds its way through some impressive ground on massive holds. Start at the base of a very steep wall on a long ledge below a short pinnacle.

1) 4a, 15m. Climb rightwards down the ledge until steep moves on good holds lead up past a large white blob to a corner. Climb a short way up the corner and then move out right around the arete to a good ledge and belay.

2) 4b, 22m. Move right and down, crossing the ramp-line (that rises to the left) to gain a short corner that leads up to the arete. An overhanging corner continues up leftwards. Follow this line, stepping left onto the wall to avoid steep ground, until large grassy ledges lead to a thread belay.

FA. Iain Peters, Pete O'Sullivan 5.5.1985

100m to the south is the dark face of Hollywood Walls.

② Quo Vadis . . . . 🔆 ⚒ ▢ **E1 5a**

An imposing line that provides some steep moves on generally good holds. Start on a small ledge just right of the descent ramp.

20m. Climb the overhanging face on big jugs to a more pressing section that ends below a thin crack in the less steep upper wall. Follow the thin crack directly to the top.

FA. Pete O'Sullivan, R.Cope 26.5.1985

③ The Goldrush . . . . 🔆 ⚒ ▢ **HVS 4c**

Exhilarating climbing on an intimidating line that is far easier than its appearance would suggest. Low in the grade. Start below an overhanging right-slanting flake-crack, 5m right of the descent ramp.

Photo on page 287.

22m. Pull directly up the overhanging wall using the flake-crack to an easing in angle. Traverse right above the flake-crack to gain the base of the much friendlier upper wall. Above is a very thin crack, move left past this and climb the blank looking wall on excellent pockets to the top.

FA. Iain Peters, Pete O'Sullivan 11.5.1985

④ Silent Movie . . . . 🔆 🔦 ▢ **VS 4b**

Although from initial impressions this line appears to be much harder than the grade, in execution it proves to be a worthwhile introduction to the rock and climbing on the Hollywood Walls. Plus, it is a very good climb in its own right. Start at a thin low flake in the steep wall just left of a right-leaning corner.

20m. From the flake reach up over the steep wall to good holds and pull up strenuously to more good holds. Move left and up to the base of an open groove and follow this to the top on huge holds.

FA. Iain Peters, A.Martin, K.Tole 31.8.1984

Tower Buttress

Gearing-up ledge

Approach from bench seat

Gearing-up ledge

Hollywood walls

1

Coastguard Cliff - Hollywood Walls

An exciting collection of climbs in an atmospheric location. Although not particularly high, the routes are fairly steep and the boisterous sea directly below makes the cliff an interesting place to visit.

Approach - From the bench seat on top of the buttress, scramble down to the right of the summit to a big flat gearing-up ledge. The climbs are directly below this ledge. To reach the base of the cliff, scramble down to the right (facing out) and then drop steeply back left down a crack until it is possible to traverse back left on easy-angled rock to below the routes.

Tides - The base of the climbs are non-tidal but they become wave-washed in moderate seas even at low tide.

Conditions - The cliff does seep a little after prolonged spells of rain. The cliff gets plenty of sun and at times can become very hot.

5 **Limelight. . . . . . .** 〔23〕 🧗 🪝 ☐ **HVS 5a**

The finest pitch on the Hollywood Walls combines some hard climbing in intimidating positions, although with good protection. Start at the arete to the right of the descent ramp below a hanging corner.

20m. Move up to below the hanging corner and, using a diagonal crack in the wall to its left, make a strenuous pull out to a small foot ledge on the arete. Step left and climb directly to the left-hand of two short corners. Climb the short technical corner to better holds and finish up the wall above.

FA. Iain Peters, Pete O'Sullivan 7.7.1985

6 **Mae West . . . .** 〔23〕 🪝 ☐ **HVS 5a**

Spacey climbing on good holds up the centre of the most impressive section of the crag. Start at a belay on a sloping ledge on the slab below the steep central section of the wall. *Photo on page 281.*

23m. Move up the slab to its apex and climb the right-slanting corner for 8m to some big holds on the left. Traverse left for 5m to a short crack and good nut. Climb up the crack and the steep ground above, slightly leftwards, to the capping roof. Traverse right under the roof to a rounded arete and make a final awkward move over the roof to finish back at the gearing-up ledge.

FA. Pete O'Sullivan, J.Barber 1.9.1985

7 **Quasimodo . . . .** 〔23〕 ☐ **E1 5b**

An unusual climb for here, where the meat of the route starts on a slab and finishes on steep ground. Start as for *Mae West* at a sloping ledge on the slab below the steep central section of the wall.

22m. Move up to just before the apex of the easy slab and pull out rightwards onto the steeper black slab. Follow the easiest line up this to its top and climb the steep crack up into a left-leaning corner. Climb the corner to the roof above then step right and pull over the roof to finish at the gearing-up ledge.

FA. Pete O'Sullivan, J.Barber 1.9.1985

Gearing-up ledge

Approach

Belays above high-water level

Avon Somerset
North Devon
Culm Coast
Inland Cornwall
Atlantic Coast
West Penwith
The Lizard
Inland Devon
Torbay
Dorset

Avon Somerset

North Devon

Culm Coast

Inland Cornwall

Atlantic Coast

West Penwith

The Lizard

Inland Devon

Torbay

Dorset

Lots of sun | 15 min | Abseil in | Tidal

Scramble easily along high ledges to access route 1

① ② ③ ④ ⑤

Coast path from Housel Bay Hotel

Coast path to Coast-guard lookout and Bass Point

Lloyds' Signal building

Access path to headland and Pen Olver

Pinnacle

Pinnacle

Escape ramp (Mod)

①

Pen Olver

A delightful area that has a good collection of routes spanning a broad grade range. The climbs are on good rock, and access to and from them is reasonably straightforward, allowing plenty of climbing time.

Approach - From the parking on the village green follow a road east (Beacon Terrace), past Anne's Famous Pasty Shop to a right turn signed to 'The Housel Bay Hotel'. Follow signs to the Hotel and join the coast path just before the entrance. Once at the coast path, turn left and follow it a short way until 200m before the distinctive Lloyds' Signal building. Walk out towards the headland on the right then, just short of the rocks at its end, head right, down the grass-slope to a rocky ridge on the right (facing out) of a wide gully. Descend the rocky ridge and traverse left (facing out) to a large slabby area, ideal for gearing-up. Do not use other descents as the slopes are very susceptible to erosion. The Amnesty Wall is easily viewed to the left, and accessed via abseil from its top. For Pen Olver, make a short abseil down a gully and crack to the right (facing out) to ledges from where all the routes can be gained via a series of sea-level ledges.

Tides - The base of the cliffs are tidal and only accessible for 3 hours either side of low water. However, in calm sea-conditions the climbs on Pen Olver (not the Amnesty Wall) can be accessed for much longer.

Conditions - The cliff gets plenty of sun and dries quickly.

① Let Her Children Play .. 🕸 🪝 ☐ **VS 4b**
The impressive thin crack in the wall next to an escape line (Mod) is a worthwhile climb, although the rock is lichen-covered near the top. Start below the crack that splits the wall at the outer end of a deep corner/chimney.
25m. Pull up a short wall to the base of the crack and climb it to an easing. Move right and then back left to the crack and a break just above. Move rightwards up a wide crack-line with care to finish.
FA. Dave Hope, D.Issitt 6.9.1997

② Bilson's Fowl Play .... 🪝 ☐ **VDiff**
Excellent corner-climbing. Start on a huge, flat ledge below two staggered corners.
20m. Climb the two corners that gradually increase in difficulty as height is gained. Well protected.
FA. D.Issitt, Dave Hope 16.6.1996

③ The People's Queen 🕸 🪝 🧗 ☐ **VS 4c**
A fairly tricky pitch that is well protected. Start below a large, flat ledge at 5m.
25m. Gain the flat ledge and climb the narrow, technical groove above it to easier ground.
FA. Dave Hope, D.Issitt 6.9.1997

④ Ocean of Tears .... 🕸 🪝 ☐ **Diff**
An impressive corner-line, best caught in the midday sun. Start below the intimidating corner at the back of a recess.
25m. Climb the corner, which succumbs to bridging, and eases towards the top.
FA. Dave Hope, D.Issitt 6.9.1997

⑤ Songs from a Gentle Man .. 🕸 ☐ **VS 4b**
A fantastic arete that looks to be much tougher than it actually is. Start below the soaring arete behind a huge pinnacle.
25m. Climb the arete on small, but reliable holds to a good horizontal break at 8m. Continue up the arete past a notch to the top. An exposed pitch.
FA. Dave Hope, D.Issitt 16.6.1996

Coastguard lookout

Pen Olver Slab

Gearing-up ledges

Amnesty Wall

Avon Somerset · North Devon · Culm Coast · Inland Cornwall · Atlantic Coast · West Penwith · The Lizard · Inland Devon · Torbay · Dorset

Pen Olver continues with an attractive slab. For tides and approach see previous page

1 Great Slanting .... 🕐 ✏️ ☐ VDiff

The left-leaning wide flake-crack is a steady lead, capped off with an airy finish. Start below the large flake-crack.
20m. Climb the flake-crack using the left wall more frequently as height is gained. Eventually the arete is reached from where a final pull up, either on the left or right, gains a good belay ledge.
FA. Dave Hope, D.Issitt 15.6.1996

2 Saltheart .... 🕐 ☐ S 4a

Slightly more pressing than the other good lines on the wall. Start at a vertical wall with a groove at 4m.
22m. Ascend the vertical wall and move up into the groove, bold. Continue up the groove, avoiding an exit left at mid-height.
FA. Dave Hope, D.Issitt 15.6.1996

3 Mile End .... 🕐 ✏️ ☐ Mod

A good pitch at the grade. Start at the base of the prominent right-slanting wide crack.
30m. Climb the sustained, but hold infested crack-line to a slightly steeper section near its end. Above, a gully leads easily to a belay on the right behind a large pinnacle.
FA. D.Issitt, Dave Hope 15.6.1996

4 Blind Pew .... 🕐 ✏️ ☐ VDiff

One of Pen Olver's most appealing lines. Start at a long groove to the right of the diagonal break of *Mile End*. *Photo on page 278.*
30m. Climb the groove all the way to a junction with the final gully of *Mile End* and finish up this.
FA. Dave Hope, D.Issitt 15.6.1996

5 A Little Gemma ...... 🕐 ✏️ ☐ Diff

A good pitch to get the feel of the climbing on this section of cliff. Start at a slim groove right of the long groove of *Blind Pew*.
20m. Climb the groove and slab above direct to a short V-groove. Pull up the V-groove and climb juggy rock to a good ledge and belay.
FA. Dave Hope, D.Issitt 15.6.1996

6 Love is Blind .... 🕐 ✏️ ☐ VDiff

The final line on this section of the cliff follows cracks on its right-hand margin. Start below a left-facing wide flake-crack.
20m. Climb the left-facing flake-crack and the slabby wall above to a another flake-crack. Climb this to a good ledge and belay.
FA. Dave Hope, D.Issitt 15.6.1996

Lots of sun | 15 min | Abseil In | Tidal

Scramble off rightwards along ledges and gullies back to the gearing-up ledges

Gearing-up ledges

Ⓐ
Line of abseil

Tidal Ledges

① ② ③ ④ ⑤ ⑥

Avon Somerset

North Devon

Culm Coast

Inland Cornwall

Atlantic Coast

West Penwith

The Lizard

Inland Devon

Torbay

Dorset

Dave Henderson on *Cian* (F4 5c) - *page 294* - at the dark Amnesty Wall, Lizard Point

① Cian . . . . 🔲 🔲 🔲 **E4 5c**

A fantastic route that combines steep, well-protected climbing with positive holds. Start just to the left of a short, narrow corner at the base of the wall. *Photo on page 293.*

23m. Climb the wall for 7m and move up right to a leftward slanting crack. Follow this to its end, below a tiny left-facing groove. Move up to the groove and climb it to a good hold. Steeper climbing on positive holds leads to the top.

FA. Dave Henderson, Carrie Hill 6.5.2001

② International . . . . 🔲 🔲 🔲 **E3 5c**

A stunning wall pitch. Start at a short, narrow corner at the base of the wall.

23m. Climb the corner to a left-slanting crack. Move up, and then make fingery moves right to some large holds. Move up and left to pockets and finish steeply up the final section of wall.

FA. Mike Raine, Shane Ohly 3.1995

Pen Olver - Amnesty Wall

An imposing black wall with a trio of excellent, hard wall climbs. Low tide and sunny evenings provide the best conditions.

Approach - Walk to the top of the wall from the gearing-up ledges and abseil directly down to the tidal ledge at the base of the wall.

Tides - The ledge at the base of the wall is tidal and only accessible for 3 hours either side of low water in calm sea-conditions. However, access is severely limited in moderate sea conditions when the ledge at the bottom of the wall becomes wave-washed.

③ Amnesty . . . . 🔲 🔲 🔲 **E3 5c**

The original route of the wall holds its own with the newer additions. Start at a crack at the base of the right-hand side of the wall.

23m. Climb 5m up the crack and gain a small ledge on the right. Move right to a rounded flake and make hard moves up to a large horizontal break (big cam). From here, climb a crack leftwards and finish up the steep wall above to the top.

FA. Pete O'Sullivan, C.Pretty 22.6.1986

From gearing-up ledges

Tidal Ledges

④ Halley's Corner . . . . . . HS 4a
A good, although isolated line that is less problematic with regard to the state of the tide than the others here. Start below the large corner on the left side of the cliff.
24m. Climb the sustained corner on good holds to the top.
FA. Ken Hosie, Paul Buttrick 16.3.1986

⑤ Dawn E4 5c
An exciting and slightly bold headwall is the main attraction of this pitch. The top pitch can be gained easily by abseil if the tides are not favourable. Start on sea-level ledges below the main buttress.
1) 4c, 16m. Traverse left and climb a crack in a slab to a ledge and belay below the steep headwall.
2) 5c, 18m. Climb up the headwall to a horizontal break and move right. Boldly climb the wall above to better holds and protection before finishing up a short lichen-covered wall.
FA. Pete O'Sullivan, Steve Bell 5.4.1986

⑥ The Cull E3 5c
A phenomenal pitch that features a steep initial section and a stunningly positioned final crack. Start on sea-level ledges below the steep corner-line.
34m. Climb the corner a short way and then the very steep flake-line on the right to less strenuous ground at 16m. Make a short traverse rightwards to a crack-system and follow it to the top.
FA. Steve Bell, Pete O'Sullivan, S.Bishop 16.3.1986

Bass Point
An enticing wall that juts out into the sea and provides the Lizard with its best known climb - *The Cull*.
Approach - From the parking on the village green follow a road east (Beacon Terrace), past Anne's Famous Pasty Shop to a right turn signed to 'The Housel Bay Hotel'. Follow signs to the Hotel and join the coast path just before the entrance. Turn left on the coast path and follow it for 400m to the distinctive Lloyds' Signal building. Walk down to the promontory directly in front of the building from where the leaning wall of The Cull is seen in profile. Descent to the base of the cliff can be made at low tide via easy climbing down the right side (facing out) of the cliff, or more usually at low to mid tide and in calm sea-conditions by abseil directly to ledges below the climbs.
Conditions - The cliff gets plenty of sun and dries quickly.
Tides - The base of the buttress is tidal, and the ledges below the 3 seaward climbs are exposed for around 3 hours either side of low water.

⑦ Lazarus E6 6b
A very impressive pitch that takes on the bulging wall on the seaward end of the cliff. The grade is for an ascent with the peg in place, although a good nut is also available but may prove difficult to place on lead and is sometimes pre-placed to back up the aged peg. Start below a steep, thin flake-crack, just right of *The Cull*.
Photo on page 280.
33m. Climb the flake to a thin horizontal break. Pull right and then up with difficulty to a peg from where more hard climbing gains a good hold. Climb with less difficulty to an overhang and thread, before moving up left to a crack that is followed to the top.
FA. Pat Littlejohn 20.5.1988

Alex Hughes launches out on the Chudleigh Rocks' jamming-testpiece *Oesophagus* (E1 5b) - *page 308* - Photo: Ian Parnell

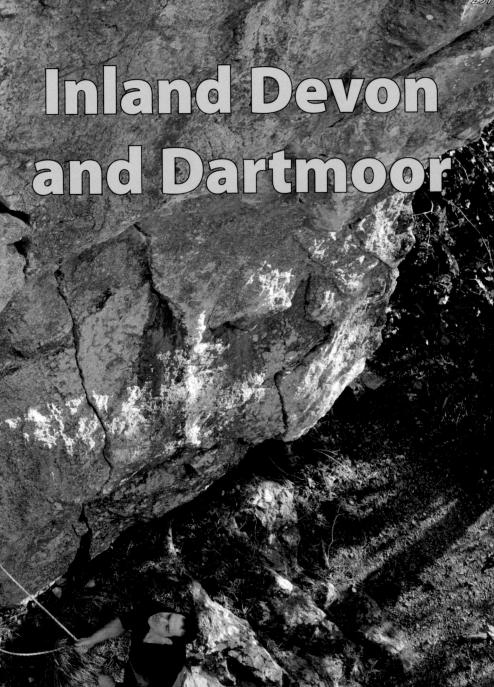

Inland Devon and Dartmoor

Avon Somerset

North Devon

Culm Coast

Inland Cornwall

Atlantic Coast

West Penwith

The Lizard

Inland Devon

Torbay

Dorset

The high, tor-capped wilderness of Dartmoor contrasts starkly with the leafy rural lanes of South Devon and this contrast also extends to the area's climbing. The lowlands are home to a couple of quaint limestone crags that offer both classic trad climbs and some high quality sport-routes. The moorland granite tors and adjacent forested valleys of Dartmoor are havens of cool when the weather is hot, and dish up a surprisingly varied number of climbs that range from some fierce 'outcrop style' lines to more gentle multi-pitch climbs in outstandingly beautiful locations. The area also has the advantage of very convenient access; many of the cliffs are close to the end of the M5. The fringes of Dartmoor have some of the best accommodation options and pubs in the West Country. They are generally close to the climbing, and make good bases for exploring both Dartmoor and the inland crags, along with the neighbouring sea-cliff climbing in Torbay.

Getting Around

Most of the climbing - both on the low-lying inland limestone and the higher moorland tors - is usually approached from the section of the A38 that runs between Exeter and Plymouth. Once off of the A38 the distances to the crags are relatively modest, although the myriad of high banked Devon lanes can make journeys seem much longer than they look on a map.

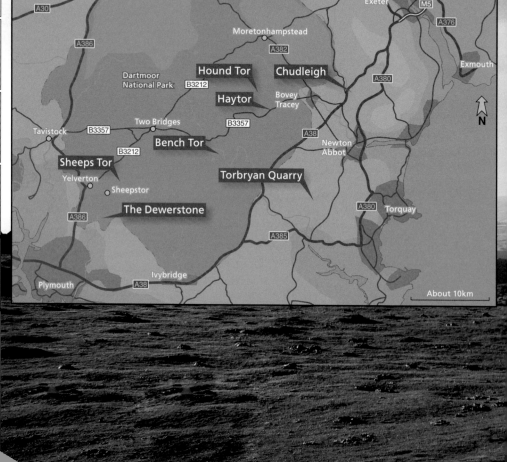

Avon Somerset | North Devon | Culm Coast | Inland Cornwall | Atlantic Coast | West Penwith | The Lizard | Inland Devon | Torbay | Dorset

Avon Somerset

North Devon

Culm Coast

Inland Cornwall

Atlantic Coast

West Penwith

The Lizard

Inland Devon

Torbay

Dorset

An early morning ascent of *Hangover* (E1 5b) on the crisp granite of Haytor on Dartmoor - *page 318* - Photo: Sean Kelly

	No star	⟨1⟩	⟨2⟩	⟨3⟩
Mod to S	1	2	2	1
HS to HVS	2	5	3	3
E1 to E3	-	3	5	4
E4 and up	-	2	1	2

Chudleigh Rocks is a very popular and picturesque crag with a rich climbing history attached to it. The 'Rocks' are composed of excellent limestone that, in general, gives well-protected climbing on sustained and technical pitches. There is something here for all, ranging from multi-pitch lower grade classics to a clutch of fingery test-pieces, plus a host of brilliant VS and HVSs. Being close to Exeter, Chudleigh is very quick to get to and more often than not has some of the best weather in the West Country. It can be a good choice to head for if the weather further to the west is poor.

Approach   See main area map on page 298

To reach Chudleigh Rocks from the north, turn off the A38 for Chudleigh. Go into the village and continue straight on through the centre to a left turn into Rock Road (by the Police Station). Continue down the road for 100m to parking by a kissing gate on the right. Parking here can be problematic: if full park further back up the road or in the village. Go through the kissing gate and follow the path to where it starts to drop down the hillside. Take the path that contours off rightwards around the slope until the shady North Face of the Rocks is seen on the right (private land). Continue a short distance and the first buttresses come into view. Descend easy rock-steps to the base of the crag and the cave of Pixies Hole. If approaching from the south, take the first Chudleigh exit off of the A38, drive into the village and turn right at the Police Station.

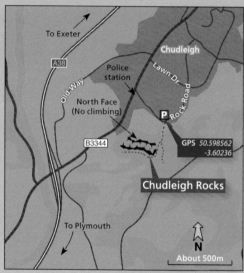

GPS 50.598562 -3.60236

Conditions

The climbing at Chudleigh described here faces south but shade can be found at most times of day. Climbing is a year-round prospect at Chudleigh and in all but the worst weather seepage is not a problem. On hot days the place becomes an oven and the polish can make the climbing harder and unpleasant. Chudleigh is in the rain-shadow of Dartmoor and receives much less rain than The Dewerstone, Haytor and Cornwall.

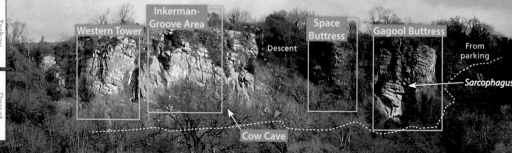

Margin tabs (left): Avon Somerset | North Devon | Culm Coast | Inland Cornwall | Atlantic Coast | West Penwith | The Lizard | Inland Devon | Torbay | Dorset

Avon Somerset

North Devon

Culm Coast

Inland Cornwall

Atlantic Coast

West Penwith

The Lizard

Inland Devon

Torbay

Dorset

Danie Rushmer high on the classic Chudleigh
VS *Inkerman Groove* (VS 4c) - *page 304*

❶ Harvestman . . . . 🔲 ❤️ ⬜ E5 6a

Intricate fingertip climbing but with big fall potential. Start at a line of flowstone on the left-hand side of the face.

18m. Climb the flowstone to a break and move right and up to a thin horizontal break and the last protection. Climb a tiny blind flake-line to its end and step left to an easing. Move up right to the top of the wall and then traverse left to exit with care onto grass. Tree belay.

FA. Robbie Warke, Rik Meek 1987

❷ Grim Reaper . . . . 🔲 🔲 ⬜ E3 5c

Technically challenging moves on excellent rock. Start at a flowstone curtain below a tiny corner in the lower wall.

18m. Climb to a good flowstone hold and thread and continue to a ledge below an open groove in the upper wall. Climb the groove, past a peg, to a small nut just before the top and finish with care onto grass. Tree belay.

FA. Nick White, Dick Thorns 10.5.1986

The Western Tower

A fine tower of good quality limestone, up which some of the area's best mid-grade, multi-pitch lines weave their way.

Approach - Walk to a flat clearing at the far left end of the crag above which the Western Tower rises.

Descent - From the summit of the Western Tower, walk off leftwards (facing out) and pick up either the tree root descent path or a little further the approach path. For the shorter routes on the left walk off along a grassy ledge and back to the base of the crag.

Conditions - The rock dries quickly after rain and gets plenty of sun however, some seepage occurs after prolonged rainfall.

❸ Stalactite Direct . . . . 🔲 ⬜ HVS 5a

A short but useful filler-in. Start below a corner with a block in it above the horizontal break.

18m. Climb the wall past the horizontal breaks to the block and finish up the short corner above.

FA. Pete Biven, Jim Braven 7.1962

❹ Great Western . . . . 🔲 🔲 🔲 ⬜ VS 5a

A popular and interesting route composed of four short but entertaining pitches that are split by accommodating belay ledges. Start at a slim right-facing corner in the middle of the face.

1) 4b, 12m. Climb the corner and wall via spaced ledges to horizontal breaks. Traverse left and pull onto a belay ledge at the base of a slab.

2) 4c, 6m. The intricate, short slab and corner lead to another good ledge with peg and nut belays.

3) 5a, 10m. Move above the belay steeply to below an overhang, peg. Move left and gain a small corner above with a bit of a struggle. Continue to a belay on the edge of the buttress at a tree.

4) 15m. Follow the cleanest line up the edge of the buttress to the summit of the Western Tower.

FA. Nev Hannaby, Eric Rayson 6.1961

Walk off

Avon Somerset · North Devon · Culm Coast · Inland Cornwall · Atlantic Coast · West Penwith · The Lizard · Inland Devon · Torbay · Dorset

⑤ The Spider . . . . `Top 50` E1 5b

One not to be missed. Two contrasting pitches wend their way up Chudleigh's biggest chunk of limestone. Start just left of a low zigzag-crack at a small corner that leads to a ledge at 3m.

1) 5a, 20m. Climb onto the ledge and take the diagonal crack left to another ledge. Arrange gear and move left and up onto a good hold in the middle of the slab. Some bold moves gain the belay ledge up on the left. Peg and nut belays.

2) 5b, 24m. From the right side of the belay ledge move up to another smaller ledge and take the white wall above to the overhang. Climb steeply around its left side on good holds to a small ledge above. Climb direct above the ledge to a small whitish groove that allows access to the thin crack on the grey headwall, good wires. Work rightwards on thin ground to a tree stump and finish up the easier wall and cracks above.

FA. Frank Cannings, Peter Biven 14.2.1965

⑦ Never on a Sunday . . . . HS 4b

A lovely climb with plenty of charm and an exposed second pitch. Start at the base of a broad buttress with small twin caves at 7m.

1) 4a, 18m. Climb up to and out of the right-hand cave via an awkward move and continue to a large ledge. Take the short vertical wall to another large ledge and belay.

2) 4b, 32m. Ascend the square-cut corner (just right of the main corner taken by *Scar*) for 4m and then move out right to the arete. Step around the arete to a small exposed ledge and climb the face right of the arete to a tree. A short wall above leads to easy climbing and the top.

FA. Dave Bassett, Alex Allen 8.1961

⑧ Scar . . . . VS 4b

Two contrasting pitches - the first requires care and the second is a testing exercise up a wide and overhanging cleft. Start at the base of a broad buttress that has two small caves at 7m.

1) 4b, 18m. Climb the steep buttress right of the two small caves on sloping holds to slabby rock, move up the slab and then traverse left to a large ledge. Take the short vertical wall to another large ledge beneath the overhanging corner and belay.

2) 4b, 31m. Climb the corner behind the stance, above a small cave, to where it starts to overhang. Climb the overhanging corner either up the wide crack or on its right wall, both options are committing. Above, easy climbing leads to the top.

FA. Nev Hannaby, Tom Patey 7.1960

⑥ The Spy E3 5c

A direct line that sees limited traffic, but gives continuously good climbing. Start at a ground-level zigzag crack.

1) 5b, 18m. Climb the zigzag crack, and move up onto a ledge on the right below a thin left-slanting crack. Climb the crack to a break and continue up the slim groove above to a good ledge and belays up to the right.

2) 5c, 22m. Move up left of the overhang above to a grassy ledge. Climb the corner to the right side of the block overhang above and pass it to gain a ledge above. Move up the short wall to the rightward leading break and follow this strenuously right to a good incut jug. Pull up to another good hold and less steep ground. Finish up the broken corner above.

FA. Pat Littlejohn, John Hammond 9.3.1968
FFA. Ed Hart 1973

Avon Somerset · North Devon · Culm Coast · Inland Cornwall · Atlantic Coast · West Penwith · The Lizard · Inland Devon · Torbay · Dorset

Avon Somerset | North Devon | Culm Coast | Inland Cornwall | Atlantic Coast | West Penwith | The Lizard | Inland Devon | Torbay | Dorset

Inkerman Groove Area

A brilliant wall of compact rock split by an alluring twisting groove in its upper section, the line of the fabulous VS *Inkerman Groove*. The walls on either side of the groove provide some fantastic single-pitch climbs and the classic *Wogs*. The routes are sustained and very technical, but the gear potential is excellent.

Approach - 25m left of Cow Cave is a flat grassy area clear of trees beneath the face.

Descent - From the top of the climbs walk off leftwards (facing out) and pick up the tree root descent or a little further on, the approach path.

Conditions - The wall is very fast drying, fairly sheltered and sunny. Seepage can occur after prolonged rainfall.

❶ Wogs . . . . **HVD**

A rare commodity on UK limestone, a classic low-grade route. The polish is testimony to the route's popularity but does not spoil the experience. Start beneath the disjointed crack-line.
1) 10m. Climb the wall and cracks to a good small ledge and sound nut belays.
2) 18m. Pull up from the belay and move through the bulge leftwards with difficulty. Head straight up to the crack and follow it to a belay on top of a pillar.
3) 12m. Easy climbing leads leftwards to below an old garden wall. Nip up this to finish.
FA. L.B.Prowse 1923

❷ Inkerman Groove . . Top 50 **VS 4c**

The curving, slim groove high on the wall is one of the best limestone VSs in Britain. Start as for *Wogs. Photo on page 301.*
36m. Follow *Wogs* to a point above the overhang at the start of its second pitch, then move up to a crack at the bottom left of the blank grey and white wall. Make a technical traverse right to the base of the slim curving groove and follow this to an easing above a small ivy patch. Exit the groove rightwards to a ledge and take the short wall above to the top. Magnificent.
FA. Eric Rayson, Nev Hannaby 11.60

❸ White Life **E5 6b**

An excellent, tough route with good gear on the crux which lies in the top third of the climb. High in the grade. Start as for *Wogs*.
30m. Follow *Wogs* to the start of *Inkerman Groove's* crux traverse. Head up the wall to the right on pockets to a good wire and a peg a little higher up. Move left to a peg, and up to another peg, then on to a thin horizontal break. Move left again and up to another peg, before a final sequence up a thin crack gains the top.
FA. Nick White, Pete Bull 30.6.1985

❹ Black Death **E4 6a**

An impressive, high standard classic on immaculate rock. Start as for *Wogs/White Life*.
30m. Follow *White Life* to its first peg. Steep moves above reach a hole containing an at times prickly bush and a good wire. Fight up through the bush (if it has not been pruned) to the top.
FFA. Pat Littlejohn 1982

Descent

Avon Somerset

North Devon

Culm Coast

Inland Cornwall

Atlantic Coast

West Penwith

The Lizard

Inland Devon

Torbay

Dorset

5 Machete Wall **E2 5c**
A sustained and much sought-after tick that follows the right-
hand side of the grey wall. Start at a short rib right of *Wogs*.
30m. Climb the easy rib just left of the shallow overhung cave
until below a short white corner. Pull up into the corner and
continue via a steep bulging wall, two pegs, to beneath an
overlap. Using a suspect block with care, pull up and left into a
corner and progress up this with interest to the top.
FA. Eric Rayson 3.61

6 Mortality Crisis **E4 6a**
Reasonably-protected wall climbing linking some subtle features
on the face right of *Inkerman Groove*. Start as for *Machete Wall*.
30m. Follow *Machete Wall* until below the short white corner.
Move up left to a ring peg and then up to a horizontal break. Take
the shallow, left-trending groove, peg, to another peg at its end
and make difficult moves left onto the edge of *Inkerman Groove* at
an ivy patch. Move right, thread, and up to meet the top of a thin
crack-line on the right, thread. Easier climbing gains the finish of
Inkerman Groove.
FA. Nick White, George Szuca 4.5.1985

Cow Cave to Space Buttress

The entrance of Cow Cave is a popular place for gearing-up. The climbs in this area cover a broad grade range but suffer from polish, although protection is usually at hand.

Approach - Walk along the base of the crag until just before Cow Cave, where a steep path leads up to the Salome Face. For Space Buttress, scramble up a gully full of tree roots on the left of the Salome Face and walk right to a large platform and the crag.

Descent - Walk off leftwards (facing out) from Cow Cave, or rightwards (facing out) from Space Buttress, and descend tree roots down a gully.

Conditions - Space Buttress is shady in the morning.

① The Slot . . . . HVS 5a

A burly pitch that follows a jamming crack up the corner on the left of the square-cut buttress that is perched above a ledge. Start by scrambling to the ledge and a belay under the corner.
16m. Enter the corner strenuously and jam away up the crack to a rightward exit near the top.
FA. Nev Hannaby 11.1960

② Barn Owl Crack . . . . HVD

One of Chudleigh's well-worn favourites that follows the wide snaking crack left of Cow Cave. Start below a short 3m wall directly beneath the crack.
22m. Climb the wall to a ledge and take on the wide crack and its right wall with conviction. At its top, move left to a narrower section of the crack that leads quickly to the top.
FA. Tom Patey, R.Grant, S.Bemrose 7.1960

③ Ash Tree Buttress . . . . . VDiff

A retiring little pitch that makes a nice continuation to *Barn Owl Crack*. Walk 8m right from the finish of *Barn Owl Crack* and belay at the base of the buttress with a tree growing out of it. Not shown on the topo.
12m. Climb steeply up to and past the tree on its right to the top. Worth seeking out.

④ Reek . . . . HS 4b

A great little route with a big reputation - best not attempted in humid conditions when the polish will make it feel a whole grade harder. Start at a corner-crack 5m left of the cave entrance.
23m. Climb the slick corner-crack to a large ledge at 3m. Place some bomber wires and pull steeply up the wall then rock up left onto the steep slab. Continue up the fine steep corner directly above and pull onto a large ledge. Belay possible. Move up easily leftwards before climbing directly to the top.
FA. Eric Rayson, B.Waistell, Nev Hannaby 1.1961

⑤ Twang E1 5b

Stylish climbing requiring good technique and a set of strong fingers. Start just left of the cave below a ledge at 3m.
1) 5b, 15m. Boulder to a ledge at 3m and move up the technical wall above it. Continue through the narrowing groove to a stance on a prow.
2) 5a, 10m. Climb up the steep crack behind the belay and then traverse wildly rightwards around the arete to finish direct on good holds.
FA. Pat Littlejohn, Ed Grindley 30.6.1968

Descent

Lots of sun | 5 min | Sheltered

Loot .... HVS 5b

The wide, overhanging crack-system sprouting from the left side of Cow Cave. Start on the left of the cave entrance.
19m. Head for the narrowing funnel. Squeeze up the funnel and onwards to the roof. Spectacular moves utilising the crack on the left side of the roof gain the top.
FA. Nev Hannaby, Eric Rayson 9.1960

Smoke Gets In Your Eyes E3 6a

The offset grooves right of the cave entrance are overcome by a perplexing series of moves. Start at the base of the grooves.
15m. Move up and left into the upper groove. Climb and exit the groove rightwards with difficulty past a number of pegs.
FFA. Pete Leedell 2.1971

Guy Fawkes Crack..... VS 4c

The wide crack right of the cave entrance is entertaining. Start at the base of the crack.
12m. The crack is steep to enter but well-protected.
FA. Nev Hannaby, Eric Rayson 11.1960

TNT. .... VS 5a

A short and popular exercise. Start below a block at 3m just right of the wide crack of *Guy Fawkes Crack.*
10m. Gain the block and climb the short, thin crack above.

Hot Ice E4 6a

A short but serious arete. Start at the arete left of the smooth wall climbed by *Seventh Veil.*
9m. Slick and balancy moves up the right side of the arete gain an easing midway. Head directly up the wall right of the arete to finish.
FA. Kev Buckley 10.1978

Seventh Veil .... VS 4c

A popular though highly-polished wall climb that has a tough initial section. Start in the centre of the face below a small crescent-moon shaped crack at 4m.
10m. Climb up past the crack to a ledge on the right at mid-height. Climb the crack and wall above to the top.

Salome .... VDiff

The ramp-line that slopes up left from the toe of the face is a very popular climb. Start at the toe of the buttress.
13m. Climb the narrowing ramp using a crack on the right in the upper section.

Major Tom E3 6a

A wild and powerful trip through some very impressive terrain with good protection and for the most part excellent holds. Start next to the large cage beneath the overhangs.
15m. Stand on the cage and pull up to a short crack then up to a peg. Make a low traverse right on finger edges to jugs. Move up steeply to a peg high on the left and make a powerful move right to gain good holds that lead strenuously to the top. The steep wall right of the cage can be bouldered out to give a difficult start.
FA. Chris Nicholson 13.4.1984

Saturn Five E2 5b

The central line of weakness through the stacked overhangs is a spectacular climb on jugs, a couple of which are a touch wobbly. Protection is good. Start at the large cage beneath the overhangs.
15m. From the top of the cage step rightwards onto the slab beneath the line. Climb on good holds to twin pegs and then another peg a little higher on the left. Grasp a large flat flange and pull around the overhang above on big holds, the top is a little higher.
FA. Steve Bell, John Grubb 27.5.1979

Avon Somerset | North Devon | Culm Coast | Inland Cornwall | Atlantic Coast | West Penwith | The Lizard | Inland Devon | Torbay | Dorset

Avon Somerset | North Devon | Culm Coast | Inland Cornwall | Atlantic Coast | West Penwith | The Lizard | Inland Devon | Torbay | Dorset

Gagool Buttress

Sarcophagus Area and Gagool Buttress

The first sighting of the main climbing area at Chudleigh is on the right after passing the rather gloomy North Face (which is on private land). The barred-off cave of Pixies Hole is a popular bouldering haunt and marks the start of the main climbing at Chudleigh. Both the Gagool Buttress and the Sarcophagus Area hold some exceptional climbs that follow either strong crack-lines and aretes or thin faces on crimps and pockets. The rock and protection is usually good. However, the most popular lines of *Sarcophagus* and *Chudleigh Overhang* are very polished and are best not attempted in hot and/or humid weather.

Approach - The footpath from the parking ends at some slippery rock steps that descend to the entrance of Pixies Hole cave. This is barred off in order to protect a bat colony. On rounding the buttress, the impressive *Combined Ops* arete and overhanging corner of *Sarcophagus* are revealed; open and light and in complete contrast to the rather chilly and polished ambience of the Pixies Hole side of the buttress.

Descent - Either walk right (facing out) and descend the tree roots to arrive back at Cow Cave or go left to meet the approach path which quickly gains the base of the cliff at Pixies Hole.

Conditions - The more popular lines are very polished and become very unpleasant in hot weather. The rock is quick drying, and there is the potential to find some dry rock in the rain.

① Greenmantel . . . . ⚿2 🪨 ⬜ Diff
A strong line and a favourite first climb that follows the tree-draped corner above a small railed-off cave. Start 20m left of the huge corner of *Sarcophagus* at a small, railed-off cave.
30m. Climb up just right of the cave to a corner at 4m. Move up and climb the right wall of the corner to ledges on the right. Climb back leftwards to below a tree in a corner. Climb the corner on good holds, past the tree (possible belay) to the top.
FA. J.Brooks, R.Cockran 2.1964

② Sarcophagus . . . . . ⚿ 🪨 👥 ⬜ VS 4b
A line and a half! The overhang-strewn corner requires a wide range of manoeuvres and, although polished to a high sheen, it is still a classic outing. Start at the base of the corner.
1) 4b, 9m. Squirm up the awkward wide crack to a cave belay.
2) 4b, 13m. Back-and-footing and bridging gains the start of a short traverse left on a hanging slab. Move left along the slab and up through a small overhang above it to a stance.
3) 9m. The narrowing-corner above ends at a stout tree belay.
FA. Tom Patey 1960

③ Oesophagus . . . . . . ⚿3 🪝 🪨 ⬜ E1 5b
The bending hand-crack in the overhanging white wall to the right of the corner of *Sarcophagus* is a great test of jamming technique and perseverance. Start beneath the crack. *Photo on page 296.*
25m. Gain the overhanging hand-crack and push on to a rest in a roof-capped niche. Pull out right and climb up and left to join the finishing corner of *Sarcophagus*.
FA. Barrie Biven, Jim Braven 7.1962

④ Combat . . . . ⚿3 🪨 ⬜ E3 5c
An extremely fine and challenging pitch that doesn't let up from the very start. Start below the hand-crack of *Oesophagus*.
20m. Move up twin cracks to the overhang and boldly swing up and right along a flake to the arete. Move up the arete, peg on the right, before traversing a short way left to the foot of a wide crack. Power up the crack and headwall past a thread to positive holds and a bolted belay above. Abseil off or finish up easy ground above (as for pitch 2 of *Combined Ops*).
FA. Pat Littlejohn, Steve Jones 2.9.71

⑤ Combined Ops . . . . 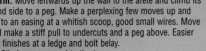 **E2 5b**

The striking arete is as good as it looks. Protection from small wires is ample and the climbing is technical and sustained. Start up the slope just right of the arete.

1) 5b, 21m. Move leftwards up the wall to the arete and climb its right-hand side to a peg. Make a perplexing few moves up and then left to an easing at a whitish scoop, good small wires. Move right and make a stiff pull to undercuts and a peg above. Easier climbing finishes at a ledge and bolt belay.

2) 11m. Climb easy ground to the top.

FA. Peter Biven, Barrie Biven, Cliff Fishwick, Jim Braven 7.1962

⑥ Gagool . . . . 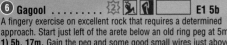 **E1 5b**

A fingery exercise on excellent rock that requires a determined approach. Start just left of the arete below an old ring peg at 5m.

1) 5b, 17m. Gain the peg and some good small wires just above. Traverse left with difficulty for 5m on small holds to an easing at a thin vertical crack. Climb the crack and move rightwards to a large belay ledge. A good and slightly easier alternative (*Logic* 5b) moves up right from the old ring peg onto the blunt arete and follows the arete to the large belay ledge.

2) 5a, 16m. Move up and stand on a block on the left, peg. Step right into an open groove and climb it past some poor rock and a very wobbly but keyed-in small block to finish on easier ground.

FA. Ian McMorrin, W.Reilly 2.65

⑦ Chudleigh Overhang 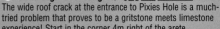 **HVS 5a**

The wide roof crack at the entrance to Pixies Hole is a much-tried problem that proves to be a gritstone meets limestone experience! Start in the corner 4m right of the arete.

1) 5a,16m. Climb up the crack and right wall to a ledge beneath the wide roof crack. A committing layback rapidly gains a ledge above the roof and a short traverse left to a stance.

2) 20m. Traverse left to the edge of the buttress and climb up easy rock to the top.

FA. Tom Patey 1961
FFA. Peter Biven, Jim Braven 1961

Descent

Easy finish just around arete

Sarcophagus Area

Avon Somerset | North Devon | Culm Coast | Inland Cornwall | Atlantic Coast | West Penwith | The Lizard | Inland Devon | Torbay | Dorset

	No star	☆1	☆2	☆3
Mod to S	-	-	-	-
HS to HVS	-	-	-	-
E1 to E3	7	3	2	1
E4 and up	5	1	2	2

Torbryan Quarry is a great little crag with a small set of exquisite sport climbs on its gently overhanging wall. The climbing is well bolted and gives sustained, fingery pitches on flowstone sheets and pockets with the two central lines of *Mayday* and *Thread Flintstone* being classics of their grade. The setting is typically rural Devon, narrow lanes, high hedges and a quaint local village blessed with a good pub.

Approach   See main area map on page 298

From the A38, drive to Newton Abbot and follow signs to Totnes on the A381. After around 3 miles turn right into the village of Ipplepen. Go through the village and 200m from the village outskirts a car park on the right is reached just as the lane enters woods. Park here. Turn right out of the car park and walk down the road, take the left fork and after 200m a gated track on the left is reached. Go through the gate and the quarry is just up the track on the left.

Access

The quarry is within a SSSI and no access to the top of the crag is allowed in order to protect the flora that grows there. Do not light fires or leave any litter.

Conditions

The quarry is tucked away in a sheltered dell and can be a useful retreat in light rain or cool weather once the sun comes around in the afternoon. It can get hot in warm weather, although the base is shaded by trees. It does seep after prolonged spells of wet weather.

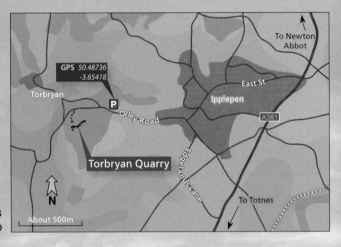

GPS 50.48736 -3.65418

Torbryan

To Newton Abbot

East St

Ipplepen

Orley Road

A381

Torbryan Quarry

Edgelands Lane

To Totnes

N

About 500m

The rural idyll that surrounds Torbryan Quarry.

Avon Somerset

North Devon

Culm Coast

Inland Cornwall

Atlantic Coast

West Penwith

The Lizard

Inland Devon

Torbay

Dorset

Carrie Hill enjoying the fantastic flowstone wall-climbing on *Boogie on Down* (6c) - *page 313* - at Torbryan Quarry, South Devon. Photo: Martin Perry

1 Peggy Potato . . . . 🔲 🖼 ⬜ **6b**
A bouldery little line. Start up the slope on the left side of the face
next to a block/flake.
12m. Move up to and climb a small slanting corner with difficulty
to a ledge and lower-off above.
FA. Paul Donnithorne 10.11.1987

2 Pebbles . . . . 🔲 🖼 🖼 ⬜ **6c**
Good, but short-lived wall climbing. Start on a high ledge at its
left end.
14m. Climb the very technical and fingery face above a ledge at
4m to a large ledge and lower-off above.
FA. Nick White 4.12.1989

3 Wages of Fear . . . . 🔲 🖼 ⬜ **6c+**
Another fingery number that packs a punch. Start on the high ledge.
15m. Climb a vague groove to the right end of a ledge at 4m.
From the ledge, trend left to finish as for the previous routes.
FA. Nick White 4.1988

4 Vicious Delicious . . . . . 🔲 🖼 ⬜ **7b**
A tough right-hand variation on *Wages of Fear*. Start on the high
ledge.
20m. Climb to the ledge at 4m on *Wages of Fear*. Move up and
right to enter a very narrow groove with difficulty and better holds
just above. Move up the wall and rightwards to finish.
FA. Nick White 15.9.1993

5 Little White Lie . . . 🔲 🖼 🖼 ⬜ **7b**
Intricate and fingery followed by a powerful crux. Start on the
right-hand side of the raised ledge.
19m. Pull up to a blob and crimp up left to better holds. Step
left to a finger-crack and make very powerful moves through the
narrow overlap above to a good ledge. Finish up the easier wall
above. A variation start climbs directly to the finger-crack.
FA. Ken Palmer 29.7 1987

Avon Somerset | North Devon | Culm Coast | Inland Cornwall | Atlantic Coast | West Penwith | The Lizard | Inland Devon | Torbay | Dorset

Lee Proctor about to move around the arete on *Bedrock* (6b+)
- *opposite* - at Torbryan Quarry, South Devon.

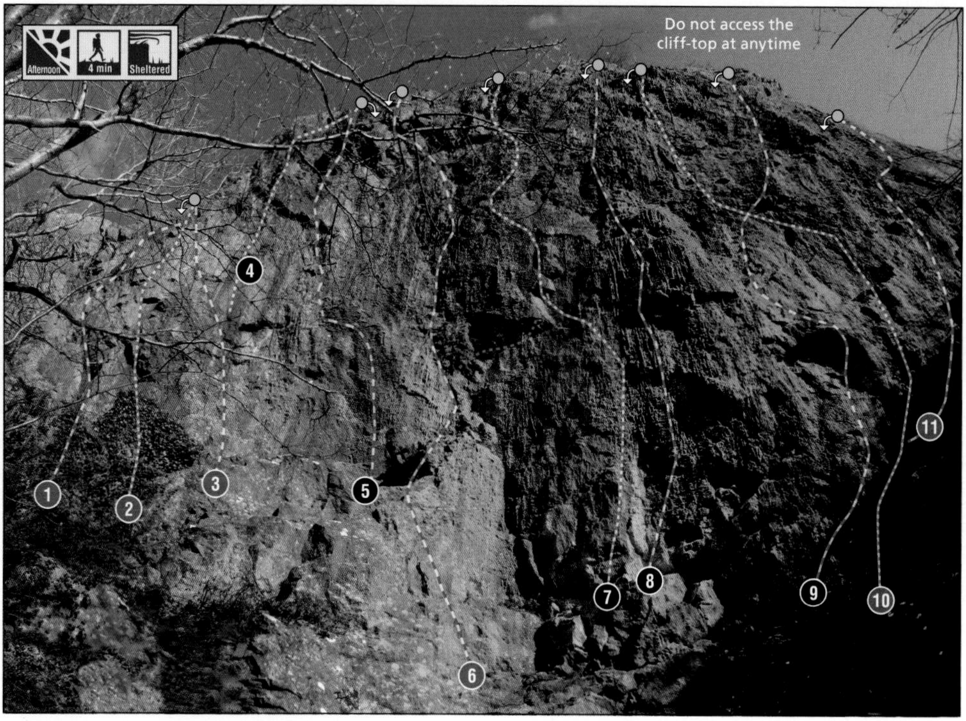
Afternoon
4 min
Sheltered
Do not access the cliff-top at anytime
1
2
3
4
5
6
7
8
9
10
11

Torbryan Quarry
Access - Do not top-out or abseil from the cliff-top.
Descent - All the climbs have lower-offs.

6 Mayday 3 **6c**
They don't come much better than this at the grade. Start below the wide central groove.
22m. Move up to a high ledge and from its right-hand side embark on the fingery and technical open groove to an easing midway. Continue more strenuously but on good holds to an awkward final layback sequence.
FA. Andy Turner 1.5.1986

7 Threadbare . . . 2 **7c+**
The narrow slanting corner and leaning wall right of *Mayday* gives some exceptional climbing on a tight line. Start just right of the base of the wide central groove of *Mayday*.
22m. Climb the wall right of the bolts to a point where a long stride left can be made into the base of the narrow stepped corner. Climb the corner, then move back left to good holds before climbing directly to the top via some fingery and then powerful moves. Can be started by moving in from *Mayday* at 7b+.
FA. Nick White 18.8.1991

8 Thread Flintstone . . 3 **7b**
Classic fingery flowstone followed by a forearm destroying upper wall. Start just right of an orange streak.
22m. Juggy initial moves quickly access a fingery and technical wall which ends at a small ledge, and a shake out. Climb the pumpy upper wall to a sting in the tail.
FA. Ken Palmer 19.6.1987

9 Barney Rubble . . . . 3 **7a+**
A delectable pitch both technical and sustained. Start on the right below a ledge at head height.
22m. Carefully stand on the ledge and pull through the small overhang on good holds. Move left and take the crimpy wall to an easing. Step right and move steeply up to gain a jug and a final couple of powerful moves.
FA. Robbie Warke 18.4.1989

10 Boogie on Down 2 **6c**
Another great route. Start 3m up the broken corner.
Photo on page 311.
22m. Use ledges to reach a left-slanting crack. Climb this to an easing. Finish directly up the steep headwall.
FA. Andy Grieve 29.7.1987

11 Bedrock . . . . 2 **6b+**
A popular pitch based on the shallow arete on the right side of the main face. Start 4m up the broken corner. *Photo opposite.*
24m. Climb the wall left of the arete on good blobs to a small finger pocket. Traverse awkwardly right to the easier-angled side of the shallow arete and finish up the still interesting walls.
FA. Tom Rainbow 2007

	No star	{☆1}	{☆2}	{☆3}
Mod to S	-	4	3	-
HS to HVS	-	3	4	1
E1 to E3	-	3	1	4
E4 and up	-	-	-	2

Haytor is Dartmoor's largest tor and, along with the Dewerstone, one of its major climbing attractions. The climbing is uniformly pleasurable and the views from the summit are impressive, although being one of Devon's most popular tourist attractions, Haytor does not include solitude amongst its many credentials.

The tor is split into two lumps - High Man and Low Man. The huge brow of Low Man is one of Dartmoor's finest faces and one of its biggest at a height of around 30m. Low Man is home to a couple of the region's best Extremes and, although not totally out of the public gaze, is much quieter than nearby High Man. High Man is also a good crag, although shorter and less impressive than Low Man and very popular with walkers and day visitors.

Approach   See main area map on page 298

From the A38 Exeter to Plymouth road, exit at the junction for Bovey Tracey. Drive to Bovey Tracey and pick up signs to Widecombe-in-the-Moor (B3387). Follow these to parking beneath Haytor just beyond the turn-off for Haytor Vale. Haytor is reached in a couple of minutes from the parking.

Conditions

Haytor is perched high on the eastern side of Dartmoor and is battered by wind and rain for much of the late autumn and winter months. Climbing is possible during the spring on calm warm days but the best time to be at Haytor is on warm summer afternoons and evenings The crags do not seep, and dry very quickly after rain.

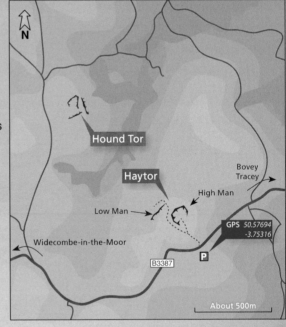

Evening sunshine on Haytor

Avon Somerset | North Devon | Culm Coast | Inland Cornwall | Atlantic Coast | West Penwith | The Lizard | Inland Devon | Torbay | Dorset

Avon Somerset

North Devon

Culm Coast

Inland Cornwall

Atlantic Coast

West Penwith

The Lizard

Inland Devon

Torbay

Dorset

Approaching the steep section of the Dartmoor classic
Interrogation (E3 6a) - *page 317* - on Low Man, Haytor.

Avon Somerset | North Devon | Culm Coast | Inland Cornwall | Atlantic Coast | West Penwith | The Lizard | Inland Devon | Torbay | Dorset

① Screw .... **VS 4c**

Balancy and poorly-protected climbing up the arete 30m to the left of *Raven Gully*. Start on a high block next to the buttress.

15m. Step boldly on to the wall, traverse right and then climb the broad rib to the top.

FA. Ed Grindley, John Fowler 2.5.1970

② Honeymoon Corner .... **S 4a**

A rather uninspiring line that sneaks up the left margin of the buttress. High in the grade. Start at a tall pedestal.

20m. Stand on the pedestal and climb the short corner above to a ledge. Move right and finish up the wall past an overlap.

FA. Geoff Sutton, Ann Sutton 11.1955

③ Outward Bound ...... **HVS 4c**

A steep but juggy pitch which travels through some wild territory at the grade. Start beneath the jutting block at the overhang's widest point. *Photo on page 15.*

24m. Climb up to the block overhang and pull out across the roof on massive holds and with excellent gear, to a grassy ledge (possible belay). From the right-hand side of the ledge, continue up the face above, heading slightly rightwards and then back left.

FA. Tom Patey 30.6.1960

④ The Flier **E1 5c**

Well-named and a good deal harder an undertaking than *Outward Bound*. The gear is good, but strenuous to place.

23m. Move up to the overhang, pull through and get established on the wall above with difficulty. Climb direct for 3m before trending right and then back left to finish as for *Outward Bound*.

FA. Pat Littlejohn 1.5.1971

Low Man

The west face of Haytor's Low Man keeps itself well hidden from the road and the day trippers milling around on the summit of the neighbouring High Man. The face is an impressive sweep of granite rising to 30m at its central point and with a band of overhangs at 6m.

Approach - Head up towards the summit of Haytor and then over to the lesser top of Low Man just to the west. Drop down to the north and around to the base of the main face which has a beautiful outlook and a grassy base.

Descent - Descend the iron rungs and walk back down to the base of the crag.

Conditions - The face is very exposed and picks up any poor weather. Summer evenings can be sublime.

⑤ Raven Wing .... **VS 4b**

Airy climbing and an eye-catching line that takes on the leaning 'feathered' arete to the left of *Raven Gully*. Start in an overhung corner directly under the arete.

23m. Pull up steeply into the corner using a hollow flake. Make a spectacular move left around the leaning arete, past a spike-runner, to easier-angled ground on the face. Pleasant climbing up the wall and breaks just left of the arete gains a large ledge. Move left from here and climb the slabby wall to the top.

FA. Frank Cannings, Pete Biven 18.3.1967

Descent

Haytor 100m

Possible belay

⑥ Raven Gully . . . . . . S
A high-moorland classic that features crack-climbing in all of its guises. It is possible to run the upper pitches together. Start on the right side of the flake that sits at the base of the gully.
1) 9m. Climb the crack and then the groove above (it is also possible to climb the left face of the groove) to a good ledge.
2) 9m. Chimney up the steep crack and exit onto a large ledge and belay.
3) 9m. The easy chimney above to finish. Belay on blocks.
FA. Tony Moulam 1951

⑦ Interrogation E3 6a
An impeccable and varied climb that takes on the full height of Low Man's central wall. Start 3m right of the base of *Raven Gully* at a protruding flake in the low line of overhangs. *Photo on page 315.*
35m. Climb past the flake and follow thin grooves to gain a horizontal break. Make a difficult couple of moves left and then up, to the base of a larger curving groove. Climb the steepening groove then make strenuous moves up left to a rest at its top. Move back right and stand on a small knobbly ledge. Technical moves away from this rightwards are rewarded with easier climbing that leads to the summit.
FA. Frank Cannings, Pete Badcock 21.8.1964 (6pts)
FFA. Pat Littlejohn 1971 (Direct start with 1pt)
FFA. Mick Fowler 1980

⑧ Aviation . . . . Top 50 E1 5b
Dartmoor's enduring classic gives sustained and engrossing climbing on perfect rock. Start at a short, square-cut pillar below a steep flake-crack.
1) 5b, 16m. Climb the short pillar to beneath the bulging and rounded flake-crack. Forceful moves into and up the crack are then followed by a delicate and technical traverse right to a hanging belay on nuts and a tied-off chickenhead.
2) 5a, 20m. Traverse a short way rightwards and climb a flake-crack and the insecure drainpipe above to easier, slabby climbing and the summit.
FA. Dave Bassett, Harry Cornish 9.1961

⑨ Rhinoceros E2 5c
The counter-line to *Aviation* is a fine but difficult proposition that is high in the grade. Start right of a blank wall below the narrowest point of the overhang.
1) 5c, 14m. Climb to the band of overhangs and use thin flakes to pull onto the wall and then move left to the hanging belay of *Aviation*.
2) 5c, 22m. Reverse the traverse of *Aviation* and take the flake at its end to the next bulge. Move right for 3m and make a very hard move up the bulging wall on tiny crystals. Easier climbing above gains the summit of Low Man.
FA. Pat Littlejohn, Sam Whimster 14.5.1971

⑩ Levitation Direct . . . . . HVS 5b
A butch and popular variation start to *Levitation*. Start below a steep, cracked bulge at the end of *Levitation's* initial traverse.
20m. Climb up to and through the overhang to join and finish as for *Levitation*. Well-protected.
FA. Pat Littlejohn, Steve Jones 1968

⑪ Levitation . . . . VS 4b
Tucked away on the right margin of Low Man is this delightful pitch. Start at a left-leaning crack just to the right of the main overhangs.
24m. Climb the awkward crack to a ledge on the left. Make a low intricate move left above the overhang to below a flake-crack. Climb the flake-crack and bulge above to easier slabs and a belay.
FA. Andy Prowling, Pat Littlejohn 4.1967

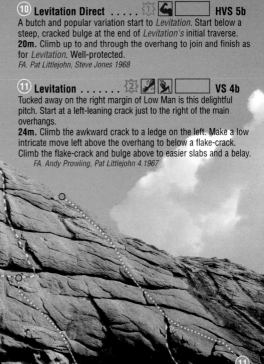

Avon Somerset · North Devon · Culm Coast · Inland Cornwall · Atlantic Coast · West Penwith · The Lizard · Inland Devon · Torbay · Dorset

① Letterbox Wall/Hangover — E1 5b

The combination of the best of two lines gives a technical and exhilarating climb not to be missed. Start at a blank wall with a hand-ledge at head height. *Photo on page 298.*

15m. Make a hard move to get established on the hand-ledge from where some stretchy moves gain a jug and then the horizontal break. Climb the leftward trending line of overhanging flakes above (good spike-runners) to a final heave over the last bulge to easier ground.
FA. Jack Denton 18.9.1955 Letterbox Wall
FA. Joe Barry 1961 Hangover

② Don't Stop Now — E2 5c

Very hard moves on the lower wall are followed by steeper stuff above. Start at a shallow 'Y' crack just right of the hand-ledge of *Letterbox Wall/Hangover*.

15m. From the top of the 'Y' crack make hard moves to the deep horizontal break and continue directly up the steep upper wall to the top.
FA. Paul Dawson 1980

③ Zig Zag — Diff

A very good climb at the grade, and furnished with comforting holds and gear. Start at the base of a right-trending ramp and crack.

15m. Move up the ramp and crack to the horizontal break. Pull up onto the wall above it and move left to less steep ground. Climb up rightwards on good holds to the top.

④ Bulging Wall — VDiff

The tallest section of the South Face is taken by this smashing climb. Start at the base of a right-leaning flake-crack.

16m. Climb the flake-crack to the horizontal break and make a tricky move to stand on a ledge above it. Move left to a flake and climb up this and the wall above to a small rounded boss. Traverse right to more good holds and follow these to the top.

⑤ Step Across — Diff

Disjointed but interesting climbing which culminates in a spectacular ending. Protection is not easy to arrange. Start at a large vertical spike at the start of a wide crack.

16m. From the spike, climb the wide crack to the base of a wide chimney. Bridge up the chimney and stride left to a good foothold on the left wall and pull across on jugs. Finish slightly left on more jugs.

Haytor - South Face

A fine face of granite sliced by some good crack-lines. The climbing is fairly intense, although for the most part well-protected and on brilliant rock. The tor is a popular tourist spot and the watching crowds can be large.
Approach - Walk up to the tor from the car park.
Descent - Walk off down the tourist steps.
Conditions - The South Face dries extremely quickly, has no seepage problems and gets plenty of sun.

⑥ Haggis — E1 5b

A compact classic that crams in a large amount of testing climbing. Start at a steep slab in the narrow buttress right of the chimney of *Step Across*.

15m. Make thin moves up the slab to good gear at the break below the first overhang. Move rightwards up through the overhang and continue past the upper overhang to a final easy wall.
FA. Robin Shaw 1961

⑦ Athos — VDiff

A well-travelled wide crack that possesses a tough but well-protected initial few metres. Start below the wide crack.

14m. Move up to the low overhang and make some steep moves to pass it. Continue up the easier widening crack to the top.

⑧ D'Artagnan — E1 5c

A hard, highball boulder problem start is the meat of this much-attempted line. Start below the low overhang right of the wide crack of *Athos*.

14m. Move up to the low overhang and make some difficult moves to get established above it. Finish direct.
FA. Pat Littlejohn 1976

⑨ Aramis — VS 4c

Well-protected, old-school crack-climbing that has been the scene of many a struggle over the decades. Start at the steep crack on the far right of the face.

14m. Climb the awkward crack to its top and pull left on good holds to an easy finish.
FA. Tony Moulam 18.5.1946

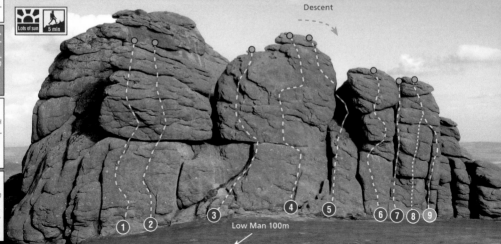

Lots of sun | 5 min

Descent

Low Man 100m

⑩ Canis . . . . VS 4c

When the upper slabs are clear of moss this is a worthwhile pitch. Start on the left side of the face next to a deep chimney that is formed by a massive flake that leans against the tor.

23m. Move up cracks in the wall left of the chimney to a spike and continue up cracks until a pull up the wall above can be made and a ledge on the left gained. Move up through a bulge and climb carefully up the mossy slab to the top. Do not attempt this section in damp conditions.

FA. Tony Moulam 8.1.1952

⑪ Vandal and Ann . . . HVS 5b

A minor moorland-classic that needs dry conditions to be enjoyed to the full. Start at two small holes below the remains of an iron spike at 5m.

1) 5b, 14m. Climb direct up the slab from the two holes, initially with great difficulty, to the summit of the huge flake. Move right to belay below the rounded crack in the upper wall.

2) 5a, 13m. Access the wide, rounded crack in the upper wall via a tricky pull through the bulge. Follow the crack and slabs above to the top.

FA. Tom Patey 7.1959 Vandal
FA. Geoff Sutton, Ann Sutton 10.1955

⑫ Bridal Piton Slab . . . . . Diff

The fine set of right-facing flakes in the easy-angled slab combined with the descent down the wide chimney gives a substantial round trip. Start at the base of the slab.

14m. Follow the flakes until moves right gain a small corner that leads to the top of a pinnacle. To descend, climb down the deep chimney to the left (facing in) which is Mod in dry conditions.

Haytor - North Face

The North Face is the least hospitable of Haytor's faces, and is rarely climbed on outside of the summer months. However, when in condition, the climbing is well worthwhile, and often much quieter than the other faces on the tor.

Approach - Walk to the tor from the car park.
Descent - Walk off down the tourist steps.
Conditions - The face receives very little sun and is generally a cold place which can be a blessing in hot weather. Some of the climbs are mossy in their upper sections.

⑬ Rough Justice E5 6a

Intricate and very bold climbing that is high in the grade. Start below a short, mossy crack on the left side of the steep wall.

18m. Gain the mossy slab above the crack and stride right to a crack. Move up to a peg and nut just above, the first and last protection. Climb the shallower crack above and then stretch for a tiny right-facing corner. Pull up and finish precariously up the final wall with great care.

FA. Pete Bull 4.10.1983

⑭ Rough Diamond E4 6a

Well named. The bottomless, rounded crack in the centre of the wall is a fine, if hard-won line. Start at a thin crack left of the bottomless rounded crack.

18m. Move up to a good, small nut placement at 3m and reach right for positive side-pulls. Make some committing moves to the crack proper and good jams and cams. Follow the sustained series of rounded cracks and breaks to the top.

FA. Pat Littlejohn, Pete O'Sullivan 7.7.1979

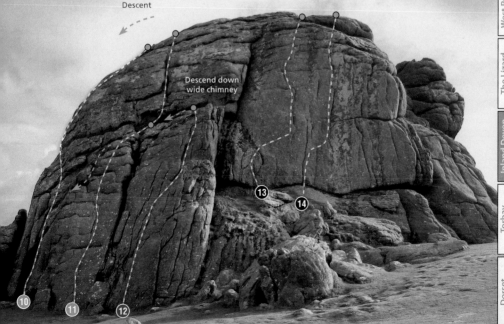

Descent

Descend down wide chimney

	No star	⚑	⚑⚑	⚑⚑⚑
Mod to S	1	2	3	-
HS to HVS	-	1	-	1
E1 to E3	-	1	-	-
E4 and up	-	-	2	-

The jumble of boulders and granite tors that make up Hound Tor hold some of the most popular climbs on Dartmoor and during days of clement weather they see plenty of attention. It has a good spread of grades and styles, although most of the climbs are steep. The environment is gorgeous, the views are expansive and the grassy paths and dells between the rocks lend Hound Tor a less-harsh feel than nearby Haytor. The place also benefits from a particularly good tea van located in the car park. The climbs are on the short side, but pack a punch and, although very much under the public gaze, a little bit of quiet can always be found.

Approach   See main area map on page 298

From the A38 Exeter to Plymouth road, exit at the junction for Bovey Tracey. Drive to Bovey Tracey and pick up signs to Widecombe-in-the-Moor (B3387) then follow this road up onto Dartmoor. Once past Haytor and its various car parks continue out across the moor for 3 miles, always taking the right turn, until the large car park of Hound Tor is reached on the left and its welcoming snack van. Hound Tor is a couple of minutes walk up the slope on the right.

Conditions

Hound Tor is extremely exposed to all the elements and is best enjoyed on warm days when the lower lying crags are gently baking. Hound Tor does not seep and dries very quickly after rain. Sun and shade can be found throughout the day.

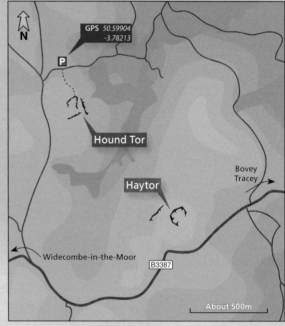

Pulpit Face

Suspension Flake Ro

The jumble of rocks that make up Hound Tor.

Avon Somerset

North Devon

Culm Coast

Inland Cornwall

Atlantic Coast

West Penwith

The Lizard

Inland Devon

Torbay

Dorset

Philippa Arding making quick work of the gymnastic moorland favourite *Suspension Flake* (VS 4c) - *page 322* - Hound Tor. Photo: Nick Arding

Hound Tor

Hound Tor is a collection of sinister-looking piles of granite boulders and buttresses that hold a small but intriguing line-up of climbs.

Approach - From the car park the approach to the Hound Tor is easily seen up a gentle grassy slope. On approaching the rocks the Suspension Flake block is on the right and the Pulpit Face is on the left. The Aerobic Wall Face is on the far right side of the rocks.

Descent - The only descent that is not straightforward is from the summit of The Pulpit Face which requires a scramble down to the left when looking out.

Conditions - The rock dries quickly after rain but is very exposed to the wind and it can be bitterly cold.

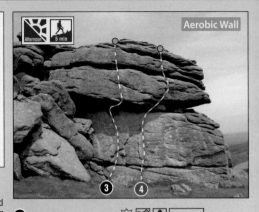

Aerobic Wall

❶ Suspension Flake . . . . . VS 4c

One of the best of Dartmoor's fun micro classics. Short, sharp and exciting. Start on boulders under the ledge below the right-slanting flake that strikes out from the base of a steep offwidth. *Photo on page 321.*

10m. Move onto the ledge and make a tough swing out right before continuing along the flake rail to a tricky move up a short crack to finish. Fun.

FA. Geoff Sutton 16.8.1954

❷ Toltec Twostep . E6 6c

A testpiece that climbs the blank face to the finish of *Suspension Flake* via some vicious and difficult to protect moves. Start below the middle section of *Suspension Flake.*

9m. Move up to a wide horizontal break. Make hard moves up to a small flake and a very difficult-to-place nut, before a long move rightwards gains a shallow groove and the finish of *Suspension Flake* just above.

FA. Pete Bull 20.4.1989

❸ Limbo Dancer. E4 5c

A popular and very committing, but potentially crippling problem. Start under the roof just left of a crack at an inconveniently situated pointed block.

9m. Nip up the wall to the roof and reach around to a hold on the lip. Pull around and proceed with caution up the rounded breaks to the top.

FA. Ken Palmer, Low Man 17.6.1986

❹ Aerobic Wall E2 5c

A far more amenable and protectable method of ascending the wall and roof, but still no push-over. Start at the thin crack beneath the roof.

10m. Climb the thin crack to the break under the roof and power up and out across the right-leaning flakes to a couple of rounded finishing overlaps.

FA. Simon Cook 8.1978

Pulpit Face - Hydraulic Arete

The Pulpit

Avon Somerset

North Devon

Culm Coast

Inland Cornwall

Atlantic Coast

West Penwith

The Lizard

Inland Devon

Torbay

Dorset

---

6 The Vice . . . . **VDiff**

A good expedition that possesses a lot of interesting and varied climbing, and a test of jamming ability on the first pitch. Start on a block ledge 5m right of *Hydraulic Arete*.

1) 10m. Move up the initial wall past diagonal breaks and then up steeper ground via some deep vertical cracks to a ledge. Move right along the ledge to a belay below a wide chimney.

2) 12m. Climb up the left wall of the chimney and stride over to the main tor on the other side of the chimney. Traverse right under an overlap until it is possible to pull up onto the summit.

7 Pulpit . . . . **HVD**

Accessing the Pulpit from the left proves to be a grunt, sandwiched between some much more pleasing climbing. Start at the foot of a short slab left of the corner below the Pulpit.

18m. Climb up the left arete of the slab and move up leftwards to an overhung crack. Grunt up onto the left end of the Pulpit using the crack and a jug in the wall above, and follow the much easier corner above to the summit.

FA. Jack Denton 1951

8 Devonleigh . . . . **HVD**

The best climb on this buttress builds to an exposed finale. Start at the foot of the right arete of the corner below the Pulpit.

18m. Climb up the arete to a point level with the Pulpit and step left onto it. From the centre of the Pulpit climb directly through the steep bulges above to the summit.

9 Paddy . . . . **Mod**

A very good piece of climbing at the grade which is well protected and satisfyingly varied. Start 2m right of the arete of *Devonleigh* at a well-worn patch of ground.

18m. Climb the wall that leads left under some small overhangs to a ledge below a much larger roof. Climb the crack on the right using big flakes to the summit.

10 Liars Dice . . . . **S**

This short hand-and-finger crack is a delight, if you can jam! Start below the crack in the right wall of the descent corner.

8m. The crack is very well-protected and furnished with jams of all dimensions.

5 Hydraulic Arete . . . . . . **HVS 5b**

The longest route at Hound Tor follows the blunt overlap-infested arete on the left side of the face. Start below a ledge and cracks on the arete.

22m. From the ledge make some steep moves up the cracks and then balance up and pull through the overhang to much easier ground above.

FA. Pete O'Sullivan, I.Thomas 6.1984

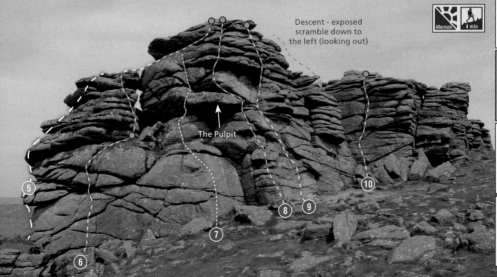

Descent - exposed scramble down to the left (looking out)

The Pulpit

	No star	⬧	⬧⬧	⬧⬧⬧
Mod to S	-	1	1	-
HS to HVS	-	1	-	-
E1 to E3	-	-	-	1
E4 and up	-	-	-	-

Tucked away on the edge of Dartmoor is one of the smaller chunks of granite to be found in the West Country. Bench Tor is a secluded, and very beautiful venue that has one particularly notable climb. This is a good spot to escape the crowds.

Approach
See main area map on page 298
From the A38 Exeter to Plymouth road, exit at the south junction for Ashburton and follow signs for Princetown. After 2 miles, turn left to Holne. Drive for 3 miles past Holne, up onto Dartmoor, and park on the right, at a large, grassy car park on the eastern side of the small Venford Reservoir. From the car park, follow vague paths northwards, until the top of Bench Tor can be seen ahead. From the summit of the tor the main face can be seen, 150m further on (15mins).

Conditions
The face is sheltered from the wind, but not the rain

Avon Somerset · North Devon · Culm Coast · Inland Cornwall · Atlantic Coast · West Penwith · The Lizard · Inland Devon · Torbay · Dorset

Mike Robertson not hanging around on the short, but action-packed *Hostile Witness* (E2 5c) - *opposite* - at the quaint Bench Tor.

Two Bridges · B3387 · N · Hexworthy · **Bench Tor** · GPS 50.52281 -3.85178 · Venford Reservoir · P Holne · About 500m

❶ Central Buttress . . . HVD

An entertaining initial move gives this steep little line merit. Start on a perched block at the left-hand end of the main face.

12m. Place some good gear. Bridge out over space and pull onto the rock using good but high jugs. This move is 4b if the jugs cannot be reached. Follow the steep wall above, just left of a crack, on good holds to the top.

FA. Andrew Borwick 1959

❷ Hostile Witness E2 5c

One of Dartmoor's finest. A gritstonesque climb that packs in some athletic and technical moves. Start on a flat-topped block below the left end of the huge overhang in the centre of the main face. *Photo opposite*.

16m. Pull up directly into the corner, left of the overhang, and place some good gear before swinging out to the arete on a horizontal break just above the lip of the overhang. Gain a flake on the face around the arete and make a couple of tricky moves to leave it and enter the base of a good crack. Follow the crack to the top.

FA. Pat Littlejohn, Dave Garner 23.4.1976

❸ Suspended Sentence. . . HVS 5b

Although this line only covers a small amount of independent ground it is still a good route in its own right. Start as for *Hostile Witness* on a flat-topped block below the left end of the huge overhang in the centre of the main face.

16m. Pull up directly into the corner left of the overhang and take the corner to an overhang at its top. Traverse right, around the arete to reach a good crack that is followed to the top.

FA. Paul Twomey, S.Scarbro 10.8.1989

❹ Oak Tree Zig Zag . . VDiff

The corner in the centre of the main face is a splendid and challenging little pitch that has a complex start. Start as for *Hostile Witness* on a flat-topped block below the left end of the huge overhang in the centre of the main face.

17m. Pull up rightwards to a crack in the face below the centre of the huge overhang and then traverse left with feet just above the low overhang to the base of the corner (this point can be gained by climbing direct as for the start of *Hostile Witness* at Severe 4a). Follow the corner to an overhang, then move left to the easier continuation and take this to the top past some saplings.

FA. Andrew Borwick 1959

Lots of sun | 15 min

Descent

	No star	⚝	⚝⚝	⚝⚝⚝
Mod to S	2	4	2	-
HS to HVS	-	4	-	-
E1 to E3	-	-	-	-
E4 and up	-	-	-	-

Sheeps Tor is a wall of vertical granite, split by cracks of all shapes and sizes. The climbs here are all worthwhile, and provide a high concentration of easy to mid-grade routes that are not too intimidating - useful for those looking to practise their first leads. As a consequence, the crag has become very popular with commercial groups, who at times dominate the cliff. The climbs are fairly polished, but in compensation the holds are positive and the protection possibilities excellent.

Approach   See main area map on page 298

From the B3212 that links Yelverton to Princetown on the south eastern side of Dartmoor, follow signs to Dousland and Burrator Reservoir. Once at the reservoir cross the dam and follow signs to the hamlet of Sheepstor. Pass though the hamlet and take the first narrow lane on the left that climbs uphill and then turns right on to open moorland. A couple of hundred metres along are various parking pull-offs. Walk up the slope to the crag (five minutes).

Conditions

Sheeps Tor is extremely exposed to wind and rain, although the rock does dry very quickly. A couple of the lines do seep but generally it is always possible to climb here if it is not raining. The face catches the sun for a good part of the day, but goes into the shade in the late afternoon.

Sidebar tabs (top to bottom): Avon Somerset · North Devon · Culm Coast · Inland Cornwall · Atlantic Coast · West Penwith · The Lizard · Inland Devon · Torbay · Dorset

Avon Somerset

North Devon

Culm Coast

Inland Cornwall

Atlantic Coast

West Penwith

The Lizard

Inland Devon

Torbay

Dorset

Meilee Rafe balances up the final moves of the crux finger-crack of *Wind Wall* (HVS 5a) - *page 328* - at the very popular Sheeps Tor. Photo: Mike Robertson

1 Workers' Wall . . . . HS 4a

A fairly tough line that has some very good moves and feels much longer than it actually is. Start at a crack-system 5m right of the edge of the crag.

16m. Climb the shallow cracks to the diagonal break. Step right and push on up the steep crack to finish.

2 Crack and Chimney . S 4a

The central line of Sheeps Tor's largest face is the crag's best route. Start below the crack at the wall's highest point.

16m. Climb the flake-crack via some balancy layaways to a diagonal break, swing right and tackle the short chimney above to finish.

3 Wind Wall . . . . HVS 5a

The thin crack in the upper wall above *Slab Route* is short but pleasant. Start as for *Crack and Chimney. Photo on page 327.*

16m. Move up the first section of *Crack and Chimney* before moving right to a good hold below the thin crack. Climb the excellent crack to easier ground.

4 Slab Route . . . . . . Diff

One of the best of its grade on Dartmoor. Start on the left side of the tapering inset slab in the corner.

16m. Move up the left side of the slab on polished rock and with little in the way of protection to where it fades. Continue up the crack on the left wall to finish.

5 Slanting Crack . . . . S 4a

A steep boot-wide crack in the wall right of the corner. Start beneath the crack.

14m. Make a powerful pull into the crack to get started, and climb to its top and easy ground above.

6 Mushroom Wall . . . . . . VS 5a

The short but tricky wall packs in some good moves. Start at the black wall just left of the central arete.

9m. A stiff few moves quickly gain the mid-height break where more steep but slightly easier moves bring the top within reach.

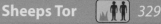
7 **Omega Crack** . . . . HVD
A good old fashioned crack. Start at the base of the first crack just to the right of the central arete.
9m. A hard start gradually eases to less steep but still challenging ground.

8 **Burdock** . . . . HS 4a
The capping overhang that runs right across the wall has a number of breaks that provide the cruxes for all of the routes that cross it. Start just right of *Omega Crack*.
10m. Follow the line of parallel cracks just right of *Omega Crack* to and through the first break in the capping overhang.

9 **Overhang Crack** . . . . . . S 4a
A much attempted line that sees some epics. Start below the cracks that point the way to the middle break in the upper overhang.
10m. Take the cracks to an awkward finish through the break in the overhang.

10 **Dandelion** . . . . S 4a
Another good little pitch that is perhaps the easiest of the three Severes on this section of the wall. Start at a crack that leads to the right end of the upper overhangs.
10m. Pull up the cracks and pass the right end of the high line of overhangs.

11 **Barking Crack** . . . . HVD
A Sheeps Tor classic that is now very polished. Start at the base of a very polished corner on the right side of the crag.
9m. The square-cut corner-crack is often a bit damp and extremely polished. A popular variation takes the wall and flake to the left of the corner at the same grade.

12 **Sheltered Crack** . . . . Diff
A well-trodden and unintimidating climb. Start at the stepped corner.
9m. The corner past a good ledge.

The wall to the right has some very short lines.

Avon Somerset

North Devon

Culm Coast

Inland Cornwall

Atlantic Coast

West Penwith

The Lizard

Inland Devon

Torbay

Dorset

Descent

Short pitches on this wall

	No star	☆1	☆☆2	☆☆☆3
Mod to S	-	2	5	-
HS to HVS	-	1	4	4
E1 to E3	-	-	-	3
E4 and up	-	-	-	-

The Dewerstone is located in one of the ancient and magical wooded valleys of southwest Dartmoor and is a wonderful place to experience some classic low to mid-grade climbing. For those who have not been to the Dewerstone before, the first sighting will come as a neck-craning surprise. The Main Face towers up through the trees above the babbling River Plym. Many of the climbs are multi-pitch, sustained and often require good crack technique. The Main Face, along with the equally appealing outcrops of Needle and Raven Buttresses, are seamed with long cracks and well defined grooves and corners. Protection is nearly always perfect and the holds are positive allowing the spectacular situations to be enjoyed to the full. The Dewerstone has plenty to offer the climber operating in the Very Difficult to E1 grade range and would make an excellent long weekend venue.

Approach   See main area map on page 298

To reach the Dewerstone from the M5 at Exeter, follow the A38 to the Lee Mill exit, just beyond the Ivybridge exit at the south end of Dartmoor. Turn off here and follow signs to Cornwood (needs care to follow correct signs after leaving the A38) and then on to Shaugh Prior. Continue through the village of Shaugh Prior and down the hill to a car park just before the road bridge over the River Plym. Walk over the footbridge just up from the road bridge and go upstream on a wide path until a smaller path leads off right and around the hill side to the crag on the riverbank (10 minutes from the parking).

Conditions

The Dewerstone lies on the lower southwestern fringes of Dartmoor and its weather is influenced by the neighbouring high ground. Nevertheless it can be a very sheltered spot, and climbing is possible year-round, although the crag is green in winter and not a good choice after prolonged rainfall. The upper buttresses are more open and dry very quickly. When the river is high, communication on the Main Face becomes difficult.

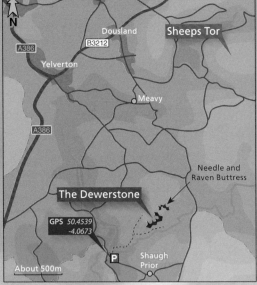

Needle and Raven Buttresses at the Dewerstone.

Side tabs: Avon Somerset | North Devon | Culm Coast | Inland Cornwall | Atlantic Coast | West Penwith | The Lizard | Inland Devon | Torbay | Dorset

Tom Skelhon about to start the hard climbing on an ascent of *Gideon* (E1 5b) - *page 337* - at the Dewerstone, Dartmoor.

Avon Somerset | North Devon | Culm Coast | Inland Cornwall | Atlantic Coast | West Penwith | The Lizard | Inland Devon | Torbay | Dorset

Pinnacle Buttress

A tall buttress that rises out of the trees and provides a number of very worthwhile, easier multi-pitch lines. The climbing gets better as height is gained.

Approach - Pinnacle Buttress is the first of the tall sections of cliff reached on the approach. The base of the buttress is in the trees, and the starts of the climbs take a little bit of finding on first acquaintance.

Descent - Walk off to the right (looking out) and go down through the trees.

Conditions - The open aretes dry quickly but the cracks can be green and damp during wet spells.

❶ Pinnacle Buttress

.... ⚃ 📷 ☐ **VDiff**

Fun and varied climbing that builds to a head spinning finish on the summit of the pinnacle. Start below a chimney crack at the foot of the ridge where the approach path begins to drop down to the main area.

1) 8m. Bridge steeply up the chimney to a large ledge.

2) 10m. Scramble easily to a belay ledge under a vertical wall with a crack in it.

3) 13m. Climb the crack to another ledge. Continue up the arete and move left to a ledge and belay below a vertical crack.

4) 10m. Make a committing step right to the arete and move up to the top of the pinnacle. Climb down and bridge across to a short finishing wall.

FA. Bob Higgins, Keith Lawder 28.1.1949

❷ Mucky Gully

.... ⚃ 📷 ☐ **Diff**

A strong line and good climbing make this a popular and impressive undertaking. Start about 10m right of the point where the approach path begins to drop down to the main area below a long corner. *Photo opposite.*

1) 18m. Climb up the corner on good holds to a smooth ledge, and a little further on another good ledge and belays.

2) 30m. Bridge and jam away up the corner above until just above a couple of large chockstones. Climb the right-hand wall to the top.

FA. Walter Parry Haskett-Smith, Scott Tucker 1894

❸ Reverse Cleft .... ⚀ 📷 ☐ **S 4a**

The eye-catching crack in the wall to the right of *Mucky Gully*. Start as for *Mucky Gully* below the long corner.

1) 18m. Climb up the corner on large holds to a good ledge and belays. This is the first pitch of *Mucky Gully*.

2) 4a, 21m. On the right wall of the gully above the belay ledge is a long crack. Climb the fine and well-protected crack to a tree belay.

3) 9m. Climb up the exposed face above the tree and bridge left over a gap to the top.

FA. Bill Higgins, Bob Higgins 3.4.1949

❹ Colonel's Arete .... ⚃ 📷 🪨 ☐ **VDiff**

An excellent expedition up the large subsidiary buttress just left of the main face. Start at a short mossy looking wall left of a large vegetated gully and just right of a crack.

1) 12m. Climb the wall on improving holds and at its top work leftwards towards the arete and belay.

2) 10m. Move up the broad face of the arete past ledges and flakes to a belay on a good ledge below a prominent bent tree.

3) 14m. Climb up to a ledge either directly past the bent tree or via a crack just to its left. Climb the steep crack which rises from the ledge. Once the first moves are made, better holds follow, then move up and left to a tree belay.

4) 9m. Climb the exposed face above the tree and bridge left over a gap to the top, this is the top pitch of *Reverse Cleft*.

FA. Jim Moulton, Skinner Saunders 7.1948

Avon Somerset

North Devon

Culm Coast

Inland Cornwall

Atlantic Coast

West Penwith

The Lizard

Inland Devon

Torbay

Dorset

Carrie Hill departs from the top of the fine corner of *Mucky Gully* (Diff) - *opposite* - on Pinnacle Buttress at the Dewerstone. Photo: Ian Parnell

❶ Leviathan . . . . 🎲3 ▨ ▨ ☐ VS 4c

The groove in the striking left-arete of the Main Face gives a stout and eye-catching route of great quality. Start at a wide crack in huge blocks below the arete.

26m. Climb to a ledge on top of the blocks beneath the groove in the arete. Follow the groove to a move right at its top and a final pull on slopers. Abseil off.

FA. Tom Patey 9.1957

❷ Vala . . . . 🎲2 ▨ ☐ HVS 5a

The staggered overlaps on the left wall of the dominating corner of *Central Groove*. Start at the base of the corner.

28m. Climb *Central Groove* for 10m and access the overlaps. Follow these to a pull over onto the cracked wall and the belay ledge a short distance above. Abseil off.

FA. Brian Shackleton, Pat Mellor 1963

❸ Central Groove . . . . ᵀᵒᵖ₅₀ ▨ ☐ HS 4b

A truly wonderful climb - they don't come much better. The climbing is intimidating but straightforward and very well-protected. Start directly beneath the dominating corner. *Photo this page.*

1) 4b, 28m. Climb the short polished wall to the base of the corner, which is followed all the way to the capping overlap. Traverse rightwards to the arete and a large block-belay.

2) 4b, 20m. Climb up and then rightwards to a ledge. Move right to below a well defined corner (possible belay). Climb the fine corner to the top, the technical crux of the route.

FA. Jim Simpson 5.2.1949

❹ Scimitar Variations . 🎲3 ▨ ⌂ ☐ E1 5b

A spectacular linkage taking on the hold plastered sheer right wall of *Central Groove*, followed by a powerful overhang high up on the cliff. Start as for *Central Groove*.

1) 5b, 28m. Climb up the initial wall of *Central Groove* and bridge out right onto a hanging slab. Immediately climb direct to the left end of the overhang above and pull through onto the vertical wall. Ascend direct on positive holds to the belay at the top of pitch one of *Central Groove*.

2) 5b, 17m. Climb up and then leftwards to below a large overhang. Tackle the overhang by moving up rightwards on large but well spaced holds to a mossy crack. Move up the crack past a small tree to a ledge. Take the short easy crack to finish.

FA. Pat Littlejohn, John Fowler 3.8.1968 (The direct start was climbed in the 1980s) The upper pitch is part of the route Extendable Arms. FA. Pete O'Sullivan 27.1.1979

Main Face

A superb crack-seamed face of clean granite with a selection of tremendous multi-pitch climbs.

Approach - Walk down the steps to below the tall sheer face above the riverbank.

Descent - Walk off left (looking out) down a steep narrow path.

Conditions - The face gets the morning sun and dries fairly quickly after rain, although seepage can be a problem. The lower section of the crag is shaded by trees.

Danie Rushmer and Mike Robertson on the first pitch of *Central Groove* (HS 4b) - *this page* - on The Dewerstone's Main Face.

Avon Somerset

North Devon

Culm Coast

Inland Cornwall

Atlantic Coast

West Penwith

The Lizard

Inland Devon

Torbay

Dorset

Morning   10 min

Upper pitch
of Central Groove

Abseil from tree Ⓐ

②

Fruitflancase
- page 336

④

Climbers' Club Direct
- page 337

③

①

5 Fruitflancase **E1 5a**

A brilliant crack-climb of sustained interest taking the steepest section of the sheer wall on the right-hand side of the Main Face. Start as for *Central Groove*. *Photo opposite*.

1) 5a, 22m. Climb up the initial wall of *Central Groove* and pull out rightwards onto a hanging slab. Climb the slab, then layback around the right end of the overhang and jam away to a stance at a large bollard on the right.

2) 4c, 18m. Climb up left to a diagonal crack, move up this and take the tricky vertical crack to a ledge. Move right to a belay below a clean-cut corner.

3) 4b, 9m. Pull up steeply left to a crack on the left arete of the corner. Move up the crack and finish up the wall slightly left to avoid vegetation.

FA. Andy McFarlane, Deryck Ball 14.9.1969

Lots of sun | 10 min | Multi-pitch

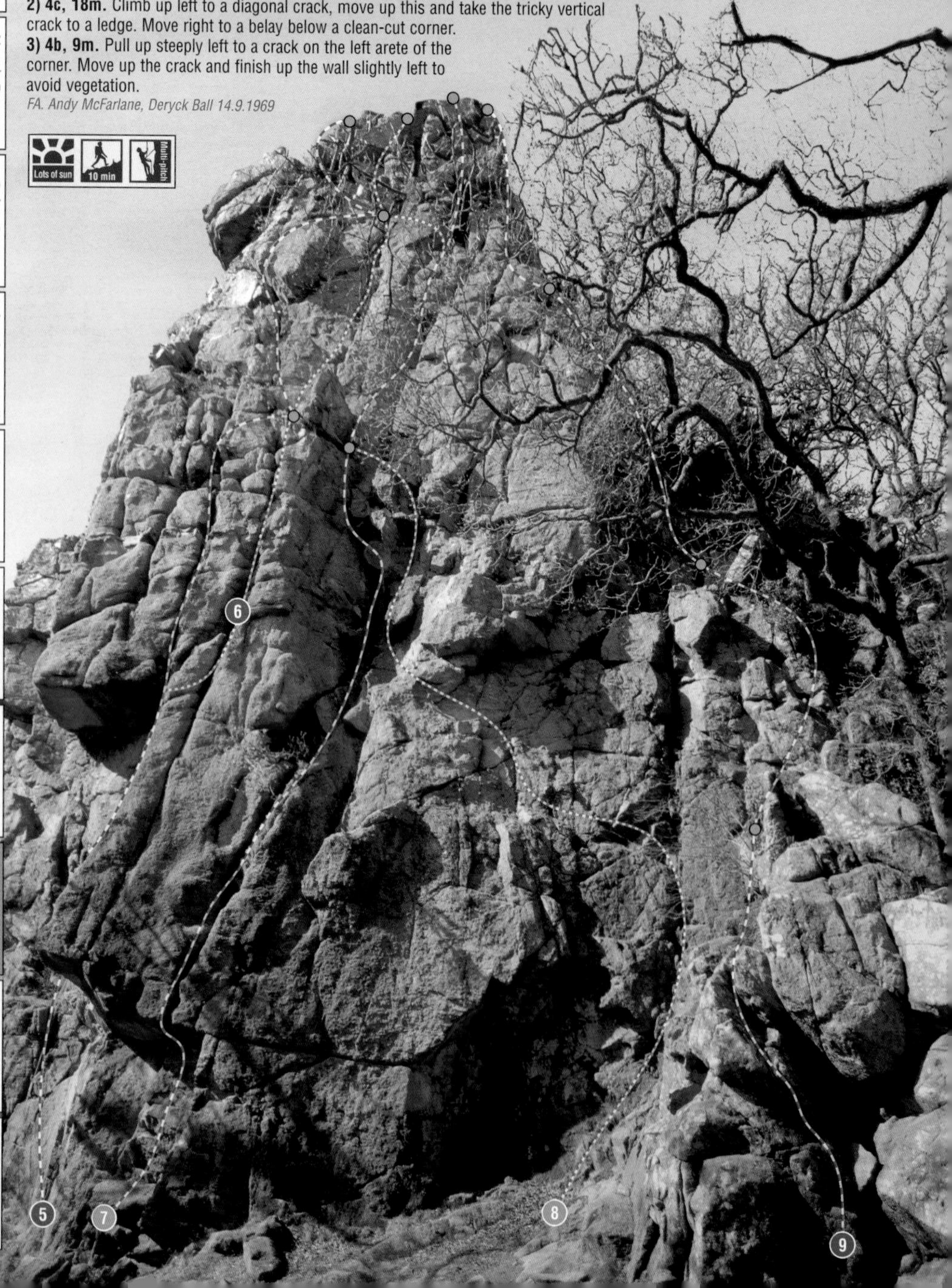

Starting out on the sustained *Fruitflancase* (E1 5a) - *opposite* - at the Dewerstone. Climber John Warner.

6 Gideon **E1 5b**

Perhaps the best of the harder routes at the Dewerstone. It features two sustained crack-pitches, each hard to fault. Start as for *Central Groove*. *Photo on page 331.*

1) 5b, 22m. Climb up the initial wall of *Central Groove* and pull out rightwards onto a hanging slab. Climb the slab and layback around the right end of the overhang. Immediately pull rightwards onto a good large spike, then climb the steep crack above with difficulty to a large bollard-belay.

2) 5a, 26m. Above the bollard is a thin crack. Take this all the way to a ledge beneath a clean-cut corner. Climb the corner to the top.

FA. Mike Rabley, John Jones 12.1962 (1pt)
FFA. Len Benstead, Dennis Morrod 1969

7 Climbers' Club Direct

. . . . **HVS 5a**

Magnificent, and one for the jamming master. A forceful couple of pitches that have taken a few scalps (and skinned a few knuckles) over the years. One of the best HVSs in the area. Start beneath the hand-crack that cuts through the low overhang at the base of the face.

1) 5a, 23m. Climb the crack strenuously and continue past a sapling to a short, overhanging corner. Climb to an overhang and exit leftwards to a good stance above.

2) 4c, 27m. Ascend the wide crack in the V-groove to the overhang at its top. Pull out right and climb the widening crack above direct to a wild finish.

FA. Robin Hodgkin, David Cox 27.9.1936

8 Climbers' Club Ordinary

. . . . **VS 4b**

The easiest way up the Dewerstone's most impressive wall is a fine series of pitches. The first pitch is serious and requires care. Start on the right of the face at the base of a small gully.

1) 4b, 24m. Climb up and traverse left to some dubious flakes. Move left, using them with great care, then climb up left to an overhanging corner. Move up this for 2m and then make a blind move rightwards, around a rib, into a parallel corner. Move up to a good stance.

2) 4b, 20m. Ascend the wide crack in the V-groove to the overhang at its top and pull out right. Move up to a widening and traverse leftwards using a thin black crack to a good ledge-belay beneath a clean-cut corner.

3) 4b, 8m. Climb the magnificently-positioned corner to the top.

FA. David Cox, Rennie Bere 2.9.1935

9 Route B . . . . **HVD**

The final exposed and sustained pitch is the best of the VDiffs at the Dewerstone. Although the line looks a little hidden away and broken from below, the climbing is varied and fairly tricky. The route is shady and needs dry conditions. Start at a small protruding buttress of blocks, right of a small gully.

1) 10m. Move up left past a low overhang and then step back right and up to a belay on a good ledge.

2) 10m. Climb the wall above the stance to ledges and a large tree belay.

3) 11m. Above is a small corner in the wall. Move right and pull back left steeply on good holds into the corner. Climb this and a short wall to a ledge and tree belay. Strenuous.

4) 18m. A brilliant pitch. Move left from the stance onto the main face and climb to below an overhanging nose on the arete. Take the slim corner just right of the nose until it is possible to work leftwards to the top.

FA. Keith Lawder, Bob Higgins 22.1.1949

Avon Somerset — North Devon — Culm Coast — Inland Cornwall — Atlantic Coast — West Penwith — The Lizard — Inland Devon — Torbay — Dorset

Avon Somerset | North Devon | Culm Coast | Inland Cornwall | Atlantic Coast | West Penwith | The Lizard | Inland Devon | Torbay | Dorset

❶ Needle Arete .... VDiff

A well-positioned and exposed route that finishes atop the needle. Start low down on the front face amongst the trees beneath a very short boot-wide layback crack.

1) 7m. Climb the crack to a ledge with some big trees on it and a low, large spike. This pitch is easily avoided by walking to the ledge from the right.

2) 20m. From the right-hand side of the low spike climb the slab to below the buttress proper and continue up a crack-system just left of the arete to a steeper final section that eases at a good spike hold. Swing right to a stance and tree belay.

3) 12m. Climb above the tree for 2m on good holds until horizontal moves left around the arete under a nose access a corner/groove. Climb this easily to the needle.

FA. Jim Simpson 5.2.1949

❷ Cyclops .... HVS 5a

The top pitch takes the rounded crack in the centre of Needle Buttress' upper wall. Start on the mossy slabs with a small wilting tree at 5m.

1) 4c, 22m. Climb the slab right of the tree to a block beneath a steeper wall with a thin left-leaning crack. Follow this and the wall and cracks above to belay on the left-hand tree.

2) 5a, 14m. Take the rounded crack on the headwall to a tricky move right. Move up and right to a groove that leads to the summit.

FA. Frank Cannings, Brian Shackleton 1.11.1964

Needle Buttress

Descent

Lots of sun | 15 min

Needle Buttress

A smart buttress with a couple of very good routes up its sunny south-east face. Well worth the 5 minute approach from the Main Face and always less busy.

Approach - From the base of the Main Face, walk up and right through the woods on a faint path.

Descent - Scramble off left (looking out).

Conditions - The lower section can remain damp under the tree cover.

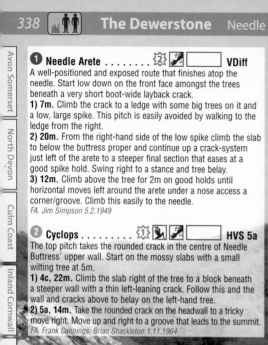

A busy afternoon on Raven Buttress with climbers finishing
Fly On The Wall (HS 4b) and *Imperialist* (HVS 5a) - *opposite*

Raven Buttress

The lower section of Raven Buttress has some really good two-pitch lines. The climbing is at times delicate, in contrast to the rest of the Dewerstone.
Approach - The buttress is across the wide gully from Needle Buttress and the starts of the routes are hard to find.
Descent - Scramble off left (facing out).
Conditions - The base of the routes can remain damp under the tree cover.

⑤ Spider's Web . . . . . 🕸🪝✏️◻️◻️◻️ **HVS 5a**

A hidden classic that weaves its way up the alternating slabs and overhangs of the front face. Start by scrambling around the base of the buttress to a tree on the right.
1) 5a, 17m. Move up to the right end of the overhangs and climb a short corner (not the square-cut longer corner to the right). Pull out left after 3m and move across the slab to a peg and nut belay.
2) 5a, 16m. Climb up behind the belay and make a thin move rightwards onto another slab before moving up to the next overhang. Restricted moves left gain the arete and much easier climbing leading to the summit.
FA. Tom Patey, Barry Page, P.Henry 5.1959

The next route starts on the col that separates the lower and upper sections of Raven Buttress.

⑥ Raven Face . . . . 🕸✏️◻️◻️◻️ **VDiff**

A very pleasant way to finish off the climbs on the lower section of Raven Buttress. Start at the col between the lower and upper buttress. The col is most easily reached by walking up the right hand side of the lower buttress and moving left to the col.
22m. Move up the broad rib above the col to a slabby section of rock beneath a prominent overhang. Traverse right under the overhang and finish up the break to its right.
FA. Bob Higgins 26.2.1949

③ Fly on the Wall . . . . 🕸✏️◻️◻️◻️ HS 4b

A well-travelled line with some impressive climbing on the second pitch. The route climbs the vertical face overlooking the gully between Needle and Raven Buttress. Start at a belay on a ramp, above a 2m high mossy wall, beneath a small tree at 5m.
Photo opposite.
1) 4b, 10m. Move past the tree and take the short crack above to a slab that leads to a tree and belay.
2) 4a, 14m. From a flake, climb up left to the overhung line leading back rightwards to the top.

④ Silken Thread/Imperialist

. . . . 🕸✏️🪝◻️◻️◻️ HVS 5a

A varied and testing hybrid which is both delicate and strenuous. Start right of *Fly on the Wall* at the base of the slabby front face.
1) 5a, 16m. Climb the thin weakness 4m right of the slabby arete to the overhangs. Move left under the overhangs to the arete and move awkwardly around it. Move steeply up and back right above the overhang and belay immediately below an overhanging corner.
2) 5a, 15m. Climb the overhanging corner and at its steepest point use good holds on the left arete to gain easier ground above that leads to the top.
FA. Tom Patey 17.11.1958 (Silken Thread)
FA. Len Benstead. Dennis Morrod 14.5.1969

Avon Somerset
North Devon
Culm Coast
Inland Cornwall
Atlantic Coast
West Penwith
The Lizard
Inland Devon
Torbay
Dorset

Avon Somerset

North Devon

Culm Coast

Inland Cornwall

Atlantic Coast

West Penwith

The Lizard

Inland Devon

Torbay

Dorset

Torbay

Avon Somerset

North Devon

Culm Coast

Inland Cornwall

Atlantic Coast

West Penwith

The Lizard

Inland Devon

Torbay

Dorset

Lee Proctor rounding the slight rib to gain the crack on the first pitch of the classic *Moonraker* (HVS 5a) - *page 347* - in the Great Cave of the Old Redoubt at Berry Head, Torbay.

Avon Somerset

North Devon

Culm Coast

Inland Cornwall

Atlantic Coast

West Penwith

The Lizard

Inland Devon

Torbay

Dorset

Setting up for the final difficult moves on *Tuppence* (8b) - *page 363* - on the Ferocity Wall at Anstey's Cove, Torquay. Climber Dave Pickford

Torbay is a major tourist centre and at either end of the bay are clusters of fantastic sea-cliffs that provide some very varied limestone and climbing styles. The rock ranges from the large slabby sections of Long Quarry Point to the intimidating stacked overhangs of the Old Redoubt at Berry Head. Between these are the hard sport crags of Anstey's Cove and the sunny more traditional venues dotted along the seashore at Daddyhole.

Approach

From the M5 at Exeter, take the A38/A380 directly to Torquay/Torbay. The cliffs of Berry Head are close to the town of Brixham, at the southern point of Torbay, whilst the other cliffs of Daddyhole and Anstey's Cove are at the northern point of Torbay on the outskirts of Torquay.

Berry Head - follow signs for Brixham and on approaching Brixham pick up signs for Berry Head and follow them to a car park (fee). From here the approaches to each cliff are described in the Berry Head section.

Daddyhole and Anstey's Cove - the best way to locate the parking on a first visit is to follow signs for Torquay Harbour, then follow signs for Daddyhole around its Marina, past the Living Coasts bird-sanctuary and up a hill. A number of signed turnings eventually lead to the Daddyhole Plain car park (free). For Anstey's Cove, also head for the harbour and pick up signs for Babbacombe. Follow the road up a hill away from the harbour for around 1.25 miles to the huge Palace Hotel on the right. About 150m past the Palace Hotel turn left into Perinville Road and park.

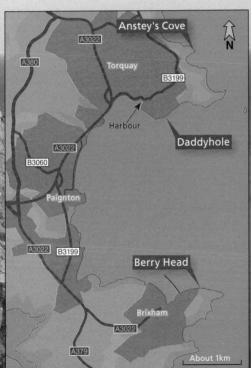

Access

The Old Redoubt at Berry Head has a restriction due to nesting birds that runs from the March 1st to July 31st inclusive. Access to the beach at Anstey's Cove is banned but the crags are unaffected.

Tides

The Old Redoubt is tidal, as is access to the Sanctuary Wall, although to a lesser extent. All of the other cliffs are non-tidal but still close to the sea.

Conditions

The generally sunny aspect, dry climate and sheltered nature of Torbay's cliffs means that it is possible to climb all year round, especially at Telegraph Hole and Anstey's Cove, though the latter does tend to seep after rain. The Old Redoubt is a more serious and shady crag and also needs a bit of wet weather to clean off all the poo once the birds have departed after the nesting season.

Avon Somerset | North Devon | Culm Coast | Inland Cornwall | Atlantic Coast | West Penwith | The Lizard | Inland Devon | Torbay | Dorset

	No star	⭐	⭐⭐	⭐⭐⭐
Mod to S	-	-	-	-
HS to HVS	-	1	3	1
E1 to E3	-	-	2	3
E4 and up	-	-	-	3

The massive yawning mouth of the Old Redoubt's Great Cave is one of the most intimidating sections of sea-cliff in the West Country; its tiered overhangs seemingly impossible to breakthrough. However, the rock is some of the most climbable to be found anywhere, and is peppered with jugs and handrails that allow the outrageous overhangs and walls to be scaled. The Old Redoubt holds some of the most sought-after long sea-cliff classics in the UK, but increasingly its flanking sea-level traverses, tackled as deep water solos, are catching up the popularity of the 'roped' routes. Should the sea-conditions or tides restrict access to the base of the Old Redoubt, the nearby Red Wall area offers some short, but pleasant pitches.

Approach

Follow signs for Brixham. On approaching the town, pick up the brown tourist signs for Berry Head and follow them to a car park on the headland (fee). Approaches to each cliff are described in the relevant section.

Access

A restriction due to nesting birds (£1000 fine) is in force from March 1st until 31st July inclusive. Red Wall is not covered by the ban.

Tides and Conditions

The starts of the routes on the main section of the Old Redoubt cliff are tidal and calm conditions are required for the approach traverse to the base of the Old Redoubt. *Rainbow Bridge* is non-tidal but requires a calm sea. The routes on The Red Wall are non-tidal. The routes are often in condition, although they can be guano-covered in places immediately after the bird-ban has finished. Seepage does occur after prolonged periods of wet weather. The sea-conditions are often benign, the bay being sheltered from westerly swell or winds.

N

Berry Head hotel

Quarry

Lighthouse

Berry Head Rd

GPS *50.396078 -3.491710*

Cafe

P

Visitor centre

Red Wall

Rainbow Bridge

Great Cave

Magical Mystery Tour

From Brixham

Gillard Road

About 500m

Avon Somerset | North Devon | Culm Coast | Inland Cornwall | Atlantic Coast | West Penwith | The Lizard | Inland Devon | Torbay | Dorset

Magical Mystery Tour

The Great Cave

Rainbow Bridge

Avon Somerset | North Devon | Culm Coast | Inland Cornwall | Atlantic Coast | West Penwith | The Lizard | Inland Devon | Torbay | Dorset

Pete Saunders finishing the crux traverse of the space-walking *Dreadnought* (E3 5c) - *page 347* - on the Old Redoubt at Berry Head, with the long crack and traverse of *Moonraker's* first pitch dropping away below. Photo: Sue Hazel

Access - A bird ban is in effect on this face between March 1st and July 31st.

Morning | 3 min | Multi-pitch | Tidal

④

③

Magical Mystery Tour
- page 350

①

②

The Great Cave

Avon Somerset | North Devon | Culm Coast | Inland Cornwall | Atlantic Coast | West Penwith | The Lizard | Inland Devon | Torbay | Dorset

The Old Redoubt

The centrepiece of the Old Redoubt is its Great Cave, one of the UK's most impressive sea-cliffs. The immense overhangs and neck-straining lines are some of the West Country's most spectacular.

Approach - From the gearing-up ledges, drop down to the right (facing out) and downclimb a steep wall (Mod) on huge hidden holds to large sea-level ledges at the mouth of the Great Cave. To approach the majority of routes a sea-level traverse of Severe standard is necessary. This is only possible for around 1 hour either side of low water. From the large sea-level ledges scramble to the back of the cave and then cross to the opposite wall and follow overhung ledges on massive holds out to the starts of the various routes. At high tide, an abseil to the start of *Moonraker* is possible.

Tides - The starts of the routes are all tidal and calm conditions are required for the approach traverse.

Conditions - The routes require calm sea-conditions and low tides. The routes are often in condition, although they can be guano covered in places.

1 Goddess of Gloom .... HVS 5a

Sustained climbing on a strong line-up the wall left of the Great Cave. Start on a good tidal ledge at the base of a large corner with two overhangs.

1) 5a, 16m. Climb the corner to below the first overhang and pass it via moves on the right wall. Continue to the overhang at the top of the corner and move right and then up to a small stance.

2) 5a, 17m. Above is a vegetated crack. Climb the wall left of the crack, then trend rightwards across the top of the crack and climb to a stance on a pedestal (this is also the second stance of *Moonraker*). If clear of vegetation, the crack itself can be climbed, lowering the grade of the pitch to 4b.

3) 5a, 26m. Make some steep moves up left into a groove which leads to a small cave. Move right out of the cave to a tiny ledge and then climb up left to a thin crack with difficulty. Climb the crack and groove above to the top.

FA. Frank Cannings, Pete Biven, Mark Springett 6.4.1968.

2 Moonraker .... HVS 5a

One of the UK's greatest HVSs. A stunning atmosphere and position, with steep climbing on big holds. Start at a hanging belay just above the high-water mark and 6m right of the first good tidal ledge reached on the approach traverse.

Photo on pages 341.

1) 5a, 27m. Make a diagonal traverse up right to a slight rib past a peg, climb round the rib to the base of a steep crack. Climb the crack to a chockstone, then traverse up leftwards across the wall to a stance on a ledge at the base of a corner-crack.

2) 4c, 17m. Climb the corner to a steepening, then head left across the wall to a comfortable stance on a pedestal. Peg, thread and sling belay.

3) 5a, 32m. Move out right to the base of a steep corner-crack. Climb the crack on good holds to an easing at its top. Move left to a smooth walled corner-crack and jam and layback up this all the way to the top. Belay on a large metal pole.

FA. Frank Cannings, Pete Biven, Pat Littlejohn 17.9.1967 (as described)

3 Dreadnought E3 5c

A phenomenally-exposed route that voyages out across the lip of the Great Cave prior to climbing the massive headwall above. Start as for *Moonraker* at its hanging stance.

Photo on pages 345.

1) 5c, 36m. Follow *Moonraker* to the chockstone at the top of its steep crack. Traverse right, out across the lip of the cave to a corner, and climb this to a roof. Traverse rightwards beneath the roof via some constricted moves to an old peg and continue for 3m to a footledge and hanging stance. Friend 3 will be useful for the belay.

2) 5b, 20m. Move back left to a steep corner/groove and climb it to an overhang at its end. Move out left and up to a deep slot before climbing the wall above, leftwards to a good ledge. The short wall on the right gains a cave and a huge thread belay.

3) 5b, 23m. Move left out of the cave and climb steep ground to a narrow groove on the right which is followed to a ledge. Ascend the leaning wall above to an overhang and pull though this with difficulty to better holds and easier climbing to the top.

FA. Frank Cannings, Pat Littlejohn 4.4.1969

4 Seventh Dread E1 5b

Although a linking pitch, this inventive section of climbing allows the magnificent lower section of *Moonraker* to be connected to the wild headwall of *Dreadnought*. Start at the top of pitch 1 of *Moonraker*.

1) 5b, 24m. Climb the corner above the stance to its top (as for *Moonraker*). Move right into a wide crack/chimney, exit this right and move down to a ledge. From the right-hand end of the ledge climb steeply to another good ledge. Finish as for *Dreadnought*.

FA. Frank Cannings, Pat Littlejohn, Pete Biven 5.4.1969 (as part of the girdle traverse The Seventh Circle.

Descent into cave

Start of
Rainbow Bridge

Approach-traverse

Large ledges

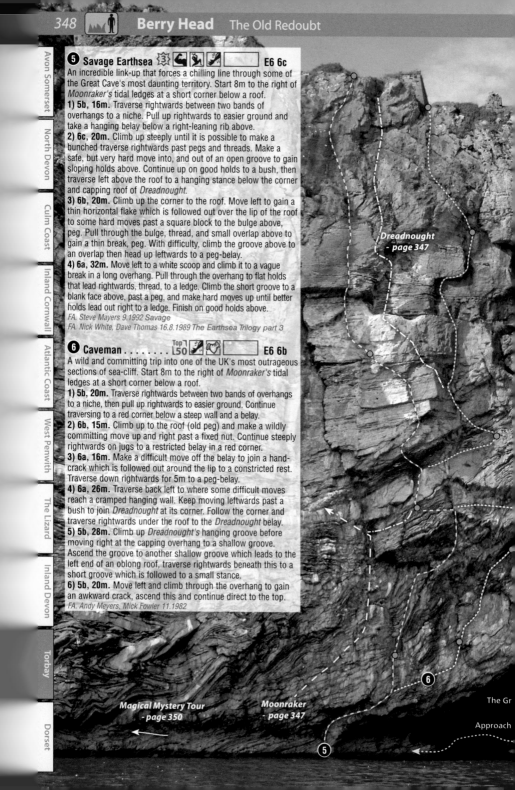

5 Savage Earthsea ⬡ E6 6c

An incredible link-up that forces a chilling line through some of the Great Cave's most daunting territory. Start 8m to the right of *Moonraker's* tidal ledges at a short corner below a roof.

1) 5b, 16m. Traverse rightwards between two bands of overhangs to a niche. Pull up rightwards to easier ground and take a hanging belay below a right-leaning rib above.

2) 6c, 20m. Climb up steeply until it is possible to make a bunched traverse rightwards past pegs and threads. Make a safe, but very hard move into, and out of an open groove to gain sloping holds above. Continue up on good holds to a bush, then traverse left above the roof to a hanging stance below the corner and capping roof of *Dreadnought*.

3) 6b, 20m. Climb up the corner to the roof. Move left to gain a thin horizontal flake which is followed out over the lip of the roof to some hard moves past a square block to the bulge above, peg. Pull through the bulge, thread, and small overlap above to gain a thin break, peg. With difficulty, climb the groove above to an overlap then head up leftwards to a peg-belay.

4) 6a, 32m. Move left to a white scoop and climb it to a vague break in a long overhang. Pull through the overhang to flat holds that lead rightwards, thread, to a ledge. Climb the short groove to a blank face above, past a peg, and make hard moves up until better holds lead out right to a ledge. Finish on good holds above.

FA. Steve Mayers 9.1992 Savage
FA. Nick White, Dave Thomas 16.8.1989 The Earthsea Trilogy part 3

6 Caveman . . . . Top 50 E6 6b

A wild and committing trip into one of the UK's most outrageous sections of sea-cliff. Start 8m to the right of *Moonraker's* tidal ledges at a short corner below a roof.

1) 5b, 20m. Traverse rightwards between two bands of overhangs to a niche, then pull up rightwards to easier ground. Continue traversing to a red corner below a steep wall and a belay.

2) 6b, 15m. Climb up to the roof (old peg) and make a wildly committing move up and right past a fixed nut. Continue steeply rightwards on jugs to a restricted belay in a red corner.

3) 6a, 16m. Make a difficult move off the belay to join a hand-crack which is followed out around the lip to a constricted rest. Traverse down rightwards for 5m to a peg-belay.

4) 6a, 26m. Traverse back left to where some difficult moves reach a cramped hanging wall. Keep moving leftwards past a bush to join *Dreadnought* at its corner. Follow the corner and traverse rightwards under the roof to the *Dreadnought* belay.

5) 5b, 28m. Climb up *Dreadnought's* hanging groove before moving right at the capping overhang to a shallow groove. Ascend the groove to another shallow groove which leads to the left end of an oblong roof, traverse leftwards beneath this to a short groove which is followed to a small stance.

6) 5b, 20m. Move left and climb through the overhang to gain an awkward crack, ascend this and continue direct to the top.

FA. Andy Meyers, Mick Fowler 11.1982

Dreadnought - page 347

Magical Mystery Tour - page 350

Moonraker - page 347

The Gr

Approach

Avon Somerset
North Devon
Culm Coast
Inland Cornwall
Atlantic Coast
West Penwith
The Lizard
Inland Devon
Torbay
Dorset

Access - A bird ban is in effect on this face between March 1st and July 31st.

❼ **Yardarm** **E2 5b**
The jutting prow that lurches out over the sea above the down-climb into the Great Cave provides the line for this sensational and non-tidal pitch. Competent seconds and some prusiks are essential. Done in a single-pitch, the grade is more like E3 due to communication and rope management difficulties. Start above the steep section of the descent route to the Great Cave where a right to left weakness gains access to the headwall.
1) 5a, 22m. A stiff pull up into the depression is followed by a rising leftward traverse for 15m to a belay at a thread on the edge of the arete.
2) 5b, 35m. Make a hard move down left to enter the bottomless bay to the left which is crossed to airy moves up the arete and into a hanging groove. Climb the groove to a roof and make the crux move past its left edge to easier ground and belays on ledges above. Walk off to the right.
FA. Pat Littlejohn, Dave Roberts 4.8.1977

Walk off

From parking

Gearing-up ledges

Descent into cave

❼

Start of Rainbow Bridge

Large ledges

Avon Somerset

North Devon

Culm Coast

Inland Cornwall

Atlantic Coast

West Penwith

The Lizard

Inland Devon

Torbay

Dorset

Avon Somerset

North Devon

Culm Coast

Inland Cornwall

Atlantic Coast

West Penwith

The Lizard

Inland Devon

Torbay

Dorset

Coast path to car park

Moonraker - page 347

Overhanging buttress

The Great Cave

Descent into cave

Blue Grotto

Green Grotto   Steep black wall

Magical Mystery Tour

The low level expedition across the base of the Old Redoubt is a memorable trip and a good introduction to the delights of deep water soloing.

Approach - From the gearing-up ledges, drop down to the right (facing out) and downclimb a steep wall (Mod) on huge hidden holds to large sea-level ledges at the mouth of the Great Cave.

Tides - The route is best started at low tide.

Conditions - The route requires calm sea-conditions and low tides.

Access - A bird ban is in effect on this face between March 1st and July 31st.

❶ Magical Mystery Tour **E1 5b**

A mighty-fine sea-level traverse that crosses the terrain from the Great Cave to the headland to the south. The climbing is steep and sustained but fun, and for the most part on huge holds. Start at low tide in the Great Cave. Given a DWS grade of S1.
Photo on page 352.

380m. Scramble into the back of the Great Cave and traverse back out steeply on its opposite wall, to gain a tidal ledge (the start of *Moonraker*). Continue on good holds and pass an overhanging buttress, either very low on barnacles, or high on more difficult ground. Continue along to a steep black wall. Climb up this, then traverse to the Green-Grotto entrance, where you may have to get damp feet to pass across its entrance to the opposite side. Follow the juggy wall all the way along to the much bigger Blue Grotto entrance. Swim 10m across the entrance and climb easily up onto the ridge of the headland. Finish by scrambling up to the coastal footpath which leads back to the car park and descent path to the Great Cave.
FA. Rusty Baillie, John Cleare 31.12.1967 (some aid)
FFA. Frank Cannings, Pete Biven 3.1.1968

Descent

Rainbow Wall   Pink Block   Crystal Cave

The Great Cave

❷

❷ Rainbow Bridge . . . E4 6b

Wonderful positions, combined with superb rock and climbing mark out this long sea-level traverse as one of the coastlines best deep water solo's (S1). As described here, the vast majority of the climbing is above deep water and the crux is very low. It is not possible to describe the route in great detail, so easily-definable sections are used.

280m. The Great Cave to the Pink Block.
From the ledges in the Great Cave, traverse rightwards, then cross a tricky corner. Drop down, then gradually rise, to drop down again onto the colourful 'Rainbow' wall. Traverse this wall on good, but spaced pockets, then drop down and strenuously exit the wall for a low resting-position under the Pink Block.

The Pink Block to the Crystal Cave.
From the Pink Block, continue along, and a little up, to pass under a large white block. Steady climbing gains the very deep Crystal Cave and a good rest.

The Crystal Cave (Crux-pitch).
Move out of the Crystal Cave to a blank wall beyond. Climb across this, first up and then gradually head downwards, to a series of big sloping holds. From the final sloping hold, stretch for a hidden finger-jug, and use it to gain the resting corner to the right. Climb the technical corner up to the upper ledges.

The Crux-pitch to the Cod Tympani Buttress.
If climbing the route as a DWS, it is recommended to escape from the cliff for this next section, then go back down the line indicated. This avoids the original (S3) traverse, which, although good, finishes over a jutting reef below the boulder-choke in the big corner. Exit the crux-pitch easily to the cliff top, then walk along the hillside to gain the top of the easy downclimb to reach sea level once more.

Rainbow Bridge
The continuously-undercut wall of multi-coloured rock that stretches eastward from the Old Redoubt's Great Cave, provides the ingredients for the West Country's best sea-level traverse. The traverse to the Crystal Cave and back is a fine 5b in its own right.

Approach - From the gearing-up ledges, drop down to the right (facing out) and downclimb a steep wall (Mod) on huge hidden holds to large sea-level ledges at the mouth of the Great Cave.

Tides - The route is climbable at any tide-state, but calm sea-conditions are required.

Conditions - The route requires calm sea-conditions as the exit-swim is long, and access to ledges is difficult in a swell. Seepage does occur after prolonged rainfall. The water from November to March will be very cold. it is at its coldest in February (7˚C) and warmest in August (17˚C).

Cod Tympani Buttress to The Wave.
Traverse easily under the roof of Cod Tympani Buttress, to reach the start of The Wave - a diagonal feature of textured strata, that soars diagonally rightwards. Either climb this strenuously, or stay low and take on the technical traverse, staying close to the sea.

The Wave to the Terminal Zawn.
Steady traversing leads to the entrance of Terminal Zawn. Traverse rightwards into the zawn to gain the hanging back wall. The final moves to gain the big white finishing ledge are slightly unsafe being above a ledge not water; use discretion here, a short swim would not be too frowned upon!

FA. Andy McFarlane, Deryck Ball 10.1973 (8pts)
FFA. Nick White 9.1991 (entire traverse)

Access - A bird ban is in effect on this face between March 1st and July 31st.

Avon Somerset
North Devon
Culm Coast
Inland Cornwall
Atlantic Coast
West Penwith
The Lizard
Inland Devon
Torbay
Dorset

Cod Tympani Buttress

The Wave

Exit

The Crux

Terminal Zawn

Avon Somerset

North Devon

Culm Coast

Inland Cornwall

Atlantic Coast

West Penwith

The Lizard

Inland Devon

Torbay

Dorset

From cafe →

Square building

The Red Wall

Long low face

Bruce Woodley approaching the Green Grotto on a solo crossing of the classic sea-level traverse *Magical Mystery Tour* (E1 5b) - *page 350* - whilst others relax at the entrance to the Great Cave where the route starts.

The Red Wall

The Red Wall is a good little section of crag, tucked away at the end of some isolated sea-level ledges. The ledges are great for sunbathing and swimming.

Approach - From the car park, head out to Berry Head. Just inside the old fort walls is a cafe, and 100m beyond this is a square building. Pick up a narrow path that drops rightwards to a long, low face. Take the path and easy slabs down right to large ledges. Walk right to the Red Wall at the end of the ledges.

Descent - Walk along to the approach path.

Tides - The routes are non-tidal, but the traverse to the base maybe wave-washed in heavy seas.

Conditions - This area can get extremely hot and is very sheltered from westerly winds.

The belays of the first three lines are easily reached via a traverse out along overhung ledges, starting from the edge of the main ledge.

1 Abbot's Way......... 2 **HVS 5a**

An exhilarating, well-positioned pitch that is steeper than first appearances suggest. Start at a belay on the ledge beneath the right-trending crack-line.

18m. Move up to the crack-line in the roof and follow it rightwards to a point level with a ledge on the right. Move out left to a thinner crack that leads steeply to the top.

FA. Dave Bassett 16.10.1961

2 Binky.............. 2 **HS 4b**

Another little gem that takes the broad hanging rib right of *Abbot's Way* on excellent rock. Start at a belay ledge just right of the corner-line of *Abbot's Way*.

18m. Move up onto the wall just right of a thin crack in its centre and trend right up the wall, left of the broad rib, to a ledge at the top of the rib. Finish up the short wall above the ledge.

FA. John Hammond, John Fowler, Fred Stebbings 6.4.1968

3 Chastity Corner.... 1 **VS 4b**

The central corner is another deceptively steep experience on good rock. Start at a belay directly beneath the wide crack.

17m. Enter the corner via a difficult move on smooth rock and continue with a little less expenditure of energy to the top.

FA. Pat Littlejohn, D.Rogers, R.Crawshaw 7.5.1967

4 Blood 2 **E1 5b**

Technical face-climbing up the appealing wall with a flowstone sheet at its base. Start at the short flowstone-wall.

18m. Climb to a block and move right and up to a small ledge. Step left and climb to the top.

FA. Pat Littlejohn, John Fowler, Frank Cannings 13.4.1969

To mid afternoon | 10 min

	No star	⟨1⟩	⟨2⟩	⟨3⟩
Mod to S	-	3	-	-
HS to HVS	-	3	3	2
E1 to E3	1	2	-	3
E4 and up	1	-	2	1

Daddyhole - 'The Home of the Devil' - is a spectacular and picturesque series of limestone sea-cliffs and quarried bays, located minutes from the hustle and bustle of Torquay's harbour. The centrepiece of Daddyhole is its Main Cliff - a large, strikingly-featured sea-cliff with several exposed multi-pitch climbs in a secluded setting. Bracketing the Main Cliff are two quarried crags perched well above the sea - Telegraph Hole and Meadfoot Quarry. These provide more in the way of open face and steep slab climbs, with the added benefit of potential for swimming and sunbathing nearby.

Approach

From Torquay's Harbour, follow signs for Daddyhole around its Marina, past the 'Living Coasts' bird sanctuary and up the hill. A number of signed turnings eventually lead to the Daddyhole Plain car park. All three cliffs are approached from here.

Telegraph Hole - Follow a path rightwards across a flat, grassy area and through a walled arch (this is Rock End walk). Follow the path for 20m or so, then drop left over the fence, down a steep, narrow and earthy path that soon emerges on the cliff-top. Take the still-narrow path rightwards on the cliff edge to a stone wall with broken glass cemented on its top. Go through the collapsed section of the wall and scramble down to the flat base of the quarry.

Daddyhole Main Cliff - Walk left (facing out) down steps and follow a small path off right. The Main Cliff now comes into view and a small, steep and narrow path on the right descends to the boulder-beach (care required). The base of the crag is a quick boulder-hop away.

Meadfoot Quarry - Walk left (facing out) down steps and follow a small path off right (as for the Main Cliff approach) to arrive at the top of the quarry on the left. Follow the edge of the cliff down to the floor of the Quarry.

Tides

Daddyhole Main Cliff is the only crag that is tidal. However, it is only at high tide that the left-hand side of the cliff is inaccessible.

Conditions

Telegraph Hole and Meadfoot Quarry are suntraps, so warm up very quickly from first thing in the morning. On hot days they are best visited in the evenings.
The Main Cliff dries quickly and receives the sun from first thing.

Side tabs: Avon Somerset | North Devon | Culm Coast | Inland Cornwall | Atlantic Coast | West Penwith | The Lizard | Inland Devon | Torbay | Dorset

Map labels: Daddyhole Rd, N, P, Rock End Ave, Meadfoot Quarry, Daddyhole Main Cliff, Telegraph Hole, About 100m

Photo labels: Daddyhole Main Cliff, Meadfoot Quarry

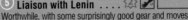

❶ Blinding Flash . . . . 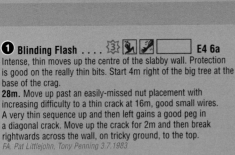 **E4 6a**
Intense, thin moves up the centre of the slabby wall. Protection is good on the really thin bits. Start 4m right of the big tree at the base of the crag.
28m. Move up past an easily-missed nut placement with increasing difficulty to a thin crack at 16m, good small wires. A very thin sequence up and then left gains a good peg in a diagonal crack. Move up the crack for 2m and then break rightwards across the wall, on tricky ground, to the top.
FA. Pat Littlejohn, Tony Penning 3.7.1983

❷ Flash Dance . . . 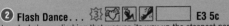 **E3 5c**
Lovely, balancy climbing that weaves its way up the steepest part of the face. Protection on the crux is from very small wires. Start 10m up the slope from the tree.
27m. Climb to a peg at 12m and then directly to a thin diagonal break. Place some very small wires, then step up onto the break and balance left up a narrow ramp to double pegs. Move slightly left again and then climb up intricately past two more pegs to finish.
FA. Pat Littlejohn, Tony Penning, Pete Cresswell 3.7.1983

❸ Crinoid . . . . . . 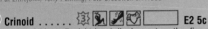 **E2 5c**
The central slabby walls right-hand rib gives yet another fine pitch requiring a technical touch. Start 10m up the slope from the tree.
27m. Climb to a peg at 12m and then move up and right to the rib and a peg. Climb the finely positioned rib boldly, past another peg, to a steepening near the top. Finish leftwards.
FA. Pat Littlejohn, Peter Biven 3.8.67

❹ The Midas Touch . .  **HVS 5a**
The ramp-line just right of the main slab offers some very pleasant climbing on compact rock. Start beneath the left-leaning open groove line at a small tree.
24m. Move up rightwards to a hollow block then move up and traverse left to better holds and gear. Continue up the line to a steep finish on positive holds.
FA. Frank Cannings, Pat Littlejohn, Peter Biven 13.6.1967

❺ Liaison with Lenin . . . . **HVS 5a**
Worthwhile, with some surprisingly good gear and moves. Start on a large flat ledge beneath the big corner on the right of the crag.
24m. Move up the left wall of the corner and step left over some vegetation to stand on a ledge and flake, good wires here. Make some pressing moves leftwards along the open groove past more good gear to a point where the groove fades and some good holds are encountered. Stand on the good holds and reach a broken flake up to the right and some handy small wires just to the left. Finish up right over slightly vegetated rock but on good holds.
FA. Bruce Woodley, Mark Glaister, Jerry Brooks 7.80

Descent

Telegraph Hole
A steep sweep of compact lime-stone is the centrepiece of this secluded and charming venue.
Approach - Descend the steep, narrow path above the slab to a stone wall topped by some vicious broken glass. Pass through the gap in the wall and scramble down to the flat grass floor.
Descent - Walk back down via the approach path.
Condtions - Telegraph Hole is a sheltered suntrap, dries quickly after rain and there is no seepage. Good sunbathing and swimming off of the lower ledges.

Avon Somerset · North Devon · Culm Coast · Inland Cornwall · Atlantic Coast · West Penwith · The Lizard · Inland Devon · Torbay · Dorset

To mid afternoon | 5 min | Sheltered

① Good Dog . . . .  **E1 5b**

An enticing and well-protected climb in an idyllic setting. Start at mid to low tide at a flat topped spike.

25m. Climb to a small roof and pull over before moving up left to a flake. Climb the flake for a short way and move right to a groove. Climb the groove and join *Tobacco Road* to finish.
FA. Dave Henderson, Craig Williams, Anthony Snow 18.4.1998

② Pinnacle Traverse . . . . **HVS 5a**

A useful way to gain the top of the crag or the nearby Telegraph Hole. Also climbed as a deep water solo (with care) at high water. Start at the left end of the crag.

25m. Climb up on good holds to gain the leftwards diagonal traverse line. Follow this, on jugs at first, to a tricky move midway. Finish by traversing to the seaward pinnacle.
FA. Peter Biven (solo) 1967

Main Cliff

Daddyhole has a big-crag feel about it, and has been bestowed a number of classic lines on good rock.
Descent - Walk steeply back up the slope to the parking area and then back to the base via the approach or abseil back to the base of the crag.

③ Tobacco Road . . . . **VS 4b**

A good little pitch that gives a gentle introduction to the climbing and atmosphere of the crag. Start behind a huge boulder below the mid-height overhang at the left side of the landward face of the cliff.

25m. Move up the wall on good holds to the golden-coloured wall beneath the big overhang. Pass beneath the overhang leftwards to the rib, then climb to the top on slightly suspect rock.
FA. Frank Cannings, Pat Littlejohn, Peter Biven 18.6.1967

To car park

Approach alo
boulder-bea

4 Gargantua E1 5b

A wild expedition up the curving left arete of the main corner. Start below the steep wall, right of a large red corner.

1) 5a, 12m. From some sandy red rock at the base of the crag, move up the right wall on good, but suspect holds to a wide crack, large cam, that ends at a large ledge and belay.

2) 5b, 16m. Climb the groove above and move up left to a rest. Climb up the steep left side of the arete and then step right to the arete. Pull into a large sloping belay-niche. An exposed spot.

3) 5a, 12m. Traverse rightwards out of the niche and pull up and then left into a corner below another overhang. Finish direct.

FA. Frank Cannings, Pat Littlejohn 9.7.1967

5 Gates of Eden .... HVS 5a

An often-overlooked sea-cliff classic that takes on the Main Cliff at its most intimidating, incorporating some juggy climbing and airy situations on great rock. The first pitch is now much harder than when originally climbed due to a rockfall. However, it is well protected and solid. Start next to the huge block leaning against the cliff beneath the massive corner. *Photo on page 359.*

1) 5a, 20m. Bridge up the wide crack between the cliff and the huge block, and at 3m, step left onto the cliff and climb a thin crack to a ledge. Negotiate the steep wall and strenuous moves directly above into the bottom of the massive corner (good nut placement before you pull round) and climb easily up to a stance in the corner.

2) 4a, 16m. Move up the corner to a point where a line leads out leftwards. Follow this on good holds between two overhangs towards the arete, then a move can be made up to the well-defined niche. Awkward belay.

3) 4a, 10m. Move left out of the niche into an exposed bottom-less corner and climb this to the top.

FA. Steve Dawson, John Hammond 29.5.1967

6 Last Exit to Torquay. HVS 5b

The dominating central corner in its entirety is a 'must do'. Start below the corner as for *Gates of Eden*.

1) 5a, 20m. Pitch 1 of *Gates of Eden*.

2) 5b, 21m. Move up the corner to the first of two overhanging sections. Pass the first with difficulty and the second via some useful holds on the sheer, right-hand wall of the corner.

FA. Peter Biven, Al Alvarez 10.6.1967

7 Suicide Blonde E6 6b

The impressive brown-and-grey-streaked wall right of the central corner of *Last Exit to Torquay*. Start as for *Gates of Eden*.

1) 5a, 20m. Pitch 1 of *Gates of Eden*.

2) 6b, 25m. In the blank right wall is a thin crack. Climb to and up this to better holds that are followed right then leftwards to a steep right-leaning groove. Move up this to flakes and pull over out of the groove and up to a peg. Gain a slight groove up right and climb this to a pocket, peg. Move up to a further peg and make difficult moves to a jug. Finish direct up the wall above.

FA. Nick White, Mark Campbell 12.5.1993

8 Zuma E4 6a

The soaring white arete to the right of the corner of *Last Exit to Torquay* is a stunning line. Start as for *Gates of Eden*.

1) 4c, 20m. As for pitch 1 of *Gates of Eden*.

2) 6a, 27m. Move up the corner until level with a small overhanging groove on the right wall. Pull across the groove, past an old peg in the groove and a good peg in the wall to the right, and climb steeply up the slim overhanging groove above to a block on the arete. Move up the right-hand side of the arete for 5m and transfer to the left side where it steepens, peg out left. Fingery moves up the wall on crimps and pockets access the final wall that is taken rightwards to the top.

FA. Pat Littlejohn, Chris King 10.1977

9 Triton .... VS 5a

A very worthwhile top-pitch up the huge right-leaning corner. High in the grade. Start as for *Gates of Eden*.
Start at the arete right of the layback crack.

1) 4a, 21m. Climb Gates of Eden until it is possible to work rightwards to a stance at the base of the corner.

2) 5a, 25m. Climb the long, wide corner-crack with the crux near the top.

FA. Peter Biven, Frank Cannings 17.6.1967

The final route is a pleasant deep water solo.

10 Plimsoll Line ..... Sev

A popular little outing that, in good weather, is usually soloed, it is given a DWS grade of S1. Start from the boulder-beach at the bottom of the descent path to Daddyhole's Main Cliff.

140m. Traverse the high-water line, sometimes above and sometimes below, to a ramp just before a gully. Climb this to the base of Meadfoot Quarry.

FA. Pat Littlejohn 20.7.1967

Avon Somerset · North Devon · Culm Coast · Inland Cornwall · Atlantic Coast · West Penwith · The Lizard · Inland Devon · Torbay · Dorset

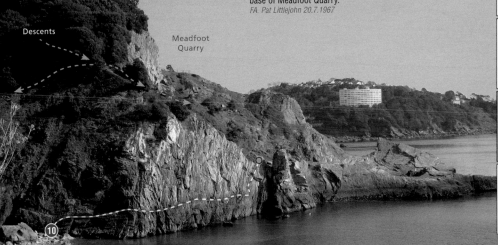

Descents

Meadfoot Quarry

10

Avon Somerset | North Devon | Culm Coast | Inland Cornwall | Atlantic Coast | West Penwith | The Lizard | Inland Devon | Torbay | Dorset

① Diamond Rib . . . .   HS 4a

The clean, smooth-looking rib is a popular outing, and luckily offers more protection than you might expect. Start beneath the easy-angled clean rib on the left side of the wall.

26m. Climb the right-hand side of the rib, which gradually gets more difficult, to a steeper section at two-thirds height. Move right and up the final wall, peg, taking care with the rock near the top.

FA: Peter Biven, Cliff Fishwick 2.6.1967

② Median Lucky. E1 5b

A hybrid pitch providing one of the best ways up the left-hand wall of the quarry. Gear is spaced. Start on a small bushy ledge, 7m up and left of a small tree at the base of the crag.

26m. Climb a shallow groove-system to a small triangular overhang at 8m. Move up its right-hand side and up to a peg. Traverse 5m left and step up to a short diagonal crack. Move up right and follow a narrow groove to a peg where it fades. Pull out left and up on small holds and finish up easy but earthy ground.

FA: S.Woolard, A.Holburn 31.5.1981

③ Nest Egg . . . .   S 4a

An interesting route climbing to the large tree just below the top of the crag and left of the quarry's impressive headwall. Start on a ledge 8m up from the small tree at the base of the crag.

1) 4a, 21m. Climb to good gear in a thin slanting crack just to the right of a slanting rectangular block. Pull up the wall right of the block and step left to a broken corner/groove-system. Now head directly for the tree on steady ground via a good nut in the base of a borehole. Belay at the tree.

2) 6m. Climb up to the overhang behind the tree and pass it on the right.

FA: T.Lindop, E.Phillips 3.6.1967

④ Tree Root. . . . .   VDiff

A well-trodden line taking in some nice positions with plenty of protection. Start by scrambling to a small ledge and nut belays beneath the headwall at the back of the quarry.

1) -,19m. Take the line of ledges and cracks leftwards from the belay, past a bush to the large tree. Belay.

2) -,6m. Climb up to the overhang above and pass it on the left.

FA: Jeff Jones, John Fowler 21.5.1967

⑤ Pegs Progress E3 5c

Exhilarating and exposed climbing up the thin crack in the leaning headwall. Start on the small ledge as for *Tree Root*.

24m. Climb 3m above the belay and then move right to a ledge. Climb the wall just left of a narrow corner to the midway break. Step left and make a committing move to a huge jug. Jam the finger-crack above to another good hold and bomber gear at its top. Step left to a ramp and force the final wall, moving right to finish.

FFA: Bruce Woodley 1983

⑥ Clotted Cream E4 6a

A thin, steep crack-climb up the headwall. Start left of the arete.

21m. Climb a left-leaning groove to the base of the crack. The thin crack proves to be a well-protected challenge, right until the very end.

FFA: Chris Nicholson, Mark Courtier 28.4.1984

Lots of sun | 7 min | Sheltered

Trees have now been felled

Descent

Viewpoint

Meadfoot Quarry

The quarry has a selection of worthwhile routes on generally good, compact limestone. It is usually quiet, and a nice place to climb.

Approach - Walk left (facing out) down the steps from the parking at Daddyhole Plain and follow a small path off right to arrive at the rim of the quarry. Follow the edge of the cliff down to the quarry floor.

Descent - Walk down the rim-path.

Conditions - The crag is very sheltered, quick drying and can get really quite hot.

Daddyhole 359

Bruce Woodley about to enter the exposed belay-niche at the end of the second pitch of the Torquay classic *Gates of Eden* (HVS 5a) - *page 357* - Daddyhole Main Cliff, Torquay.

Avon Somerset

North Devon

Culm Coast

Inland Cornwall

Atlantic Coast

West Penwith

The Lizard

Inland Devon

Torbay

Dorset

	No star	⚝	⚝⚝	⚝⚝⚝
Mod to S	-	-	-	1
HS to HVS	-	2	-	-
E1 to E3	-	1	3	4
E4 and up	-	-	6	15

The climbs of Anstey's Cove, Long Quarry Point and the linking sea-cliff of the Sanctuary Wall are about as diverse as possible in such a small area. The styles range from the ultra-modern and desperate sport-climbs of the Ferocity Wall to the huge, technical slabs of Long Quarry Point. Between are the leaning trad pitches on the Sanctuary Wall. The setting for all the crags is magnificent and the beach is only a stroll away.

Approach
Across the road from the entrance to Perinville Road is Otter Nurseries, to the right of its entrance is a public footpath that leads to open ground above the crags.
Anstey's Cove - bear right to the top of the descent path which is clearly marked 'closed'.
Long Quarry Point (LQP) and Sanctuary Wall - continue across the open ground to a white shelter and pick up a small path behind it that leads steeply down to the quarry floor.

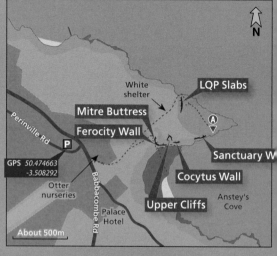

Access
The climbs at Anstey's Cove are approached down a path that is clearly marked as closed due to rockfall. The rockfall is predominantly from the slope right of the descent path and above the beach, and does not affect the crags described here. Climbing has gone on unhindered for many decades and, as long as a relatively low profile is adopted, this should not be threatened.

Tides and Conditions
Only the approach to the Sanctuary Wall is tidal, whether via *The Long Traverse,* or more easily from Long Quarry Point. The Sanctuary Wall and Anstey's Cove get plenty of sun and are good choices in cool weather, whereas in the summer they can become extremely warm. Long Quarry Point gets less sun and seeps after rain.

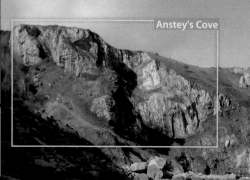

Anstey's Cove

Long Quarry Point

Avon Somerset
North Devon
Culm Coast
Inland Cornwall
Atlantic Coast
West Penwith
The Lizard
Inland Devon
Torbay
Dorset

Avon Somerset

North Devon

Culm Coast

Inland Cornwall

Atlantic Coast

West Penwith

The Lizard

Inland Devon

Torbay

Dorset

Dave Turnbull starting up the leaning prow of *Might and Main* (6c+)
- *page 362* - on the Mitre Buttress at Anstey's Cove, Torquay.

Avon Somerset | North Devon | Culm Coast | Inland Cornwall | Atlantic Coast | West Penwith | The Lizard | Inland Devon | Torbay | Dorset

❶ Heathen Man 7b
Very good, if a little sharp on the finger tips. Start on the fallen slab, near the top of the steep path beneath the wall.
17m. Move up to the stuck-on pancake of rock and move rightwards with difficulty to a line of sharp, shallow pockets. Continue up the overhanging wall to finish via a mono.
FA. Martin Crocker 8.5.1988

❷ Empire of the Sun . . . . . Top 50 7b+
One of the West Country's great sport-routes. Low in the grade, but very pumpy and a touch polished. Start beneath a pocketed weakness.
20m. Move up the weakness on good pockets and then swing right to good jams in the horizontal break at 6m. Make a hard move to a good pocket then lurch up the wall, first leftwards and then back right to a final heave onto easier ground.
FA. Nick White, Pete Bull, Andy Turner 3.1988

❸ Avenged . . . . 7c+
Brilliant moves up the highest section of the wall just right of *Empire of the Sun*. Start 3m left of the arete.
22m. Stretch up right past deep horizontal breaks, before moving left and up via some fingery moves to an easing and a shake out. Head leftwards to join the final moves of *Empire of the Sun*.
FA. Nick White 4.6.1989

❹ Might and Main . . . . . . 6c+
The huge bow-shaped arete has lots of difficult moves punctuated with good rests. Start at the base of the arete. *Photo on page 361.*
23m. Boulder-out the leaning arete to a ledge. Move left and climb the arete to a rest on the right. Move to the left of the arete again and make some long moves to another good rest. Continue up the arete before making a fingery move left to positive holds and a lower-off just above.
FA. Nick White, Bruce Woodley 1.6.1989

❺ The Mitre E3 6b
A snaking line featuring exposed positions and very steep climbing. Start 2m right of the base of the arete.
25m. Powerful moves on slopers, past a bolt, lead to an overhung niche on the arete. Pull directly out of the niche and climb past another bolt to beneath more steep ground. Traverse left to a spike on the arete. Continue up the arete before making a fingery move left to positive holds and a lower-off just above.
FA. Frank Cannings, Peter Biven, Pat Littlejohn 1968
FFA. Steve Bell, Bruce Woodley 1979

❻ How the Mighty Fall . . . 7a+
Unusual climbing on large sloping holds gains a heart-stopping finish. Start 2m right of the arete.
18m. Move up and right to stand on a good ledge. Head left into a cramped niche and pull out insecurely on slopers. More steep moves gain a ledge and a brief breather. Climb the final wall on pockets and hard to spot finger-edges. Lower-off just above.
FA. Nick White, Mike Barnes 6.6.1988

❼ Devonshire Cream E5 6a
The eye-catching left arete of the wall is a stunning, but bold undertaking. Start beneath the arete on its right-hand side.
16m. Pull onto a slab, then head through the overlaps prior to making a hard move to get established on the wall, and clip the first bolt at 8m. Fine but easier climbing remains passing one more bolt. A skyhook placement is possible before the hard move.
FA. Chris Nicholson, Nick White 2.4.1984

8 La Crème . . . . 7c+

The white, overlap-strewn groove provides a classy piece of technical climbing. Requires crisp conditions. Start just down and right of the arete.

16m. Move up the open groove on hidden holds and pull through the overlaps on slopers, before making long moves right and up to a welded on block. Follow the wall above to finish.
FA. Nick White 7.12.1988

9 Tuppence 8b

A superb testpiece taking on the centre of the wall. Start right of a thin right-slanting crack. *Photo on page 342.*

15m. Dynamic moves gain a good hold. Fingery and very technical climbing above leads to another reasonable hold before a final slap up and left allows the top to be reached.
FA. Ken Palmer 22.11.1990

10 A Fisherman's Tale 8b

An improbable line up the steepest and blankest section of the Ferocity Wall. Start at a sloping shelf that cuts in from the right.
14m. Make hard moves up to a left-slanting fault-line. Pull over a small overhang before moving rightwards to an undercut and finish direct.
FA. Ken Palmer 2.6.1991

11 The Cider Soak 8a

A very impressive sport route. Start at the sloping shelf that cuts in from the right.
14m. Stand on the shelf and move up to a thin break. Move right and use a finger-crack and sloping holds to reach a good finger pocket. Use the pocket to gain a jug that allows a shake-out before the final bouldery upper wall.
FA. Nick White 1988

Mitre and Ferocity Walls
The showpiece crag of southern Britain for state-of-the-art hard sport-climbs. The streaked wall overhangs for its full length, and the climbs are as ferocious as they appear.
Approach - Walk along for 25m from the base of Mitre Buttress.
Descent - All of the routes have lower-offs.
Conditions - The wall is a suntrap but due to its steepness is nearly always just about in the shade during the summer months. Stays dry in light rain.

12 Brian . . . . 8c+
The hardest sport climb in the south of the UK takes in the crux of *Tuppence* and a whole lot more hard climbing. Start as for *The Cider Soak*.
21m. Move up to the overhang and traverse left to join *A Fisherman's Tale*. Now go left and down slightly to join and follow *Tuppence* to just above its last hard move. Go left and finish direct.
FA. Ken Palmer 2003

13 The Lynch . . . . . . 7b+
Brilliant and brutal. The overhanging groove and crack on the right-hand side of the wall is a classic of its genre. Start beneath the crack-line.
14m. Boulder up to the slim overlap and make difficult and wild moves into, up and then out of the groove to a wider crack. Jam this to the top.
FA. Nick White 7.11.1987

Sun and shade 9 min

Upper Cliffs and Cocytus Wall

In contrast to the other crags at Anstey's Cove, the Cocytus Wall and Upper Cliffs are composed of steep walls and the odd slab. The rock is generally good but care is needed where the climbs top-out. The best routes are extremely technical and will only fall to the strong-fingered.

Approach - The Cocytus Wall is easily approached down a small path from below the Ferocity Wall, whilst the Upper Cliff requires an easy scramble up a line midway down the approach path to the Cocytus Wall.

Descent - The Cocytus Wall routes that top out end at an abseil station. The Upper Cliff routes finish on the top of the crag and it is easiest to walk back down via the general approach.

Conditions - The crags get a great deal of sun and are often dry, although seepage does occur after prolonged rainfall. The Cocytus Wall is also usually very sheltered from the wind.

① St Gregory the Wonder Worker

HS 4b

The long, low-angled slab on the left-hand side of the hanging basin provides the only easyish 'up' route of note at Anstey's Cove. The climbing is open, but also serious with minimal protection, and requires a steady leader. Start at the base of the slab.

1) 30m. Head up the middle of the slab to a belay on a metal quarry-spike where the upper wall rears up. The slab is straightforward but lacks any significant protection.

2) 4b, 23m. Traverse left for 4m to an arete and climb this to a ledge below the upper overhangs. Traverse rightwards to clear the overhangs and climb easy, but broken rock to the top and a fence post belay.

FA. Mark Springett, Peter Biven 5.11.1967

② The Lumpy Universe

E3 5c

An interesting and well-positioned outing that wanders up the wall above and left of the orange stained cave at 8m. Start at a belay beneath the cave.

25m. Climb up a flake-line to the cave and a thread. Move up left to a peg, and another down to the left. Make some difficult moves left and up to a thin break and then stretch left to a juggy pocket and good thread. Move onto the slab above and climb the bulge, past a peg, to another slab below the final short and steep wall, which is supplied with good holds. Fence-post belay well above.

FA. Chris Nicholson 3.1986

Approach

3 Moonshot E1 5b
The original route of the wall is an action-packed pitch, exiting the orange cave via some fairly bold climbing. Start at a belay beneath the cave as for *The Lumpy Universe*.
20m. Climb up to the thread in the cave, as for *The Lumpy Universe*. Make a move left, then traverse right, low on the lip of the cave, then reach up to a small vegetated ledge. Climb up above the ledge, then head leftwards up the wall to the top. Belay on a tree a long way back from the edge.
FA. Pat Littlejohn, John Hammond 22.12.1968

4 American Express . . 7a+
Tendon-twanging technicalities are the order of the day on this fine micro challenge. Start just left of the slim groove of *Cocytus*.
13m. Boulder up to a pocket and the first bolt. Make progress on tiny crimps to a long reach for a good hold at the base of the steep finishing corner. Lower-off.
FA. Chris Nicholson, Nick White 5.1984

5 Cocytus E3 6a
A superb route featuring two contrasting pitches; the first is technical, and the second steep. Start beneath the slim, smooth corner/groove.
1) 6a,13m. Climb the immaculate, smooth groove past two bolts and swing left at its top to a bolt belay on a sloping ledge.
2) 5b, 15m. Move up left from the ledge, then traverse steeply rightwards to find and use a borehole on a sloping shelf to access the base of a short steep corner. Climb this to the vegetated slope above. Bolt belay in an outcrop over to the right. Abseil off.
FFA. Pat Littlejohn, Dave Garner 31.5.1976

6 More Steam, Bigger Women!!!
. . . . 7b
A stout exercise with a problematic initial wall, and a gradually steepening finale. Start just right of the *Cocytus* groove beneath a tiny corner/ramp.
22m. Climb the deceptively-difficult ramp boldly to the first bolt, then make some fierce, fingery moves above this to an easing. The arching wall above is furnished with some decent, but spaced holds. Lower-off.
FA. Nick White 30.5.1988

7 Blonde Bombshell . . E5 6b
A hard and serious lead, taking on the 'blonde' wall left of the huge overhanging corner. Start below and right of a lone bolt 5m right of the groove of *Cocytus*.
23m. Move up leftwards to the bolt, then continue to a short, thin crack. Climb insecurely up rightwards on sloping shelves until a move right can be made towards the corner. Continue up the left wall of the corner with difficulty to the top. Bolt belay in an outcrop back from the edge. Abseil off.
FA. Pat Littlejohn, Tony Penning 29.5.1983

8 Acheron . . . . HVS 5a
Good physical climbing, despite the rather vegetated appearance from below. Start by scrambling up the slope, past the base of the huge corner, to a belay below a layback-flake.
22m. Layback the flake to a sloping ledge and then enter the left-leaning corner which succumbs to good, old-fashion udging. At the top of the corner, traverse left to a bolt belay in an outcrop. Abseil off.
FA. Pat Littlejohn, Ed Grindley, John Taylor 27.1.1968

From mid morning | 10 min | Sheltered

Upper Cliffs

Bolt for belay and descent

Avon Somerset · North Devon · Culm Coast · Inland Cornwall · Atlantic Coast · West Penwith · The Lizard · Inland Devon · Torbay · Dorset

Avon Somerset

North Devon

Culm Coast

Inland Cornwall

Atlantic Coast

West Penwith

The Lizard

Inland Devon

Torbay

Dorset

Sanctuary Wall

The main, central section of the crag is 30m high and overhangs at around 30 degrees. The climbs are serious, and although the holds are generally good, the routes are incredibly sustained. The majority of the routes rely on a good deal of fixed gear for protection, which should always be backed up if possible.

Approach - *The Long Traverse* is used to access the Sanctuary Wall itself, either from Anstey's Cove or Long Quarry Point.

Descent - Either walk up the steep and thorny slope via a faint path, or from the iron spike used as part of a belay at the top of the routes, carefully descend the 10m wall (VDiff) to the quarry floor. The spike can be used to top-rope down this section.

Conditions and Tides - The wall is accessible via *The Long Traverse* from low to mid-tide. The base of the climbs are not tidal in calm sea-conditions. At mid to high-tide, a short abseil from an iron spike on the edge of Long Quarry Point gains the non-tidal ledges. The wall is a suntrap and does not take much seepage.

❶ The Long Traverse . . . . **VDiff**

A journey beneath some of the UK's most adventurous climbing terrain. Usually accomplished as a DWS. Start at sea level in Anstey's Cove down and left (looking out) of the *Cocytus* buttress. Mid to low tide only at the given grade.

250m. Traverse rightwards on huge holds to a steeper section. Once past this point, a 'ridge like' reef is encountered that provides an excellent view of the Sanctuary Wall. Cross a couple of inlets and traverse wildly below the wall on massive holds, to where some scrambling and boulder-hopping leads to an exit onto the Long Quarry Point floor just beyond a pinnacle. Note that at high-tide the section beneath the Sanctuary Wall itself can be gained via a short abseil from an iron spike on the rim of the quarry floor.

FA. John Worsley 1962

❷ Sacrosanct **E1 5a**

A serious but spectacular line whose first pitch needs a careful approach. Start a few metres to the right of the fault-line at a massive block forming two slabby corners about 5m above the high-water line. The right-hand corner has a cramped ledge at its base. A good belay can be found here.

1) 20m, 5a. Move up the slabby corner to dirty ledges on top of the block where a line of good flakes leads left across a steep wall. This point is below a more distinct horizontal flake/crack. Make a committing hand-traverse left along the flakes, and gain a resting position in the fault-line with difficulty. The short steep corner of the fault leads up to a good ledge, Peg and nut belay.

2) 50m, 5a. Move right across the slab and climb up its right edge, until it is possible to move across right to a cramped ledge. Climb the steep crack above to easier ground. Keep moving up right to gain a ridge. A difficult nut-belay can be made here or move up back left to a notch, peg and tree well back.

FA. Pat Littlejohn, Ed Grindley, Peter Biven 15.2.1969 (pitch 1 added by Steve Jones 1974)

Upper Cliffs

Cocytus Area

Approach

Long Quarry Point

Sanctuary Wall

❶

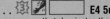

❸ Free the Spirit . . . .  **E6 6a**

An awesome route taking the middle of the Sanctuary Wall at its most intimidating. The climbing is superb. Much of the gear is in place but the climb is a serious undertaking especially in its lower reaches. Start on the highest belay ledge beneath the steepest and blankest section of the wall, 7m left of the corner of *Call to Arms*.

28m. Climb the wall to the right of the groove. The first peg is visible as it always has a bit of tat hanging from it. Move up and strike out left to a thin seam marked by an insitu thread and a peg. Follow the seam and then move up left to gain a thread on an overhung ramp-line that cuts across the face. Climb the steep wall above, to gain merely vertical ground just below the top. Nuts and an iron spike just below the ridge.

FA. Martin Crocker, Nigel Coe 3.4.1988

❹ Caribbean Blue . . . **E6 6a**

An outrageously-positioned line that links a series of good holds up the seemingly blank and severely overhanging wall. The climbing is serious in its lower half, and care is required with the protection. Small friends useful. Start on the lower ledges 3m left of the corner of *Call to Arms*.

30m. Move onto a big ledge at 3m. Make a steep pull up right to a good hold in the pink streak, poor peg up right, and then move leftwards to another peg. Continue up slightly leftwards via good holds to a jug-rail and place a long sling over the rail here for protection. Make a difficult move up and stretch left to a jug below a thin crack-line adorned with a good deal of fixed gear. Tackle the sustained wall on edges, jugs and pockets to a final pull onto an overhung ramp. Finish up the less-steep crack above. Nuts and an iron spike just below the ridge.

FA. Ken Palmer, Mark Campbell 30.10.1991

❺ Call to Arms **E4 5c**

The severely overhanging, narrow corner that dominates the main section of the Sanctuary Wall presents a daunting line. Very strenuous. Start directly beneath the corner.

1) 5c, 18m. Climb the corner strenuously, past pegs on the right, to a stance and belay on an exposed ledge.

2) 5c, 10m. Move up to the overhang and pass it on the right. Nuts and an iron spike just below the ridge.

FA. Steve Monks, Ed Hart 5.80 (pitch 2 Steve Lewis, John Codding 1983)

❻ Incubus **E1 5b**

A lesson in adventure on a route with a fearful name and reputation gives a sensational trip onto the Sanctuary Wall at a reasonable grade. Start at the notch on the landward side of the Sanctuary Wall. *Photo on page 1.*

1) 5b, 9m. From the notch, step down over the void, and make a tricky move left onto an easier ramp. Follow this a short way, peg, to a flat ledge and belay.

2) 5b, 20m. Take the corner above and pass the overhang on the left by via a steep layback. Easier climbing gains the top. Nuts and an iron spike just below the ridge.

FA. Pat Littlejohn, Peter Biven 30.3.1968

❼ False Gods **E5 6a**

The best introduction to the harder routes on the wall provides reasonably protected climbing on good holds. It is advisable to back up the insitu pegs and some of the rock requires a cautious approach. Start approximately 8m right of the corner of *Call to Arms*, below a peg at 5m. The route is also identified by its hanging groove near the top.

20m. Climb to the peg, move slightly left then continue up to a second peg. A few pulls up the wall above lead to a juggy break and another peg. Move right then climb quickly up the hanging groove above. Head up and leftwards to finish up a short groove.

FA. Nick White, Pat Littlejohn 28.04.1988

Descent

Long Quarry Point

Avon Somerset · North Devon · Culm Coast · Inland Cornwall · Atlantic Coast · West Penwith · The Lizard · Inland Devon · Torbay · Dorset

① Up the Styx, Without a Paddle
. . . . 🔲🔲🔲 **7b**
A tough little number on good rock. Start below a bolt-line on the left of the smooth bulging wall.
27m. Thin face-moves up right are immediately followed by some hard moves up the short, steep wall to an easing above it. Move up right and climb direct to a large flake. Finish up the slab.
FA. Nick White, Andy Turner 19.5.1987

② Shadow Beast . 🔲🔲🔲🔲 **7c+**
A stunning but desperate climb that follows the most sustained section of the smooth bulging wall. Start at the wall's lowest point.
27m. Climb the thin wall to a hard move up and left, and a rest. Very thin moves rightwards, bolt, and up to a thin crack, peg, lead to an easier slab and the lower-off. Linking the start into the finish of *Up the Styx* gives a fine 7c pitch.
FA. Nick White 5.9.1987

③ Renegade . . . . 🔲🔲🔲🔲 **E4 6a**
A very sustained route that has a good deal of excellent climbing, although the protection, from numerous ageing pegs, should be treated with caution. Start left of a tree at the base of the wall.
1) 6a, 27m. Climb sloping holds boldly to a vegetated diagonal-break and a peg above it. Move left below the peg, then climb a pocket-line to a thin crack, peg. Move up the crack to an open groove and ascend it boldly to a bolt and peg-belay on a slab.
2) 6a, 27m. Follow thin cracks rightwards to a small ledge from where bold moves access a ledge on the left and a medium size cam placement. Make hard moves to a poor peg and traverse rightwards below it to holds that gain a peg. Continue to another peg from where hard moves past a further peg end at a blank slab. Climb a thin flake up on the left to easier ground and a traverse rightwards to a bolted belay.
FA. Nick White, Pete Bull 11.7.1986

Long Quarry Point Slabs
The large, quarried headland is backed by a massive sweep of compact slabs reaching 50m in height. The climbing is good, although many of the original routes have gradually become overgrown.
Approach - From the white shelter, cross the fence and descend a steep and narrow path to the quarry floor.
Descent - For the multi-pitch lines make a 45m abseil to the ground or scramble off rightwards, then walk down the approach path. For the single-pitch lines, lower-off or abseil.
Conditions - The slabs dry very quickly and catch the sun from first light. There is a lot of vegetation visible on the crag but this does not spoil the climbs described.

④ Black Ice . . . . 🔲🔲 **E3 5c**
The centre of the huge sweep of 'boilerplate' slabs provides some exquisite slab-climbing. Start directly beneath the smoothest part of the face, just to the right of a small tree. *Photo opposite.*
1) 5c, 30m. Move up past some pink stains to a good peg in a thin diagonal break. Go right to another peg, before climbing leftwards to a shallow niche, then a large vegetated break just above. Move right 2 metres, and climb the wall above a short way, before traversing left, past a peg, to gain a thin, intermittent crack-line. Follow this to a difficult sequence just below the belay-ledge.
2) 5c, 23m. Climb up rightwards from the belay to a ledge, slightly loose. Move up to an undercut flake. Take this leftwards, then follow the steep, fingery wall to another flake-crack on the left. Climb more easily to a bolt-belay. Either move right to the descent path or make a 45m abseil to the ground.
FA. Pat Littlejohn, Keith Darbyshire 2.1973

Descent-path down to quarry floor

Abseil or lower off

45m abseil or scramble off to the right

To The Sanctuary Wall

Avon Somerset

North Devon

Culm Coast

Inland Cornwall

Atlantic Coast

West Penwith

The Lizard

Inland Devon

Torbay

Dorset

Climbers on the smooth boilerplate-slabs of the first pitch of *Black Ice* (E3 5c) - *opposite* - at Long Quarry Point, Torquay.

Dorset

Avon Somerset
North Devon
Culm Coast
Inland Cornwall
Atlantic Coast
West Penwith
The Lizard
Inland Devon
Torbay
Dorset

Portland is now the most popular sport-climbing destination in the West Country, offering a wide grade-range, and some of the most reliable climbing conditions in the UK. Barry Humphreys on *Pump Hitler* (7a+) - *page 382* - Battleship Back Cliff.

Avon Somerset | North Devon | Culm Coast | Inland Cornwall | Atlantic Coast | West Penwith | The Lizard | Inland Devon | Torbay | Dorset

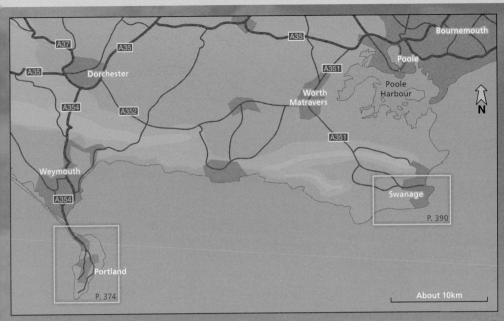

Avon Somerset

North Devon

Culm Coast

Inland Cornwall

Atlantic Coast

West Penwith

The Lizard

Inland Devon

Torbay

Dorset

Dorset climbing is confined almost exclusively to its limestone sea-cliffs, with the vast majority of its traditional climbs being centred on Swanage to the east and its sport climbing on the Isle of Portland to the west. The limestone is very different to that found in Somerset, Avon and Devon, being softer and yielding a huge diversity in structure that ranges from monumental corner, roof and crack climbs to intricate and weirdly-featured faces of flowstone. Swanage is a massive cliff-line that has many hundreds of climbs of all grades along its length. Much of the climbing is at the adventurous end of the game and the climbs, although not being particularly high or tidal, require respect due to the abseil approaches, the tough style and the often-harrowing exits.

In recent years Portland has become the focus of sport climbing in the West Country and its huge collection of routes attracts visitors throughout the year.

Getting Around

Dorset has the accolade of being a county with no motorway and this severely affects the ease with which the climbing sites can be accessed - especially from the north and the west. Travel along the coast to both Swanage and Portland is on slow roads which become hideously congested in the summer months - an early start is essential to beat the hoards on the way to the beaches.

Good tides and perfect weather on the classic *Wall Street* (HS 4b) - *page 397* - at Cormorant Ledge, Swanage. Climber John Warner

Avon Somerset | North Devon | Culm Coast | Inland Cornwall | Atlantic Coast | West Penwith | The Lizard | Inland Devon | Torbay | Dorset

Portland is a one of the premier sport climbing destinations in Britain with several hundred well-bolted routes across the grade range. The climbs are on faces often skimmed with flowstone, which provides some brilliant hold-plastered drapes of rock. Other faces consist of clean white rock, most being vertical, giving sustained, technical climbing. In recent years Portland has become even more popular and most weekends will see the main crags packed with climbers from all over the country.

Tides
Only Wallsend is tidal and even this is only inaccessible for an hour or so either side of high water.

Conditions
Portland is one of the West Country's most reliable venues, its rock dries remarkably quickly, rarely seeps, and shelter from sun and wind can be found throughout the day. In hot weather the temperatures can become unpleasant and the rock soapy.

Guidebook
There are hundreds of sport routes on Portland and only the prime sectors are described in this guidebook. The Rockfax Guidebook to Dorset gives full coverage of all the sport routes on Portland and is available from www.rockfax.com. (New edition 2011).

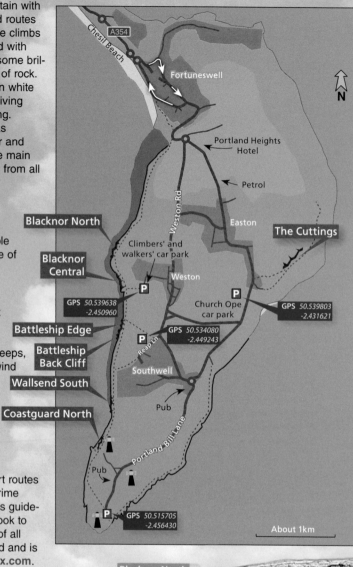

Chesil Beach — A354 — Fortuneswell — Portland Heights Hotel — Petrol — Easton — The Cuttings — Blacknor North — Climbers' and walkers' car park — Weston Rd — Blacknor Central — Weston — Church Ope car park — GPS 50.539638 -2.450960 — GPS 50.539803 -2.431621 — Battleship Edge — GPS 50.534080 -2.449243 — Reap Ln — Battleship Back Cliff — Southwell — Wallsend South — Coastguard North — Pub — Portland Bill Lane — Pub — GPS 50.515705 -2.456430 — About 1km — N

Blacknor North

	No star	⚜	⚜⚜	⚜⚜⚜
Mod to S	-	-	-	-
HS to HVS	-	2	7	4
E1 to E3	2	11	19	7
E4 and up	2	13	17	10

Approaches   See main area map on page 373

Once on Portland, follow signs to Portland Bill, then, as the road reaches the top of the island at a roundabout, either follow signs for Weston, Easton or Portland Bill.

Blacknor North - Approach from the climbers' and walkers' car park (fee) - sign posted from Weston (opposite the shops). Walk to the cliff-top path and turn right. Continue for about 500m, past a walled concrete-fort, to where the path drops down slightly into a quarried area. Locate a narrow, steep path at a break in the cliff, which doubles back left under the face. Walk for 200m to reach the sector.

Blacknor Central - Approach from the climbers' and walkers' car park (fee) - sign posted from Weston (opposite the shops). Walk to the cliff top. Turn right onto the cliff-top path, after a few metres a quarry just below the path comes into view. Scramble down into the quarry, through a large block-wall, and then down a narrow gully at the far end of the quarry. Turn right at the base of the gully and follow a narrow path under the cliff for 100m to the sector.

Battleship Edge and Battleship Back Cliff - Drive through Weston to a small roundabout and turn right into Reap Lane and park on the roadside. DO NOT PARK DIRECTLY OUTSIDE THE HOUSES AND DO NOT CHANGE CLOTHES IN FRONT OF THE HOUSES. Walk along the path opposite the houses to the coast path and turn right. After few metres, take a steep path down the hillside. The cliffs are on the left, the first is Battleship Edge, and a little further on Battleship Back Cliff. It is also possible to approach from the climbers' and walkers' parking using the cliff-top path (see map).

Wallsend Central and Coastguard North - Drive to the Portland Bill car park (fee). Walk back up the road past the Pulpit Inn and head out leftwards towards the Coastwatch Lookout. Just before the Lookout, go left across grass to the cliff edge then descend a steep and precarious path past a promontory to below Coastguard Cliff. For the Wallsend sector, boulder-hop north under the cliff for around 250m to the sector. This approach is cut off for around 1 hour either side of high water.

The Cuttings - Drive through Easton to the Church Ope car park. Walk back up the road for 50m and at the tiny Portland Museum turn right onto Church Ope Road. Follow the road under an arch and down to a flat area with some benches. From here, take the coast path (not the path to Church Ope Cove) to a wide track which leads to The Cuttings.

Side tabs (top to bottom): Avon Somerset | North Devon | Culm Coast | Inland Cornwall | Atlantic Coast | West Penwith | The Lizard | Inland Devon | Torbay | Dorset

Approach

Blacknor Central

❶ Downtown Julie Brown . 　　　　　 **6c**
A splendid, but testing pitch that incorporates a good number of both technical and fingery moves on fine flowstone. Start just to the right of the blunt arete.
22m. Climb direct, just right of the bolts, to good holds. Proceed with more difficulty via some thin wall-climbing and a small undercut to an easing at better holds on a flowstone curtain. Finish leftwards.
FA. Pete Oxley 12.9.1992

❷ Reptile Smile . . . . 　　　　　 **6a+**
The Portland flowstone-classic that powers its way up the centre of the frozen cascade. Start below the steep upper wall.
21m. Climb easily up slightly rightwards, past a thread (occasionally missing) to the first bolt. Ascend the steepening wall above on a variety of flowstone features and some poor footholds to an easing towards the top.
FA. Pete Oxley 12.9.1992

❸ Slings Shot . . . . 　　　　　 **5**
More stunning flowstone, and one of the best grade 5 climbs around. Start below the line of weakness in the centre of the face.
22m. Follow the easy-angled lower wall to a deep flake. Climb up this to finish up some more unusual rock-formations. A link-up from the second bolt on *Reptile Smile* is possible at 5+.
FA. J.Tookey 1975. FFA. Nigel Coe 24.9.1988. The line was bolted by Pete Oxley 11.5.1994 and claimed as 'The Scales of Balance"

❹ Crocadilia . . . . 　　　　　 **6a**
A neat pitch that is very close to *Slings Shot* in its lower reaches. Start at the line of bolts just right of *Slings Shot*.
23m. Climb the wall until steep moves right at the mid-height overhang gain a large protruding flange of flowstone. Pass this with care and continue to the top a short way above.
FA. Gary Gibson 10.2005

Blacknor North
The big pull here is the amazing wall of flowstone that provides a number of brilliant pitches.
Approach - Walk along the base of the cliff to below the unmistakable flowstone wall.
Descent - All routes have lower-offs in place.
Conditions - The afternoon sun creeps around onto the face later than other west-coast sectors. It is often a much cooler spot than others nearby.

❺ Spanner Eyes . . . . . 　　　　　 **7b**
Some pressing manoeuvres mark this line out as the most difficult on this section of wall. Start under the large flowstone pipes high on the right-hand side of the cliff.
21m. Move up, then left to steeper ground. Climb a crack, then move left and up with difficulty to a nasty mantle move. Finish more easily.
FA. Will Jones 8.1996

❻ England's Dreaming 　Top 50　 **7a+**
A 'flowstone-fest' of the highest quality. Start as for *Spanner Eyes*. *Photo opposite.*
21m. Move up and right before steep, fingery moves gain a position below the fatter section of flowstone at mid-height. Make a powerful stretch up right and then head left and up yet more brilliant flowstone to finish.
FA. Pete Oxley 4.9.1992

❼ Cake Walk . . . . 　　　　　 **6a**
A well-featured climb worth tracking down. Start at a wide crack on the right-hand side of the flowstone face.
22m. Climb up past the bolts and move leftwards to the base of a massive pillar of flowstone. Climb the pillar and finish leftwards with difficulty.
FA. Steve Taylor 11.10.1992

Avon Somerset

North Devon

Culm Coast

Inland Cornwall

Atlantic Coast

West Penwith

The Lizard

Inland Devon

Torbay

Dorset

Midway up the flowstone classic *England's Dreaming* (7a+)
- *opposite* - Blacknor North, Portland.

Blacknor Central

A big wall that, although slightly spoilt by some broken rock and vegetation in its lower reaches, is nevertheless a great sector. The best climbing is both fingery and sustained.

Approach - Walk along the base of the cliff from the bottom of the descent gully to below the wall.

Descent - All routes have lower-offs in place.

Condtions - The sun hits this wall much earlier than any other on the west coast, and is a great place to head for if a bit of early warmth is required.

❶ Cybernetic Orchard . . . . **7a+**

A good, strong line that gradually increases in difficulty with height gained. Start left of a low overhang, at a bolt above a vegetated ledge.

28m. Climb up vegetated ground to a long groove line and follow it, passing a bulge on the left, to the top.

FA. Pete Oxley 29.5.1995

❷ I Walk the Line **7b**

Intricate and sustained climbing up the wall just to the right of the long groove of *Cybernetic Orchard*. Start right of a low overhang below a difficult-to-see bolt.

28m. Climb up broken ground to the main wall. Climb the wall directly, past some hard climbing in its middle section.

FA. Gary Gibson 4.5.2006

❸ Portland Heights. . . **7a**

A popular and sustained face climb. Start right of a low overhang below a difficult-to-see bolt.

28m. Climb up broken ground, then head up right to a line of bolts. Sustained climbing up the bolt-line, past a fingery and technical section at mid-height, gains a fine finish.

FA. Pete Oxley 14.5.1989

❹ Grand Larceny . . . . **7a+**

An eliminate line. Start at a bolt-belay above broken ground, which is gained by abseil. Alternatively, climb up the initial broken wall of routes either side and traverse to the belay.

28m. The steep prow on small pockets and edges to a slabby finish, without straying across to *Portland Heights*.

FA. Dave Pickford 9.1999

❺ Burning Skies. **6c**

A first-class climb that features some great climbing on very good rock. Start at a horizontally-placed staple, just to the right of a crack.

28m. Climb up to a steep groove and continue with difficulty to a less steep, but still high-quality finish.

FA. Pete Oxley 18.6.1995

6 Isle of Slingers....... 6c+
A popular line with good moves and rock. Start at a crack-line in the lower wall.
28m. Move up the lower wall and climb directly up the wall above to a technical finish on the head-wall.
FA. Nic Hellyer 18.4.1999

7 Lord Stublock Deepvoid Breaks the Chain of Causation............ 6b+
A really good, long wall-pitch on fine rock. Start at a crack-line in the lower wall.
28m. Climb the gradually-steepening wall to a thrilling finish.
FA. Pete Oxley 18.6.1995

8 Dusty Bedrock in Need of Careful Preparation
.... 7a+
A big pitch that crosses the wide chimney. Start left of the wide crack that becomes a chimney higher up.
30m. Climb the wall via cracks to a ledge. The upper wall on the opposite side of the chimney provides the meat of the pitch.
FA. Gary Gibson 4.5.2006

9 Cocteau Phenomena
.... 7b+
An impressive line up the steep wall to the left of the dominating arete. Start just to the right of the wide crack.
28m. Climb up and right into the centre of the wall, then climb this to a hard finish. Finishing on the right is 7b. The lower-off is situated on the ledge above the route.
FA. Pete Oxley 11.5.1989

10 The Chronicles of Vladimir.... 6c+
A steep start gains the hanging arete. Start below the roofs.
29m. Climb up through the stack of overhangs and then climb the arete all the way to a difficult finish.
FA. Gary Gibson 2.5.2006

11 Ausfahrt........... 6b+
A much-travelled favourite. Start below a wide crack on the right of an overhang at 4m.
29m. Climb up past the overhang at 4m, and then pursue a line leftwards to a long groove just right of the arete. Follow this to an overhang and finish via some difficult final moves.
FA. Mike Robertson 6.5.1995

12 Screw the Roses, Send me the Thorns
.... 7a+
Sustained wall-climbing on a direct line at the lower limit of the grade. Start at the wall just right of an overhang at 4m.
28m. Climb the wall and broken ground to the upper face which gives some blind and fingery climbing.
FA. Nic Hellyer 1998

13 The Shells, The Shells 7a
Eliminate in style, but worthwhile climbing. Start below a diagonal crack and a bolt between two staples.
28m. Climb the lower wall and continue to the upper face, which gives good moves, though on a very tight line.
FA. Gary Gibson 16.9.2004

14 Driven Like the Snow .. 6b+
A Portland gem. Start at a boulder on the path.
28m. Climb the lower wall to below a long crack-line. Move up the crack until a line leads out left onto the wall and small ledge. Climb the slabby wall above the ledge until a tricky mantel move gains the lower-off.
FA. Pete Oxley 14.9.1991

15 Return to Roissy........ 6b+
The long crack is a good route. Start at a boulder on the path.
28m. Climb the lower wall to below a long flake-crack. Climb the accommodating crack to a tricky bulge at its end. Finish up a perplexing groove in the headwall.
FA. Pete Oxley 13.8.1995

16 Last Rose of Summer .. 7a
Pleasant climbing punctuated by some fairly tough moves. Start below a semi-circular cut-out above the first break.
28m. Climb to below the upper wall. Sustained climbing gains a small ledge from where one last blind move reaches easier ground and the top wall.
FA. Pete Oxley 21.8.1988

Approach

Avon Somerset | North Devon | Culm Coast | Inland Cornwall | Atlantic Coast | West Penwith | The Lizard | Inland Devon | Torbay | Dorset

① Evening Falls . . . . 🏷️ 📷 ☐ **6a+**
The large, overhang-capped corner on the left margin of the wall is a strong line and popular pitch. Start beneath the corner. *Photo opposite.*
18m. Make some tough moves up the initial wall to get established in the corner proper, then climb to beneath the roof. Traverse rightwards along the horizontal break and make a steep move up to a jug.
FA. Pete Oxley 17.12.1988

② Victims of Fashion . 🏷️ 📷 🧗 ☐ **7a+**
A finger-stamina test of the highest calibre. Start below the blunt rib right of the corner of *Evening Falls*.
18m. Move up the pocketed lower wall. Then, from a small finger-ledge, make some tricky moves up to a shallow groove in the final section of the rib. Make a couple of blind moves to reach the horizontal break and pull through the final bulge to a jug.
FA. Pete Oxley 10.5.1989

③ Barbed Wire Kisses. . . . 🏷️ 🧗 ☐ **7a+**
Another strong corner-line with a hard crux sequence midway. Start below a shallow corner just right of the rib of *Victims of Fashion*.
19m. Climb the lower wall into the base of the corner-line. Move up and make a hard move through a slight bulge to gain easier ground.
FA. Pete Oxley 13.11.1988

④ Monoculture. . . 🏷️ 🧗 🧗 📷 ☐ **7c+**
A classic tendon stretching testpiece. Start left of a grey streak.
19m. The lower wall sets the scene prior to the technical, and extremely fingery, blind moves over the upper bulge.
FA. Pete Oxley 12.88 FFA. 17.4.1993

⑤ Reve d'un Corbeau . . . . 🏷️ 🧗 ☐ **7a**
The hard lower wall has a stopper move. Start below a square-cut groove in the upper wall with a black streak running down it.
20m. Difficult moves going left to the base of the interesting upper groove prove to be the undoing of many.
FA. Pete Oxley 19.11.1988

🌙 Afternoon | 🚶 10 min

⑥ Lazy Days and Summer Haze
. . . . 🏷️ 📷 ☐ **6a+**
A testing pitch that is rounded off by a steep and exposed finish. Start below a prominent flake at two-thirds height.
18m. Move up to the right and then back left to the shallow corner below the flake. Climb the corner and layback-flake to the horizontal break. Move leftwards through the upper flowstone bulge to a lower-off.
FA. Pete Oxley 8.5.1989

⑦ Norfolk Coast . . . . 🏷️ 🧗 ☐ **7a+**
An eliminate up the steep slab just right of *Lazy Days and Summer Haze*. Start just right of the prominent flake.
18m. Technical moves up the slab lead to a tricky finish.
FA. Gary Gibson 4.5.2003

⑧ Pinch an Inch . . . . 🏷️ 🧗 ☐ **6a**
Pleasing and precise climbing on great rock. Start in the centre of the grey wall below a small right-facing corner at 4m.
18m. Move up the wall with care to the corner and make some long moves via good holds to an easing at a thin crack. Climb the thin crack and move rightwards to a ledge at the horizontal break from where one last move up gains a lower-off.
FA. Pete Oxley 21.8.1988

⑨ Inch Perfect, Inchworm . 🏷️ 🧗 ☐ **6b+**
An equally good, but tougher, wall-climbing experience to *Pinch an Inch*. Start below an open groove at 4m.
18m. Climb to positive holds in the groove. Make a series of technical moves up and right and then back left before easier ground leads to the upper horizontal breaks. One last pull gains a jug and lower-off.
FA. Crispin Waddy 8.8.1987

⑩ Serious Music . . . . 🏷️ 🧗 ☐ **6c+**
An 'all out' start is the key to more intricate and well-positioned climbing above. Start left of a shallow arete right of the grey wall.
18m. Move up to a high bolt and make a powerful pull, with little for the feet, to better holds. Traverse rightwards to the arete and climb it and the wall above the horizontal break to a lower-off.
FA. Pete Oxley 19.11.1988

11 **Margaret on the Guillotine** . . . . . 🔦 📋 ⬜ **6a**
Surprisingly varied climbing which requires an eye for route finding.
Start just right of an arete at mid-height.
17m. Start left of the first bolt, then move up and traverse rightwards
before stepping back left to the shallow corner above. Climb the corner
to a horizontal break where a long move gains the next break and a
lower-off on the wall above.
FA. Pete Oxley 22.4.1989

12 **Gratuitous Lies Here** . . . . 📋 📋 ⬜ **6c+**
Good, hard climbing, but unfortunately rather runout. Start 4m right of
an arete at mid-height.
17m. Move up to the first bolt which is shared with the previous route.
Follow the thin groove up right to the break and finish via some difficult
and bold moves through the overhang.
FA. Martin Crocker 22.4.1989

13 **Keel Haul** . . . . 📋 📋 📋 ⬜ **7b**
A good line but escapable. Start at a blunt arete.
17m. Climb the blunt arete via some hard pulls.
FA. Damian Cook 16.2.1993

14 **Out of Reach, Out of Mind** . . 📋 📋 📋 ⬜ **6c**
The rounded groove is one of Battleship Edge's best climbs. Start
below the groove with a doorknob insitu!
18m. The pocketed groove passing, but not using, the doorknob ends
at the upper break. Make some steep and committing moves to finish.
FA. Pete Oxley 13.11.1988

15 **No me Comas el Coco** . . . . 📋 📋 ⬜ **7a**
A good, varied pitch with a fingery start and butch finish. Start below a
faint groove 2m right of the insitu doorknob.
18m. Climb the thin groove and wall above it to the upper break.
A powerful sequence up the bulging headwall gains the top and a
lower-off.
FA. Jon Biddle 7.2.1993

16 **Come, Armageddon, Come** . . . . 📋 📋 ⬜ **6c+**
Unusual moves on the lower wall. Start below a small corner to the left
of a wide bolted groove.
18m. Layback the chunky pinch-grips, to a steep finish.
FA. Pete Oxley 22.4.1989

North Somerset
Avon
North Devon
Culm Coast
Inland Cornwall
Atlantic Coast
West Penwith
The Lizard
Inland Devon
Torbay
Dorset

Battleship Edge

A long, low wall of fantastic rock with an enticing line-up
of routes. The base of the cliff is flat and the climbs
themselves are generally well supplied with face holds
and pockets.
Approach - Walk along the base of the cliff from the
base of the descent path to below the wall.
Descent - All routes have lower-offs in place.
Condtions - The cliff dries extremely quickly.

Topping out on *Evening Falls* (6a+)
- *opposite* - Battleship Edge, Portland.

Avon Somerset | North Devon | Culm Coast | Inland Cornwall | Atlantic Coast | West Penwith | The Lizard | Inland Devon | Torbay | Dorset

① Nihil 7b

The well-defined rib in the upper wall has good climbing and plenty of exposure. Start 3m left of a low flake.
27m. Climb the lower wall past a bulge to a rest below the upper wall. Make difficult moves through a larger bulge above and climb the arete on its right-hand side to easier ground on the final wall.
FA. Pete Oxley 16.4.1993

② No Man is an Island . . . 6c

A long established Portland favourite. Start between two low flake-cracks under a long narrow roof at 6m.
27m. Climb to the narrow roof and pass it on the right before making some fingery moves back left above it to an easing. Continue to the base of the upper corner and follow cracks up this, exiting leftwards along the breaks at its top.
FA. Pete Oxley 10.7.1990

③ Always Have the Edge 6c

Another gem with sustained climbing after a hard start. Start at a low left-facing flake.
26m. Climb through the low overhangs with difficulty and continue up the sustained wall above to a rest below the upper wall. Move up into the wide corner above and follow this to a steep finish past a pocket.
FA. Pete Oxley 10.7.1990

④ Pump Hitler . . . . . . 7a+

Exciting situations combined with technical climbing. Start at a low, left-leaning flake-crack. *Photo on page 370.*
26m. Climb up and stretch past the low roof. Continue up the sustained wall to blanker rock. Clip a high bolt and then traverse left on finger pockets before rocking up into a small corner. A final balancy wall and roof round off this great pitch.
FA. Pete Oxley 14.4.1993

⑤ Buoys Will Be Buoys . . . 6b+

A long stamina climb that is one of the region's best grade 6 sport climbs. Start at a small left-facing corner. *Photo opposite.*
27m. Move up to the overhang and negotiate it on the right before heading up the wall above to a corner with a good crack in it. Climb the corner and the left-trending groove above to a roof and swing right along the breaks until it is possible to pull up onto the headwall and finish rightwards.
FA. Pete Oxley 10.7.1990

⑥ Shape Shifter 7c

A hard upper-wall. Start 3m right of a small left-facing corner.
26m. Climb easily to the mid-height ledge. Step left and climb direct up the wall via a powerful sequence to finish at the lower-off of *Buoys Will Be Buoys*.
FA. Bob Hickish 31.8.2008

←— To Battleship Edge

7 Jurassic Shift 7a
A good but unbalanced route. Start 3m right of a small left-facing corner as for *Shape Shifter*.
27m. Climb easily to the mid-height ledge. Climb the teasing shallow groove above to a steep finish.
FA. Pete Oxley 16.4.1993

8 The Fun Factory . . . 7b
Excellent and varied groove climbing with an almost gritstone-like mid-section. Start at a small ground level corner.
26m. Climb poor rock until above the wide chert band. Move up and then left into a corner/groove and follow it to a steep finish that is overcome by a big reach.
FA. Pete Oxley 4.6.1997

9 Info Freako . . . 7b+
Varied and technical moves up a thin crack in the impressive headwall. Start as for *The Fun Factory*.
27m. Climb the easy lower wall on poor rock to below the start of the thin crack. The crack succumbs to a series of precarious moves until better holds are gained in the upper break. Finish up the steep bulge via an enormous reach, the 'short of arm' may prefer to finish up the arete to the right.
FA. Pete Oxley 18.7.1990

10 The Racing Line . . . 7b+
An excellent climb with plenty of technical sequences. Start at a bolt-line just to the right of a low corner.
27m. Climb the lower wall taking the left bolt-line past a flake to a shallow, left-facing groove. Make technical moves up this and then right to a thin crack and tiny corner. Climb the crack and left-hand bolt-line up the wall to finish.
FA. Pete Oxley 4.6.1997

11 Zinc Oxide Mountain 7b+
One of Portland's very best routes, ascending the white headwall via some exquisite moves. Low in the grade. Start at a bolt-line just to the right of a low corner as for *The Racing Line*.
28m. Climb the right-hand bolt-line up the lower wall and then make a rising traverse left to a thin crack and tiny corner. Climb the thin crack and finish up the right-hand bolt-line.
FA. Pete Oxley 25.7.1990

Battleship Back Cliff
One of Portland's biggest and best walls featuring some fine, long routes. The lower section of the wall can be a bit dusty at times but the upper wall more than compensates for this.
Approach - From the base of the descent path, walk under Battleship Edge, to below the wall.
Descent - All routes have lower-offs in place.
Condtions - The cliff dries extremely quickly, but the base is a bit of a wind tunnel and can be a chilly spot in cool weather.

On the exposed finish of *Buoys Will Be Buoys* (6b+) - *opposite* - Battleship Back Cliff, Portland. Climber Lee Proctor.

Wallsend South

A superb line-up of long sport-routes on one of Portland's tallest sections of cliff. The atmosphere is very much that of a sea-cliff, as the approach is tidal.

Approach - From the base of the descent path, walk and scramble over boulders past a tidal section to flat, non-tidal ledges below the wall.

Access - There is a bird restriction on the route *Halfway to Heaven*. No climbing from March 1st to July 31st.

Descent - All routes have lower-offs in place.

Tides and Conditions - The approach to the base of the cliff is tidal and access is cut off for around 1 hour either side of high water. Conditions can be very soapy in humid weather.

1 Child of Light . . . . 6c+

A left-hand finish to *Immaculata*. Start at a break in the low overhang right of the huge curving groove.

27m. Climb to a groove high on the wall, then break out left and surge up the impending face.
FA. Mick Ward 10.9.2009

2 Immaculata 6c

Intricate climbing that builds to an exposed final wall. Start as for Child of Light.

27m. Climb, on slightly dusty rock to the upper wall. Move right into a corner, and climb this to a step left and a final push up the exposed headwall.
FA. Mick Ward 31.3.2003

3 The Watchman 6b

A testing line that features some hard moves low down, and a brilliant upper corner. Start just to the left of a corner in the low overhang.

27m. Execute a technical, but short-lived sequence to better holds on the wall above, then follow this to the mid-height break. The clean-cut corner and headwall above are the icing on the cake.
FA. Pete Oxley 31.12.1989

4 Waiting for the Barbarians . . 6b+

The wall above the short corner is worthwhile. Start at the short corner in the low overhang.

27m. Move up through the overhang and pull left to a sloping ledge. Follow the shallow groove and wall above to a ledge below the upper wall. Climb the wall direct to finish.
FA. Mick Ward 8.8.2008

5 Peace in the Nineties . . 6b+

The rightward trending line above the short corner is much easier in its upper reaches. Start at the short corner in the low overhang as for *Waiting for the Barbarians*.

27m. Move over the overhang and trend rightwards across the wall above it, until a direct line can be followed to the straightforward upper wall.
FA. Pete Oxley 31.12.1989

6 Some Velvet Morning 7a

The wall and blunt arete right of *Peace in the Nineties*. Start at the short corner in the low overhang as for *Waiting for the Barbarians*.

28m. Start up *Peace in the Nineties* and continue beyond its traverse above the low overhang before ascending the face, blunt arete and headwall above to finish.
FA. Mick Ward 8.8.2008

7 The Enchanted Path . . . 6c

A powerful pull through the initial overhang is followed by far more pleasant climbing above. Start just to the left of an overhang sentry-box.

27m. Heave over the low overhang and ascend the wall above to twin corners in the upper wall. Finish via the left corner, turning the final overhang on the left.
FA. Brian Tilley 13.7.1989

8 Once Upon a Time in The West
. . . . 6c

A neat pitch. Start as for *Best Fingers Forward*, in an overhung sentry-box.

27m. Climb *Best Fingers Forward* to clear the overhang, then weave up the wall to the obvious groove. Climb the groove to an exit via some of the most amazing holds on Portland.
FA. Mick Ward 19.9.2009

9 Best Fingers Forward . . 6c+

A brilliant pitch that features a forceful finger-crack. Start in an overhung sentry-box.

27m. Move up and right to clear the overhang and gain the wall above. Climb the wall rightwards on good finger-holds to the base of a thin crack in the upper wall. The fine, thin crack is climbed with difficulty to a short headwall.
FA. Pete Oxley 11.7.1989

10 Blue Faced Booby 6c

Exposed and committing climbing up the wall's right-hand arete. Start just to the left of the arete.

27m. Make a tricky series of moves over the low overhang and then climb rightwards up the wall to meet the upper arete. Make committing moves up the arete to an easier finish.
FA. Pete Oxley 21.5.1996

11 Tea Cakes Calling . . 7a

A pitch with a hard lower crux. Start just right of the wide, broken corner-crack.

28m. Climb the wall direct with a bouldery move on the steep initial wall.
FA. Pete Oxley 21.5.1996

12 The Jewel of the Isle . . . 6b+

A magical wall-climb. Start in the middle of the steepest section of the wall.

28m. Climb up the fingery lower wall with conviction to finish up a thin crack-line in the compact face above.
FA. Pete Oxley 25.6.1995

⑬ Stalker's Zone . . . . 🎖️📷 6a+

The right-hand line of the lower wall is another terrific face-climb. Start below ledges and a left-leaning corner under an overhang. The first bolt is high.

28m. Climb carefully to the first bolt and then proceed with less caution up the wall to finish up a flake-crack.
FA. Pete Oxley 30.4.1989

⑭ Trad Free World . . . . . . 🎖️📷 6a+

A Wallsend classic that sees plenty of ascents. A lovely pitch on great rock. Start at the left end of a high ledge below a shallow corner.

28m. Climb the rib just left of the corner and the wall above to a thin crack. Climb the thin crack to a short, leaning headwall.
FA. Pete Oxley 7.11.1992

⑮ Genuflection . . . . . 🎖️📷 7b

Gradually steepening climbing with an intense sequence midway. Start at the left end of a high ledge, below a shallow corner.

28m. Climb the shallow corner for 10m until a line of bolts on the left leads up to a bald wall just above an overhang. Thin moves up the wall gain easier but bulging ground that leads to the top.
FA. Pete Oxley 11.5.1996

⑯ Reverence . . . . 🎖️📷 7a+

When in condition, the central depression and upper cracks offer a brilliant experience that is low in the grade. Start at the left end of a high ledge below a shallow corner.

28m. Climb the technical central groove to a more defined section of the depression, where the difficulties build before the final impending headwall is reached and climbed on more positive holds.
FA. Pete Oxley 5.7.1989

⑰ Outside the Gate. . . 🎖️📷 7b

The left-leaning open corner in the middle of the bulging section of the upper wall splits the difficulties of this good route. Start below the blank wall directly below the corner.

28m. Climb the fingery wall and flake to below the midway corner. Inch up to easier ground in the corner and climb this to more tricky climbing at its end, where the overhang and headwall provide a spectacular finale.
FA. Pete Oxley 5.7.1989

> **Restriction (Halfway to Heaven) -** *No climbing March 1st to July 31st because of nesting birds.*

⑱ Halfway to Heaven . 🎖️📷 7b

Another Portland classic, with continuously interesting and varied moves on superb rock. Start at a vertical wall directly below a clean cut corner in the upper wall.

28m. A hard move to a good hold gains easier ground that leads to the midway horizontal break. Pull up leftwards into the base of the square-cut corner. Climb the corner steeply to a difficult exit out right and up to gain the finishing headwall.
FA. Pete Oxley 29.4.1989

Avon Somerset · North Devon · Culm Coast · Inland Cornwall · Atlantic Coast · West Penwith · The Lizard · Inland Devon · Torbay · Dorset

Coastguard North

A cliff that possesses a combination of fabulous rock, excellent climbs and is set right down next to the sea, but is not tidal.

Approach - Carefully scramble down the very steep path to the boulder-beach below the cliff.

Descent - All routes have lower-offs in place.

Tides - The base of the crag is non-tidal.

Conditions - The cliff does suffer from seepage more than most on Portland after wet spells. Conditions can be very soapy in humid weather.

❶ Retaining the Ashes . . . 🔆 🖾 ☐ **6b**

Lurking just around the corner from the main face is this testing pitch that follows a slightly leaning, thin crack up the wall. Start at a short wall under the crack-line.

22m. Climb the short wall to a ledge below the thin crack. Climb the technical crack to a steep finish. This line can be unpleasant in damp or humid conditions.

FA. Steve Taylor 7.3.1993

❷ Into the Groove . . . . 🔆 🖾 ☐ **6b+**

A short, but useful link-up. Start as for *Retaining the Ashes*.

23m. Start up *Retaining the Ashes*, then move right past a single extra bolt. A touch fluttery.

FA. Pete Oxley 2000

❸ Nothing but the Groove . 🔆 🖾 ☐ **6c+**

The soaring groove on the left-hand side of the wall is a fine line, although the groove itself is relatively easy. Start directly below the groove. *Photo opposite.*

24m. Nip up the bouldery lower wall and pull steeply left to below the groove line. Move up with difficulty to the groove proper and continue up it more easily to the top.

FA. Pete Oxley 8.8.1988.

❹ Running It In . . 🔆 🔆 🖾 🖾 ☐ **7b+**

A very direct line that involves a good deal of fingery and technical moves with little in the way of respite. Start below a pocket.

23m. Climb to the pocket and then on up to a very thin crack. Follow this with difficulty to a rest, then continue more easily up the remainder of the crack to moves left and the top.

FA. Martin Crocker 10.6.1990

❺ Superfly Guy . . . . 🔆 🖾 ☐ **7a**

A quality pumpy pitch that is packed with good climbing. Start at a low ledge that protrudes from the face.

22m. Climb up and then left, past some good pockets to a large hold below the upper wall. Make some difficult moves on hard-to-see holds up and right to a slim groove. Follow this, and the wall to its right, to the top. The lower pockets seep at times.

FA. Pete Oxley 8.8.1988

6 Lost in Rock . . . . 🗒️ 📷 ☐ **6c+**
Quality rock and good technical moves are the main ingredients of this often-overlooked route. Start just to the right of a low, protruding ledge.
23m. Climb the initial wall, then pull rightwards over the bulge to an easing below the upper wall. Make some perplexing moves up and across the left-leaning groove before finishing up a thin crack.
FA. Pete Oxley 17.7.1992

7 The Man Who Never Found Himself
. . . . 🗒️ 🔧 ☐ **6a+**
The central corner is an enjoyable climb, however it does seep badly during wet periods. Start below and left of the corner.
23m. Ascend the steep lower wall and bulge to arrive at the base of the corner. Follow the corner in its entirety to the top.
FA. Pete Oxley 15.8.1988

8 Van People . . . . 🗒️ 📷 ☐ **7a**
A fine climb, although a little runout in places. Start at some dark grey streaks.
22m. Climb straight up the wall and bulges to meet a very shallow depression on the upper wall. Climb the shallow depression to a hard finish.
FA. Brian Tilley 20.8.1989

9 Fantasy Island . . . . 🗒️ 🔧 ☐ **6c**
An unusually-tough layback which is sometimes damp. Start at the bottom of the mud slope.
22m. Climb up through bulges to the open corner/groove. Climb the corner/groove all the way to the top and then traverse rightwards to a lower-off.
FA. Mark Higgs 28.5.1993

10 La Usurpadora . . . . . . 📷 🔧 ☐ **7c**
An artificial eliminate up the wall right of *Fantasy Island*. Start just up the mud slope below a steep wall.
20m. Climb the fingery wall direct until a traverse rightwards joins the finish of *Shining Heart*.
FA. Pete Oxley 25.5.2000

11 Heartland . . . . 🗒️ ☝️ 📷 🔧 ☐ **7c**
A short but significant link-up. Start just up the mud slope below a steep wall as for *La Usurpadora*.
19m. Move a short way up the wall and break right to join *Shining Heart* at its powerful crux.
FA. Pete Oxley 17.5.2000

12 Shining Heart . . . . . 🗒️ ☝️ 🔧 ☐ **7b+**
A well-positioned power problem. Start up the mud slope under the right end of a small horizontal overhang.
18m. Move up the wall and step left. Powerful moves up the rib allow a crack to be grasped. Climb awkwardly up this and finish up the easier wall above.
FA. Pete Oxley 20.8.1989

13 Frenzied Detruncation . . 🗒️ 🔧 ☐ **7b+**
A tough start is the entry price to the fine groove line above. Start below a groove with a small overhang at mid-height.
18m. Make technical and fingery moves on tiny crimps and smears to the overhang, then continue up the groove to the top.
FA. Pete Oxley 27.7.1989

Avon Somerset | North Devon | Culm Coast | Inland Cornwall | Atlantic Coast | West Penwith | The Lizard | Inland Devon | Torbay | Dorset

Trev Ford on the crux of *Nothing but the Groove* (6c+) - *opposite* - Coastguard North, Portland.

Avon Somerset | North Devon | Culm Coast | Inland Cornwall | Atlantic Coast | West Penwith | The Lizard | Inland Devon | Torbay | Dorset

❶ **Blowing the Gimp** . . . . . 7a+
A difficult move mid-pitch is a major obstacle. Start below two small, right-facing corners.
17m. Climb the corners and the very short crack in the headwall to a difficult sequence that brings easier climbing within reach.
FA. Pete Oxley 23.11.1994

❷ **The Sears Tower** . . . . . . 7b+
A short, but tough wall that involves some fierce crimping. Start at a bolt-line below a blank wall left of a recess.
17m. Climb to the upper wall and proceed up it using tiny crimps and smears.
FA. Pete Oxley 4.11.1990

❸ **The Holy Hand Grenade**
. . . . 7a
An awkward climb up an open groove and finger-crack that takes a bit of working out. Start at a bolt-line below a high finger-crack.
17m. Gain the open groove and climb it awkwardly to a fine finish up the finger-crack.
FA. Mike Robertson 26.11.1995

❹ **Brief Encounter** . . . . 6a+
A really good climb with a sting at the start! Start at a bolt-line that leads up into the right-hand side of the recess.
18m. Climb the wide groove, mainly on its right-hand side. The start is a boulder problem at about **V2**.
FA. Tim Dunsby 6.10.1991

❺ **Infernal Din** . . . . . . 7b+
The wide prow gradually builds in difficulty to a tenuous finish. Start below a bolt above the left end of a low overhang.
19m. Climb direct to the upper section of the wide prow, from where two equally tricky sequences must be executed to finish.
FA. Pete Oxley 2.10.1996

❻ **European Flavour** 6b
An excellent and hard-won line. Start below a bolt above the widest part of the low overhang.
19m. Boulder up past the bolt to a ledge. Climb up the left-hand side of the recess to a steep finish out to the left.
FA. Pete Oxley, Barry Clarke 2.10.1996

❼ **The Breathing Method** 8a
Hard and powerful moves through the mid-height overhang mark this out as The Cuttings' testpiece. Start below the left side of the mid-height overhang.
20m. Climb steeply to a narrow corner on the lip of the mid-height overhang. Make powerful moves up the groove and small blunt rib above to an easing at some flowstone.
FA. Pete Oxley 24.4.1994

❽ **Hall of Mirrors** 7c
A great pitch that requires good conditions. Low in the grade. Start below two short grooves in the mid-height overhang.
20m. Climb to the mid-height overhang. Pull up into the right-hand groove, then make difficult moves into, and up the left-hand groove. Quit the groove leftwards and finish easily.
FA. Pete Oxley 3.11.1990

Avon Somerset

North Devon

Culm Coast

Inland Cornwall

Atlantic Coast

West Penwith

The Lizard

Inland Devon

Torbay

Dorset

❾ Want Out . . . . 〔3〕 7b

The overhang-laden groove is a very fine and technical climb. High in the grade. Start directly below the corner/groove.
20m. Climb the lower wall to a small ledge. Continue up the fingery and technical corner/groove to a strenuous finish over the upper overhang.
FA. Martin Crocker 24.3.1991

❿ New Saladin . . . . 〔3〕 6c

Spectacular moves on good rock. Start directly below the corner/ groove, as for *Want Out*.
20m. Climb the lower wall to a small ledge. Wild moves up the crack and hanging corner on the right gain easier ground. Move up and finish leftwards.
FA. Pete Oxley 13.1.1991

⓫ Hurricane on a Millpond
. . . . 〔3〕 7c+

A smooth, highly technical wall-climb that requires crisp conditions. Start below two grey streaks in the upper wall.
19m. Climb the lower wall to a ledge and then get stuck into the perplexing crux-wall.
FA. Pete Oxley 21.11.1996

The Cuttings

An incredibly reliable cliff that gets plenty of morning sun and has a line-up of clean and challenging climbs.
Approach - Walk along the track to the sector.
Descent - All of the climbs have lower-offs.
Conditions - A very quick drying cliff that also stays dry in parts during light rain.

⓬ Consommé. . . . . . . 〔3〕 6a+

The long, thin layback-flake in the upper section of the climb is an outstanding line. Start at a bolt-line left of some hanging ivy.
19m. Climb up and then make difficult moves left and up to a good ledge below the layback flake. Climb the clean-cut flake and cracks to their end and finish rightwards to a lower-off.
FA. Unknown. Unearthed and reclimbed by Jim Kimber 6.9.1997

⓭ Haute Cuisine. . . . . 〔3〕 7a

A tricky little wall-climb. Start just left of a blocky corner.
17m. Climb the broken lower wall and then make technical face-moves based around the very thin crack in the upper wall.
FA. Martin Crocker 16.4.1990

⓮ The Mouth Waters . 〔3〕 7a+

A harder but equally worthwhile right-hand variant on *Haute Cuisine*. Start just left of a blocky corner as for *Haute Cuisine*.
17m. Climb the initial broken wall and then head right up the thin wall before moving back left to finish.
FA. Martin Crocker 16.4.1990

Avon Somerset

North Devon

Culm Coast

Inland Cornwall

Atlantic Coast

West Penwith

The Lizard

Inland Devon

Torbay

Dorset

At around four miles long, Swanage's sea-cliff is the largest in the West Country. Its sheer and overhanging line of off-white limestone drops down to boulders that buffer its base from the sea for most of its length. The climbs are generally exhilarating and reasonably protected, although the rock is not uniformly solid, so care is required, especially when exiting the cliff-top. The approach is often via abseil which lends the climbing an air of seriousness, although much of the climbing is non-tidal. The range of difficulties and variety of styles is broad, with classic trad and sport climbs that span the full range of grades. Swanage is officially one of the sunniest places in the UK. This, combined with the fast drying nature of the rock, makes it a reliable venue that, even in the depths of winter, can provide a fair number of warm days for climbing.

Approach   See main area map on page 373

The approaches to the various cliffs radiate from the town of Swanage. Swanage lies at the end of the A351 and is a very popular seaside resort.

Access

Climbing restrictions are in place on some of the cliffs due to nesting birds. These are described in the individual cliff introductions.

Tides and Conditions

Access to most of the climbing is only marginally tidal during calm sea-conditions. Swanage faces south and can get very hot. On humid days the rock can become soapy.

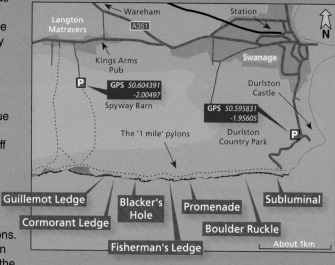

Wareham
Langton Matravers
A351
Station
N

Kings Arms Pub
Swanage

P
GPS *50.604391 -2.00497*
Spyway Barn

Durlston Castle

GPS *50.595831 -1.95605*

The '1 mile' pylons
Durlston Country Park
P

Guillemot Ledge
Cormorant Ledge
Blacker's Hole
Fisherman's Ledge
Promenade
Boulder Ruckle
Subluminal

About 1km

Boulder Ruckle

Marmolata Buttress p. 348

Tim Dunsby nearing the final few feet of the stupendous second pitch of *Behemoth* (HVS 5b) - *page 411* - in the Boulder Ruckle with the chalked holds of *Soul Sacrifice* (E3 5b) on the right. Photo: Mike Robertson.

Avon Somerset

North Devon

Culm Coast

Inland Cornwall

Atlantic Coast

West Penwith

The Lizard

Inland Devon

Torbay

Dorset

	No star	⛶	⛶	⛶
Mod to S	-	-	-	-
HS to HVS	-	-	2	3
E1 to E3	-	-	2	3
E4 and up	-	-	-	1

Guillemot and Cormorant Ledge are two sections of adjoining cliff that have individual approaches. Guillemot Ledge is divided into two distinct parts (the abseil line is conveniently located between the two). To the west, the cliff has a number of Swanage's harder multi-pitch lines that are some of the longest hereabouts. To the east of the abseil, Guillemot Ledge is at its most friendly with more multi-pitch climbs but in the mid-grades and with solid finishes. Cormorant Ledge is a superb section of Swanage that has two brilliant climbs that wend their way up some incredible ground on massive holds.

Approach   See main area map on page 390

Guillemot and Cormorant Ledges are approached from Langton Matravers. From just outside Swanage, turn off the A351 towards Langton Matravers. Once in the village, go past the post office and turn left into Durnford Drive. Drive 300m to a free car park (on a track for the last 150m). From the parking, walk south on a good path past four fields and Spyway Barn. After the 4th field, the coast path is reached. Turn left (looking out) and follow the path to just past the next stone wall. Drop diagonally right, down a steep hillside to reach another stone wall. Follow the valley bottom to reach a rickety stile in the cliff-top fence.

Guillemot Ledge - cross the stile to find the lower cliff-top quarry on the left. The main abseil and gearing-up ledge lies at the base of the deep gully on the right (looking out) of the stile. Steep rock-steps lead down a gully to a small ledge. There is an abseil stake cemented into the back of the ledge.

Cormorant Ledge - from the rickety stile, follow the fence line left to a wall. Continue along the fence line and cross the fence at the 4th wooden stile (about 150m from the wall). Drop down a steep path into a small quarry. An abseil stake is in the floor of the quarry 25m from where the path enters.

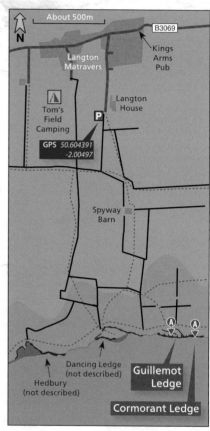

Access

All the routes on the Guillemot Ledge West cliff have restrictions due to nesting birds. **No climbing from March 1st to July 31st.**

Tides and Conditions

The bases of the cliffs at Guillemot Ledge are non-tidal, however the approach to Guillemot Ledge West is cut off for a short time around high water. The base of Cormorant Ledge can be accessed for 4 hours either side of low water in calm sea-conditions. Both cliffs can get very hot.

Left margin tabs: Avon Somerset | North Devon | Culm Coast | Inland Cornwall | Atlantic Coast | West Penwith | The Lizard | Inland Devon | Torbay | Dorset

Avon Somerset

North Devon

Culm Coast

Inland Cornwall

Atlantic Coast

West Penwith

The Lizard

Inland Devon

Torbay

Dorset

On the first pitch of *Tensor II* (VS 5a) - *page 396* -
Guillemot Ledge, Swanage.

Guillemot Ledge West

A large and fairly serious section of Swanage that has some very good, harder multi-pitch lines.

Approach - From the base of the abseil, boulder-hop right (looking out) around a large buttress for 100m to below the towering white face. Left of this is a massive sea-cave.

Tides - The boulder-beach below the face is non-tidal but calm seas are needed to get to the face from below the abseil point.

① Tudor Rose E2 5b

A remote route that takes a looping line across the hanging wall above the sea cave, then back across the capping white wall high on the face. Start at the right-hand end of the sea cave overhangs.
1) 5b, 42m. Move onto a ledge and pull up a short, steep wall to a slab on the right. Move steeply up left to a crack-line and jugs. Traverse left to a tiny short corner and rest ledge at its top. Move left to a short right-facing corner, then traverse left once again to the base of a corner/groove line. Climb this past the mid-height fault-line to a belay on ledges above.
2) 5b, 25m. From the right-hand end of the ledge move up a flake, and into a shallow groove on the left. Make a tricky move to a good horizontal crack above, then traverse rightwards to a narrow ledge. Move right along the ledge to a blocky corner and climb this with care to the top. Belay on fence posts.
FA. Richard Crewe, P.Charman 5.5.1974

 Access - A bird ban is in effect on this face between March 1st and July 31st.

② Facedancin' E3 6a

Stupendous wall-climbing up the best line on the face. The climbing is hard, and high in the grade, but the gear is very good on the hardest sections. Start as for *Tudor Rose* at the right-hand end of the sea cave overhangs. *Photo opposite.*
1) 6a, 25m. Follow *Tudor Rose* to the good, small rest-ledge on its traverse and then climb up to a narrow overhang. Move up to the groove above and make a very hard move to enter it and exit right to a good hold. Climb the short wall above to the fault-line and a hanging belay on nuts, cams and a thread.
2) 6a, 25m. From the fault-line, move up right for 5m and then step left to a footledge. Move up to the base of the white wall, then climb thin breaks and flakes, past twin pegs, to another peg, and a final, long move to a good hold just below a long ledge. Stand on the ledge, and traverse rightwards to a blocky corner. Climb this with care to the top. Belay on fence posts.
FA. Martin Crocker, Jim Robertson 8.1.1983

③ Warlord E4 6a

A great top pitch that heads up the leaning white headwall at its highest point. Start on the huge boulders right of the sea cave.
1) 5a, 22m. From the top of the boulders, move out left across a slab to the base of a broken crack-line. Follow the crack-line, past a niche, and move right to a belay on a ledge on the slab.
2) 6a, 24m. Move diagonally left, then back rightwards above an overhang to a small ledge and a peg. Follow the tapering crack above, past a large, wedged 'cornflake', to fingery moves that gain the final, slightly broken wall. Belay on fence posts. The crack has lots of pegs insitu, however some of them have very narrow eyes, so some narrow krabs will be useful to clip them.
FAA. Brian Snell, Keith Knight 21.2.1976
FFA. Steve Monks, Steve Findlay 28.11.1981

Avon Somerset

North Devon

Culm Coast

Inland Cornwall

Atlantic Coast

West Penwith

The Lizard

Inland Devon

Torbay

Dorset

Marti Hallett heading up the superb wall climb of *Facedancin'* (E3 6a) - *opposite* - at Guillemot Ledge West, Swanage. He is just below the point where *Tudor Rose* (E2 5b) heads left.

1 Sapphire .... ⟨3⟩ 🦀 ▮▮▮▮ **E1 5b**

A much-attempted route that features a spectacular and powerful top pitch. Start beneath a huge rectangular depression that meets the overhangs at the mid-height break.

1) 4b, 18m. From right of the low overhangs, move leftwards above them and climb the steady wall, with little in the way of gear, to a thread and nut belay in the rectangular depression.

2) 5b, 16m. Gain the fault beneath the overhang and move left to an arete. Pull over the roof (2 pegs) to reach the next roofs. Traverse rightwards underneath these and finish up a crack, past a bulge to the top.

FA. George Smith, Kenny Winkworth 3.4.1972

2 The Spook .... ⟨3⟩ ✏️ ▮▮▮▮ **E1 5b**

A sustained, varied climb and one of the best E1s at Swanage. Start under a prominent smooth-sided corner.

1) 5a, 18m. Climb a corner to the roof, and swing right to beneath the smooth-sided corner. Climb the fine corner to the mid-height break on a ledge to the right.

2) 5b, 15m. Step right onto the wall and climb up to the chert band, and an old hidden peg. There is a small cam placement around to the right and a large nut up and left; these protect the pull through the overhang. Finish up the bold wall.

FA. Richard Crewe, P.Sharman 31.3.1974

3 Tensor II .... ⟨3⟩ ✏️ ⛏️ ▮▮▮▮ **VS 5a**

One of the very best VSs at Swanage. Both technical and sustained, but furnished with good protection. Start at a raised ledge below a corner next to a massive boulder. *Photo on page 393.*

1) 4c, 20m. Climb the corner until level with an overhang on the left. Traverse beneath this and pull up the wall on good holds to a good ledge and huge flake belay.

2) 5a, 15m. Stand on the flake, then either climb with difficulty direct to the next wide break, or at about the same difficulty, step left and move up to the break. Climb past the overhang above on its left, and finish up the corner above.

FA. Brian Snell, W.Lyons 8.12.1973

Guillemot Ledge East

A popular area with easy access, good mid-grade routes and clean finishes. The routes are a bit shorter than on the West Face and many have a friendly feel.

Approach - The routes are reached along the boulderfield below the wall from the base of the abseil.

Tides - Non-tidal.

Conditions - It can get very hot.

4 Ledgend Direct .... ⟨3⟩ ✏️ ▮▮▮▮ **HVS 5a**

A popular, but exhausting route up a gear-packed corner, 9m right of *Ledgend*. It has taken a lot of scalps over the years and fully merits its HVS grade.

1) 5a, 18m. Climb a wall to gain the corner which leads steeply to a ledge on the left, as for *Ledgend*.

2) 4a, 15m. Step right off the ledge then move up for 5m. Traverse left to reach the quarry. Care required with loose flakes.

FA. D.Burgess, J.Allen, R.Colledge 11.4.66 Ledgend
FA. P.Neame, A.Monnery 12.2.67 Ledgend Direct

5 Batt Crack .... ⟨2⟩ ▮▮▮▮ **VS 4c**

A popular route. Start just right of *Ledgend Direct*.

1) 4c, 18m. Climb a short wall to a ledge, then move right to enter and follow a corner to an overhang. Go right to belay.

2) 4a, 18m. Ascend a groove and flakes, then move right and up to a ledge. Pass another ledge and a small roof on the left.

FA. D.Hadlum, G.Reynolds 25.3.1967

6 Yellow Wall .... ⟨3⟩ ✏️ ▮▮▮▮ **E1 5b**

More fine wall-climbing. Start just left of a big groove.

1) 5b, 20m. Climb the wall, trending left to a down-pointing spike. Move left past a bulge and a peg, into a shallow groove. Belay on the left.

2) 5b, 20m. Trend steeply right under blocks, then move over to a small ledge. Move on and rightwards, around an arete, into a corner with a large flake. Finish up this, exiting left.

FA. Richard Crewe, A.Wilde, P.Crewe 3.4.72

Lots of sun | 25 min | Multi-pitch | Abseil

Avon Somerset | North Devon | Culm Coast | Inland Cornwall | Atlantic Coast | West Penwith | The Lizard | Inland Devon | Torbay | Dorset

Descent

Ledgend

Line of abseil

⑦ Quality Street . . . . ❄ 🔧 ▭ **HVS 4c**

A marvellous pitch on excellent holds and with the added benefit of a solid finish. One of Swanage's best HVSs.

30m. Move up the wall on great holds to a flake at 10m, before climbing rightwards on steeper ground to gain the fault-line (possible belay). Gain the steep wall on the left above the fault-line and take this to an overhang. Go left and up into a shallow corner with difficulty, before easier bridging and crack-climbing gains a solid finish.

FA. Richard Crewe, P.Charman 10.2.1974

⑧ Wall Street . . . . ❄ 🔧 ▭ **HS 4b**

Impressive wall-climbing in a remote setting provides a memorable Swanage experience at the grade. Start down and left of a crack in the wall. *Photo on page 372.*

1) 4b, 21m. Good holds lead up and right to meet the crack. Climb the crack to the fault-line and traverse rightwards until it is possible to move up on good holds to a stance on ledges on the arete.

2) 4b, 10m. The steep, shallow corner above gains a solid top-out.

FA. Richard Crewe, Kenny Winkworth 29.3.1970

| Lots of sun | 25 min | Multi-pitch | Abseil in | Tidal |

Cormorant Ledge

A superb section of cliff that hides two of Swanage's best mid-grade climbs. Can be easily combined with the neighbouring Guillemot Ledge.

Approach - The routes are reached by abseil. The line of the abseil is 3m right of the stake down a corner (facing out).

Tides - All the climbs are possible at low to mid tide and in calm seas.

Conditions - A sheltered bay that is a suntrap.

Avon Somerset · North Devon · Culm Coast · Inland Cornwall · Atlantic Coast · West Penwith · The Lizard · Inland Devon · Torbay · Dorset

⑦   ⑧

Avon Somerset

North Devon

Culm Coast

Inland Cornwall

Atlantic Coast

West Penwith

The Lizard

Inland Devon

Torbay

Dorset

Gavin Symonds on the outrageous 45m prow of *Infinite Gravity* (8a+) - *page 401* - at Blacker's Hole, Swanage. One of the UK's most impressive sport-climbs. Photo: Mike Robertson

Blacker's Hole, Fisherman's Ledge and The Promenade are a formidable trio of steep cliffs. The majority of the climbs described are very hard sport-climbs. All of the routes are extremely steep, most emerging from massive caves or tackling gravity-defying buttresses that lurch out over the sea. Fisherman's Ledge is also one of the UK's most popular deep water soloing venues - its overhanging walls, solid rock and blue waters making it the ideal starting point for dipping a toe (or a bit more!) into this thrilling off-shoot of sea-cliff climbing.

Approach   See main area map on page 390
Drive through the centre of Swanage, and pick up signs for Durlston Castle and Country Park. Drive to the Country Park car park (fee). Walk west along the tarmac road from the car park to the coast path. Head west (right, looking out) along the coast path to two 'one mile' pylons. The various approaches are described from here in the individual cliff introductions.

Access
Access to all the routes in the Polaris and Great Cave area is restricted because of nesting birds.
No climbing from March 1st to July 31st.

Tides and Conditions
The caves are all susceptible to dampness and can take time to dry out. However, once in condition they stay sheltered from the rain, although they are a longish walk from the car park.

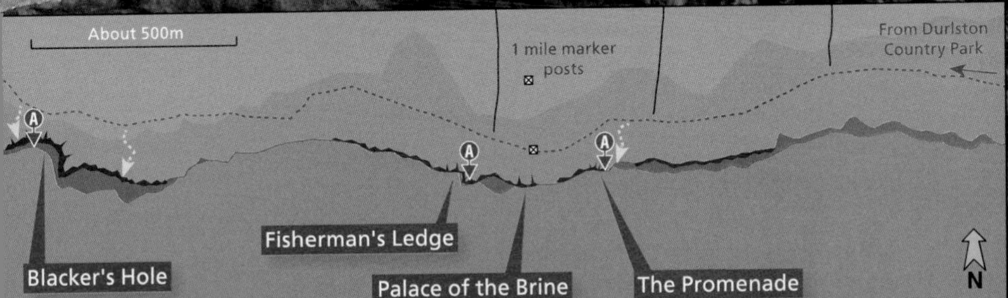

Avon Somerset

North Devon

Culm Coast

Inland Cornwall

Atlantic Coast

West Penwith

The Lizard

Inland Devon

Torbay

Dorset

About 500m

1 mile marker posts

From Durlston Country Park

Blacker's Hole

Fisherman's Ledge

Palace of the Brine

The Promenade

N

Avon Somerset

North Devon

Culm Coast

Inland Cornwall

Atlantic Coast

West Penwith

The Lizard

Inland Devon

Torbay

Dorset

Blacker's Hole

Two very impressive routes that lie at either end of the gaping mouth of Blacker's Hole.

Approach - Walk past the 'mile' pylons and around a wide bay. Cross two walls and 200m past the second wall locate a hidden descent ramp that leads down to the base of a quarry. Walk right (facing out) and then traverse around a buttress (E1) and into Blacker's Hole and a boulder-beach below the route. There is sometimes a rope in place.

Polaris approach - 150m west of Blacker's Hole locate a stile on a 90 degree bend in the fence, cross over the stile and go directly downhill for 40m to a big stake. Gear up and abseil down the very steep grass to a pair of stakes, from where another abseil gains the base of the route.

Tides - Blacker's Hole is non-tidal, although lower tides are preferable. For *Polaris,* a low to mid tide is needed for the sea level ledge to be exposed.

Conditions - Blacker's Hole takes time to come into condition.

Belay stake up grass-slope

Abseil down grass to this point

Ⓐ

Ledge covered at high tide

①

Lots of sun | 45 min | Abseil in | | Tidal

Access - A bird ban is in effect on Blacker's Hole between March 1st and July 31st.

Afternoon | 45 min

Descent-ramp to quarry

Boulder-beach above high tide

②

Approach (E1)

❶ Polaris . . . . 〈3〉 [icons] E5 6a

A Swanage classic. High-calibre traditional adventure that gains the large open corner above the left side of Blacker's Hole. The climbing on the upper pitches is steep and exposed, but the protection is reasonable. Abseil to a stance at sea level.

1) 4c, 30m. Climb the left-hand crack past an overhang to the fault-line and traverse rightwards to the arete (or better, traverse rightwards at a slightly lower level). Continue the traverse to a belay below a large open groove.

2) 6a, 15m. A very exposed pitch. Move down onto the main arete and climb a steep thin crack to a hand traverse line across a leaning wall. Follow this right to a final tough move onto a belay ledge above the huge roof.

3) 5c, 25m. Climb the wall 2m right of the corner to a hidden peg. Move left and follow a slanting crack to a rest at the bottom of the big upper corner. Climb the sustained corner past a bulge to a slab and finish up steep grass to a stake belay.
FA. Arni Strapcans, Gordon Jenkin, Frank Farrell 13.8.1978

❷ Infinite Gravity . . . . Top〈7〉 L50 [icon] 8a+

The awesome 'ship's prow' that protrudes from the depths of Blacker's Hole is a stellar line, and one of the UK's best sport climbs. The line is fully equipped with staple bolts. Start at the base of the 45 degree overhanging prow. *Photo on page 398.*
45m. Follow the very steep groove to a shakeout and then proceed through the overhangs via a crack to another shakeout. The last section follows an arching crack and horizontal breaks leftward to some final pressing moves.
FA. Pete Oxley 4.1992

Fisherman's Ledge

A fantastic deep-water-soloing arena that has two of the very best, one on each of its walls. The ledges on top are spacious, and swimming off the lower ledge is safe.
Approach - Locate a stile just before the 'mile' pylons. Cross the fence, follow a path on its seaward side and then follow a slight ridge down towards the sea and the ledges atop the cliff. Abseil or downclimb to the base of the cliff.

❸ The Conger . . . . . . 〈3〉 [icons] E2 5c

The entire pitch is above a fathom or ten of water, so when the sea is inviting it is usually soloed (S1). The climbing is varied, and the rock, apart from the final few easy metres, is perfect. Start on a sea-level ledge at the base of the descent.

30m. Traverse the low break just above sea level into the cove itself, until moves up a chimney allow the hanging wall on the left to be accessed. Traverse the wall to a corner, then make a tricky sequence of moves around the arete, and into a bottomless chimney. Bridge across the chimney, then pull over onto the opposite wall from where an easy ramp above leads leftwards to the top.
FA. Richard Crewe 7.9.1969
FFA. Frank Farrell 9.1979
FSA. Nick Buckley 26.6.1983

❹ Freeborn Man . . . . . 〈3〉 [icons] E4 6a

Brilliant and committing climbing that increases in difficulty as height is gained. Often climbed as a DWS (S1). Splashdowns from the final steep moves are not uncommon! Start on a sea-level ledge at the base of the descent.

20m. Traverse the low break just above sea level into the cove itself, until about halfway to the back and below the gradually steepening wall. Climb up the slab and the pocketed wall above to a hole. Make a committing move leftwards, and climb up onto the finishing slab.
FA. Nick Buckley, Kevin Turner 8.1979

Abseil or down-
climb (Diff)

Avon Somerset · North Devon · Culm Coast · Inland Cornwall · Atlantic Coast · West Penwith · The Lizard · Inland Devon · Torbay · Dorset

❶ Impending Gleam E4 5c

A sensational pitch that climbs the continuous crack in the left wall of the cave. Start from the wave-washed platform on the left of the cave under a steep groove.

25m. Climb the steep groove to a niche at 5m, and make a hard move out of it. The strenuous crack and groove higher up give little respite. The lower section of the route can be greasy if big seas have been running.

FA. Nick Buckley, N.Stein 1983

❷ Temple Redneck . . . 7c+

A tremendous route. Start at an arete on the left-hand side of the cave.

30m. Climb the right-hand side of the arete to a roof, then move up left through it to a rest. Continue out across the overhang and leaning wall above to a break and then swing left to a lower-off station.

FA. Pete Oxley 21.2.1993

❸ The Mind Cathedral. E6 6b

The original line through the cave roof is a masterpiece. Start at a chimney on the left side of the cave.

1) 6b, 27m. Climb the chimney and overhanging groove above to the roof of the cave, 2 threads. Using flakes move out left to a handrail, thread, and continue, thread, to a belay in a niche. This is also the lower-off station for *Temple Redneck*.

2) 5a, 7m. Finish up the short wall.

FA. Pete Oxley, Steve Williams 21.5.1988

❹ Palace of the Brine . . . . 8a+

An incredible roof climb that follows a severely overhanging groove out to the lip of the cave. Start on a high ledge at the back of the cave.

30m. Climb a wall, crack and flake to the roof. Move out to the main groove-line in the roof, and work out along this to the lip of the cave. Pass the lip and climb the short wall to the top and a stake belay.

FA. Pete Oxley 21.9.1991

Palace of the Brine

A huge cave with an array of big and burly pitches.

Approach - At low water, walk to the routes from the base of the Fisherman's Ledge abseil-decent. At high tide *Palace of the Brine* can be approached by abseiling directly to the ledge below the left side of the cave (looking out). The abseil is from 2 stakes about 20m below and east of the pylon. From the ledge at the bottom of the abseil, traverse to a small stance 5m up the wall.

Tides - The approach and cave floor are tidal.

Conditions - Finding good conditions in the cave can be difficult once it becomes damp.

Sun and shade | 40 min | Abseil in | Tidal

High tide access from base of abseil

Approach...

❺ Waves Become Wings . . ⏱🪝☐ **7b+**

When in condition, this is a superb pitch. Start under the left side of the gently overhanging white wall.

25m. Step over the trench and climb the wall to some hard, fingery moves midway. Finish up a groove and wall with less difficulty.

FA. Pete Oxley, Mark Higgs 19.6.1994

❻ Birth Pains of New Nations

. . . . ⏱🪝🪝☐ **7b**

Fine climbing and rock but no give-away at the grade. Start below the centre of the face.

25m. Step over the trench and climb the leaning wall past a hand-ledge to a groove. Finish up the groove and wall above as for *Waves Become Wings*.

FA. Pete Oxley 8.10.1986

❼ Tessellations . . . . . ⏱🪝🪝☐ **7b**

The bulging arete of the buttress is a fantastic climb. Start on a protruding section of the ledge below the arete.

25m. Climb the lower wall to steeper rock on the arete. Move up a steep groove and then work rightwards, on sloping holds, and pull up into a narrow corner. Climb the corner and easier wall above to a lower-off.

FA. Pete Oxley, Crispin Waddy 10.7.1986

The Promenade

The Promenade is one of Swanage's most extensive sections of cliff, predominantly devoted to sport climbing. Most of the better pitches are in the harder grades. The centrepiece is the severely bulging buttress to the west of the descent.

Approach - From Durlston Car park, follow the road towards the lighthouse then turn west (right, when looking out) along the coast path. Continue to a stile, just before the two 'mile' pylons. From here, drop down a steep grass-gully to a ledge above a large rock amphitheatre. Descend this (Diff) past a tricky step at the bottom to gain the platform. There are abseil bolts if required (the rope can be pulled down afterwards) and this is probably advisable on a first visit.

Tides - The base of the buttress is non-tidal, although it is wave-washed in moderate or rough seas.

Conditions - The west face needs a bit of afternoon sun on it to burn off any moisture, whilst the front face is one of the more reliable sections of cliff to find in good condition.

❽ Total Seizure . . . . . ⏱🪝🖐☐ **7c+**

A super-steep and spectacular pitch that weaves through the tiered overhangs on the front of the bulging buttress. Start on a protruding ledge.

20m. Climb an easy groove to the roof. Cross the large roof before moving rightwards and then back left up steep ground to a lower-off.

FA. Pete Oxley 11.6.1994

Downclimb or abseil

Approach along broken ledge

Avon Somerset · North Devon · Culm Coast · Inland Cornwall · Atlantic Coast · West Penwith · The Lizard · Inland Devon · Torbay · Dorset

	No star	☼	☼☼	☼☼☼
Mod to S	-	-	-	-
HS to HVS	-	-	3	5
E1 to E3	-	-	1	8
E4 and up	-	-	2	2

Avon Somerset

North Devon

Culm Coast

Inland Cornwall

Atlantic Coast

West Penwith

The Lizard

Inland Devon

Torbay

Dorset

Nearing the finish of the long and very sustained pitch of *Mother Africa* (E4 6a) - *page 407* - at the Ocean Boulevard Wall, Swanage. Climber Dave Henderson.

Swanage's Boulder Ruckle is the place to head for some memorable and challenging trad-climbing. The style of climbing is predominately on steep faces and cracks, and is generally strenuous, but on the whole well-protected. Many of the climbs are multi-pitch, and all require an abseil approach to the base of the cliff. The abseils are long and free-hanging, which adds to the feeling of commitment of the routes in 'The Ruckle'.

Approach   See main area map on page 390

Drive through the centre of Swanage and pick up signs for Durlston Castle and Country Park. Drive to the Country Park car park (fee). Walk west along the tarmac road from the car park to the coast path. Head west (right, when looking out) along the coast path. A cliff-top track runs below the coastal path, and the abseil stakes are found near this lower path. The first area is a 10 minute walk, and the furthest area takes 20. Details of the various approaches are listed with the individual cliff introductions.

Access

There are restrictions in the Old Faithful Area from March 1st to July 31st due to nesting birds.

Tides

Most of the areas are untroubled by the tides due to the line of huge blocks and boulders along the bottom, but avoid Boulder Ruckle entirely if the sea is rough.

Conditions

The whole cliff faces due-south, and is a big suntrap. This is good in winter, but may be too hot in summer, although it is shady after 6pm.

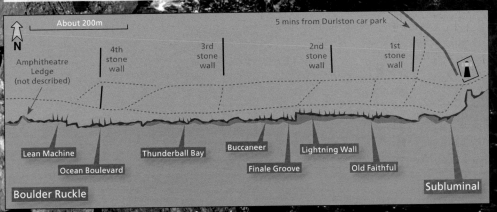

5 mins from Durlston car park

About 200m

N

4th stone wall   3rd stone wall   2nd stone wall   1st stone wall

Amphitheatre Ledge (not described)

Lean Machine
Ocean Boulevard
Thunderball Bay
Buccaneer
Finale Groove
Lightning Wall
Old Faithful
Subluminal

Boulder Ruckle

Avon Somerset | North Devon | Culm Coast | Inland Cornwall | Atlantic Coast | West Penwith | The Lizard | Inland Devon | Torbay | Dorset

Avon Somerset | North Devon | Culm Coast | Inland Cornwall | Atlantic Coast | West Penwith | The Lizard | Inland Devon | Torbay | Dorset

Ocean Boulevard Area

Two fantastic overhanging walls, which provide some long, and very pumpy wall-pitches of the highest quality. Protection and the rock quality are both excellent.

Approach - Follow the coast path to the 4th stonewall. Just before it, a small grass-gully leads a few metres down towards the cliff edge and numerous stakes. Abseil from the stakes to the base of the cliff. The abseil ends at the base of *Ocean Boulevard*. For *The Lean Machine,* walk 50m beyond the 4th wall (17 fence posts). Climb over the fence and head down through a break in the bushes to the cliff edge. 5m to the right are two stakes. Abseil from the stakes to the large boulder at the start of the line.

Tides - The area is non-tidal in calm conditions. It is only possible to walk between the walls at low tide.

Conditions - The rock dries quickly but can be sandy in the breaks after storms or if the routes have not had much traffic.

Lots of sun | 20 min | Abseil in

30m from coast path

Poor rock

Belay and pull out on abseil rope

Non-tidal boulder

① Ocean Boulevard (50m) →

② ③ ④

Thunderball Area 200m →

❶ The Lean Machine E5 6a

An incredibly steep and pumpy climb that wends its withering way up a series of well-protected cracks in the centre of the wall. Start on top of a massive boulder at the base of the abseil.

40m. From the boulder, climb a thin crack to the low horizontal break. Move left and climb the accommodating crack-line rightwards on good holds until a move up left gains a small right leaning overhang. Move out right up the wall via a thin crack and then up to belay on the abseil rope where the angle drops back. Pull out on the rope to finish.

FA. Martin Crocker, Jim Robertson 11.6.1983

❷ Ocean Boulevard ..... Top 50 E3 5b

An outstanding Swanage classic, which follows the steep cracks and mid-height bulge towards the left-hand side of the wall. Very pumpy but also very well protected. Start at a slab just right of the base of the unrelenting crack-line.

40m. Follow the slab easily left to the base of the crack-line and climb it to the mid-height horizontal break. Pull through the steep bulge above to a shake out at a good hold on the left. Continue up the thinner, but less steep, crack above the good hold to a point where a step left gains easier climbing and the top.

FA. Kevin Turner, Nick Buckley, S.Bartlett 3.1979 (with a belay midway)
FFA. Steve Monks, Gordon Jenkin 21.11.1981

❸ Mother Africa E4 6a

Superbly sustained climbing taking an intricate line up the very centre of the wall. Start at the base of the wall, below a thin crack with a rope sling at the midway horizontal break. *Photo on page 404.*

40m. Climb the first few easy-angled metres to the start of the thin crack. Make hard, but well-protected moves up the crack to the horizontal break and an insitu rope-sling. Move left, then up, past good holds and a peg before gaining a thin crack-line on the left. Follow the crack-line past four more pegs to finish.

FA. Martin Crocker, Jim Robertson 5.6.1983

❹ Wall of the Worlds . E5 6a

A truly fantastic pitch. Sustained, well protected and with a pressing crux-move high on the wall. Start below the very thin line of cracks in a slight depression on the upper wall and just right of the rope sling at the midway break on *Mother Africa*.

40m. Move up the wall on good holds to a narrow ledge. Harder climbing past white blotches gains the horizontal break above, from which sustained moves through the bulge and up the line of thin cracks lead past a jug, but without much respite, to a bulge. A hard couple of moves up and right past a peg gain a thread and the final short wall.

FA. Martin Crocker, Jim Robertson 12.6.1983

❺ Thunderball E1 5b

An incredibly intimidating line that requires good route-finding on the second pitch, which snakes through the upper overhangs. Start 7m right of a large roof capped corner.

1) 5a, 16m. Pull up through bulges to a rest above. Climb rightwards to an arete, then move around it to a corner that ends at the fault-line and a belay.

2) 5b, 19m. Climb the wall on the left, past a small overhang, then move right to below a roof. Pull strenuously through the roof at a break to a corner. Follow this to a final overhang which is passed on its left side. Stake belays in place above.

FA. P.Bell, T.Goodfellow 11.7.1963

❻ Jo .... HVS 5a

A brilliant climb. Varied, well protected and in a remote location. Start at the back of the bay at a cave.

1) 4c, 17m. Climb the right wall of the cave to a ledge. Bridge up past a roof and continue up a corner to a belay at the fault-line.

2) 5a, 19m. Move up onto the wall above the stance and head rightwards, thread, to a bulge, Pull over the bulge to a corner and finish up this. Stake belays in place above.

FA. Richard Crewe and team 16.6.1968

Avon Somerset | North Devon | Culm Coast | Inland Cornwall | Atlantic Coast | West Penwith | The Lizard | Inland Devon | Torbay

← Ocean Boulevard Area 200m

Lots of sun | 20 min

Thunderball Area

An intimidating bay that is capped with some large overhangs through which the routes find a way.

Approach - Follow the coast path to the 4th stonewall, just before it a small grass-gully leads a few metres down towards the cliff edge and numerous stakes. Abseil from the stakes to the base of the cliff. The abseil ends at the base of *Ocean Boulevard*. Scramble left for 200m (facing out) along the boulders at the base of the cliff to the Thunderball Bay.

Tides - The area is non-tidal in calm conditions.

Avon Somerset · North Devon · Culm Coast · Inland Cornwall · Atlantic Coast · West Penwith · The Lizard · Inland Devon · Torbay · Dorset

❶ Mickey Mouse E3 6a

Well-positioned climbing with a generous helping of exposure on the top pitch. Start at the base of the right-leaning crack that rises to meet the large corner, which is around 170m to the west of the abseil descent. The corner itself is the line of *Buccaneer*.

1) 5b, 20m. Climb the crack to meet up with the corner. Climb the corner, via a strenuous section to pass a bulge, to reach the fault-line. Traverse left to a ledge and belay.

2) 6a, 25m. Climb the wall above the belay to a flake and follow it rightwards to a corner. Move up the corner a short way, until a leftward-trending line across the corner's left wall can be followed to reach a good hold on the arete, peg. Move up onto the hanging slab before climbing left and up more easily to finish.

FA. Brian Snell, Richard Crewe, T.Tanswell 8.2.1975
FFA. Arni Strapcans, Gordon Jenkin 1.1978

❷ Buccaneer E2 5b

The huge roof-capped corner is a magnificent line that gradually increases in difficulty with height, and features a thrilling and airy finale. Start at twin cracks in the corner.

43m. Climb the cracks to the fault-line, and continue (past a possible belay stance) to below the roof. Climb up under the roof to a massive thread. Drop back down and climb out left and up via steep and sustained ground to a still difficult final crack.

FA. Richard Crewe, Kenny Winkworth 7.6.1969
FFA. Gordon Jenkin, Richard Harrison 2.1978

❸ Finale Groove . . . . HVS 5a

West of the abseil-descent is an eye-catching, tapering corner-groove that runs up the full-height of the cliff. This is the line of *Finale Groove*. As a bonus, it also has good rock and gear. Start at the base of the corner that is 70m to the west of the abseil descent.

42m. Climb the wide corner-crack to some steeper ground, which leads to the narrower corner above the fault-line. Follow the corner to the top. The climbing is low in the technical grade, but there is a lot of it.

FA. George Smith, D.Hadlum 12.4.1966

Finale Groove Area

A steep section of cliff that is seamed with corner-cracks and a liberal smattering of overhangs which make for some exhilarating climbs.

Approach - About 400m (22 fence posts beyond the 2nd stone wall) along from the lighthouse is the jutting Marmolata Buttress. Make a free-hanging abseil, from stakes, down its East Face (left looking out). The Finale Groove Area is to the right of the abseil (looking out) and the Lightning Wall Area is to the left.

Tides - Non-tidal in calm seas.

Conditions - A very hot spot in warm weather.

❹ The Heidelberg Creature . . . VS 4c

An outrageously steep corner-line that is well protected but high in the grade. Start on a small ledge below the corner.

1) 4c, 20m. Climb the corner and make a steep pull up left to a ledge below an overhang at 8m. Continue steeply up the corner on good holds to a ledge and belay at the fault-line.

2) 4b, 20m. Pull through the overhang using a finger-crack and move up to a slim corner. Climb the sustained corner to a sloping ledge on the right at its end. Place some good gear and finish carefully up the short, loose wall above.

FA. Tony Willmott, A.Heppenstall 18.9.1966

❺ Tatra . . . . VS 5a

The best VS in Boulder Ruckle. A great expedition with diverse climbing and situations. Well protected but at the upper limit of the grade. Start on a ledge below a large sentry box.

1) 5a, 18m. Climb up until a move right can be made to the base of a crack in the right wall of the sentry box. Climb the crack and pull right to an easing at the right-hand side of the overhang above. Follow the steep crack to a ledge and thread belay.

2) 4b, 10m. Move right along a footledge to a short vertical crack. Pull up the crack to the break and make a strenuous traverse along this to a ledge and belay just around the arete.

3) 4c, 20m. Climb the large corner above the belay via some wide bridging, past a wobbly hold to a ledge and finish up a short, steep corner. *Photo opposite.*

FA. Barry Annette, P.Kemp pre 1963

Gearing-up spot on the top of Marmolata Buttress

100m to Finale Groove

40m free abseil

A

① ② ③ ④ ⑤

Carrie Hill negotiating the crucial moves out of the sentry box on the first pitch of the Boulder Ruckle classic *Tatra* (VS 5a) - *opposite* - Swanage.

Avon Somerset

North Devon

Culm Coast

Inland Cornwall

Atlantic Coast

West Penwith

The Lizard

Inland Devon

Torbay

Dorset

Lightning Wall Area

The impressive sheer wall to the east of the summit of Marmolata Buttress is one of Swanage's most popular sections of cliff. The climbs are all very sustained and most are fairly strenuous.

Approach - About 400m (22 fence posts beyond the second stone wall) along from the lighthouse is the jutting bulk of Marmolata Buttress. Make a free-hanging abseil, from stakes, down its East Face (left, when looking out). The Lightning Wall Area is to the left of the abseil (looking out).

Tides - Non-tidal, and very well shielded from the sea by a substantial boulder-beach, which means access is possible in most seas.

Conditions - A very hot spot in warm weather.

❶ Lightning Wall . . . . ⌗ 🗲 ☐ HVS 5a

An intimidating, but essential tick of the Boulder Ruckle. The route climbs the vast wall that is easily viewed from the abseil point and gearing-up spot on top of the Marmolata Buttress. Start below a groove, just left of a deep corner 25m from the base of the abseil.

42m. Enter the groove and follow it to the fault-line. Move right and up through a bulge into a short corner. Move right onto the wall above the roof and traverse this up rightwards on good holds to the arete. Follow the arete to a niche, old peg, move up and then head right to an easier corner that leads to the top.

FA. George Smith, A.Webster 10.4.1966

❷ Elysium . . . . ⌗ 🗲 ☐ E1 5b

A great, technical pitch. Well protected, with good rock. Start 5m right of a large corner, beneath a huge roof at the fault-line.

38m. Climb a crack to a ledge at the base of a thin crack in the smooth wall below the roof. Climb the thin crack past a peg to the roof, traverse rightwards to below a corner and climb this strenuously to another corner (or climb the wall just right of the corner which is less awkward). Move left around the arete to join and finish more easily up *Lightning Wall*.

FA. Richard Crewe, Kenny Winkworth 7.1.1968

❸ Dune Dust . . . . ⌗ 🖾 ☐ E4 6a

A good route that maintains interest throughout both its pitches. The pegs are old but there is good gear available to back them up. Start below an overhung, right-leaning corner.

1) 6a, 25m. Move up the right-leaning corner for 5m, then pull straight up through the bulge to gain a horizontal break. Climb the thin black streak above, 2 pegs, to the main fault-line. Move right and up through a bulge to a corner and a stance.

2) 4c, 12m. Climb up and leftwards around an arete to enter and finish up a corner.

FA. Pete Oxley, J.Preston 5.9.1986

❹ Gypsy . . . . ⌗ 🗲 ☐ E2 5b

Well-travelled and protectable climbing, being sustained but never desperate. Start below a slim right-facing corner in the smooth face, below the main fault-line.

1) 5b, 16m. Pull up strenuously onto a ledge and move up a corner to an overhang. Climb another overhang and the slim corner to the fault-line and belay.

2) 5b, 22m. Step right and pull through the overhang into a open groove. Follow the groove to an overhang before moving right and climbing to the top.

FA. Richard Crewe, Kenny Winkworth 29.10.1967

❺ Vortices. . . . . ⌗ 🗲 ☐ E2 5c

A mix of the sustained and strenuous on a strong line makes this a route worth tracking down. Start right of a corner, below a large roof.

1) 5c, 20m. Move up the thin wall to a large hanging flake. Move right into a short corner, and traverse rightwards again, until just beyond a vertical crack. Climb the wall on reasonable holds to the fault-line and belay.

2) 5b, 20m. Pull onto the wall above, follow it to a corner, and take this to the top.

FA. Pete Finklaire, D.Glover 21.4.1985

Line of abseil descent down Marmolata Buttress

Ⓐ

Old Faithful Area

A secluded and rather special section of cliff with a number of steep and airy climbs. The routes have the added benefit of reasonably solid finishes.

Approach - 14 fence posts after the first stone wall passed on the coast path, a small path leads straight down to a number of abseil stakes. The abseil ends at a large fin-backed boulder.

Tides - The boulder-beach is non-tidal, but keep away in moderate seas when getting along the crag base is tricky.

⑥ Ximenes . . . . 🔲📷🔲 E2 5c

One for those who relish steep and well-protected crack-climbing. Start below the line of steep jamming cracks that cut through the two huge overhangs 10m right of a large corner. The base of the route is tidal.

1) 5c, 18m. Climb up a narrowing chimney and jam or layback with determination up the overhanging crack above to a cramped stance in the fault-line.

2) 5b, 20m. Pull over the roof above on good holds and climb a corner above it to yet another overhang. Move right and pull over the roof before climbing the right-hand of two grooves to an easier finish.

FA. George Smith, Richard Crewe 4.9.1971 (5pts)
FFA. Kevin Turner, Nick Buckley 1977

⑦ Old Faithful . . . . 🔲📷🔲 VS 4c

A good route, featuring great positions and spectacular climbing. Start at the fin-backed boulder at the base of the abseil line.

1) 4b, 13m. Climb the bulging crack-line above the fin-backed boulder to a ledge. Belay at the fault-line.

2) 4c, 21m. Continue up the crack above to a roof. Pull out around the roof and climb the crack to a ledge on the left. Move right into a corner to finish.

FA. R.Kent, Richard Crewe, Kenny Winkworth 4.5.1969

⑧ The Golden Fleece . 🔲📷🔲 HVS 5b

A great HVS, with the added attraction of it being located in a less frequented section of Boulder Ruckle. Start 15m right of the fin-backed boulder at the base of the abseil, at an undercut buttress.

1) 5a, 15m. Move up a steep corner on the right to a ledge on the left. Continue up the tricky wall above to the fault-line and belay at a ledge on the prow to the right.

2) 5b, 22m. Make some hard, but protectable moves off the ledge to gain better holds up on the right. Pull up into a groove above and climb to a ledge on good holds, from where a corner leads to the top.

FA. Richard Crewe, Scott Titt 2.8.1975

⑨ Behemoth . . . . 🔲📷🔲 HVS 5b

Stupendous climbing and positions on the second pitch - up a juggy, overhanging corner. Start at a right-facing corner, 30m right of the base of the abseil. *Photo on page 391.*

1) 5a, 17m. Climb the corner-crack to the roof, then make a tricky little traverse left to a stance at the base of the main corner.

2) 5b, 22m. Climb the magnificent corner, past a bulge, and up the sustained crack to exit right onto a cleaned ledge and belay.

FA. Richard Crewe, George Smith 14.11.1971
FFA. Howard Lancashire, Falco Rech 1.1975

⑩ Soul Sacrifice . . . . 🔲📷🔲 E3 5b

Swanage rock at its very best. A tremendous pitch that features diverse and sustained climbing with reliable protection. Start at the corner-crack of *Behemoth*.

37m. Move up the corner and then take thin cracks in the wall on the right to the fault-line. Make awkward moves up the very narrow chimney in the overhang to a rib, peg. Climb the rib and white headwall on pockets to the top and a cleaned belay ledge.

FA. Martin Crocker, Jim Robertson 2.2.1983

Lots of sun | 15 min | Abseil in | Non-tidal

Access - A bird ban is in effect on this face between March 1st and July 31st.

Line of abseil descent down Old Faithful

Ⓐ

⑩

⑦

⑧

⑨

Large fin-backed block at base of Old Faithful

Avon Somerset · North Devon · Culm Coast · Inland Cornwall · Atlantic Coast · West Penwith · The Lizard · Inland Devon · Torbay · Dorset

	No star	☆	☆☆	☆☆☆
Mod to S	-	3	2	1
HS to HVS	-	1	4	1
E1 to E3	-	1	3	1
E4 and up	-	-	1	-

Avon Somerset

North Devon

Culm Coast

Inland Cornwall

Atlantic Coast

West Penwith

The Lizard

Inland Devon

Torbay

Dorset

Alison Martindale enjoying the lovely upper wall of the Subluminal classic *Freda* (VS 5a) - *page 415* - Swanage.

Subluminal is a very friendly sea-cliff, which has a substantial collection of good, lower-grade trad routes. The majority of the climbs follow strong lines, and for the most part are on sound rock. Subluminal is a popular destination due to its ease of access, pleasant cliff-top ledges and sunny aspect. Just to the east, and directly below the lighthouse is the Black Zawn, offering a very different experience to Subluminal. Black Zawn is a dizzying sight when viewed from its rim and holds some exceptional routes that require both commitment and experience.

Approach   See main area map on page 390

Drive through the centre of Swanage and pick up signs for Durlston Castle and Country Park. Drive to the Country Park car park (fee). Walk west along the tarmac road from the car park to the coast path and walk over to the lighthouse. From the lighthouse, a track leads diagonally right (looking out) down the grass slope to cliff-top ledges situated directly above Subluminal and 100m west of the Black Zawn. The best abseil line is down *High Street*, which also doubles as a good escape route, although other abseil lines exist.

Tides

All the routes, apart from *Avernus*, are non-tidal. A lowish tide and calm seas are required in order to reach the base of *Avernus*.

Conditions

There are no seepage problems at Subluminal, and all the routes face south. *Avernus* can be greasy. The Black Zawn can be damp and slow to dry due to its recessed and sheltered nature. The crag can be very popular at times.

5 mins from Durlston car park

1st stone wall

Black Zawn

Avernus

Subluminal

About 50m

Avon Somerset | North Devon | Culm Coast | Inland Cornwall | Atlantic Coast | West Penwith | The Lizard | Inland Devon | Torbay | Dorset

Subluminal

The solid rock and easily accessible climbing found here are enhanced by a commodious cliff-top ledge to lounge about on, and a high belay ledge that stays dry even in moderate seas. The flat cliff-top is strewn with small shattered rocks so care must be taken to protect those below.

Approach - To reach the belay ledges, abseil from above the chosen climb, take care with teams below. The belay ledge runs under all the climbs, although there are some exposed sections across gaps that some may feel more comfortable roping up for. A downclimb descent can also be made to the left (looking out). For *Avernus* scramble down and around to its base via sea washed ledges. There are many stakes to belay from which vary in quality, so always use a minimum of two, properly equalized.

Conditions - The belay ledges are well above the sea and are often dry in moderate seas. *Avernus* is only accessible at lowish tides and in calm seas.

① **Transcript Direct...** ☒2 🧗🔧⬜ **HVS 5a**
Continually pressing moves but with plentiful protection. A good first taste of Swanage's signature style. Start below the overhang-strewn corner.
13m. Start up the corner and then step left and up into the constricted upper corner-crack to finish.

② **Balcony...........** ☒2 🔧⬜ **HS 4b**
Sustained climbing up to and around the isolated mid-height overhang. Start below the overhang.
13m. Climb the diagonal line leftwards to below the overhang, then move around its right-hand side to stand above it. Move right and climb a good flake-crack to the final short wall.

③ **Gangway..........** ☒1 🔧⬜ **S 4a**
A varied pitch both steep and delicate. Start where the ledge narrows at some steep flakes.
14m. Climb the steep flakes to meet up with the narrow 'gangway' on the right, then follow this to the top.

④ **Stroof.........** ☒2 🔧🧗⬜ **E1 5c**
A much-coveted Subluminal testpiece. Start where the ledge is at its narrowest, below a thin crack in a smooth calcite-mottled wall.
13m. Pull directly through the low bulges to a position under a small roof. Fortify your position with as much gear as you like, before launching up the crack via a hard sequence, until flat holds are reached, where things ease, just below the top.
FA, Tony Willmott 12.1965

⑤ **Spreadeagle.......** ☒2 🧗⬜ **VS 5a**
A technical and well-protected route. Start at a thin crack where the ledge narrows.
13m. Climb the thin crack to a short corner under a roof. Step right and up to below a recessed crack. Climb the well-worn crack via some tricky moves to the top.

⑥ **High Street.........** ☒1 🔧⬜ **Diff**
A popular first-lead at Subluminal. Start at the widest part of the ledge.
13m. Climb onto a squat pedestal and up the well-protected, broken crack. Continue passing some small, projecting ledges and finish up a corner.

Lots of sun	10 min	Abseil in

Many belay stakes on cliff-top

Exposed step across chimney

⑦ Slip Road . . . . 🏃 [____] **VS 4c**
An exposed pitch up the steep buttress at the right-hand end of the wide ledge. Start just left of the 'exposed step' below a flake.
14m. Climb the flake, step right and pull through the overhang with difficulty. Finish up a corner in the upper wall.
FA. Dave Hope, Ed Hart 16.12.1971

⑧ Double Chockstone . . . . 🏃📷 [____] **HVD**
The deep gap in the ledge crossed by the 'awkward move' is capped by a short hanging slab, start below this.
14m. Step up onto the short hanging slab and move up into a massive niche. Climb the chimney above via awkward moves past the chockstones to finish in the cliff-top crevasse.

⑨ First Corner . . . . 🏃📷 [____] **S 4b**
The first of two well-protected, classic corner-lines. A good introduction to the area. Start at the bottomless corner that forms the left hand side of the sheer wall, left of 'The Bad Step'.
14m. Pull straight into the corner, or move in from the left, then climb directly to the top past an awkward bulge at half-height.

⑩ Philatus. . . . . 🏃📷 [____] **E3 5c**
The central line of the sheer wall between *First Corner* and *Second Corner* gives sustained climbing with good, but hard-to-place gear. Start below the wall just right of *First Corner*.
14m. Use the diagonal crack to reach the first overlap, move straight through and pass a second overlap on its right to reach a small niche. The final wall gives a fitting finale.
FA. Tony Willmott 7.1965

⑪ Second Corner . . . . . . 📷 [____] **S 4a**
A well-protected pitch. Start at the shallow corner and crack directly above 'The Bad Step'.
14m. Step in from the right and use twin cracks to gain the corner which gives both enjoyable and thought provoking moves all the way to the top.

⑫ Freda . . . . 📷📷📷📷 [____] **VS 5a**
One of the best of its grade hereabouts. Start just right of the 'The Bad Step', below a thin crack with an old peg in place at 4m.
Photo on page 412.
14m. Climb the thin crack with difficulty, past the peg, to its end. Move slightly left, then head rightwards up the blank looking wall above on good holds to exit past ledges just below top.

⑬ Grandma's Groove . 🏃📷📷 [____] **E2 5c**
A good pitch with a bold lower wall. Start just right of the thin crack of *Freda*.
14m. Climb the fingery lower wall to meet a slim groove that starts on the right-hand side of a tiny overhang at 7m. Climb the groove to ledges just below the top.
FA. Tony Willmott 7.1965

⑭ Avernus . . . . 📷📷 [____] **S 4a**
Unusual in the extreme. A climb that thinks it's a caving trip! Some choose to use a head torch. Start near the back of the cave.
20m. Climb up the chimney and out across the roof on big but difficult-to-spot holds to emerge through the blow hole onto the cliff-top. A memorable trip.
FA. M.Hurn, F.Higgins, D.Partridge 22.8.1971

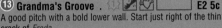

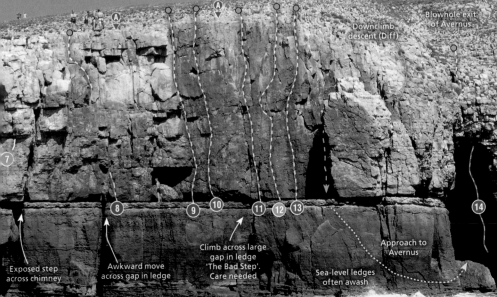

Lighthouse and
Black Zawn 70m →

Many belay stakes
on cliff-top

Downclimb
descent (Diff)

Blowhole exit
of Avernus

Climb across large
gap in ledge
'The Bad Step'.
Care needed

Approach to
Avernus

Exposed step
across chimney

Awkward move
across gap in ledge

Sea-level ledges
often awash

Avon Somerset | North Devon | Culm Coast | Inland Cornwall | Atlantic Coast | West Penwith | The Lizard | Inland Devon | Torbay | Dorset

Black Zawn

Black Zawn is an atmospheric cliff that features some big feeling and long routes, requiring abseil approaches and a degree of commitment significantly higher than the nearby Subluminal. The Black Zawn should be considered a place for more experienced parties only.

Approach - The Black Zawn is the section of cliff below the lighthouse. To reach the abseil stakes, follow the cliff-top path from Subluminal leftwards (looking out) to a small ledge above the zawn. All the climbs are accessed by a 20m abseil. It is best to view the wall from the opposite side of the zawn before abseiling in. The abseil leads down the overhanging line of *Astrid* to its hanging stance (place directional runners to keep in contact with the crack on the abseil). Keep the ropes out of the sea so that they do not become snagged in the boulders.

Tides - The routes are non-tidal in calm sea-conditions.

Conditions - The zawn is prone to dampness owing to its enclosed nature. Do not enter in rough seas or on damp days when the zawn can become very greasy.

The routes all start from the same belay; a spike and nuts, 4m above the sea at the base of Astrid.

❶ **The Peccary** E2 5b
A smashing climb that is, for the most part, on good holds and has plenty of gear. Start at the hanging stance.
25m. Traverse left from the belay for 4m to below a thin crack. Climb the thin crack up the wall on fine holds to a niche. Finish up the wall above.
FA. George Hounsome, Martin Barnicott 31.5.1976

❷ **Astrid** . . . . HVS 5a
The easiest of the lines on this wall has bags of atmosphere and good climbing. Start at the hanging stance.
25m. Climb the well-protected groove and crack-line in the centre of the wall to the top.
FA. Richard Crewe, S.Garner, Tim Dunsby 11.8.1974

❸ **Melpomene** E4 5c
Wild climbing which is both steep and pumpy, but well protected with it. Take care to avoid rope-drag. Start at the hanging stance.
30m. Climb diagonally rightwards above the fault-line into the corner of *Mars*. Move up rightwards under a roof using flakes to reach the arete. Sprint up the leftward-slanting cracks to a small ledge. Finish up cracks in the headwall, staying right of a square-cut groove. *Photo opposite.*
FA. Pat Littlejohn, Chris King 1978

❹ **Mars** E2 5b
A simply awesome zawn-climb on excellent rock, with sound protection and a stunning position. Start at the hanging stance.
1) 5m, 5b. Traverse rightwards along the fault, or drop down to sea level, then back up to a sloping ledge beneath the roofs.
2) 26m, 5b. Climb the intimidating roofed-corner and the sustained groove above to the top.
FA. Richard Crewe, Tim Dunsby 11.8.1974

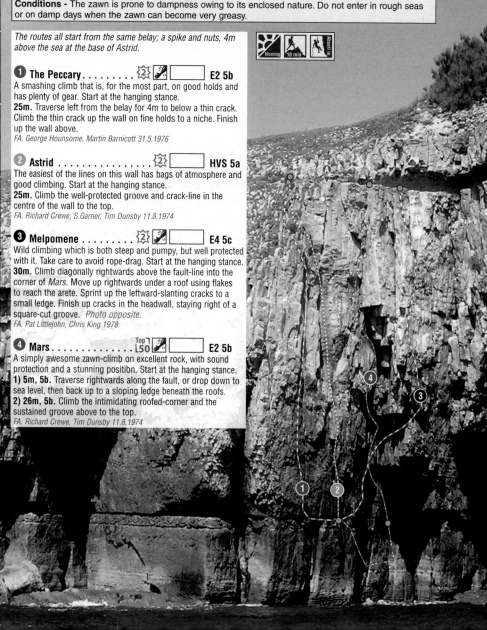

Avon Somerset

North Devon

Culm Coast

Inland Cornwall

Atlantic Coast

West Penwith

The Lizard

Inland Devon

Torbay

Dorset

Marti Hallett moving away from the corner of *Mars* (E2 5b) on the super strenuous *Melpomene (E4 5c)* - *opposite* - in the Black Zawn, Swanage. Photo: Sue Hazel

Avon Somerset | North Devon | Culm Coast | Inland Cornwall | Atlantic Coast | West Penwith | The Lizard | Inland Devon | Torbay | Dorset

Avon Somerset · North Devon · Culm Coast · Inland Cornwall · Atlantic Coast · West Penwith · The Lizard · Inland Devon · Torbay · Dorset

Avon Somerset · North Devon · Culm Coast · Inland Cornwall · Atlantic Coast · West Penwith · The Lizard · Inland Devon · Torbay · Dorset

Avon Somerset | North Devon | Culm Coast | Inland Cornwall | Atlantic Coast | West Penwith | The Lizard | Inland Devon | Torbay | Dorset

Avon Somerset | North Devon | Culm Coast | Inland Cornwall | Atlantic Coast | West Penwith | The Lizard | Inland Devon | Torbay | Dorset

Avon Somerset

North Devon

Culm Coast

Inland Cornwall

Atlantic Coast

West Penwith

The Lizard

Inland Devon

Torbay

Dorset

Climbers running together the two pitches of Sennen's most celebrated climb, *Demo Route* (HS 4b) - *page 227* - Photo Duncan Skelton/Offwidth Images

M4
M5
M4
Cardiff
Bristol
Bath
Exmoor
National Park
M5
A303
Lundy
A361
Barnstaple
A377
A39
A37
Bournemouth
A35
Swanage
Dartmoor
National Park
A38
Portland
Bodmin
Plymouth
Glasgow
A394
Penzance
Dublin
Manchester
London

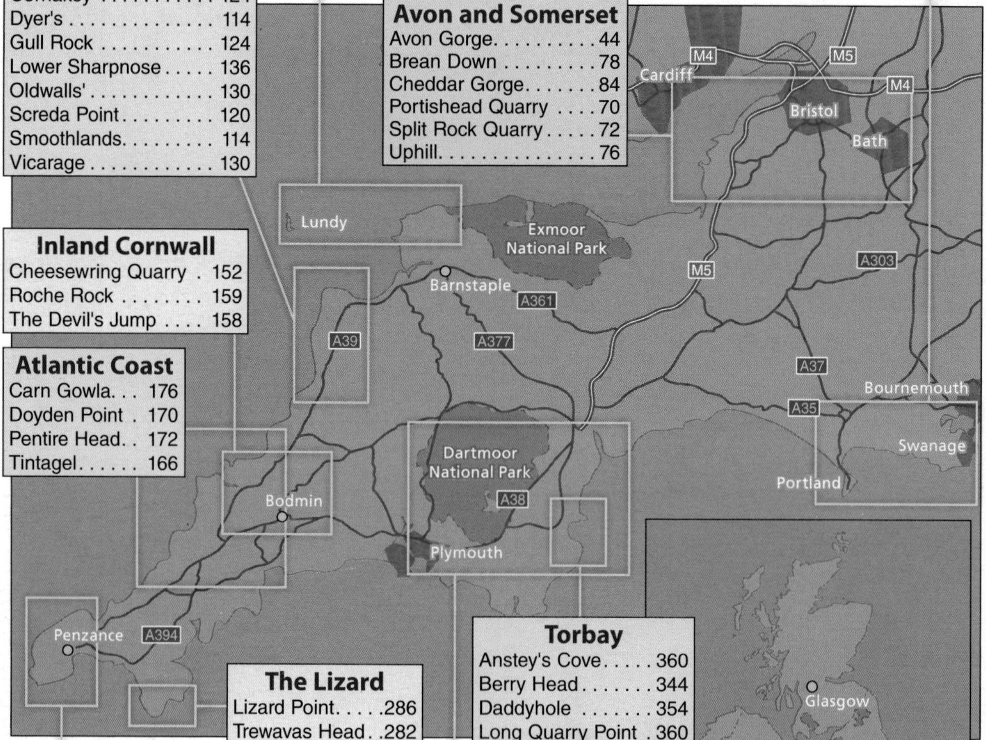

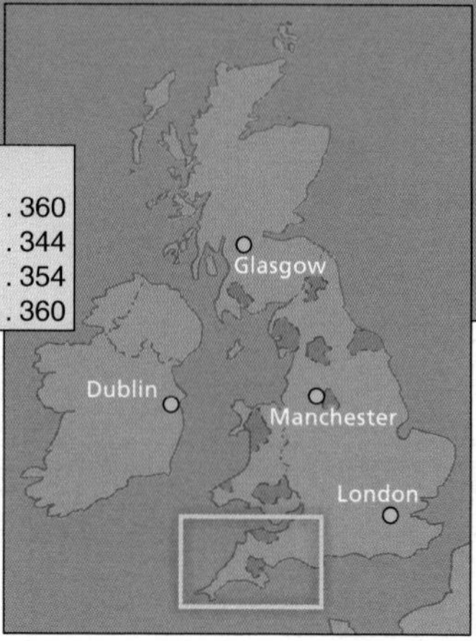

Avon Somerset
North Devon
Culm Coast
Inland Cornwall
Atlantic Coast
West Penwith
The Lizard
Inland Devon
Torbay
Dorset